CW00393136

God's Biologist

God's Biologist

A Life of Alister Hardy

David Hay

David Hay

To Jimmy + Betta, good companions
and lovely people.

DARTON·LONGMAN + TODD

First published in 2011 by
Darton, Longman and Todd Ltd
1 Spencer Court
140 – 142 Wandsworth High Street
London SW18 4JJ

ISBN: 978-0-232-52847-3

A catalogue record for this book is available from the British Library

Phototypeset by Kerrypress Ltd, Luton, Bedfordshire
Printed and bound in Great Britain by CPI Antony Rowe, Chippenham

For Michael and Belinda

Firstly Michael and I would like to thank David very much for all his hard work in producing this biography of our father.

We would also like to mention what an important part our mother played in his life. How fortunate he was to have met and married her. She was not only a wonderful mother but a wonderful wife to him. She was very supportive, completely unselfish and tried very hard to persuade him to put the brakes on occasionally!

Our father had a terrific sense of humour and she had a pretty good one too, which helped them cope so well in their old age. They had great respect and love for each other. After our father died in May 1985 our mother lived on for only five months, dying in October of that year.

Belinda Farley
6 September 2010

Contents

Foreword

Professor David Wulff is based in the Psychology Department at Wheaton College in Massachusetts. He is internationally recognised as one of the most gifted contemporary students of the psychology of religion. David is best known as the author of the magisterial Psychology of Religion: Classic and Contemporary (2nd Edition; Wiley, 1997).

Honoured many times over for his work as a marine biologist, an ecologist, and an authority on plankton, Sir Alister Hardy (1896–1985) was privately preoccupied with a different agenda: reconciling evolutionary theory and spiritual awareness, which he was convinced is the universal heritage of humankind. As a young student facing the prospect of going to war, he had solemnly vowed 'to what [he] called God' that, should he survive the great conflict, he would devote his life to achieving a reconciliation sufficient to convince the scientific world. As David Hay points out in this authoritative, sympathetic, and deeply engaging biography, it was only 70 years later that Hardy was able to overcome his understandable reticence and to acknowledge this vow publicly. Meanwhile, he laid firm foundations for the project by establishing his authority as a scientific observer and a specialist on evolutionary theory and by earning the respect of peers and the loyalty of friends on which he would later draw.

Hardy was above all a naturalist – a meticulous observer who, by means of enormous patience and considerable inventiveness, contributed substantially to matters of real practical importance. Initially put off by the pettiness he saw in academic circles, he first applied his Oxford training in zoology under Julian Huxley by joining the Ministry of Agriculture and Fisheries. Soon, still in his twenties, Hardy was appointed the chief zoologist to the famous expedition to the Antarctica on the British Royal Research Ship *Discovery*, which was undertaken from 1925 to 1927 to study the ways of southern whales and eventually to establish a policy for conserving them. It was during this expedition that Hardy first developed the Continuous Plankton Recorder, an apparatus for establishing the feeding habits of the whale and for which Hardy would become universally known among marine biologists.

The *Discovery* trip had required Hardy to give up the security of his earlier position, but as fate would have it, a generous benefactor had underwritten the establishment of a new university in the city of Hull, and Hardy was offered his first full professorship, in zoology. The challenges were considerable – from gathering a collection of specimens to creating a comprehensive library of books and journals, meanwhile accommodating the needs of the first students to arrive – but through a combination of hard work and good fortune, Hardy was able to meet them. In the midst of this activity he was awarded the degree of DSc by Oxford and, a year later, in 1939, the first Scientific Medal of the Zoological Society of London. He was elected a Fellow of the Royal Society in 1940.

In 1943, Hardy accepted the Regius Chair in Natural History at the University of Aberdeen, but only four years later he was lured back to Oxford, to take up the Linacre Chair of Zoology and Comparative Anatomy. In that position he was also to head the Department of Zoology. Among his publications during his years at Oxford was a widely admired work, *The Open Sea: Its Natural History* (1956–1959), the first volume of which is dedicated to plankton and the second, to fish and fisheries; intended for the wider reading public, both volumes were illustrated with Hardy's own sensitive watercolors. Drawing on his old journals, among other sources, Hardy then revisited the *Discovery* explorations in *Great Waters: A Voyage of Natural History to Study Whales,*

Plankton and the Waters of the Southern Ocean (1967), a volume likewise illustrated with Hardy's artistic renderings of the sea and rugged coastlines. Hardy relinquished the Linacre Chair in 1961 and retired as Professor and Head of the Department of Zoological Field Studies two years after that. Over the years, Hardy received a number of additional honors, including a knighthood for his services to the fishing industry; honorary doctorates from the universities of Aberdeen, Southampton, and Hull; and honorary memberships or fellowships in British, American, and Indian professional societies.

It was yet another honor, the invitation in 1962 to give the Gifford Lectures in Natural Theology at Aberdeen University that finally provided Hardy with the opportunity and incentive to give sustained public expression to his ongoing private preoccupation with issues on the borderland between science and religion. As Hay remarks, it was 'a courageous and innovative decision' to appoint Hardy to this highly prestigious lectureship, for at that time 'his views on the biological basis of religion were both radical and little-known'. Fortunately, Lord Gifford's terms for the lectureship were extremely liberal, hence they easily accommodated the critical realism that Hardy shared with most other empirical scientists and his determination to approach religion from the perspective of evolutionary science. The first series of lectures, intended for a general audience as Lord Gifford had specified, were given in 1963–1964 and published in 1965 as *The Living Stream: A Restatement of Evolutionary Theory and Its Relation to the Spirit of Man*. The second series, given in 1964–1965, appeared in 1966 as *The Divine Flame: An Essay Towards a Natural History of Religion*.

Subject from childhood to intimations of a spiritual dimension and later confirmed as a member of the Church of England, Hardy had grown increasingly estranged from the Church as he came more clearly to see how, in its conservatism, it served to protect the powers that be while impeding the work of scientists. He was repelled, he said bluntly, by much that he saw in orthodox Christianity; were he alive today, Jesus would surely be no Christian as many now understand the term. In time Hardy would reluctantly drop his membership in the Church of England – his heart, he said, remained in it – and join the Unitarians, in whose company he realized his mind had long belonged. Still, he was less concerned with institutional differences or theological subtleties than, in Hay's words, 'finding his way towards a generic view of religion.' At the very least, Hardy thought, biology might be able to test out the notion of a common core in all of the religious traditions, a spiritual disposition with relationship at its center. That human universal, he was convinced, had become repressed in western society, a theme he explored in a series of unpublished and highly revealing stories. Recovery of that spirituality, he believed, was essential for the nation's social and political well-being.

In preparing his Gifford lectures, Hardy saw himself as building on the work of his distinguished predecessor William James, whose own Gifford lectures, published as *The Varieties of Religious Experience: A Study in Human Nature* (1902), were among the most influential works on religion in the twentieth century, as well as on Edwin Starbuck's *The Psychology of Religion: An Empirical Study of the Growth of Religious Consciousness* (1899), which Hardy likewise saw as a contribution to the natural history of religion.

In his first series of lectures, Hardy reviewed the development of evolutionary theory from the ancient Greeks through Darwin to the present time, and then addressed the notion that natural selection proceeds exclusively by means of impersonal mechanism. Surveying a wide range of cases of animal camouflage, he pointed to what he considered a far more significant dynamic: conscious selection on the part of adapting organisms. In choosing which insect to eat, for example, predators play a major role in the evolution of these insects. Hardy called the interaction between such changes in habitual behaviour and the process of natural selection *behavioural selection*, in contradistinction to genetic selection. In the evolution of human beings and other higher animals, Hardy concluded, conscious choice is the more important factor. In such a system, he believed, there is room for theism, understood not as belief in an anthropomorphic deity, but as the conviction that genuine contact with a power greater than the individual self is possible. The Darwinian position, in other words, does not compel a strictly materialistic interpretation but leaves room for a spiritual dimension.

Hardy's second series of lectures addressed the question of whether there is a reasonable prospect of establishing a natural theology on a genuinely scientific foundation. The ten lectures,

Hardy said at the outset, would be dedicated to surveying the ground on which such a science might be established. Over the courses of several of the lectures, he drew on various classic authorities on religious experience, including not only James and Rudolf Otto but also well-known sociologists and anthropologists, and he argued that 'the numinous, the love of nature, and the inspiration of art,' while not identical, are closely enough related to require like attention. A critical lecture largely on Freud and those influenced by him, another on religious devotion as akin to animal submission, and two others – on the promise of psychical research and in rebuttal to critics of natural theology – culminated finally in an argument for a science of theology that is guided by an experimental faith, a faith grounded in experience rather than in a dogmatic past.

Coming at the end of his distinguished career as a zoologist, Hardy's Gifford lectures set the stage for his final project: becoming once again the naturalist, but this time in search of as broad and representative a sample of religious or spiritual experiences as he could muster. But what, in this context, would be the equivalent of his Continuous Plankton Recorder, the precisely submergible device that, on a moving band of silk, rolled up and preserved plankton as they came streaming through it? Hardy conceived of a research centre at Oxford that would gather first-hand reports of spiritual experiences and subject them to systematic analysis, as a contribution to a natural theology and confirmation of his own conviction regarding the biological, and thus universal, character of spiritual experiences.

The obstacles Hardy faced were considerable, as Hay documents in some detail. They were first of all political and financial; Hardy no longer had the clout that he had possessed as the holder of the Linacre Chair. Some obstacles were also religious. His eagerness to investigate the spiritual life was met with polite scepticism by scientific funding agencies, on the one hand, and the heterodoxy of his religious views troubled the religious establishment, on the other. He had become associated with Manchester College, the bastion of Unitarianism at Oxford, but members of its council worried about the potential financial burden and the threat the Unit represented, if it became dominant, to the college's Unitarian character.

Hardy remained determined, however, and in due time he was granted a run-down but serviceable cottage on the College grounds in which to set up the Religious Experiences Research Unit. Although the centre remained financially precarious, the main challenge became obtaining a sufficiently large and diverse collection of documents, establishing some means for classifying them, and finally using them to address research questions. After a modest start, usable documents came flooding in from diverse quarters, and in due time, a series of book-length studies appeared as publications of the Unit, several authored by Hardy, others by co-workers. The Unit was also finally able to finance a national survey on religious experience in the United Kingdom, which was carried out in 1976. In 1970, Hardy had invited Edward Robinson, a lecturer in Divinity, to join the Unit in a senior position, and in 1976, Robinson took over as director, even though Hardy found it difficult to let go of the reins. Hardy was felled by a severe brain haemorrhage in 1985, at age 89, and at that point Robinson resigned from the directorship. It was only a few days before Hardy died, ironically, that he was awarded the munificent Templeton Prize for his work at the intersection of science and religion. Unable himself to use the money, which was pegged always to be higher in monetary value than the Nobel Prize, Hardy left the sum to the Unit to secure its future.

David Hay, who became director of the unit after Hardy's death, is, like him, a zoologist. He is author of *Something There: The Biology of the Human Spirit* (2006), and is no less interested in examining the hypothesis that religious or spiritual awareness is part and parcel of the human endowment, a testament to the survival value of such awareness. Thus the vivid portrait that he offers in this book is enriched by his extended first-hand acquaintance with Hardy much as it is by his judicious selection of quotations from Hardy's unpublished correspondence and autobiography. In a postscript, Hay offers an historical account of the progressive submersion of relational consciousness, or spiritual awareness, by commercial and intellectual pressures that have increasingly heightened scepticism and the individualism of western culture . Thus Hay notes with some satisfaction the growing prominence of empirical research on spirituality, notable examples of which he briefly introduces here and discusses at greater length in *Something There*.

Foreword

This book is itself evidence of the vitality of the human spiritual disposition – in the life of Alister Hardy, first of all, but also in the work of his biographer, David Hay. Whether or not one concurs with them that spirituality possesses a universal evolutionary advantage, one cannot but come away from their writings with the impression that they are truly on to something.

David M. Wulff

Preface and Acknowledgments

I first met Alister Hardy in 1956 when I was an undergraduate studying Zoology at Aberdeen University. I was in my second year and had the (mistaken) idea that I would take up a career in marine biology. Accordingly I organized a summer vacation job at the Torry Marine Laboratory. A major perk of working at Torry was the chance to go to sea for an extended period and I was assigned to the *Explorer,* a research trawler owned by the Lab. On the day that I was due to embark it so happened that Hardy had also arranged to join the ship. His purpose was to paint watercolours of freshly caught fish, for use as illustrations for *Fish and Fisheries,* the second of a pair of volumes he had written on *The Open Sea.*

Although I was the most junior member of the crew, I had the privilege of dining in the Officers' Mess owing to my status as a university undergraduate. One evening early on in the trip I found myself sitting next to Hardy at dinner. He was already a famous figure in the biological world, soon to be knighted for his services to the fishing industry, and I felt overawed. Conscious of a need to avoid talk about his specialism lest my ignorance was exposed, I sought for alternative topics of conversation. In my confused embarrassment, for some unaccountable reason I asked him if by any chance he shared an interest of mine – utterly remote from marine biology – namely the writings of a German philosopher/ theologian, Rudolf Otto? Not that I knew very much about Otto, but

I remembered him being talked of in a General Studies class at school as the inventor of the term 'numinous' to refer to the experience of the sacred. To my surprise, Hardy burst out excitedly, 'Good heavens, you're not interested in Otto, are you?' I thought the game was up, but we continued talking into the early hours of the morning, oblivious of the time, for we were sailing in the company of the midnight sun in latitudes to the north of Shetland.

Looking back, I now realize that the conjectures Alister shared with me on the biological roots of religion predated the current scientific interest in the subject by more than half a century. I was thrilled by what he had to say and from then on our paths repeatedly crossed until eventually I came to work with him in Oxford at his Religious Experience Research Unit. When Hardy died in 1985, I was appointed Director of the Unit. I had known Alister for nearly thirty years.

Perhaps for this reason, Marianne Rankin, the Chair of the Alister Hardy Society sent a letter to me in November 2003 to ask if I would consider writing Alister's biography. I was flattered, but doubtful of my competence to do the job. It was only when Hardy's son and daughter told me that they too would be happy for me to make the attempt that I decided to start a serious investigation of his personality and life-story.

By temperament Hardy was a light-hearted, joyful man and at one level the unfolding narrative of his life reads like a rip-roaring schoolboy's yarn. I hope something of this comes across in the succeeding pages, but the major purpose of the book lies elsewhere. Alister's story brings the mounting problems of Western religion into unusually sharp focus, but unlike a number of other contemporary critics he had no wish to abandon it. On the contrary, he was convinced of the radical social and political importance of paying attention to the spiritual dimension of our human experience. It is this part of his legacy that I have tried to make clear.

There are many angles from which a biography of Hardy could and no doubt will be written, for he was a man of many parts. My purpose in this case is to present a readable account of his life that goes some way towards an understanding of the religious preoccupations of a great biologist. Therefore, although I go into considerable detail in introducing many of Alister's major ideas in zoology my coverage is by no means comprehensive. Nor do I mean it to be. The primary purpose of the discussion is to illuminate the interaction between his biological and theological conjectures. His conviction was that this gulf could be crossed in either direction without sacrificing one's intellectual integrity. The extent of my success or failure in clarifying this point is for the reader to judge.

I am not a professional biographer, nor am I a theologian. Even in my own field of zoology there are large gaps in my knowledge. Crossing academic divides is notoriously hazardous. Consequently, over the lengthy period during which the book was gestating, I have had to depend on a variety of institutions and a large number of knowledgeable colleagues for guidance and information. My ability to err has remained undimmed over the years, and none of my remaining mistakes are to be attributed to anyone but myself.

Those who deserve thanks are more than I can enumerate in this introduction, though I have tried to note my gratitude to as many as possible in the notes to the chapters. I apologize if I have mistakenly missed out anyone who assisted me.

There are two major written resources for the student of Alister Hardy's life. Hardy's main archive is held in the Bodleian Library in Oxford. I am most grateful for the help of the library staff in the Modern Manuscripts Reading Room, in particular Colin Harris who dealt patiently with many of my puzzlements over the years. The second important resource is the typescript of an autobiography that Hardy began in his late eighties. At the time of his death he had completed a sequence of brief chapters mostly referring to that part of his life leading up to and including his return from the Discovery Expedition. I have included as many direct quotations as possible from his typescript, since they convey tangibly both his humour and the flavour of his developing political and religious thought.

Besides these two rich collections of data, an important series of letters between Hardy and Julian Huxley (along with several between Hardy and Juliette, Huxley's wife) is preserved in the archives of Rice University in Houston, Texas. I am particularly grateful for the generosity of Amanda Y. Focke of the Woodson Research Center in the Fondren Library, who abstracted all the material relating to Hardy contained in Huxley's archive and sent it to me free of charge.

The archive of Sir James Wordie, held in the National Library of Scotland in Edinburgh is an important source of background information on the circumstances surrounding Hardy's role as Chief Zoologist to the Discovery Expedition of 1925–27 and the wrangling over his appointment. For information about Hardy's colleague, Rolfe Gunther, I was able to consult his archive in the Maritime Museum Library at Greenwich. Generous help was also given to me by the librarians responsible for: the Garstang archive in the Library of the University of Leeds; archival material held in the Brynmor Jones Library of the University of Hull; material held in the Rare Books Department in Aberdeen University (where I wish to record my particular thanks to Michelle Gait); and the archives of the Society for Psychical Research held by the University Library at Cambridge. Finally the extensive archival material on the history of the College, and the founding of the Religious Experience Research Unit was of great value to me in writing Chapter 10.

I am also conscious of a debt to many individuals. First and foremost I must mention Michael Hardy and Belinda Farley. From the beginning I was in regular telephone contact with both of them. Their reminiscences about their father and mother, plus the feedback they gave after reading each chapter as it was written was fundamental to the task of monitoring the accuracy of the text. Other extended family members who helped include Jane Winship, who as the granddaughter of Alister's brother Vernon, provided reminiscences of him from a slightly different perspective. Michael Stewart kindly gave me a copy of his family tree, along with notes drawn from his very thorough genealogical studies of the Clavering family.

I must also record my heavy dependence on the work of the late John Keeble, whose extensive research on Hardy's life preceded my efforts* and saved me from much footslogging. Only his early death prevented him from writing a full-length biography of his own.

For valuable conversations on the political and social history of the East Midlands I am indebted to one of Nottingham's leading local historians, Ken Brand. Ken also helped me by tracking down individual members of the Hardy family, as did Peter Rattenbury of

---

* see, *This Unnamed Something*, 87pp. R.E.R.C., 2000; ISBN 0 906165 36 9

the Nottingham Family History Society. John Baggaley was helpful with his first hand knowledge of Colwick House, having lived in the house as a young man. He was kind enough to provide a photograph of the building, which is now no longer in existence.

I wish to thank Radica Mehase, for her research in Port-of-Spain, Trinidad, on the early adult life of Hardy's mother.

For information and unique photographs of the Robin Hood Rifles, I am indebted to Eddie Edwards, Archivist of the Sherwood Foresters' records, near Nottingham. For medical advice on the health problems of Richard Hardy, I thank Drs Paul Denny and Sandy Pringle. My gratitude is due to the librarians in the local history department of Sowerby Bridge for advice on the education of Hardy's father, Richard at Ripponden College, near Halifax in Yorkshire.

I am grateful for help from the then headmaster of Bramcote Preparatory School, Scarborough, Andrew Lewin and his wife Debbie. At Oundle I received particularly generous help from Stephen Forge, the School Archivist.

Ian Rankin was helpful with information about Solomon J. Solomon who was in charge of the camouflage-training unit to which Hardy was assigned during the First World War. I am also grateful for Ian's advice to me as a novice biographer, 'Don't try to put everything in'.

My thanks are due for hospitality from the authorities at CEFAS (Centre for Environment, Fisheries & Aquaculture Science) in Lowestoft, the much-enlarged descendant of the fisheries laboratory known to Hardy.

For generously supplying information on the fate of the specimen collections made on the Discovery Expedition of 1925–27 and its outcome I must thank Professor Phil Rainbow and his colleagues at the Natural History Museum in London. For background information on Hardy's close colleague on the *Discovery*, Rolfe Gunther, I am indebted to Kay F. Sturt at the Dragon School in Oxford and to Rosalind Marsden, who is Gunther's daughter. For an important conversation about Joseph Stenhouse, the skipper of the *Discovery*, I am grateful to Stephen Haddelsey, Captain Stenhouse's biographer. I am also grateful to Niall Cooper who kindly gave me a personal guided tour of the *Discovery* in Dundee, where she forms the centrepiece of the excellent Discovery Visitor Centre.

I am very grateful to Dr Chris Reid, to whom I paid a visit shortly before he retired from the Directorship of SAHFOS (Sir Alister Hardy Foundation for Ocean Science) in Plymouth. He and his colleagues gave me a most interesting tour of the laboratory and a practical demonstration of the operation of Hardy's Continuous Plankton Recorder.

I am much in debt to Alan Gauld for providing background information about the Society for Psychical Research, particularly during the period when Hardy was its president.

On Hardy's time in Aberdeen I was given wise advice by, among others, Jimmy Adams, Sir Fred Holliday, the late Bob Ralph, Andrew Lucas and Hans Kruuk.

I was able to have personal conversations with a number of former colleagues or students in Hardy's department at Oxford. The following were particularly helpful: John Blaxter, Barbara Brunet, Bryan Clarke, Quentin Bone, John Davies, Richard Dawkins, Mary Grice, the late David Hardy, Michael Hardy, Hans Kruuk, Desmond Morris, David Nichols and finally Sheila O'Clarey, who was for some years Alister Hardy's secretary.

On a trip to South Wales I visited Elaine Morgan, who gave me generous help on the question of Hardy's 'Aquatic Ape' hypothesis.

For help with the story of the Religious Experience Research Unit, I benefited from the history of the Unit written by John Franklin, from Sue Skillicorn of the Library Staff in Harris-Manchester College, Oxford and to Polly Wheway, for some years the loyal secretary of the Unit.

I greatly appreciate the help of the following people who read and commented upon some or all of the draft chapters of the book: Ken Brand, Adrian Bullock, Jean Cameron, Belinda Farley, Bernard Hamilton, Michael Hardy, Jane Hay, Fred Holliday, Gerry Hinchliffe, Liz Moran, Rosemary Peacocke, Denis Rice and Glyn Yeoman.

I would like to thank Virginia Hearn, my editor, for her openness, warmth and enthusiasm as my editor, and all the team at Darton, Longman and Todd.

Without the financial backing of the trustees of the Religious Experience Research Centre in the University of Wales at Lampeter I would have taken much longer to finish my task. I offer them my grateful thanks. I also owe a debt of gratitude to Marianne Rankin for her constant kindness and encouragement and similarly to

Peggy Morgan and Paul Badham, two former directors of the Centre. I have also valued the friendship and support of two colleagues at Lampeter, David Greenwood and Anne Jenkins.

Finally, I am grateful to Jane, who deserves much more than a conventional nod of thanks. She accompanied me on many of my research trips, read and criticized successive drafts of every chapter, cajoled me into getting on with the task of writing, and provided all the home comforts. I could not have completed the book without her.

David Hay   Monday 11 October 2010
King's College
Aberdeen University

List of Plates

Cards and line drawings made by Hardy appear on pages 70, 229, 264 and 365.

CHAPTER ONE

A Child of the English Midlands

If you had been standing at the junction of Holywell Street and Mansfield Road in Oxford during the 1970s on any morning of the working week, you would be quite likely to spot a gentleman of advanced years pedalling a similarly aged bicycle towards you. Dismounting at the corner, he wheels his bike into the entrance of a small cottage, dwarfed by the bulk of New College across the road. He is attired in what used to be the regulation three-piece tweed suit of an Oxbridge don, plus a pair of thinking man's specs – smallish lenses in austere metal frames – the ensemble rounded off with a pair of cycle clips, an old raincoat and an extremely battered trilby hat. He is very tall, slenderly built and his personal style, accent and ingrained courtesy coincide with what one might expect of some-one at the heart of the British academic establishment. This indeed is where his ambition has led him, for the elderly gent is Sir Alister Hardy FRS, Emeritus Professor of Zoology at Oxford University, and widely recognised as the outstanding marine biologist of his day.

On the face of it, the story of Sir Alister's life is about the privileged existence of a member of the scientific elite. The son of a wealthy Nottingham architect, he went up from Oundle School to Exeter College, Oxford in 1914, initially to study forestry, but he changed his mind and turned to zoology. He was to become one of the first pupils, and the lifelong friend, of Julian Huxley – grandson of Charles Darwin's most vigorous advocate, T. H. Huxley. Hardy's subsequent career led to pioneering discoveries in marine biology and his appointment as the first Professor of Zoology and Oceanography at the University of Hull in 1928 at the age of thirty-two. From there he became Regius Professor of Natural History at Aberdeen University, was elected to a fellowship of the Royal Society and eventually was made Linacre Professor of Zoology and Comparative Anatomy at Oxford University. In 1957 the Queen knighted him at Buckingham Palace for services to the fishing industry via his zoological research. These achievements came to pass for the sake of an ulterior motive, which governed the whole of his adult life, and which for much of the time he kept hidden from his colleagues and even from members of his immediate family. The cottage into which Sir Alister disappeared with his bicycle had nothing to do with marine biology; it was the headquarters of the Religious Experience Research Unit that he set up in 1969.[1]

Hardy's dominating concern, which continues to be a matter of serious and often bitter public debate today, was the perceived conflict between Darwin's theory of natural selection and religious faith. The arguments had raged from 1859, when the publication of *The Origin of Species* made Darwin's idea available to the general public.[2] Many thoughtful people became convinced that it was irreconcilable with religious belief. Several hitherto devout individuals felt forced to renounce their faith, often experiencing great anguish at the loss, as A. N. Wilson vividly demonstrates in his book *God's Funeral*.[3] Another large group refused to look at the scientific evidence and retreated into biblical fundamentalism. Differing opinions on the subject have continued to generate anger ever since, but rather suddenly the arguments have become much more acute in the years following the Millennium.

One major source of hostility to religion is not directly connected with the dispute over evolution. I am referring to the terrorist atrocities committed by people claiming to act in the name of Islam, most spectacularly in the destruction of the World Trade Center in New York on 11 September 2001. Though this particular example of fanaticism is only indirectly associated with arguments over Darwinism, it fuels the conflict by creating fear of the power of religion to close down free thought. [4] A popular stereotype reduces the debate to an ill-tempered row between the so called 'New Atheists'[5] and the 'Christian Right'. This is probably most nearly an accurate description of the situation in the United States, where it has become a political issue because of partly successful attempts by religious groups to prohibit the teaching of evolution in schools.

The limitations of the 'atheistic Darwinism versus religious fundamentalism' simplification are revealed in Sir Alister's stance towards the debate. Throughout his academic career he held to a thoroughly mainstream line on natural selection, and personally chose to present that view in a lecture course that he gave to all first year zoology undergraduates. At the same time – in sharp contrast to the split I have outlined – he was deeply convinced that religious belief could not be dismissed as a delusion; indeed, it was essential to human wellbeing. In an astonishing letter written towards the end of his life he confessed to a friend that he had always been more interested in religion than zoology. Not surprisingly, in attempting to bring together his Darwinian orthodoxy and his religion, Hardy found himself at odds with powerful guardians of what is proper to both science and religion. The purpose of this opening chapter is to place him in the historical and social context that shaped his assumptions about the nature of religion and which eventually turned him into an unlikely outlaw within the scientific establishment.

Sociologists tell us that it is out of the primordial images absorbed in early life that our notions of reality are constructed[6] and from which many of our most enduring axioms and motivations arise. This is especially true for someone as vividly imaginative as Alister Hardy, but he was for the most part tantalisingly reserved about his own spiritual life. Therefore in this narrative, which purports to offer an account of his deepest personal commitments, it is important to be as explicit as possible about the social and cultural factors that underpin those loyalties. Awareness of this background will provide a yardstick for judging the accuracy of the intuitive judgements unavoidably made in trying to understand Hardy's life story.

Alister was born in Nottingham, in the English East Midlands, on 10 February 1896. The surname Hardy is common in the Midlands, so it is quite possible that his ancestors had lived in Nottinghamshire for many generations.[7] They would thus have been particularly heavily immersed in one of the most potent folk legends in Europe, the tales of Robin Hood. Historians have concluded that the evidence for Robin's existence is very thin, but scholarly dismissals have utterly failed to destroy the archetypal belief that Robin, Maid Marian and the Merry Men are out there in the greenwood of the human imagination, vowed to an eternal struggle against injustice. From his secret lair in Sherwood Forest, Robin launched attacks on the rich and powerful, stealing their wealth and giving it to the poor and dispossessed – seemingly an improbable renunciation since Robin himself was said to have come from the ruling elite. The corrupt members of that aristocracy were not passive in the face of these trespasses on their privileges. They are symbolised by the wicked sheriff who, if he had his way, would lock the outlaws in a dungeon in Nottingham castle and throw away the key.

This story had more than mythical significance for young Alister Hardy for, in spite of the scholars, the physical setting of the tales of Robin Hood is by no means all make-believe. As a lover of the countryside, Alister knew it well. Fragments of Sherwood Forest survive to this day in the north of Nottinghamshire as an expanse of shattered oak trees, huge and strange. There is still a Sheriff of Nottingham, and, above a tall cliff-face alongside a well-to-do Victorian housing estate called the Park, stand the remains of the mediaeval castle. William the Conqueror ordered the first *motte* and *bailey* to be built there in 1068, just two years after the battle of Hastings. The skyline confronting modern rail travellers as they draw into Nottingham Midland Station continues to be dominated by the castle rock, now crowned with a baroque mansion house that was once the property of the Duke of Newcastle.[8] To Alister all of this was part of his everyday reality, giving richness to the Robin Hood story as one of the most prominent features of his mental landscape. The social snobbery that he inherited from his family made it easy for Alister to imagine himself simultaneously in the role of the rebel aristocrat, protecting the rights of the deprived and downtrodden common people.

Leaping the centuries, another equally powerful influence on Alister's imagination was his awareness of the history of the immediately preceding generations of his family. The stark gulf between wealth and poverty that accompanied the industrialisation of England during the eighteenth and nineteenth centuries was particularly keenly experienced in Nottinghamshire. This turbulent history had an undeniable impact on the Hardys as they attempted to cope with the shock of the social changes and the inevitable violence surrounding them. Fortunately the practice of keeping increasingly detailed public records during the Victorian era makes it possible to picture the lives of the two or three generations immediately predating Alister's birth. His forebears seem to have been more aware than many of their fellows that they were entering a radically new kind of social reality, in retrospect labelled the Industrial Revolution. More and more people were abandoning the countryside and heading into Nottingham or moving further afield. Sheer poverty was the driving force for many, but this does not seem to have been the major factor influencing Alister's immediate ancestors.

In Hodson's directory of Nottinghamshire for 1814 there is a reference to someone called William Hardy, describing him as a victualler in the Maypole Hotel on Long Row, close to the Market Square in the centre of Nottingham.[9] The coincidence of surname, address and occupation makes it likely that William was related to Alister's great grandfather, John Hardy. John was also a victualler at the Maypole and eventually became its landlord. At the time of the first English national census in 1841 he was aged 65,[10] and described as an innkeeper residing with his wife Mary, daughter Emma and six servants in the Maypole Yard. Though he was a townsman he was sufficiently well off to retain a foothold in the countryside, for he also lists himself in Glover's directory of 1844 as a gentleman farmer, freeman and owner of Woodclose Farm in the parish of Basford, now a suburb of Nottingham. The records are not explicit but one might hazard a guess that John (and possibly William before him) supplied the Maypole with produce from his farm in Basford. It seems that he passed on the business to his son, also called John, for the 1851 census lists another John Hardy of the right age, 38, named as a hotelkeeper, also living in Maypole Yard. John Hardy junior and his wife Mary had four sons. The youngest listed was Richard, an eleven-month-old infant who in the future would become the father of Alister Hardy. The total household on the day of the census also included ten servants and a further nine people who were clearly guests in the hotel. The available statistics suggest that the Hardys had adapted in response to a changing environment and seized the opportunities offered by that change. In other words, they made a conscious and calculated choice. In some ways it was analogous to what Alister would one day call 'behavioural selection', a process that he believed was a major factor in evolutionary success.

The Hardy family probably had a better informed picture of the commercial and political realities of national life than many in their social class, for the Maypole was an important coaching inn, one of seven staging posts clustered in the centre of Nottingham. At their busiest these inns serviced nearly forty regular timetabled coach routes connecting with other parts of England, including the capital. For example, the stagecoach known as the Nottingham Commercial ran to the *Swan with Two Necks* in Lad Lane in London. It had an armed guard because of the fear of highway robbery and took nearly fifteen hours and ten changes of horses to complete the 130-mile trip. Several of the major coach routes started from the Maypole and, at its busiest, the yard would have been rather like a modern bus station. Coaches arrived every morning and evening, disgorging passengers who would naturally be inclined to seek the hospitality of the adjacent hotel after their exhausting journey. The feel of setting out on a long distance coach from the Maypole is caught in the opening of a description of a journey to Cambridge:

> Our coach, the *Red Rover*, stood at the Maypole Inn, and the coach office was on the east side of the yard opposite the hotel. The coach started at 5.15 in the morning and it used to be drawn up on Long Row, where the horses were put in at the last minute. Passengers used to stand under the pillared arcading, their luggage being piled on the pavement outside. The ladder was then put up the side of the coach and the hangers-about-the-coach-yard, a ne'er do well lot, handed up the packages and made themselves generally useful.[11]

That description comes from 1838, when John Hardy senior was landlord of the Maypole. He could see out of his window the unemployed people hanging about in the yard who could only dream of travelling in a long haul coach like the Red Rover. The cost of a trip to London was about a pound, a large fraction of the annual wage of someone lucky enough to have a menial job as, let's say, a chambermaid in the Maypole. The commercial position of the landlord of a coaching inn thus placed him at a particularly sharp meeting point between the wealthy and destitute members of Nottingham's citizenry. The precariousness of one's social position was all too obvious and it bred a kind of social distancing from the lower classes that lingered on into Alister's generation, and was to cause him distress.

By 1838 the bustling profitability of the stage coaches was about to be blown away. In 1839 a railway line was opened, linking Nottingham to the nearby town of Derby, thereby connecting up with the rapidly expanding national rail network. The trains were much faster than the stagecoaches and could carry many more passengers in greater comfort, quite apart from an increased capacity to handle heavy goods. Consequently the 35 daily coach services from Nottingham listed in the 1832 edition of White's directory were soon under threat. By 1853, just 21 years later, they were almost extinct. The one service left was the Sheffield Royal Mail, which still ran from the Maypole.

John Hardy junior may have had a sentimental regard for an age that was dying, but he was by temperament an entrepreneur and protective of the status of his family. Consequently he was also one of those quickest off the mark in adapting to the arrival of the railway. Very soon after the line opened he initiated the first regular transport from the railway station to the middle of the town – a horse drawn omnibus advertised in the local press as linking the Maypole with every arriving and departing train on the timetable. John's connection with the railway continued to strengthen as his family grew. He was still in charge of the Maypole in 1861, as indicated by the census for that year, but was now also listed as a 'railway agent'. He was 48 years old and, with his 38-year-old wife Mary, he had a family of eight children, six of whom (two boys and four girls) were living at home, including the now ten-year-old Richard, Alister's father.[12] Five years later an entry in the 1866 edition of Wright's directory of Nottinghamshire tells us that John had negotiated his way into taking charge of the Parcel Office of the Midland Railway Company. He was obviously good at his job for eventually both the Parcel Office and the main Booking Office of the company were shifted to the Maypole Yard, an arrangement that persisted into the early twentieth century, when the Maypole was demolished.

Behind the individual stories of the Hardys lay the industrial revolution, which had a devastating effect on the quality of life in
Nottingham. In the eighteenth century Daniel Defoe, author of
Robinson Crusoe, had visited the town and was delighted by its
broad boulevards and beautiful gardens. He judged it to be one of
the loveliest county towns in England.[13] At the beginning of the
nineteenth century, Nottingham had a population of less than
30,000, but the gracious municipality Defoe had admired was
about to become a victim of the industrial boom. Alister Hardy's
parents and grandparents must have anxiously witnessed this rapid
change, bringing with it new dangers as well as opportunities. By
the time of the 1901 national census, when Alister was five years
old, Nottingham had metamorphosed into a chronically over-
crowded city of nearly a quarter of a million souls, disfigured by
some of the worst slums in the nation.

Several factors made Nottingham especially vulnerable to the
more unpleasant effects of the industrial revolution. Apart from
farming and coal mining, the most important means of making a
living in the region had been the production of hand-made stock-
ings and lace. Both items could be considered as semi-luxuries, in
the sense that when the economy took a downturn and people
were short of money, these were the kinds of goods they would
choose to go without. Consequently, Nottinghamshire hosiers and
lacemakers had always led an up and down existence compared
with most other people because their income was geared so closely
to the economic cycle. To this uncertainty was added a more lethal
threat, the invention of machines that could manufacture these
items rapidly and much more cheaply, and it brought the cottage
industries to an end.

The country people who had lost their livelihood, and made their
way in increasing numbers into Nottingham, were primarily seeking
work in the new mechanised hosiery and lace factories. The
resulting rapid upsurge in the population triggered a further crisis
because severe restrictions, peculiar to Nottingham, prevented the
expansion of its boundaries. Compared with many other English
towns, Nottingham was surrounded by unusually large tracts of
common land, jealously guarded by those who used them to graze
their animals.[14] Therefore the only way to accommodate the influx

of people was to subdivide the available space into smaller and smaller living units. This produced disastrous suffering among the poor and turned Nottingham into one of the towns named and shamed by Friedrich Engels in his classic study of *The Condition of the Working Classes in England*.[15]

Engels' book was published in 1844 at a time when the squalid state of the new industrial conurbations finally began to be of concern to the government. In that same year a commission was set up to look into the state of the large towns of Britain, including Nottingham. Thomas Hawkesley, Borough Water Engineer for the town, testifying to the Commissioners, said explicitly that the slums in Nottingham made it 'the worst town in England'. J. R. Martin spelled this out in the Commissioners' final report:

> I believe that nowhere else shall we find so large a mass of inhabitants crowded into courts, alleys, and lanes, as in Nottingham, and those, too, of the worst possible construction. Here they are clustered upon each other; court within court, yard within yard, and lane within lane, in a manner to defy description, – all extending right and left from the long narrow streets above referred to. The courts are always, without exception, approached through a low-arched tunnel of some 30 or 36 inches wide, about 8 feet high, and from 20 to 30 feet long, so as to place ventilation or direct solar exposure out of possibility on the space described. The courts are noisome, narrow, unprovided with adequate means for the removal of refuse, ill-ventilated, and wretched in the extreme, with a gutter, or surface-drain, running down the centre: they have no back yards, and the privies are common to the whole court: altogether they present scenes of a deplorable character, and of surprising filth and discomfort. It is just the same with lanes and alleys, with the exception that these last are not closed at each end, like the courts. In all these confined quarters, too, the refuse matter is allowed to accumulate until, by its mass and its advanced putrefaction, it shall have acquired value as manure; and thus it is sold and carted away by the 'muck majors', as the collectors of manure are called in Nottingham.[16]

With nowhere else to put it, human excrement was piled up in a central midden and the resulting unsanitary conditions meant that fever was endemic.

The poverty and desperation of life in the slums contrasted starkly with the affluence displayed in the architecturally superb factories going up in the Lace Market, set round the mediaeval parish church of St Mary. It is true that some of these factory owners had a social conscience, none more so than Thomas Adams, a Christian philanthropist, who, as well as showing concern for his employees' physical needs, had a chapel built for them in his warehouse in Stoney Street, for which he supplied and paid the salary of a chaplain.[17] But not all owners behaved so responsibly. The new machines were making them conspicuously prosperous and at a time when the assumptions of free market economics were dominant,[18] the 'have-nots' of society could in general expect little sympathy from those who had made good. In some cases, manipulation of the political system and intimidation were resorted to by those in power, as in the aggressive activities of the notorious 'Nottingham Lambs', a gang of street hooligans employed by politicians of the time to enforce their electoral ambitions. The resulting pervasive sense of injustice produced a social climate in which radicalism flourished and the threat of violent disturbance simmered very near the surface. One person who had lived in the town during that period for seventeen years noted that, equivalently, seventeen serious bouts of civic disturbance took place.

In the early 1800s the Luddites (followers of another mythical defender of the poor, Ned Ludd) were active in Nottingham, both celebrated and reviled for their attacks on stocking frames and lacemaking machinery. These actions were not primarily to prevent the development of more efficient manufacturing methods, as was popularly believed, but to warn owners who paid less than a living wage that there would be retribution for their misdeeds. However the most physically destructive of the Nottingham riots was more closely connected with access to parliamentary voting rights. The trouble exploded after news reached the town in October 1831 that the second Reform Bill had been rejected by the House of Lords. The intention of the Bill was to extend the franchise, and parliament's refusal to countenance the reform infuriated radical opinion in Nottingham. A protest meeting was called in the Market Square, just a couple of hundred yards from the Maypole Hotel. The gathering happened to coincide with the annual Nottingham Goose Fair, also held in the Square, and as a result attracted a particularly large crowd.

The level of excitement was high and a crowd of hotheads felt moved to punish those whom they saw as having opposed the reform, beginning with John Chaworth-Musters, the owner of Colwick Hall, a large mansion to the east of Nottingham. They marched through pelting rain to Colwick; only to find that Chaworth-Musters himself was not there. In frustration they looted the building and set fire to part of it while Mary Musters and her daughter Sophia hid shivering in rain-soaked terror among bushes nearby. The marauders then returned to the centre of town where they broke into the Duke of Newcastle's house on the castle rock and set it alight, leaving it a burned out wreck.[19] Even then the fury of the mob was not exhausted, for the next day they made their way to Beeston on the west side of Nottingham and burned down a silk factory.

In subsequent years the Chartist movement[20] found a welcome in Nottingham and was the source of another violent incident. There was a huge altercation in 1842, commemorated as the Battle of Mapperley Hills, when around 5,000 people gathered to hear a speech from the leader of the Chartists, Feargus O'Connor. The crowd was confronted by the law in the form of a contingent of soldiers who, in their attempts to disperse the people, ended up arresting several hundred of them. The Chartists continued to be strongly supported for some years, to the extent that O'Connor was elected MP for Nottingham in 1847. Unfortunately for the reputation of the movement he became mentally deranged and, in 1852, two years after the birth of Richard Hardy, he was formally declared insane and committed to a lunatic asylum. In the following years Chartism declined as a political force in Nottingham, but political radicalism left its imprint on later generations of the Hardy family.

John Hardy saw for himself all these spectacular changes growing up round him and they had a strong influence on his politics and his hopes for himself and his family. One effect seems to have been a fierce ambition to better himself. The close proximity of the Maypole Inn to scenes of appalling poverty and frequent violent social upheaval fuelled John's longing to rise up the social ladder as a means of insulating himself from the chaos. We have seen that this was not a complete remedy, for even the Duke of Newcastle's property had not been immune from the fury of the mob. All the same, climbing the social scale was a partial protection and the conviction that class was important passed down the generations to become in due course a matter that disgusted his grandson Alister and had an important effect on his attitude to human relationships. This in turn spilled over into other parts of Alister's life, including religion.

Along with the other miseries of slum life in Nottingham, there was a serious problem of drunkenness, as there was throughout the country in regions of chronic deprivation. In a legislative effort to curb the resulting alcoholism, the government decided somewhat bizarrely to make it easier for people to brew beer, and in 1830 it introduced the Beer Act. The act abolished the duty paid on beer, and payment of a two-guinea fee allowed anyone who wished to sell it from their home premises. The idea behind this curious liberalisation seems to have been to discourage drunkenness through gin drinking and replace it with more moderate beer consumption. Unsurprisingly, the legislation backfired and magnified the problem. Within two years, 42 new beer houses came into existence in Nottingham, in addition to the 120 or so licensed premises that already existed in the town.[21] Public alarm led to the launching of organisations that tried to combat alcohol abuse, many of them initiated by the churches. One of the leading campaigners was the founder of the Salvation Army, William Booth, who was born in Nottingham in 1829 and was thus a younger contemporary of the second John Hardy.

Whatever the opinion of Booth[22] and others, John Hardy's business instincts[23] saw the passing of the Beer Act as a commercial opportunity and he decided to start brewing his own beer on the premises of the Maypole. Then, in 1850, two brothers, William and Thomas Hardy, who at the time were living in Heanor in Derbyshire, founded what was eventually to become the Hardy & Hanson Brewery in the small Nottinghamshire town of Kimberley. They began by setting themselves up as wholesale beer merchants, purchasing their stock in bulk from brewers in Nottingham and Derby.[24] It is tempting to imagine that some of their supplies came from John Hardy and that possibly William and Thomas were none other than John's two oldest sons. They certainly had an office in Maypole Yard, but unfortunately the ages recorded for them do not coincide with those of John's family.[25] What is known for certain is that John's youngest son Richard did carve out a career for himself in the brewing industry.

Richard was born in 1850. Information about his early life is scanty, but he has a key role in this story because he was the father of Alister Hardy. It would be interesting to know about his intellectual accomplishments, as the parent of a child who was to become an eminent Oxford don, but there is almost nothing available about his schooling or his everyday life before the age of 16. A single passing reference reveals that he was sent away to school at Ripponden College in the West Riding of Yorkshire. The college went out of existence in the nineteenth century, but during the period when Richard would have been there it was presided over by William Dove, a remarkable headmaster who introduced democratic ideas that were well ahead of their time.[26] No doubt the enlightened curriculum enlarged Richard's vision and the fact that his parents chose to send him to Ripponden suggests that they recognised his talent and thought carefully about the best way to nurture it. As to his self-education in the school of everyday life, we can be reasonably sure that living close to the centre of events in the busy town meant that he was better informed than most small boys about the internal politics of Nottingham. His first ten years were spent in the Maypole premises, just over the way from the Exchange Building, which was where the town council conducted its business and which fronted onto the Market Square. Consequently the Maypole Hotel itself was bound to be a busy place and no doubt a number of local government officials from across the road were regulars in the bar.

By the time Richard was three years old the era of the stagecoach was over, but the hotel continued to be a hive of activity, politically and in other ways. The Constitutional Club, which always began its proceedings by drinking a toast to Robert Peel, held regular meetings in the Maypole, making it likely that the Hardys, though perpetually alert to the security of their social position, were benevolently disposed to the idea of political emancipation. They were probably one-nation Tories who admired Peel for having eventually seen the Reform Bill through the House of Commons.

A glance through Nottingham newspapers of the time for adverts of events at the Maypole reveals other kinds of enthusiasms of which young Richard would have been aware. Horse racing was a major interest, for there were regular announcements of auctions of thoroughbred stock in the yard. Notifications in the press also instructed those who wanted to compete in the South Notts Hunt's race meetings to apply to the Clerk of the Course, whose office was based at the Maypole. Sometimes top-level billiards matches were held on the premises and it was there that in 1867 the English champion William Cook made the largest break of his career, 394, in a match against his great rival, John Roberts. Cycle club and athletic club meetings also took place, and, following the foundation of Nottingham Forest Football Club in 1865, it set up its offices in Maypole Yard. Most famously (though shortly after John Hardy's time) in 1878, the first nationally representative Australian cricket team to play against Nottinghamshire at Trent Bridge chose to have their accommodation at the Maypole.[27]

There was another feature of Nottingham life that must have affected Richard and, in this case, as we shall see later, the enthusiasm was passed directly to his son Alister. One of the best-known local sporting heroes at the time was 'Bendigo', William Abednigo Thompson. His colourful life would have been exciting to a small boy, for he was a prize-fighter, the bare-knuckle boxing champion of England, celebrated in Arthur Conan Doyle's verse:

> You didn't know of Bendigo?
> Well that knocks me out!
> Who's your board schoolteacher?
> What's he been about?
> Chock a block with fairy tales;
> Full of useless cram,
> And never heard of Bendigo
> The Pride of Nottingham [28]

Bendigo's last fight, which he won in the forty-ninth round, was in 1850, the year Richard was born, but he lived on at his home in

Beeston until his death in 1880. After giving up boxing, Bendigo turned to drink, but he underwent religious conversion and became an evangelist. Although illiterate he was a powerful preacher; he used to take up a boxer's stance alongside his trophies, saying: 'See them belts? See them cups? I used to fight for those, but now I fight for Christ.' On one memorable occasion a bunch of his former mates were standing jeering and heckling at the back of the chapel where he was preaching, till he could stand it no longer. He shut his Bible, looked up and prayed:

'Good Lord, Thou knowest that since I gave up my wicked ways I have devoted my life to Thy service, and have given Thee the whole of my time. But now, seeing what's going on in this room, I'll take with Thy kind permission just five minutes off for me sen [my self].'

Then he vaulted from the pulpit into the crowd and restored order 'the prize fighting way'.[29]

Violence of a more controversial nature was also evident in Richard's youth. It is conceivable that he could have been a spectator at the last public execution in Nottingham, which took place in 1864 before a crowd in front of the Shire Hall on High Pavement when Richard was 14 years old. But the most common-place violence that he would have encountered daily was in the misery and degradation inflicted on the people living in the slums. He could not avoid knowing about the Rookeries, one of the very worst areas of slum property in Nottingham, for they were jammed into an area between Long Row and Parliament Street hardly more than a hundred yards from the Maypole. These slums were not cleared until the mid to late 1880s and some of the ragged people hanging about in Maypole Yard were probably identical to, or descendants of, the ne'er-do-wells from the stagecoach era, now hoping to earn a few coppers from assisting railway passengers with their luggage. The combination of adjacent poverty, disagree-able smell, dirt, disease and the occasional eruption of violence, persuaded Richard's parents to find somewhere to live away from their place of work. The fact that their business interests were prospering meant that they could afford to move to a new home in the countryside. Perhaps it was this change in fortune, enabling the family to get away from reminders of poverty that caused Richard to further emphasise his father's desire to make a gulf between the 'haves' and 'have-nots', and implicitly led Alister in his early youth to feel himself a cut above the proletariat.

Probably around 1860, when Richard would have been ten, John Hardy purchased Colwick House,[30] the largest farmhouse in what was then an agricultural hamlet not far from Colwick Hall, where the rioters had created havoc some 35 years previously. This might suggest that a move to Colwick was a move into insecurity, but the riots were a long time ago and John probably foresaw that Colwick would soon have a new railway line, enabling him to commute easily to work in Nottingham. The move was a success and enabled the family to live in some style. The 1861 national census lists the household as consisting of 48-year-old John, Mary, his 38-year-old wife, two sons – William, 20, and Richard, 10 – and four daughters – Mary, 6, Helen, 5, Hannah, 2, and Flora, 9 months. In addition, they had six servants – a gardener, groom, cook, laundry maid, nurse-maid and house servant.

When he was 15 or 16 years old, Richard had to think seriously about choosing a career. He decided to train to become an architect and was fortunate to be accepted as a pupil of Richard Charles Sutton, one of Nottingham's leading architects. Sutton's office was in Bromley House on Angel Row, just off the Market Square and a few hundred yards from the Maypole. After five years of being apprenticed to Sutton, Richard's studies took him to London, where he worked for eight months in the office of Messrs Cubitt and Company and, more briefly but significantly, with Sir Arthur Blomfield.

The interlude in Blomfield's office, though very short, must nevertheless have been pivotal in Richard's life. As the son of a provincial hotelkeeper, albeit an ambitious one, he had the novel experience of meeting and personally impressing someone close to the heart of the architectural establishment. Blomfield was the son of the Bishop of London, had been educated at Rugby and Trinity College, Cambridge, and was a prolific church architect. He was proposed for a fellowship of the Royal Institute of British Architects by George Gilbert Scott, the leading neo-gothic architect of his day; he won the Gold Medal of the RIBA, was knighted for his services to architecture and, on the death of J. E. Street, was involved in completing the Law Courts on the Strand. Blomfield certainly took to Richard, for on 2 May 1872 he was the chief signatory of a proposal to elect him to membership of the Institute at the young age of 22. The accompanying letter tells us something about the milieu of the RIBA at that time, for it says nothing about Richard's architectural accomplishments, merely remarking that 'I know Mr Hardy personally, and I think him a gentleman'. After he qualified, Richard decided to specialise in buildings for the brewing industry and was responsible for a number of breweries throughout central England, several of which are still in use.

I suggested that Richard's rise up the establishment ladder at least partly explains the attitude of social exclusiveness that Alister inherited and later rebelled against so strongly. There are almost no such clues available when it comes to religious matters. To the puzzled biographer there is an almost complete blank on Richard's opinions, which is unfortunate in view of the centrality of religion in the life of his son Alister. It would be very helpful to know how the family influenced his views, but beyond the fact that they were practising Anglicans there is nothing to add. Richard Hardy's association with his architect mentor, Richard Sutton, gives us almost the only conceivable hint as to his religious opinions. At least it does so if choosing to co-operate closely with someone over a prolonged period implies a degree of sympathy with their philosophy of life. Richard Sutton was the brother of Henry Septimus Sutton, who, although almost entirely forgotten today, was held in high esteem during his lifetime. Henry was a prolific writer of poetry,[31] and a follower of the eighteenth-century scientist and student of religious experience, Emmanuel Swedenborg. He was also a close friend of the poet Coventry Patmore, who became a committed Roman Catholic towards the end of his life, and he was an admirer of the deeply religious and somewhat eccentric Scottish writer, George McDonald. Furthermore, Richard Sutton transcribed a large body of his brother's correspondence on these subjects,[32] which suggests a kindred interest on his part. One might assume that some of this would rub off on Richard Hardy, or coincide with his interests, especially since his son would one day emulate Swedenborg in being both an eminent scientist and a mystic.

Richard's time in London was crucial, but there were other events around this period that must have contributed to his feeling that his life was entering a very different phase. In December 1871, a few days before Christmas, when presumably Richard was home from his studies in London, his father died at the house in Colwick at the relatively young age of 59. The death certificate records that Richard was present and that the cause of his father's decease was judged to be 'disease of the brain and heart', which usually means a stroke, so the death may have been sudden and unexpected.

Adjusting to this loss, Richard returned home to Nottingham in 1872 and for some reason decided to join the Robin Hood Rifles, the local volunteer military unit. Like many other such contingents throughout Britain, the Robin Hoods had been founded during the 1850s in response to an increasing and, as it turned out, mistaken suspicion that Napoleon III was planning to launch an invasion of the British Isles. They drilled regularly in the grounds of Nottingham Castle and paraded through the city from time to time, where they were on occasion the objects of ridicule and stone throwing from small boys. There was a Victorian amateurism about them that has been remarked on by historians, illustrated for example by the occasion when the officer in charge of a parade through the city square realised he had forgotten the correct military term for a manoeuvre ('left wheel') and finally, in exasperation, shouted: 'Dammit men, go up King Street!' In time they gained a more professional image: they were active in the Boer War and subsequently the First World War, where outstanding courage brought the Victoria Cross to members of the unit, most famously the young air ace, Albert Ball.[33]

Richard remained with the Robin Hoods for the rest of his life and eventually achieved the rank of Lieutenant Colonel, though the historian of the unit described his passage through the ranks as 'by no means meteoric'. Even so, he was considered prominent enough to appear in a set of biographies of Nottingham worthies, with a portrait photograph of him looking impressive: balding but handsome, rather stiff and perhaps a touch pompous in his military uniform, and sporting a set of Dundreary whiskers. Why did he join up, and why did he prefer to be listed in *Contemporary Biographies* for 1900 as a military man, rather than in the section for architects? Again there is no information available, but with the passing years membership of the unit almost certainly became socially useful to him and may even have been a refuge from domestic pressures. And that brings us to consider Elizabeth Hannah Clavering, the woman he married and who became the mother of Alister Hardy.

Still a bachelor in his early thirties, Richard happened to be visiting Scarborough one summer, probably in 1883. He was staying at the Prince of Wales hotel on the Esplanade, the most exclusive establishment of its type in Scarborough. Among his fellow guests was Elizabeth Clavering, and it was not long before he found himself in conversation with her and discovered that she had a remarkable and tragic story to tell. Although she was only 23, and ten years younger than Richard, she had already been married and widowed. She was the fifth child of Thomas Clavering, an Englishman who had settled in Glasgow. Alister Hardy believed that on his mother's side he was connected with the aristocratic Clavering family who had made their fortune from coal mining in County Durham, and whose seat was at Axwell Park near Blaydon.[34] That assumption may or may not have been correct. The records that are available name Tom Clavering's parents as Matthew Clavering and Elizabeth Hannah Turnbull. Investigation of the family history has so far uncovered only one couple fitting that description, and in their case Matthew was in much humbler circumstances, making his living as a coal miner and butcher.

Whatever his true origins, Tom was a prominent figure in the Glasgow business community who had made himself independently wealthy as a stock market trader in imported metal. He was also a merchant banker who had a reputation as a charming rogue specialising in offering financial assistance to companies in difficulty, and a hard nut in foreclosing on the loan as they sunk further into debt. At least that is what one would judge from his appearance in one of the satirical 'Clydeside Cameos' published in 1885 in *Fairplay,* where the following dialogue occurs:

> 'I hear McSplutter and Diddle are down.'
> 'Is that a fact? Bad?'
> 'Very. Been buying on credit and pledging for cash.'
> 'Ah! Uncle Tom in?'
> 'Oh! Of course. Heavy.'[35]

The Claverings lived in a large house on Woodside Terrace in a fashionable part of the city. Across the road were the Turnbull family, the patriarch of whom was Gregor Turnbull, one of the richest men in Glasgow. Gregor owned numerous sugar plantations in Trinidad, and one of the largest fleets of merchant ships on the

Clyde. He was in many ways a stereotypical example of a Scotsman 'on the make', than which, as the saying goes, there are few people more formidable. He is remembered today as the founding father of Furness Trinidad Limited, one of the biggest trading companies in Trinidad. What could be more natural than for the Claverings and the Turnbulls to get to know each other, and for Gregor's son, Gregor McGregor Turnbull, to fall in love with the girl across the road? And, indeed, they became engaged.

In 1879, in the midst of this fairy tale of wealth and privilege, Gregor Turnbull senior died while on a visit to his assets in Trinidad. In his will he made it clear that he wanted young Gregor, then 24, to be the major heir to the business, and after a suitable period of mourning, the young man and his 20-year-old fiancée were married in 1880 according to the rites and practices of the Free Church of Scotland. They set out together for Trinidad and soon after arrival it seems that Elizabeth was expecting a child. Then utter disaster struck. There was a Yellow Fever epidemic sweeping through Trinidad at the time and both Gregor and Elizabeth succumbed to the disease. In the trauma that followed, Elizabeth lost the child she was carrying but eventually recovered. Gregor was less fortunate and within a very few days of becoming infected he died a miserable and agonising death.

Quite apart from the personal catastrophe suffered by Elizabeth, there was evidence of extreme negligence on the part of the medical personnel. The tone of the news articles in the local Trinidad press was accusatory and directly identified those they deemed to be at fault, including a Dr de Wolf, who was meant to be treating Gregor. The policy of the chief medical officer seemed to be to deny that there was any kind of emergency. The *Port of Spain Gazette* for Saturday, 27 August 1881, had a leading article on the crisis, beginning:[36]

> Trinidad, under the medical leadership of Dr Crane, is fast becoming a bye-word for medical incapacity and bad faith in the eyes of the neighbouring Islands. In Martinique they laugh at our clean bills of health and will not even look at them.

Fear of the disease, from which there was no protection at the time, led some doctors to behave with criminal neglect towards their patients, and such was the case with young Gregor. Referring to three particularly disgraceful examples of cowardice, the leading article goes on to say:

> They all, we regret to say, resulted fatally. It is not our intention to attribute these deaths to Dr de Wolf, but we contend that they were cases in which the assistance of the doctor attending should have been available at the very shortest notice ... In the [...] case of Mr Turnbull, Dr de Wolf [...] attended, and although the progress of the disease resulting in death was most rapid, Dr de Wolf absented himself not only in the day, but slept in town [i.e. out of touch] although he had left his patient delirious.

The apocalyptic tone of the leading article in the *Gazette* for the previous Saturday conveys something of the terror felt in Trinidad in the face of the epidemic:

> When the future historian of Trinidad brings his description down to the period embraced by the last six or eight months, he will, as he deals with that time of disease and death, be forcibly struck by one peculiar feature in its history; and that will be the sad, the almost inexplicably sad circumstances which have surrounded most of the recent deaths. Romance and romance alone will furnish him with any prototype of the deathbed scenes ... Where will he find a parallel even in romance to the sad sad case of Mrs Gregor McGregor Turnbull – *wife, mother, childless*, and a *widow* in less than one short year; and of how many others might similar things be said.

Aged just 21, Elizabeth emerged from the nightmare in Trinidad and returned home to Britain, initially convalescing in Plymouth under the care of her father. She must surely have been purged of any naïve optimism she may have borne as someone nurtured in a highly privileged environment. In the following year, no doubt still in search of physical and emotional recovery from her ordeal, she came to Scarborough and met Richard Hardy. We can see from photographs that she was a good looking young woman, while at the same time she must have been struggling with a quite exceptional degree of grief. How her sorrow affected Richard when he first encountered her we cannot know, and we can only guess at the nature of what passed between them, but it led eventually to their decision to become engaged. Certainly the extreme trauma through which she had passed was to affect her emotional state and she appears to have been an unsettled and demanding person who did not become easier over the years. One of her grandsons remembers that she was known in the family as 'very cantankerous and difficult'.[37]

Richard and Elizabeth got married on 27 November 1884, not in Glasgow or Nottingham as might be expected, but in St Barnabas Anglican church in Kensington in London. Why they chose London is not clear. Was it too painful for Elizabeth to contemplate a second wedding in Glasgow, the scene of a blissful relationship so soon to be brutally destroyed? Was there felt to be something not quite proper about her relationship with Richard? Did one family or other disapprove of the match? Among the descendents there is no testimony or even rumour available as to the facts. After the wedding the couple returned to Nottingham, and here, in 1885, Elizabeth gave birth to the first child of the marriage, christened John Clavering Hardy, but always known in the family as Jack. Approximately eight years after Jack was born, in 1893 she had a second son, Vernon Clavering Hardy, and three years after that, on 10 February 1896, her third son was born. She and Richard chose the Gaelic form of Alexander – though with a simplified spelling – as the first name for the new arrival, and once more he was given the second name of Clavering. It is not known why the parents made the rather unusual decision to give all three sons the same name, but perhaps it was to underline their supposed connection with the titled branch of the family in County Durham.

On 10 June, four months after he was born, in a ceremony conducted by the vicar of the near-by All Saints Anglican church on Raleigh Street,[38] the infant was baptised and christened Alister Clavering Hardy. We shall see that each of the tangled elements of the history described in this opening chapter will play an important part in the formation of young Alister's character and outlook.

CHAPTER TWO

From Infancy to Oundle

On the February day when he was born, Alister's mother no doubt cradled her third son tenderly in her arms and looked down to meet his gaze for the first time. At that moment she must have felt a small surge of anxiety, for she would have seen that the infant had a squint. Nowadays this would be treated by an operation, but Alister never had it corrected. His parents took him to see a specialist in London when he was a small child, and in a fragment of the unpublished autobiography that he began writing in his late 80s he records with some bitterness that they were told that he would 'grow out of it'. He did not, and the opinion at the time was that after approximately the age of nine it was too late to do anything about it. Some photographs from his early childhood look as if they were taken in profile to conceal the fact that one eye was turned inwards. In later years he ceased to worry, to the extent that his squint almost became part of his personal signature. Elizabeth's response, revealed in her subsequent letters and actions, was a flood of maternal concern. Alister was vulnerable, and she was determined to protect him as well as she could. Others had similar emotions.

Whatever the problems caused by his disability, the infant Alister was well protected, both spiritually and socially. His baptism at All Saints dealt with the former, while his social standing was guarded by the peculiarity already mentioned, that all three brothers were given the second name Clavering, an insistent public reminder of their grandfather Clavering's claim to aristocratic origins. It seems that Richard, aware that his social status was on the rise, was keen on any way of bolstering his position, including securing a fashionable address. When they were first married, Richard and Elizabeth had lived on Clinton Terrace at the top end of Nottingham Park, which, it will be recalled, is adjacent to the castle. It is a well-to-do estate laid out in Italian style and occupying the former deer park of the Duke of Newcastle. Later the family moved to Waverley Mount, a cul-de-sac off Waverley Street alongside Nottingham Boys High School.[1] Number 7 on the Mount was designed by Richard himself and it was here that Alister first saw the light of day.

Like the Park, Waverley Mount was situated on what was then the fashionable outer rim of the city, above and removed from the bustling squalor of the centre. Just below the Mount was the Arboretum, an extensive and rolling urban park which still exists and forms a buffer zone separating the inhabitants from the middle of the town. Ada Richards, Alister's nanny, regularly used to push his pram through the Arboretum to where there was a duck pond, alongside a collection of exotic caged birds that fascinated the infant. Alister's earliest memory was of an incident when they were leaving after a visit to the cages. He spotted two flashes of bright colour that he assumed to be birds and screamed petulantly till his nanny stopped, only to be disappointed for they were nothing more than pieces of coloured paper in a wire litter basket. He never lost the strength of his childhood passion for intense colour, particularly in relation to animals, and it evolved into his life-long interest in mimicry and camouflage as well as his major hobby, watercolour painting.

Apart from his nurse, Alister's closest companion was his brother Vernon, who was three years older than him. The two of them slept in the night nursery and, as small boys do, they enjoyed frightening each other after lights out:

> ... we used to talk of floor ghosts; sometimes there was a draught under the door, which made the mat ripple and seeing this we would cry: 'quick, quick, get into bed or the floor ghosts will get you'. Then again there were strange creatures which inhabited the bath, or so we imagined ... these were the simple effects of pulling the plug when the

long spiralling funnel of water disappeared down the hole with a curious noise and we called them 'quires'.[2]

At that time the Boer war was the salient political event, signalled as far as the boys were concerned by having rosettes pinned to their white sailor suits with pictures of Kitchener, Buller, Baden-Powell and other famous military leaders. In the nursery they played at soldiers, imitating incidents in the war and firing toy guns at each other's forts. For a short time they took up the dangerous practice of using wax matches purloined from their father's matchbox as ammunition. They worked out how to make the matches catch fire on release from the guns, with the aim of setting their targets alight, a practice soon to be banned by their horrified elders. Another leisure pursuit was the production of plays in a toy theatre, especially pantomimes at Christmas time. Alister was the artist who drew and coloured the paper figures that were pushed on stage with little cardboard strips, while Vernon, as the practical member of the family, looked after the lighting.

More significant than these entertainments were the measures Alister's parents took to boost their sons' interest in natural history. Of the three boys, Alister was the one who needed no encouragement. He was steeped in it, even assuming that a popular music hall song of the day, 'You are my honeysuckle, I am the bee', was about entomology. He got additional advice on collecting insects from William Ryles, who was a teacher at the Boys High School and lived two doors away at Number 11. Ryles was an internationally acclaimed entomologist and he taught Alister how to identify and preserve the specimens he had collected.

Vernon and Alister often played together in the garden, digging deep holes in search of insects, spiders and other invertebrates. In his unfinished autobiography Alister gives many instances of ecstatic encounters with nature in and around Waverley Mount:

> Our day nursery was on the top floor, and on the
> right-hand side of the house, bordering the garden, were
> three tall lime trees. I sharply recall the wonderful effect of
> the sunlight streaming down on the young spring leaves,

and ever since, I have experienced a feeling of delight at seeing the new leaves of lime trees in the springtime sunshine. Some of the leaves grew close against the nursery window, and sometimes when I looked out at them I would suddenly see looper caterpillars, which I watched with great interest. They usually appeared just before we were going on holiday, otherwise I think I would have tried to keep them in jam jars, as indeed I did so often later on. In the front of the garden there was a fine copper beech tree and next to it a beautiful red may tree. I can remember my excitement on going out of the garden gate, which was against the may tree, and seeing for the first time on the pavement outside, the caterpillar of the gold-tailed moth, whose black and white body was streaked with scarlet (a warning colouration of course, against its exceedingly irritating hairs). I picked it up, much to the consternation of my nanny, who said I would get 'bug rash' as a result of handling it. Some people do, but I have never been affected in that way. I returned it to the may tree from which it had fallen; then, just in the same place, coming out of the cracks between the paving stones where these joined the garden wall, little bronze-brown, almost golden coloured beetles ran hither and thither, giving me great delight.[3]

Astonishingly, some relics of Alister's childhood interests are still in existence, in the form of tiny booklets hardly more than an inch square, filled with drawings of animals and plants. One has the title 'Egg Book', and written on the inside front cover, in block capitals, the words 'by Alister Hardy'. The touching illustrations in the uncertain hand of a small boy include an ostrich egg (large), a sparrow egg and robin egg (small) and various other eggs, and the booklet concludes on the last page with the words 'The End'. His mother probably sewed the booklets together for him, since another of them, entitled 'Flower Book', begins patriotically with drawings of a Scottish Bluebell and a Thistle.

We have already seen that, apart from Vernon and his mother, Alister's mainstay was his nanny, Ada, who was just five years younger than Elizabeth and was one of three servants in the house. She accompanied him on outside trips, sometimes in a hansom cab, with Alister dressed up in his Little Lord Fauntleroy suit, to attend a children's party in one of the big houses in the park. She was a favourite with the Hardy family and, when she died, Elizabeth made arrangements to provide a headstone for her grave. Her death occurred in 1918, several years after Alister left home, but he obviously retained tender memories of her, for in a letter of condolence to her brother he quoted these lines borrowed from Robert Louis Stevenson:

> For the long nights you lay awake
> And watched for my unworthy sake:
> For your most comfortable hand
> That led me through the uneven land:
> For all the story-books you read:
> For all the pains you comforted:
> For all you pitied, all you bore,
> In sad and happy days of yore —
>
> My second Mother, my first Wife,
> The angel of my infant life —[4]

Alister's father was less in evidence, since he spent much of the time away from home, either overseeing the construction of a brewery or on manoeuvres with his beloved Robin Hood Rifles. Nevertheless, according to Alister, Richard was a good sport with a sense of fun when he *was* able to share his life with his family. In the evenings he would do quick sketches on the backs of envelopes to entertain the boys, and a postcard surviving from that time, sent to Alister by his father, is touchingly addressed to him as 'Mr Beetle' with, in place of the word, a sketch of a beetle in a top hat. Richard was also behind one of the other mementoes from childhood: a hand-made assembly of 39 numbered pages, sewn together to contain Alister's next attempt at a publication, entitled 'INSCETS' (sic). The text includes pages of pencil and wax crayon illustrations, labelled 'plates', a little bookmark, and it even has an index at the end. Where did he get the idea? Richard had the same interest in natural history as his son, and among his books was the Reverend W. Houghton's *Sketches of British Insects* published in 1877.[5]

Alister delighted in Houghton's anatomical descriptions and even before he could read had loved to have them read out to him. A glance through the pages, especially the illustrations, tells you at once that this is where he drew the inspiration for his first efforts at book production. In his adult years Alister thought his little book, spattered with ink blots and presented with the wholehearted naïvety of childhood, had enough resemblance in style to his New Naturalist books on *The Open Sea* (published in the 1950s[6]) for him to remark on the similarity.

Though Richard Hardy was often away from home, there were other precious moments of companionship. On one occasion he came up to the nursery at the top of the house and showed Alister something he had not realised before, that the marble mantelpiece was full of the bullet shaped fossil *Belemnites*. Because of the way the marble had been cut and polished it was possible to see many places where the saw had sliced across the animal to reveal the internal structure of chambers subdividing the body. Richard explained that these fossils used to be thought of by country people as thunderbolts, but they were in fact the remains of marine animals, millions of years old, and related to the modern sea-living *Nautilus*. Looking back, Alister thought his father had been trying to explain something about evolution, but the small boy was too young to comprehend what was being said to him.

Sometimes father and son would go on outings, as on the occasion when they took a boat trip on the river Trent to visit Colwick Hall, which Richard knew well since it was not far from his childhood home in Colwick House. On this particular trip Alister remembered him emptying the matches from his metal matchbox so that he could bring home some specimens of brightly coloured *Chrysomelid* beetles that they found in their hundreds, crawling all over the flower heads of some hogweed growing near the Hall.

Another meeting point was the family holiday. Summer vacations were complex events, involving the packing and transport of all but the kitchen sink and extending for three months, from mid-June to mid-September. During Alister's earliest childhood the custom was to spend June and July in Hackness, about six miles outside Scarborough, perhaps because his parents had discovered the village at the time of their first meeting. To this day, in the right sort of weather, the road from Scarborough to Hackness has an unusually magical atmosphere and to travel along it is to feel as if one is entering into a timeless wonderland. Hackness itself is distinctly unlike other villages, with a channelled stream running along part of its sandstone walled street and there, at a turn in the road, stands the Red House where the Hardys set up their summer headquarters.

Alister's older brother Jack was at that time a boarder at Malvern School, but when the summer term ended in July he came north to join them. Little mention is made of Jack in the autobiography and he comes across as a somewhat enigmatic figure, lacking the boisterous enthusiasm that came so easily to Alister. Nevertheless, in line with the family's preoccupation with natural history he had a butterfly collection of sorts and when he lost interest he passed on his setting boards to Alister. It was also Jack who took his brother up the hill behind the Red House one day when, for the first time and unforgettably, they came across a group of Humming Bird Hawk Moths gathering nectar from a tall blue flowering plant. These moths look like the birds after which they are named, and hover like them, and the beat of their wings makes a humming sound. They are truly a wonderful, almost numinous sight and the gift of that memory must have made Jack seem less distant from his younger brother.

When we consider the intensity of Alister's religious commitment in adult life, and the overtly religious purpose of his unfinished autobiography, it is yet again tantalising to find in its pages almost no mention of his own earliest religious practice and beliefs. One exception is his lyrical description of his time in Hackness, which makes it easy to empathise with his own conviction, expressed in his autobiography: that what was emerging here was a conscious awareness of a spiritual dimension to his experience, though unexpressed because of the lack of a language or an adequate metaphor system. This kind of spiritual empiricism was to be the lifelong focus of Alister's character, the importance and centrality of which he would not become fully aware until his teenage years.

Scarborough remained the second port of call for the family each August up until Alister was four or five years old. All that can be gleaned of religion in his description of holidays there, is a passing reference to churchgoing on Sunday morning. He notes how, after morning church (expressed in such a way as to imply that more or less everybody attended divine service), young people were in the habit of strolling languidly along the sea front, self consciously putting themselves on display. Alister's biographical essay stimulated him to recover other remote vignettes. Often he relates them in a disjointed, dream-like manner, for example he remembered as an isolated fragment a man in white trousers and blazer, standing in the street selling whiting. On another day in the midst of a violent thunderstorm he saw (or, he wondered, did he imagine it?) a fireball rolling its way slowly across the Scarborough cliff edge.[7] Then he retrieved a strange and slightly unsettling image of men dressed in brightly coloured jockey clothes sitting astride horses that are drawing carts along the sea front.

Another more coherent kind of childhood memory fits more directly with Alister's subsequent working life. Recalled and first put down on paper in old age, it is perhaps not surprising that his ordering of his memories fits rather easily with the structure of his career. He writes vividly of seeing the South Bay filled by luggers, with 'their deep brown, almost red, sails, come south from Scotland after the herring, bringing their catches in to be gutted by the fishwives at the harbour'. He remembered too the cliff tram which operated on a hydraulic principle and carried people 150 feet up to the Esplanade at the top of the cliff. Aboard the tram he was thrilled to see more and more of the bay coming into view as the carriage rose upwards and all kinds of other sailing vessels – brigs, barques, perhaps full-rigged ships – appearing over the horizon; and then; when it was pointed out to him; came the realisation that he was witnessing the curvature of the earth.

Animal life continued to dominate his attention. There was a large glass shelter at the top of some steps leading up from the beach. It was meant to provide protection from sudden showers of rain, but its main attraction to Alister was that in bad weather it acted like a gigantic trap which became filled with insects. Other holidaymakers might have shuddered, but Alister was never disappointed when it rained because 'I then had a wonderful chance of examining those window panes, which had literally hundreds of insects on them'.

Most vividly of all, he recalled the rock pools:

> As the tide went out it left quite large pools, each one a magic aquarium of different coloured seaweeds which,

when lifted up, revealed crabs, shrimps and little fishes. Then of course there were the beautifully coloured sea anemones, and starfishes, and if the tide was going far out one would get sea urchins in the deeper pools.[8]

Around the turn of the century, a shadow began to pass over the joyfulness of Alister's childhood. His parents started taking trips together, unaccompanied by the boys. Ostensibly, for this is what they told Alister and Vernon, they were looking for new places to go on holiday in Yorkshire. What they did not mention was the deterioration in Richard's health that is noticeable in photographs from the period and it may be guessed that part of the reason for the excursions was to seek for alleviation or a cure for his illness. One formal portrait of him, probably taken when he was in his mid-forties, gives a hint of a lifestyle that was less than ideal, for while he looks prosperous and the very image of a Victorian business man, his face is fuller than is compatible with good health and suggests that in matters of food and drink he was less than abstemious. Another informal snapshot from about the same time has him in military uniform, slouched in a chair somewhere out of doors, so presumably at camp with the Robin Hood Rifles, and here he looks very obviously overweight.

By 1901, when Alister would have been five, and thus old enough to have clear memories of his father, Richard's appearance had changed again. A photograph held in the archives of the Robin Hood Rifles portrays him, as he then was, the Commanding Officer of his Unit. He is in civvies, a white suit and a straw hat, looking thin and pale, while around him in relaxed pose, but in full military uniform, are his brother officers. The intuitive response on seeing this photograph is that Richard must have been convalescing from serious illness and therefore the picture commemorated a welcome back after a prolonged absence. Eventually, in 1904 at the relatively young age of 54, he died of Bright's disease, as recorded on his death certificate. The main symptom of Bright's disease is a chronic inflammation of the kidneys and there is a family rumour that Richard's condition resulted from overindulgence. According to medical advice[9] there is no link between alcohol consumption and Bright's disease but still, more than a hundred years later, there is a feeling in the family that grandfather drank too much.

The funeral service took place in All Saints Church on 11 October 1904, and was conducted by the vicar, the Rev. T. W. Windley. The chief mourner was Jack, and Richard's three sisters were also present, but most prominence is given to the large number of officers and men of the Robin Hood Rifles who had turned up to pay their respects. In the obituary that appeared in the *Nottingham Evening Post* for that day, Richard is described as a colonel in the Robin Hoods and nowhere is there any reference to the fact that he made his living by designing breweries.[10] The one small reminder of his profession was the presence of Richard Sutton, the architect to whom he had been apprenticed in his teens. Was Richard Hardy's military commitment entirely disinterested or did his emphasis on the army derive from embarrassment at his link with the licensed trade, perhaps aggravated by Elizabeth's Presbyterian disapproval? Neither Elizabeth nor his two younger sons were present at the service. It is tempting to speculate that Elizabeth's grief was made particularly severe through reactivating her traumatic feelings of loss when her first husband died in Trinidad. Whatever the reason for her absence, she was in any case protected from censure because newly widowed Edwardian wives were often expected to feel too distraught to attend. Alternatively, perhaps she needed to absent herself in order to give attention to the distress of the boys.

In his autobiographical writings Alister keeps questions of life and death, and in this case his own feelings at the death of his father, at arm's length. He reports his father's passing briefly but beyond a standard statement about loss, he sets aside any reference to what cannot have been other than a personal catastrophe to an eight year old boy.[11]

The person most practically affected by Richard's death was of course Elizabeth. Perhaps because she was in mourning, or because she was undecided on a course of action, she made no move throughout most of 1905, but something had to be done to ensure that Vernon and Alister received an education. Jack was out of the picture, having apparently left home. Working on hints, we may gather that his relationship to his parents was not a happy one. As I mentioned earlier he was sent to Malvern School, but the records show he was only there for five terms.[12] It seems that the family had hoped that he would study architecture and follow on in the business, for this expectation appears in the section of the archives of the RIBA devoted to Richard Hardy.[13] In the 1911 census Jack does record his profession as that of architect and at that time he was living as a boarder in a house on Derby Road in Nottingham. Whatever the reason, he failed to continue in the profession and followed a career that kept him remote from his relatives, reportedly spending a long period in Canada. During that time he all but disappeared from the awareness of the family, though in his later years he returned to London and re-established contact with his brothers, particularly Vernon who also lived in the capital.

Though Jack was the chief mourner at his father's funeral, we do not know how dutiful he was towards his mother or where her main emotional support was located. Her financial position was relatively sound since she had inherited a reasonable legacy following Richard's death. She was nevertheless unsettled and towards the end of 1905 she left Nottingham and rented four rooms at 40 Harlow Moor Drive, in Harrogate in Yorkshire, taking the loyal Ada Richards with her as her housemaid. The address was respectable and the house solidly built, but it was a come-down from the residence in Nottingham and thoroughly confusing to small boys used to the luxury of Waverley Mount.

An accidental discovery gave Alister a further reason to feel disoriented. One day, some months after his father's death, he was helping his mother to clear the house in Nottingham in preparation for the move to Harrogate, when he came across a faded watercolour painting of a bungalow, apparently in tropical surroundings. When he asked Elizabeth about it, she sat him down and gently began to explain something that she had never told him previously; the fact that she had been married to someone else before she met Richard, and about the tragic events in Trinidad. What Alister made of it, we do not know, but following the death of Richard he must have had the strong feeling that the supposedly solid foundations of his world were in reality precarious.

Elizabeth told her children she had chosen Harrogate because it reminded her of Scotland, but in that case why did she not return to Glasgow where her family was still living? One reason may have been that she wanted to be relatively close to Vernon and Alister, whom she had decided to send as boarders to Bramcote School in

Scarborough where Jack had been a pupil. Bramcote is today an elite prep school[14] sending boys on to most of the major British public schools, but its beginnings were very small. The Hardy family may have discovered it during their holiday visits to Scarborough and they had perhaps met Samuel Servington Savary, the founder, in 1893 when he opened the school with just three pupils. Jack Hardy was sent there in 1897 when it could not have had time to become widely known. Subsequently the school was patronised surprisingly often by parents from the Nottingham area, possibly because the name was the same as that of the village of Bramcote near Nottingham (now a suburb of the city) and it was therefore presumed to have some connection with the East Midlands.

In the vacations, Alister and Vernon came home to the rented rooms in Harrogate where their mother was still living out of packing cases and confined for living space to the crowded sitting room. She could not seem to make up her mind what to do, with the result that the boys went through parallel feelings of frustration and unhappiness. They felt quite lonely and had to depend on each other for company, for most of their friends were in Bramcote School. When they were entertaining themselves indoors at Harlow Moor Drive, the cramped conditions meant that they filled the whole of the sitting room with their clutter – in Vernon's case magazines and books about cars, while Alister took up a new interest in aeronautics. They also produced a journal which they called *The Holiday Chat*, made up of cuttings from magazines glued into an exercise book, with added editorial comments. Alister remembered the rush they had every week to get their publication out in time for Saturday morning. All this took place in the same room that other household activities like meals took place, leading to the constant exhortation from their mother, 'Now boys, pack up your traps!'

In spite of the emotional upheaval, Harrogate was in an interesting part of Yorkshire and the brothers frequently took the opportunity to cycle over the moors to local beauty spots like Bolton Abbey or Pateley Bridge. Alister also remembered the two of them going out onto the hills to fly very large box kites. In the evenings they might stroll down into town, often stopping at a bandstand that lay en route, where Mr Fred Coleman's Pierrots performed on a stage built out from the stand. Their mother loved the theatre, so sometimes she would take them to matinée performances of popular musical comedies at the Royal Opera House, such as *The Merry Widow*, *The Arcadians* and *The Quaker Girl*. There were symphony concerts, which Alister confessed he didn't always understand, also ballet, and interesting lectures. He was enthralled on one occasion by Sir Ernest Shackleton, newly returned from the Antarctic and talking about his adventures. After his lecture he was besieged by small boys, including Alister, seeking his autograph. Alister was not to know that he himself would one day make an epic journey into the great waters of the Antarctic.

It seems that Elizabeth shared her children's discomfort with the restricted living quarters in Harrogate, for the little family returned to Nottingham every year for the duration of the Christmas holidays, receiving hospitality from their numerous relatives. Alister saw this as a return to normality and enjoyed the parties and dances that always took place, along with trips to the pantomime at the Theatre Royal as well as clandestine visits to the music halls.

It was in his home town that he made a hit in a fancy dress competition at a charity ball, being presented with the first prize by the Duchess of Portland for his appearance as a penguin. A photograph shows that the outfit, designed by himself, completely enveloped his body, with a beak and head that lifted up like a cap and with his arms hidden inside the flipper-like wings. These could open to allow his hands out when he wanted to dance. He looked ludicrous, which delighted him. The fact that his mother could afford to have the penguin suit manufactured for him by a top London company at great expense was a reminder that the restricted conditions at Harlow Moor Drive were only temporary.[15]

He enjoyed wandering round the Art Gallery in Nottingham Castle and visiting the natural history museum, which when he first went there was associated with the University College and housed in Shakespeare Street.[16]

Whatever murmurings of unsettlement there may have been in Alister's consciousness when he and Vernon first arrived at Bramcote, they were soon suppressed and the two seem to have been very happy there. Savary's name amused the giggling Hardy boys, who fondly liked to imagine that his first name was really Arthur, giving the initials A. S. S. He was said to have a lovable and gentle personality but there must have been some steel in him, for he also had a reputation as a firm disciplinarian. When Alister was at Bramcote, Savary was a man in his forties.[17] A photograph of 1910 shows him with the assembled group of 58 boys in the school. Alister stands in the back row, tall but otherwise unremarkable. He is about the same height as his best friend Archie Paul further along the row. On Sundays, as the two tallest boys, Alister and Archie led their 'crocodile' to divine service at the nearby St Martin's church. They were dressed in their Sunday best with Eton collars and top hats, no doubt thinking of themselves as a cut above the local *hoi polloi*. If so, it didn't prevent them from fooling about. To their delight the teenage girls of Queen Margaret's School[18] also marched to church in crocodile on Sundays and converged on St Martin's. Alister remembered:

> On the way there was a corner we had to turn, always known as 'Amen Corner' because we were not allowed to speak after rounding it and Archie and I would lead our crocodile faster and faster, to try to cut the girls off at Amen Corner. Furious messages came from the headmaster telling us to slow down because the [little] boys at the back were running.[19]

Savary's idea of education was traditional and classical but in some ways he was an eccentric, at least by comparison with the norms of other similar establishments. For example, he would not allow sports fixtures with other schools, on the grounds that they generated ill-feeling. On the other hand all the boys had to participate in compulsory boxing every Wednesday. He neglected science at a time when it was becoming increasingly important in the educational curriculum. Nevertheless, most boys were interested in railways or in new mechanical devices like motor cars which were just beginning to appear on the roads. The result was that Alister felt discouraged from continuing with his interest in insects and instead turned his enthusiasm towards man-made flight, whether by balloon, airship or aeroplane. His wholehearted nature ensured that he quickly became very knowledgeable on the subject, and in 1908 he started collecting all the newspaper cuttings he could find on the subject, filling four large scrapbooks which, though tattered, still exist. In 1910 he and his brother Vernon went to Doncaster and for the first time saw an aeroplane flying at only the second air show ever to take place in Britain. Flight remained an enthusiasm for the rest of his life and many years later he would write a book about ballooning.[20]

In one respect Alister kept in touch with his interest in animals. His pleasure with manned flight made him curious about the way birds were able to keep themselves in the air, and with his collector's delight he filled two notebooks with sketches of birds in flight, some soaring on rising air currents, and he adds remarks about the infrequent wing beats. There is another survival from those days that indicates the wisdom of a teacher and also Hardy's scholarly exuberance at an early age. Presumably as part of a class exercise (since it is contained in a Bramcote School exercise book and there are corrections of spelling errors in another hand), he and Archie each invented an imaginary country and provided it with the apparatus necessary to survive and prosper. Alister's invention takes the form of a large island, Harland, divided into districts and provided with towns (the main one called New Waverley after the home he had left behind in Nottingham), villages, roads, railways with different kinds of rolling stock, a monetary system, postage stamps (old and new issues), factories (including a gunpowder works), coal mines, civic buildings, an army with a variety of units and uniforms, a navy similarly complex, a merchant fleet, all ruled over by King Hardy and Queen Ethel. One of the most striking aspects of his invention is the way he regularly presents a plan of an area of Harland and provides a picture of the landscape represented by the plan. There is stern competition between these imaginary nations, sometimes outright war. The main rival is Arcland, Archie's invented country, against which, in times of peace, there are sporting competitions – always won by Harland, or so Alister would have us believe.

This delightful exercise book points to one of Hardy's great strengths, already evident in childhood: his prolific creativity. In view of what he became we might expect him to feature in prize-giving days and to be given a leadership role in the activities of Bramcote School, but a thorough search of the archival material failed to uncover any evidence of such success. As one teacher remarked, 'He hid his light under a bushel', and Alister himself thought he was a late developer. He did however succeed in gaining entrance to Oundle School in the small market town of that name in

Northamptonshire, and in the spring term of 1911, approaching the age of 15, he joined his brother Vernon there in Sidney House.

We do not have explicit information on why Alister's mother chose Oundle, but the reputation of the school at that time is explanation enough, for the headmaster was a remarkable man called F. W. Sanderson. The patron of the school was the Grocers' Company and its members showed considerable courage in appointing Sanderson, who was just 35 years of age in 1892 when he left his post as senior physics master at Dulwich College and took over at Oundle. He was said to have had problems with class control as a young teacher, to have an uncertain temper, and to speak in a somewhat halting manner without the traditional rhetorical skills. Yet H. G. Wells, who sent his sons to Oundle and wrote a biography of Sanderson, said of him: 'I think him beyond question the greatest man I have ever known with any degree of intimacy'.[21] He was the first non-clergyman to be given the headship of Oundle, though he had studied theology at Durham University, preached regularly in chapel and ran classes in religious education. Apart from the burning sincerity of his care for his pupils, Sanderson's vision and creativity turned a mediocre school into a highly successful and oversubscribed institution, famed for its innovations in science education and for the workshops where boys were introduced in the most practical way to engineering and technology.

Alister's arrival there was accompanied by a frightening initiation. Sanderson's liberal ideas did nothing to get rid of the unpleasant and potentially dangerous ritual that Alister had to endure. He found he was sharing a dormitory with a dozen new boys, and along the middle of the room was a row of chests of drawers. The procedure was to force new boys to get inside a large laundry basket which was standing on top of one end of the row of drawers. Gradually the basket was tipped over the edge, so that the boy inside had to leap out at the last moment before it crashed to the ground, to avoid injury.[22] Luckily Alister chose the right fraction of a second.

Apart from this painful memory, Alister's recollections of life at Oundle were in many respects positive. He was thrilled by the emphasis given to science and appreciative of the opportunity to return to the biological interests that had been suppressed while he was a pupil at Bramcote School. He took up once more his previous enthusiasm for entomology, aided by the richness of insect life in the surrounding countryside and abetted by the concurrent publication in fortnightly parts of W. F. Kirby's *Butterflies and Moths of Europe*,[23] for which Alister paid ninepence per copy at the local newsagent. His absorption stayed with him throughout his years at Oundle, and his interest in insect camouflage and mimicry led to the setting up of an exhibition on the subject on a school open day. It also catalysed his friendships, most notably with Alan Gardiner, son of the Cambridge botanist, Walter Gardiner. They got to know each other when Alan arrived at Oundle. He was unpacking a butterfly net when Alister happened to be near by, and characteristically remarked: 'Goodness me, are you interested in butterflies too?' Similarly his love of aeronautics led to his friendship with Geoffrey Vickers, another enthusiast for aircraft and the son of a wealthy lace manufacturer in Nottingham.

The friends he made and the care taken of him ensured that Hardy enjoyed his time at Oundle and as a boy at the school he had greatly admired Sanderson. In later years he became more critical. While he honoured the ideals of the headmaster he felt that, with the exception of Ault, who was the Chemistry master (and perhaps George Olive, who taught Alister biology), the quality of the teaching staff was not good enough to put them into practice. Somewhat surprisingly he was even more dismissive of the famous system of workshops that Sanderson introduced:[24]

> ... boys were allowed to spend what I felt, on looking back, was far too much time in laboratories and workshops ...
> One could if one wished – though I was never that way inclined – spend long periods working with lathes and other tools, making some beautifully finished metal or wooden object. It was ... only afterwards that I realised that Sanderson, by introducing these workshops, was cashing in on the training of the boys [sic: sons of the owners?] of the great engineering firms of the north – Newcastle, Sunderland, Sheffield, etc. The leaders of these firms could boast that their sons 'went through the shops' ...
> Afterwards I was so convinced that boys were spending far too long in workshops and laboratories that I decided,

> although I had enjoyed my days at Oundle enormously,
> that if and when I had a son I would not send him there
> …[25]

In retrospect, Alister was equally unimpressed by the education he received over and above science. Even within science, beyond the realm of biology, he found he was easily bored. Rather remarkably for a future Oxford professor of science he admitted that among the school friends he met later in life 'it was those on the classical side that I found most interesting; those on the science side could talk about little else but carburettors and sparking plugs'. As for the arts curriculum, the main result of the English classes he took was to have Shakespeare ruined for him by reducing the study of a play to a line by line search for examples of the clever use of words, aided by a commentary. Art classes were an even greater farce; more or less non-existent, Alister felt. Miss Creaser, the art mistress,

> … painted in watercolour in the most dreadful, finicky
> style. She rested on her laurels after getting a picture of
> some geraniums in a flower pot accepted by the Royal
> Academy for one of its summer exhibitions. How it got in I
> can never imagine.[26]

Though Miss Creaser taught him nothing, Alister became a talented amateur watercolourist with a recognisable vivid style. In part he made up for the gap in Oundle by taking lessons from a watercolour artist in Harrogate during the summer vacation. No doubt he also inherited or imitated his father's architectural drawing ability and in addition his squint gave him an unexpected skill, for the lack of stereoscopic vision made his eyes act as a natural *camera lucida*. That is to say, he could look at a scene with one eye and see it projected onto the paper on which he was drawing with the other eye. This meant he never had problems with perspective or the proportions of what he was drawing and, incidentally, in micro-scope work at university he was similarly well equipped to make accurate reproductions of what he saw on the slide.

Religious education at Oundle was a major interest of Sanderson's and here he may well have had a strong influence on Hardy, in the first place through his sermons in chapel. Though Sanderson was himself passionately religious, he was anything but conservative and surprisingly egalitarian in his views. Here is part of his oft quoted indictment of imperialism, delivered in a sermon juxtaposing it with the Beatitudes:

> Blessed are they that mourn, for they shall be comforted.
> Rule Britannia!
> Blessed are the meek, for they shall inherit the Earth. Rule
> Britannia!
> Blessed are the peacemakers, for they shall be called the
> children of God. Rule Britannia!
> Blessed are they that have been persecuted for
> righteousness sake. Rule Britannia!
> Dear souls! My dear souls! I wouldn't lead you astray for
> anything.[27]

Parallel to his religious belief was his conviction of the importance of science, leading him to urge upon his hearers its absolute centrality as a means to understanding divine creation. He likened the great figures of science to modern saints:

> Mighty men of science and mighty deeds. A Newton who
> binds the universe together in uniform law; Lagrange,
> Laplace, Leibnitz with their wondrous mathematical
> harmonies; Coulomb measuring out electricity … Faraday,
> Ohm, Ampère, Joule, Maxwell, Hertz, Röntgen; and in
> another branch of science, Cavendish, Davy, Dalton,
> Dewar; and in another, Darwin, Mendel, Pasteur, Lister,
> Sir Ronald Ross.[28]

Significantly, from the young Hardy's point of view, Sanderson placed Darwin among his saints, apparently happy to sweep aside the clash which others saw between evolutionary theory and Christian doctrine. H. G. Wells, whose relationship with Sanderson became very close, thought he saw a growing religious agnosticism appearing in his teaching over the years. He notes in his biography a gradual diminishing of the doctrinal content of his sermons and a greater emphasis on the man Jesus, implying that if Sanderson had lived longer he would have completely discarded his religion. We cannot know if Wells correctly understood the nature of Sanderson's faith and whether he genuinely believed that he had reconciled it with the Darwinian account of evolution. In the case of Alister Hardy himself, potential conflicts with Christian doctrine were beginning to emerge, at this point only obscurely, though it would not be long before the problem led to a personal crisis.

Sanderson also gave a scripture class every Sunday after chapel, in the period preceding lunch. To attend the class, boys had to have supporting scholarly apparatus, for example Hardy mentions being required to have a copy of Canon Driver's commentaries on the Old Testament as well as a catalogue of Babylonian antiquities in the British Museum. Driver was Regius Professor of Hebrew at Oxford University and Hardy remarks that the intellectual status of Sanderson's classes was such that it was rumoured that when Wells' sons were at the school he charged them with the task of taking down the weekly content in shorthand and sending it to him.

In summary, religious education obviously had a key role in Oundle when Hardy was there. To leave matters at this formal level is nevertheless to ignore what Alister saw as the most important dimension of the spiritual life – direct experience. His lifelong commitment to this view came about almost by accident as the result of his mother's persisting conviction that her son was physically delicate. Before Alister first went to Oundle she persuaded her family doctor to write a letter to Sanderson requesting that the boy be excused from sporting activities. Alister was certainly relieved by his mother's action and it is conceivable that he urged it upon her, for he loathed games. His squint, as previously mentioned, meant that he lacked stereoscopic vision and was therefore unable to perform the basic skills like catching and kicking required in ball games. Sanderson accepted the GP's request and while other boys were on the games field, Alister was sent on solitary walks in the surrounding Northamptonshire countryside.

These extended spells of solitude were of pivotal importance in the shaping of his interpretation of reality for it was here, in the intensity of adolescence, that he discovered and was convinced by an unmistakable spiritual dimension to his experience. The vagueness of the term 'spiritual experience' lies not in the vividness of the experience itself, which to the experient is undeniable, but in the difficulty of putting it into words. In Alister's case, the language available came from the Christian religious culture into which he had been inducted steadily if unostentatiously, from infancy, through schooling at Bramcote and now at Oundle. I have mentioned Hardy's reticence, and his account of these episodes in his autobiography constitutes one of the very few direct references to his spiritual experience of which I am aware. He shyly remarked that only now, in his late 80s, did he feel able to admit to the depth of his response. I quote from his most extended description:

> There was a little lane leading off the Northampton Road to Park Wood, as it was called and it was a haven for different kinds of Brown butterflies. I had never seen so many all together. The common Meadow Browns of course were everywhere in the fields, but here also were the Lesser Meadow Brown or Gatekeeper, the Wall Brown and Marbled White, which belongs to the same family. As one approached the wood there was a small covered reservoir with grass banks leading over it, and this was always the home of many Ringlet butterflies, of which I seem to remember there are two forms recognised as a variety. I specially liked walking along the banks of various streams, watching, as the summer developed, a sequence of wild flowers growing along their brims. I was attracted by several streams lying in different directions from Oundle. I wandered along all their banks, at times almost with a feeling of ecstasy. There is no doubt that as a boy I was becoming what might be described as a nature mystic. Somehow, I felt the presence of something which was beyond and yet in a way part of all the things that thrilled me – the wildflowers, and indeed the insects too. I will now record something which I have never told anyone before, but now that I am in my 88th year I think I can admit it. Just occasionally when I was sure that no one could see me, I became so overcome with the glory of the natural scene, that for a moment or two I fell on my knees in prayer – not prayer asking for anything, but thanking God, who felt very real to me, for the glories of his Kingdom and for allowing me to feel them. It was always by the running waterside that I did this, perhaps in front of a great foam of meadowsweet or purple loosestrife.[29]

Alister commented that such mystical experience in nature, akin to that described by the poet Wordsworth,[30] was infrequent, but affected the rest of his life. The context of these rare and intense moments was when he was immersed in the deeply loved world of insects. The psychologist of childhood spirituality, Rebecca Nye, has remarked on the way that the personality and interests of someone in their everyday life have a recognisable continuity with the style of their spiritual experience, which she refers to as that person's 'signature'.[31] In turn, people who are advanced in the spiritual life are quick to point out that maturity involves ascetic practice and a gradual diffusion of the sense of presence beyond these isolated episodes into all the other areas of ordinary experience. This habitual awareness seems to have been the case with Alister Hardy – for he says so in the introductory pages of his autobiography. Ultimately, to use the language of the Jesuit spiritual tradition, he came to see 'God in all things'.

In the same passage of his autobiography, Hardy then makes an interesting remark about what some would call an example of Jungian synchronicity:[32]

> I had been hunting the sallow bushes for the caterpillars of the Eyed Hawk Moth, which I felt sure must be there. I didn't succeed until, rising from prayer, level with my eyes on a stem of sallow, was a large Eyed Hawk Moth caterpillar; of course it was ridiculous to suppose that it was in any way connected with the prayer, but there it was. I just record it to illustrate the extraordinary temptation there might have been to misinterpret events, and this must be borne in mind when looking at further events in my life and one's interpretation of them.[33]

Hardy is clearly uneasy with what he sees as an enticement to interpret the conjunction of prayer and the discovery of the Hawk Moth as meaningful, for of course the incident could be explained perfectly adequately as being due to chance. However, his apparently total dismissal of the possibility of alternative interpretations runs counter to his claim that his whole life had been guided in this way, and suggests a continuing tension within him between the exclusive claims of empirical science and alternative realms of meaning. Or was he protecting himself from the all too predictable jeers of sceptical fellow scientists?

Like many of his colleagues in the scientific profession, the wonders uncovered by scientific research delighted Alister during his childhood. He writes movingly about the way that a simple drop of water became much more interesting to him when he learned why it grew larger and larger until it dripped and another drop began to form. He had not realised that it was only when the weight of the drop was sufficiently great to overcome surface tension that it would fall.[34] But do phenomena like synchronicity and the sense of presence belong within the empirical realm – really and substantially part of Alister's experience – or are they the result of false or mistaken interpretation, since they seem to have no regularity and are unpredictable?

Another important question raised by his youthful nature-mysticism is its relationship to the formal religion that he was studying in Sanderson's classes and hearing preached from the pulpit. Hardy talks of a gulf that he experienced between the two. Although in the years to come he was to find the presence of God in the stillness of an empty church – which he describes as 'that extraordinary sense of the numinous' – even more strongly than in nature, it was never during a church service. He was bored by the ritual of the liturgy and wondered if it might be different when he was at an age to be confirmed and could take part in Holy Communion. In fact his most abiding memory of his own confirmation service, conducted by the Bishop of Peterborough, was of being convulsed with suppressed laughter:

> I remember so well his address before we were confirmed.
> 'Looking around me' he said, 'I see no two boys alike;
> everyone quite different – different expressions, different
> outlooks, different ways of life, yet all preparing for the
> great task before them ... ... etc, etc.' We went up to be
> confirmed in pairs, and the first two boys to do so were
> the Gulliland brothers, who were actually identical twins –
> you couldn't tell them apart![35]

Immediately following confirmation, Alister did feel differently about the God of the Church, but the change did not last, though

the imagery continued to haunt his imagination. In spite of the
deficiencies of the art department at Oundle, his watercolours were
to increase in number and quality and for a time he visualised
himself as a great painter. He thought that, perhaps after training,
he might paint a representation of a recurring image that came to
him at this period of his life: He saw in his mind's eye a scene of a
boy shortly after confirmation 'kneeling at the altar rail with a
stream of coloured light coming through the eastern window,
illuminating him in a brilliant kind of aura'. But another way forward
began to impress him.

There was a small group of pre-medical students at Oundle who
were taught biology by George Olive, and because of his love of
insect life Alister had asked if he could join the class. Olive's
personal preference was for botany, but Alister's devotion to
entomology impressed him and he welcomed him in. When the
time came to consider the future, Olive felt that Alister's route was
obvious:

> My boy, your career is made; they are crying out for forest
> botanists in India, Burma and other places. What I advise
> you to do is to go to Oxford and take part of the course to
> learn the elements of forestry and then specialise in the
> study of forest insects and become a forest entomologist.[36]

Alister was excited by the thought of studying insects in the great
tropical rain forests. It seemed too good to be true, for his heroes
were naturalists like Charles Darwin whose marvellous travel book
The Voyage of the Beagle[37] fired his imagination with its descriptions of the teeming insect life of the Brazilian forest. Alfred Russel
Wallace, fellow author with Darwin of the very first public statement
on natural selection at a meeting of the Linnean Society in 1858,
had spent years in the forests of the Malay Archipelago and wrote
about them in *Tropical Nature*.[38] Another admired explorer was
Henry Walter Bates who voyaged up the Amazon with Wallace on a
collecting trip in 1848 and, after branching out on his own, sent
home more than 14,000 specimens, many of them insects, of
which 8,000 were new to science. Alister had read about Bates'
adventures in his book *Naturalist on the Amazons*,[39] was fascinated by his studies of mimicry in butterflies and probably knew that
much of his collection was stored in the Natural History Museum in

London. What teenage schoolboy with Alister's interests would not be thrilled by the prospect of following in the footsteps of these famous men?

CHAPTER THREE

Oxford, the Army and a Vow

Alister's career as a forest entomologist seemed to have been handed to him on a plate, except that he now had the problem of gaining entry to Oxford University. According to the Oundle records, while he was reasonably sound academically he did not stand out particularly strongly. There are two references to him in the prize list for 1912, where he is named as the recipient of a Form Prize and another award in Mathematics, but apart from these successes he gets no other mention. The task facing him was challenging in another way because it meant a return to studies he thought he had left behind in prep school. To pass the Oxford entrance examination called Responsions he had to show competence in Divinity, which in turn required him to translate passages taken from the original Greek of the New Testament into English. Alister had done a small amount of Latin in Bramcote and almost no Greek. But at this moment he was a young enthusiast swept along by his dream of leading expeditions into the depths of the great rain forests; a new Adam in the Garden of Eden, discovering and naming insect species as yet unknown to science. The Forestry Department at Oxford it had to be.

Perhaps on the advice of his biology master he decided to drop out of school and concentrate solely on preparing for Responsions. The idea was to set aside the spring and summer of 1914 to preparing for the exam in September, and the school acceded to his request. Although the records state that he left Oundle in the autumn of 1914, in fact he was permitted to withdraw from formal classes a year earlier. And so at the age of seventeen he went home to his mother's cramped quarters in Harrogate and became virtually an academic hermit. He was far from the social whirl of school and from the companionship of his brother Vernon, who had gone off to Newcastle to study engineering. Often Alister must have felt lonely, but he was used to solitude and it gave him the freedom to map out an ambitious programme of study for several months ahead.

From early spring through to midsummer in 1914 he dedicated the weekday mornings to the task of mugging up Classics with the aid of a paid coach. He spent the afternoons preparing himself for the Diploma in Forestry by self education in systematic botany. His routine was to sling his botanist's tin *vasculum* over his shoulder and cycle his way methodically over the countryside within about ten miles from Harrogate, searching for plant specimens. He was able to gather a comprehensive collection of the species found in the area, including examples of different stages in their life-cycles. Each evening when he returned with his haul he made identifications using the standard text, Bentham and Hooker's *British Flora*.[1] He preserved the plants by pressing them and by the end of the summer his collection was impressively large.[2]

The admirable maturity of Alister's study plan did not mean that he lost his boyhood sense of the ridiculous, and there were occasional laughable disruptions to his programme. He recalled one incident when he was finding difficulty in tracking down specimens of the yellow water lily. Late one afternoon while several miles from home, he took a chance and sneaked into a private estate between Ripley and Ripon[3] where he knew there was an ornamental lake that might contain his quarry. Sure enough, the water lilies were there, but too far out to be reached from the shore. Determined not to be beaten and checking to see that there was nobody about, he undressed and swam out to where the lilies were. As he was helping himself, a pair of ladies emerged from behind some rhododendron bushes and caught the young thief red-handed. One of the matrons inspected him disdainfully through her lorgnette and said to the other: 'Oh, look! There is someone after our water lilies!' Shivering in the water, Alister called out: 'I am so sorry, I should have asked for permission. I am a botanical student and am taking just one flower and a leaf.' They laughed and continued to stare at him, until he shouted: 'I am getting very cold. Please let me come out. I have got nothing on and in addition to trespass you could possibly have me up for indecent exposure.' After what felt like an age they went away, though Alister wondered whether they lingered behind the bushes to spy on him.

Another more spectacular escapade stuck in his memory. He was still passionately interested in flight and he sometimes took time off to wander down to the Stray, a large expanse of open meadow in the middle of Harrogate. In the early days of flight the Stray was used as a landing ground, and among the well-known pilots Alister remembered seeing were Roland Ding, in an early Handley-Page bi-plane, and Harold Blackburn, flying an almost new Blackburn monoplane, built in 1912. Only coincidentally having the same name as the pilot, the Blackburn was one of the earliest mono-planes of British manufacture and looked very fragile, which no doubt fired Alister's love of adventure.[4] The sight of the aircraft made him long for an opportunity to fly – and at that moment he had what seemed to him an extraordinary piece of luck. The *Yorkshire Post* ran a lottery, the prize for which was a fifteen minute free flight from Bradford to the adjacent city of Leeds. Wholehearted as always, Alister poured his pocket money into buying copies of the newspaper containing the lottery coupons and collected over one hundred to send in. On the day the results were due to be published in the *Yorkshire Evening Post,* he recalled:

> I walked down the hill towards the paper shop and there met the paper man coming up. Fluttering in the wind was a placard advertising the *Yorkshire Evening Post* for Wednesday, July 22 and in bold headlines were the words 'HARROGATE MAN WINS FREE FLIGHT'. 'Gracious, it couldn't be me', I said to myself. I bought a copy at once, and to my astonishment I found it was. I hadn't told my mother, and I thought I wouldn't tell her until it was over, as I didn't want to cause her unnecessary anxiety, but next morning, before breakfast was hardly finished, a representative of the *Yorkshire Evening Post* called at the door, and he was astonished to find that I was a boy of eighteen. 'Good gracious', he said, 'we have to get the signature of an adult to release us from all responsibility.

Are your parents in?' I said 'Good heavens, I haven't told my mother. Leave the paper for a moment will you.'[5]

The man agreed and went off, saying he would call later that day to collect Mrs Hardy's signature, leaving Alister to break the news.

At first his mother was appalled by the potential hazards facing her supposedly delicate son. Powered flight was still a novelty. Only five years previously, in 1908, Wilbur Wright had carried the first ever passenger on a flight in America. In the same year Thomas Selfridge had the distinction of being the first passenger to die in a plane crash,[6] when Wilbur's brother Orville lost control of a prototype aeroplane designed to carry two passengers. But Mrs Hardy found it difficult to deny Alister anything he asked for and, knowing how fascinated he was by all aspects of flight, she eventually gave way. Next morning, when the trip was due to take place, the weather turned out to be very windy. Alister tried to reassure his mother by suggesting that the flight would be cancelled, but that nevertheless courtesy demanded that he should go to meet the pilot and see the machine. So, with his special invitation card in his pocket, he travelled to Leeds to be photographed for the *Yorkshire Post* as he was being driven round the city in a special car with a large banner reading: 'WINNER OF THE FREE FLIGHT FROM BRADFORD TO LEEDS'. Alister was in a daze of excitement; he had never felt so important.

Mrs Hardy had reason to feel anxious, for Alister's flight did take place. A report in the *Yorkshire Post* for Friday, 24 July 1914, has the heading: 'FLYING UNDER DIFFICULTIES; UNSUCCESSFUL ATTEMPT TO REACH BRADFORD'. It goes on:

> Unfavourable conditions, including a strong breeze, occasional showers, and generally hazy weather in the Bradford district, interfered with the previously arranged timetable of cross-country flights by Mr Sydney Pickles for the *Yorkshire Post* and the *Yorkshire Evening Post*. Mr Pickles was only able to accomplish the complete journey to Bradford and back once, and only in one direction did he carry a passenger. [Arriving at Bradford after a journey that had given the plane a severe buffeting and taken fourteen minutes] ... at one o'clock he was away on the return journey to Leeds, taking with him Mr A. C.

Hardy, of Harlow Moor Drive, Harrogate. This was
Mr Hardy's first flight, and he appeared to be very keen to
experience the thrills ... Mr Pickles estimated that the
machine had developed a speed of 100 miles an hour
during the brief return journey. Mr Hardy was delighted
with his experience. 'It was,' he said, 'the most thrilling
time of my life. It was a bit rough, but I did not feel
particularly scared.'[7]

Eighty-nine-year-old Alister admitted in his autobiography that the
last remark was false; he had been terrified. He added some
personal details: he was taken to the Quarry Gap ground, a piece of
open land near Bradford, to await the arrival of the plane from
Roundhay in Leeds. The plan was to fly over the showground and
perform some aerobatics that involved spinning the plane round to
display the words *Yorkshire Post* painted on the wings, then drop
copies of the newspaper into the crowd below, before flying back to
Leeds. In due course the plane arrived, sure enough minus a
passenger, for the unfortunate man had been deemed too heavy to
travel safely in the treacherous weather conditions. Alister weighed
less than 12 stones (168 pounds), the upper permitted weight limit,
but at six feet and three inches he was a tight fit in the passenger
seat which was in front of the pilot.

Pickles gave a last warning that the flight would feel bumpy and
did Alister mind? No, he didn't mind, but inwardly he found himself
wondering what would happen if the engine stalled. The engine
roared and, after bumping across the grass, Alister felt the plane
rise into the air. So far, so good, but then, half way back to Leeds,
without warning, the engine did indeed stop and Alister saw the
worst of his fears materialising. They started to dive steeply and
now the only sound was the whistling of the air through the struts
and wirework. He half heard the pilot shout something like 'Hold
on! Hold on!', but in that heart-stopping moment all he could
concentrate on was a group of three factory chimneys rushing
towards them. He instinctively ducked down, and just at that
moment the engine sputtered into life again and eventually they
landed safely at Roundhay, where a large crowd had gathered to
watch their return.

Although the flight was dramatic, Alister was not in as much
danger as he thought. The report in the newspaper reveals that

Pickles intentionally switched off the engine at one point so that he could make himself heard, shouting a warning to his young passenger to hold on to his hat. Afterwards Pickles thanked him for responding to his request, but Alister had not heard him clearly, being too caught up in what he assumed to be a lethal dive. The pilot had been concerned that the force of the wind could blow Alister's cap off so that it might fly back and get caught in the tail controls, which *could* have been dangerous. Fortunately Alister had instinctively clutched his cap to him when they began to dive.

Many years later, visiting the Shuttleworth Collection[8] and seeing the actual plane he had flown in preserved there, Alister remembered the smell of the oil shooting back from the engine and the wind screaming through the steel cables and thought to himself: 'That was really flying in those days!'

There is no evidence to suggest that at this time Alister was in the slightest degree interested in politics, but international events were soon to force their way into his consciousness, for in August 1914 the British government announced that the nation had entered the First World War. The likelihood of military service meant that Alister's forestry plans had to be put on hold, though he decided to continue with his attempt to gain entrance to Oxford. Responsions was at the end of September, and if he was successful he decided that he would complete his first term at university before thinking about the army. He would join the university Officer's Training Corps (OTC) to try for a Commission, and leave at Christmas.

When the time came for the exam, he travelled down to Oxford, arriving on a brilliantly sunny autumn morning and he was at once overwhelmed by the beauty of the colleges, many of them in those days covered with Virginia Creeper.[9] His hard work paid off. He did well and was accepted as an undergraduate at Exeter College, matriculating formally in early October. He was allocated rooms on the ground floor, embellished with beautiful oak panelling by a previous student whose father was in the timber trade. His study looked out onto Broad Street where hansom cabs were waiting in line just outside his window, for horse-drawn transport still predominated. Across the street he could see the lawns of Trinity College and, glancing to his left, he could catch a glimpse of Balliol

College. On the same side of the street as Exeter College was the Sheldonian Theatre, designed by Christopher Wren and, beyond that, the towering pillars of the Senate House. At the back, his bedroom looked out on to the College quadrangle, its walls also covered in Virginia Creeper. Alister loved it and was soon making friends. In no time at all they had formed a society with ten members, calling themselves 'The Decimal Club'. They had a special tie made up for them in green, brown and white, and they met once a week in each other's rooms for 'wine-drinking and discussions'. Once during the term they had a dinner, for which Alister designed the menu, decorated with caricatures of the members. It was so like the conventional image of undergraduate life at Oxbridge that for a brief moment it was literally a dream come true.

Hardy arranged to take introductory courses in geology, botany and forestry. Professor Sollas, who gave the geology lectures, was already elderly when Alister attended his lectures and, as was permitted in those days, he continued in post until his death in 1936 at the age of 87. Sollas interested Alister for he was a man of extremely wide scientific interests, with biological investigations to his name ranging from freshwater ecology to human evolution. He was also a member of the group of scholars involved with the discovery of 'Piltdown Man' and for a time he was thought to be implicated in the fraud, but was eventually exonerated.[10] Already absent-minded when Alister encountered him, Sollas subsequently became famous for the occasion when he greeted his principal technician, a man who had been with him for 25 years, with the words 'And now my man, what can I do for you?', not recognising him at all. Hardy nevertheless revered him as a great geologist and was upset by the behaviour of some of his classmates who treated the old man as a joke. For example when Sollas passed round some heavy fossil ammonite specimens to the students seated in the steeply-canted lecture theatre, a wag at the back thought it witty to drop the fossils so that they bounced – bang – bang – bang – all the way to the bottom of the room. Sollas continued to lecture, apparently unperturbed.

The introductory botany lectures were given by Professor Vines, and Alister expected the classes in the Forestry Department would similarly be given by the head of department, another senior citizen, a German-born naturalised Englishman, Sir William Schlich. Schlich had founded the department and was a powerful influence on the development of forestry in Britain, being responsible for the five volume standard text in the subject.[11] He was not there to greet the new students and Alister never met him, leading to the (incorrect) speculation that Schlich had been interned as a former German national. Instead, the class was introduced to the subject by a junior member of staff, who, rather than lecture, took the students to Bagley Wood,[12] two or three miles to the south of the city, to acquaint them as practically as possible with the nature of woodland.

Alister seems to have liked these outings to Bagley Wood well enough, but after his herculean efforts to enter the Forestry Department he felt a growing sense of disappointment, and indeed he was quietly in the process of changing his mind about a career in forestry. One consideration may have been the fact that the highest qualification open to forestry students at Oxford at that time was a Diploma.[13] But there was a much more serious reason behind the fading of Alister's romantic vision. All was not well with his inner life, for under the successful surface lay an accumulation of intensely troubling uncertainties. His discomfort was symbolised by the picture he had chosen to hang on the wall in his room in Exeter College, a copy of *Hope,* the well-known painting by George Frederick Watts, completed in 1886.[14] Hope is portrayed as a young woman under an overcast sky, seated on the rust-coloured globe of the earth, blindfolded, with her head bowed down. She is attempting to play a lyre, but every string except one is broken. The darkness of the mood is extreme, to the extent that the picture would be more appropriately entitled 'Desolation' or 'Despair'. Looking back in old age at his youthful choice of an appropriate work of art to hang where he could see it every day, Alister realised that it was an unconscious representation of the state of depression which lay hidden below his excitement at coming to Oxford.

The source of his brooding was of course the clash between evolutionary theory and religion that had already begun to make him feel uneasy while he was at Oundle. His brief first term at university brought home to him the realisation that his difficulties were not merely personal, or localised; they were an expression of a cultural predicament affecting any religious believer who was in touch with the history of western thought. He started reading extensively the publications of the Rationalist Press Association, including the directly biological works of Darwin, T. H. Huxley and Haeckel, as well as secularist works such as Grant Allen's *Evolution of the Idea of God* and Ernest Renan's *Life of Jesus*.[15] He began to see that what came to be called the European Enlightenment[16] implicitly challenged the religious basis of every aspect of daily life: social structure, law, ethics and, more fundamentally, the sense of living within a universe unfolding benignly and meaningfully according to the will of God.

For people thoroughly reconciled to the secularism that dominates contemporary Western life, the distress caused by this critique may be difficult to comprehend.[17] In Chapter One I mentioned A. N. Wilson's fine book *God's Funeral*. It is helpful in documenting the unhappiness and at times suicidal agony created in the lives of those Victorians who felt their religion ebbing away in the face of the critique.[18] The bleak resignation of Matthew Arnold's poem *On Dover Beach*, written in 1867, less than a decade after the publication of *The Origin of Species*, seemed to many to be the best response available:

> The Sea of Faith
> Was once, too, at the full, and round earth's shore
> Lay like the folds of a bright girdle furled.
> But now I only hear
> Its melancholy, long, withdrawing roar,
> Retreating, to the breath
> Of the night wind, down the vast edges drear
> And naked shingles of the world.
> Ah, love, let us be true
> To one another! for the world, which seems
> To lie before us like a land of dreams,
> So various, so beautiful, so new,
> Hath really neither joy, nor love, nor light,
> Nor certitude, nor peace, nor help for pain;
> And we are here as on a darkling plain.
> Swept with confused alarms of struggle and flight,
> Where ignorant armies clash by night.[19]

Alister's conventionally religious upbringing at the end of the nineteenth century meant that he was in touch with these sentiments. His dogged resistance to the secular challenge was at this stage partly based on his optimistic temperament and, somewhat more solidly, on his personal experience. He knew, or thought he knew, about spirituality very directly from his solitary walks in the Northamptonshire countryside. The discovery that his experience was rejected as claptrap by a number of prominent academics, particularly within the biological sciences, violently disconcerted him. Eventually, at the end of the autumn term in 1914, just before he left the university to join the army, he made a promise which was to affect every aspect of his subsequent career:

> During the term I had become more and more convinced of the importance of bringing about a reconciliation between evolution theory and the spiritual awareness of man. At the end of the term I made a most solemn vow; it wasn't actually in the form of a prayer, but I vowed to what I called God that if I should survive the war I would devote my life to attempting to bring about such a reconciliation that would satisfy the intellectual world.[20]

The naive tone of Alister's Vow – his overconfident aspiration to 'satisfy the intellectual world' – may cause us to smile. Many people in the intensity of youth have had lofty ambitions and made promises that are soon forgotten. The difference in Alister's case was that he never forgot, though it took a further seventy years of his life before he felt able to admit to his Vow in public. Even his son and daughter were unaware of his commitment until they read his autobiographical essay in the 1980s.[21]

The dynamic effect of Alister's remarkable pledge was to drain away the motivation that had made him struggle so hard to enter the Forestry Department. His new priority, assuming he came back safely from the war, was to put himself in a position where he could engage as directly as possible with the issues that troubled him. He decided to try to negotiate a move to the Zoology Department, where he would have the best opportunity to make a detailed study of Darwin's ideas. Whether he knew it or not, Oxford happened to be a highly appropriate location for Alister's investigation. On 30 June 1860, in the year following the publication of *The Origin of Species*, it had been the scene of a notorious public argument at a meeting of the British Association held in the Oxford Museum.[22]

The main protagonists were 'Darwin's Bulldog', T. H. Huxley, and 'Soapy Sam' Wilberforce, the Bishop of Oxford and, at least according to the popular legend, the argument was won by Huxley,[23] Alister wanted to clarify for himself the religious and scientific issues that were at stake and, with the serendipity that seemed to accompany so many of the decisive moments in his life, Alister's wish was granted in full. When he negotiated his return to Oxford after the war, the tutor appointed to oversee his studies just happened to be Julian Huxley, grandson of the great 'T. H.'

The immediacy of the war and his sense of patriotic duty forced Alister to shelve these profundities for the time being. But how best to serve? Shortly after leaving Oxford at the end of 1914 he travelled to the north of England to visit his brother. Before the outbreak of war, Vernon had begun studying engineering at Armstrong College in Newcastle, then a part of Durham University. Like Alister, he had joined the OTC at the college and enlisted with the Northumberland Fusiliers as a reservist. When war was declared in 1914 he was called up for training, with the expectation that he would be sent to the front around Christmas time. Elizabeth Hardy was now in her mid-fifties, still unsettled and naturally worried by Vernon's approaching posting to France. She had moved to Newcastle, at first staying in a hotel, but subsequently she rented rooms just off the Jesmond Road. It was here that Alister joined her and they both went on several occasions to see Vernon where he was in training in East Boldon, south of the river Tyne not far from Jarrow.

In another of her motherly efforts to ensure the welfare of her offspring, in this case Vernon, Elizabeth had taken the trouble to get to know the colonel in charge of the Armstrong College OTC. Here Alister felt that providence once more took a hand. Dr Frederick C. Garrett lectured in chemistry at the college but, like Elizabeth's late husband, his great love was the army. He also knew a lot about military history and when he met Alister the conversation naturally enough focused on soldiering. It transpired that Garrett had recently been appointed colonel in charge of a new military unit called the Northern Cyclists' Battalion (NCB) and was in the process of recruiting officers. Alister must have given some hint that he was interested in a commission, for suddenly Garrett asked him how he would fancy the life of an officer in a cyclists' battalion. With his vivid imagination, Alister probably already had a madcap image of hundreds of soldiers on bikes, pedalling into battle and outwitting the enemy by their sheer speed and panache. As a keen cyclist he saw himself as ideally suited to membership of such a cavalcade and thought: 'What a splendid idea it would be to make war on a bike!' So there and then he accepted Garrett's offer and became a second lieutenant in the NCB.

Alister's youthful notion of going to war on a bicycle as 'a splendid idea' tends to jar on the ear of subsequent generations who are aware of the immense suffering and loss of life sustained in the First World War. In the event, his idea of cycling into battle proved to be no more than fantasy. Attempts had been made to use cyclists in this way at the front, and there are newspaper photographs recording members of the NCB undergoing bayonet training and target practice in preparation for this possibility.[24] Unfortunately, while bicycles were excellent for transporting soldiers on paved surfaces, experience showed that the moment they entered a battlefield they tended to get bogged down, leading the men to abandon their bikes in large numbers and join the rest of the PBI[25] on foot. In practice the NCB, like many cyclist units, was given the task of constructing coastal defences on the British mainland, although men were regularly withdrawn and sent to France, especially when there were sudden shortages of manpower due to severe losses at the front.

The cyclists were to be billeted in the isolated village of Saltfleet on the north Lincolnshire coast but before that they undertook basic training at Bamburgh on the Northumberland coast. As an officer Alister was lodged in Bamburgh Castle, spectacularly sited on the rocky shore. The mediaeval great hall was turned into a dining room for the regiment and renovated at considerable expense by the wealthy industrialist, Lord Armstrong, after whom Armstrong College in Newcastle had been named. From his bedroom Alister could see the Farne Islands which he had visited from Holy Island when he was staying with a school friend.

The experience of command proved to have an extremely important and lifelong effect on Alister's personality. He was

eventually promoted to the rank of acting captain, in charge of C
Company, and around this time he had his photograph taken in
peaked cap, greatcoat and puttees, carrying his officer's swagger
stick. He was amused by the idea of playing the hero, modelling
himself on what he hoped was the pose of Donatello's statue
of St George. Under his command the company gradually worked
its way down the flat Lincolnshire coast, at first making its headquarters in the village of Chapel St Leonards, then moving, via
Skegness, favourite destination for day-trippers from Nottingham,
towards Boston, with the great stump of St Botolph's church
soaring above the fenland, just north of the Wash. In his old age
Alister could still picture every inch of it.

Over the weeks the officers and men were beginning to get to
know each other and, especially in Alister's unit, a remarkably close
bond developed. We can gather something of the mood from the
introduction and references in a *Memoir* of the Company that
Alister wrote and had printed for distribution to his men after the
war, when he had returned to Oxford. The preface to the *Memoir*
opens in hearty English style:

> After leaving the good old NCB, I have so often thought of
> all you splendid cheery fellows who made up C Company,
> the company with which I was most concerned and latterly
> had the honour to command, etc., etc.[26]

A message from Colonel Garrett continues in the same vein with
some added jingoism about 'our incomparable battalion':

> We were denied our ambition to go to France as a unit,
> but the battalion did great things ... I watched you at
> Bamburgh; I knew you on the coast; when you went
> overseas I followed your doings as closely as I was able ...
> Some did not return; of them one can only say with
> Sir Richard Grenville: 'If thou art brought back with all thy
> wounds in front I shall weep for thy mother, but shall have
> never a tear for thee.' For what better fate would one
> wish?

Garrett's opinion is debatable. Wilfred Owen's bitter denunciation
of 'The old Lie; Dulce et Decorum est Pro patria mori' had already

been written[27] and expressed the views of increasing numbers of people disgusted by the carnage of the war. Beneath Garrett's patriotic rhetoric, the picture of the NCB left in the mind is more mundane: a group of youths – officers and men – who were often bored stiff, but were uneasily aware that they had found a comfortable billet well away from enemy fire. At the same time they could not predict when they themselves might be called to face death at the Front. The reality of this threat is illustrated by the fact that of the men listed in Alister's *Memoir*, approximately ten per cent were eventually killed in battle and many more were wounded.

The boredom lay in the repetitive tasks involved in creating the coastal defences – digging trenches and filling sandbags all day – and with little else to occupy their minds the men were inclined to fantasise. For example, one of the security tasks assigned to the unit was to patrol the roads during the night. The rumour was that enemy agents were living under cover in Lincolnshire and acting as guides for German zeppelins on their way to bomb strategic installations. The agents were supposed to have lights strapped to the roof of their cars so that as they drove, for example, to Grimsby, the zeppelins could follow them and hence find their targets more easily. For all their anxiety the patrols never came across a single spy. Alister too was caught up in the boredom, but he also recalled occasional ecstatic moments, like the joy he once felt after being on watch all night. As the sun was rising on a glorious spring morning, the air filled with the dawn chorus and then, from somewhere across the fens, he heard the sound of a solitary cuckoo.

Another insight into Alister's life at this time comes from ex-RQMS Ed McConnell who was with the battalion throughout the war until he was demobbed in January 1919. He wrote a brief history of the doings of C Company which was published as part of the introduction to Alister's *Memoir*. It is written in an affectionately amused tone, in the mode of 'many are the tales I could tell – and a few more that are not repeatable in polite company!' It includes a recollection of young 2nd Lieut. A. C. Hardy in difficulties. One of the least popular jobs with the men was taking turns getting up very early each morning to be on guard in the defensive trenches an hour before dawn. McConnell writes:

Receiving information to the effect that Section Billet 8, at White House, were absent from their post in the trenches,

Lieut. Hardy decided to give them a visit himself. So off to the billet he went. Each step made him more determined to give them such a rouse as they had never before experienced. Arriving at the billet he attempted to find the stairs (once he tried the chimney). At last, worked into a state of temper most of us have experienced one time or another, he got up to the first floor and, going into the first room on his right feeling in the dark for the bed, then its contents, he swished down the clothes and 'Why the devil aren't you in the trenches?' To be frightened in one's sleep is no joke, and so thought the landlady's daughter, for sure enough, sitting up in bed with her locks … flowing round her shapely shoulders, was none other than but the daughter of the billet. Of course our OC who was at all times the essence of civility, apologised and beat a hasty retreat.[28]

One can almost feel Alister's animation as he shared the yarn with his Quarter Master shortly afterwards. It was frequently said of him that he never really grew up and laughter was usually close to the surface His experience of the pervasive joyousness of life is summarised in an introductory note to his autobiography where he wonders whether he ought to entitle it 'For Fun and for Joy' and it often seemed that his delight with life would lead him to burst out with a 'Yippee!'

It is therefore important to emphasise that alongside Alister's sunny nature there was another less public facet of his temperament, which we already noted in the hints of an underlying depression during his preliminary term at university. There were other tensions when he took up his duties as an army officer and there is no doubt that the stressful process of getting to know the men was one of the most important formative experiences of his life. The soldiers for whom he was responsible were mostly young coal miners of much the same age as himself, many from Ashington in Northumberland, with several others from County Durham.

What must have been the thoughts of this privileged nineteen year old when he realised that he had been given charge of men from the pits, and what doubts must they in turn have had about him? He had most probably never met a miner before, although there were thousands employed in the Nottinghamshire coalfields. Some of them worked in collieries within the Nottingham city boundary, and thus not far from his boyhood home. But the history of the Hardy family's successful campaign to better themselves, generation by generation, meant that he learned to think of himself as separate from and superior to manual labourers.

Alister's accent was that of a public schoolboy, his vocabulary cultured and extensive, and his voice was rather high pitched, with a slight hesitancy that never quite became a stutter. It contrasted strongly with the very distinctive Geordie dialect of the men from the Northumberland and Durham coalfields, and as a result he could hardly understand a word they said. Eventually he began to make sense of the dialect and the resulting encounter led to a most remarkable change in what had hitherto been a standoffish approach to his men. He writes movingly of his discovery of their generosity of spirit, putting up with any hardship provided they judged an officer was doing his best for them. He meditated with increasing resentment on how he had been misled on matters of social class:

> I became extremely angry with the way I had been brought up. I was brought up as so many were at that time, especially at a big public school, to look upon the working classes as if they were quite a different race almost. They were never treated at all like social equals – one should never mix with them, and … as an officer one could not do so. But … I was determined to try and break down what I called the barrier of class. These men lacked the education of the middle or upper classes but they were extraordinarily intelligent and really were men of great character.[29]

It is not clear that Hardy was correct in emphasising Oundle as the chief source of his youthful snobbery. If the ethos was as he claims, it was most probably in spite of the headmaster. On studying the life of Sanderson and hearing what he had to say about the human condition, it is hard to credit him with an 'aristocratic' standpoint. At least within the confines of Oundle his aim was to encourage mutual respect between all people. A more plausible candidate was the stance of the members of the Hardy family, whom we have seen had successfully struggled for several generations to reach a secure membership of the well-to-do middle class. Having got there, they had no intention of losing hold of their emancipated status. This view would almost certainly have been abetted by Alister's mother, aware as she was of the discomforts of a social come-down in her own life. This was initially so in her second marriage to Richard Hardy and perhaps equally drastically when temporarily reduced circumstances forced her to live cooped up in rented accommodation in Harrogate.[30]

Whoever or whatever were the sources of Alister's youthful snobbery, the important point is that it was swept away by his experiences with the northern cyclists. Associated with his changed view of the class system were further questions about the nature of friendship. Alister had explained to the company that the requirements of military discipline meant that as an officer he had to keep a distance between himself and his men, but he made clear to them that the relationship he personally wished for was one of friendship. Once the war was over he sincerely hoped that their relationship would continue on that basis (as indeed it did).

But what was the nature of friendship? The complexity of human relationships had already begun to become clear to Alister when he was thinking about the task of leadership. He cites Donald Hankey as one of the people who had most influenced him. Hankey is almost forgotten today, but during and after the 1914–1918 war he was admired in much the same way as poets like Wilfred Owen and Siegfried Sassoon.[31] Though Hankey had too many rigidly conservative views for Hardy's taste, he wrote perceptively about relationships. Alister found his short essay *The Beloved Captain*[32] helpful because it offered a model of sensitive leadership that he could put into practice. I reproduce part of the section Alister particularly commended, which describes the way a young, newly arrived captain set about fulfilling his role:

> He came in the early days, when we were still at recruit drills in the hot September sun. Tall, erect, smiling: so we first saw him, and so he remained to the end. At the start he knew as little about soldiering as we did. He used to watch us being drilled by the sergeant; but his manner of watching was peculiarly his own. He never looked bored

and from the first he saw that his job was more than to give the correct orders. His job was to lead us. So he watched and noted many things, and never found the time heavy on his hands. He watched for the right manner of command, the manner which secured the most prompt response to an order; and he watched every one of us for our individual characteristics. We were his men. Already he took an almost paternal interest in us ... There was a bond of mutual confidence and affection between us, which grew stronger and stronger as the months passed. He had a smile for almost everyone; but we thought he had a different smile for us. We looked for it and were never disappointed ... it was a wonderful thing that smile of his. It was something worth living for ... the fact was that he had worked his way into our affections. We loved him. And there isn't anything stronger than love, when all's said and done.[33]

This passage was of great importance to Alister and had a long-term effect on his own style of management for it raises profound questions about the nature of intimacy, especially between men. In the cultural climate of today, speculations of this kind would probably lead to a discussion of a homosexual dimension to such experience.

Alister's thoughts took him in another direction for, in an obscure way, he seems to have linked this closeness with the immediacy and undefended directness he experienced in his spiritual experience. Alister's companions during this search were, first and foremost, the cyclists of C Company which, following Hankey, he named the 'Beloved Company'. Apart from taking the unusual step of printing and publishing the *Memoir* I mentioned earlier, he travelled annu-ally to their reunions in Ashington. Almost to the end of his life he designed an NCB Christmas card, different each year, and had it printed and sent out to all the remaining old pals. The associated letter writing was on a grand scale and in some cases continued after the soldier died, with his children and even grandchildren.

The theme of relationship is one that we shall come across again and again in Alister's life, but while it had its roots in his religion, it came to have less and less to do with institutional authority. An oft-repeated phrase of his was: 'My heart is in the Church of

England but not my head'. In association with this weakening of the link, his still extensive reading on religion during the second part of his military service gives the impression of a last ditch effort to find reasons for remaining within the Church of England. Among those whom he admired was the Reverend Philip 'Tubby' Clayton, founder of the charity Toc H and provider of many houses of hospitality for military personnel. Clayton was committed to doing away with class distinction and made this clear in the first house he opened to offer friendship to soldiers. He insisted that it was a place where the men could meet and relax regardless of rank and a notice at the front door bore the message: 'All rank abandon, ye who enter here'. Another influence was the writing of G. A. Studdert-Kennedy,[34] or 'Woodbine Willie' as he was nicknamed because of his practice of handing out cigarettes when he was talking with soldiers. Studdert-Kennedy served as an Anglican chaplain at the front, where he was moved to write some of his most interesting poetry, in dialect, and labelled by him, 'rough rhymes'. His outstanding courage at the front won him the Military Cross.

While Alister esteemed the bravery and honesty of these men, they did nothing to hold him in the Church. Far more important to the aspiring scientist was the empirical aspect of religious life; his exploration of the direct experience of the sacred. His reflections on the implications of it for human companionship fed into his lifelong search for transparency in relationships. It was both his greatest strength and a weakness – through his vulnerability to the unscrupulous behaviour of one or two of the people he befriended.

During the period when Alister was pondering these matters, the everyday life of the NCB plodded on, though one piece of news stopped him short. Mrs Hardy received news from the War Office that Vernon had been captured following the first large scale gas attack by the Germans at the second battle of Ypres in 1915. Fortunately, there was an arrangement permitting relatives to communicate with prisoners of war, and one postcard sent by Alister to his brother in a prison camp in Halle survives, presumably brought home by Vernon when he was released. Alister's message is both affectionate and unguarded about revealing military information:

Thank God you are safe – mater and I had such an
anxious time waiting for news and it was such a relief to
know that you are safe. You must have had a fearfully hot
time of it the last week or so before you were captured.
You were mentioned in an article in the *Daily Mail* for
your great coolness! We are all so proud of you. May I be
the same when occasion demands.

On the front of the postcard was a photograph of a windmill at
Saltfleet and the scribbled information that the unit was still there.
The family had no further need to worry. At the end of the war
Vernon was repatriated to Holland where he was one of a large
group of men who were exchanged for a similar number of German
POWs.

Meanwhile, the work of C Company had reached a stage where
the coastal defences were mostly in place and in any case the
likelihood of invasion had greatly receded, so that the cyclists'
battalion was coming to the end of its usefulness. Small drafts had
already gone off to join the machine gun corps and to different
infantry battalions. Alister began wondering about finding another
unit as there was no possibility of his beloved company staying
together. At just that moment, out of the blue, a confidential note
arrived on the Colonel's desk from the War Office. Under the
heading 'Royal Engineers/New Special Works', the note invited
applications from volunteers with the following qualifications:

- They must be prepared to fly as observers over enemy
  territory
- They must have a good knowledge of photography
- They must have a knowledge of the principles of art

He had no idea what 'New Special Works' meant or what this
invitation was about, but he was still desperately keen to fly and he
concocted a letter that in places was edging on being 'economical
with the truth'. For example, having recently gone for his one and
only fifteen-minute free flight from Bradford to Leeds, he felt this
permitted him to say that he was not without experience of
cross-country flying. With rather more confidence he wrote about
his exploits with a plate camera, since he had taken, developed and
printed many photographs as a boy. As I have mentioned, Alister

was also a keen amateur watercolourist, and here his letter pulled out all the stops with an unblushing technical essay on such matters as light and shade, colour, contrast, texture and the like.

Somewhat aghast at his own presumption, Alister sent off his letter to the War Office. Just at the point where he was about to give up hope of reply, he received an instruction asking him to report as soon as possible to the Special Works School in Kensington Gardens in London. Without further ado he dashed off to London and found his way to a group of huts in a fenced-off part of the park. Knocking on the door of one of the huts, he was met by an effusive and somewhat portly gentleman in the uniform of a colonel. He was Solomon J. Solomon,[35] Royal Academician and one of the best known artists in Britain. A confusing exchange took place:

'I have come to report; I am Captain Hardy.'

'Oh! Hardy, Hardy! You are from the Herkomer School,[36] aren't you? Come in.'

'I'm very sorry, but I'm not.'

'Oh, aren't you? I picked you specially because … Never mind, never mind, come in.'[37]

And so, to his surprise, Alister found himself on the training programme of the Camouflage School. He got the impression that his new colleagues on the programme were all well-known artists, chosen for their skill to work as camouflage officers, and he wondered if he was about to find himself out of his depth. At the same time he was astonished by the appropriateness of the chapter of accidents that led to his recruitment by Solomon. The unique background knowledge he brought with him on the methods of concealment used by animals to protect themselves from predators, made it thoroughly appropriate for him to be on the course.

Alister and his fellow artists underwent a month's concentrated education in all aspects of camouflage, with particular emphasis on the interpretation of aerial photographs, where a professional artist's knowledge of perspective and shadow ought to be of assistance.[38] To his further surprise and gratification he gained top marks in the examination at the end of the course. Alister assumed that, having done so well in his examination, he would now be sent to France as a full time observer, flying over enemy territory on a regular basis. Instead, he received a letter informing him that the examiners had been interested in one of his answers because it suggested that he might be creative in the invention of camouflage to protect new large scale coastal batteries to be built north of Newcastle.

At the time, Alister's response was one of deep disappointment, expressed strongly in the words: 'Then an awful thing happened'. Thinking about it in maturity, he saw the turn of events as, once again, providential and he was convinced that he was being guided. 'It was extraordinary, as though fate were controlling my affairs.' At last he was attached to the Royal Engineers and began work on assessing the need to camouflage gun emplacements on the North East coast, and where necessary using his expertise to direct the construction of concealment. Sometimes the arrangements were elaborate, as when he discovered that one battery was easily visible from the sea, silhouetted against the sky and thus highly vulnerable to attack. He arranged for the Royal Engineers to build a mock silhouette, painted to look like a continuation of the landscape with roads and houses, to be erected behind the guns, thus concealing their outline. The whole complicated construction was supposed to be supported by telephone poles and had slits in it to reduce wind resistance. Alister later heard that the Engineers had been greatly upset when the contraption was blown over in a gale.

After a year in the north east, Alister was called south to the Special Works department in Kensington for a revision course, to find that Solomon J. Solomon's views had been discredited and he was no longer in charge. The new director impressed Alister and he felt he came away from the course with a much broader perspective than before. He was called upon to give many lectures on camouflage, but his work on gun emplacements was finished, and he wrote to the Special Works Section of the Royal Engineers, begging to be allowed to go to France, They agreed, but by that time the war was coming to an end and there was not much for him to do. He toured the French camouflage factory at Villefranche. After the Armistice he and an artist friend Alan Beaton toured some of the scenes of appalling devastation at the Front. Then by a curious coincidence, and on the basis of his single term in Oxford, Alister was appointed Assistant Education Officer to the 13th Army Corps and sent to Paris to purchase educational equipment. He made the most of the trip and hugely enjoyed himself, and when he returned he was ordered – of all things – to join a special course being given for Army Education Officers in Oxford, where he was already making arrangements to return to Exeter College.

Alister regarded this as part of an unfolding sequence of events that was 'meant' and himself as on a divinely given path. He was stubbornly unimpressed by sceptical explanations in terms of coincidence for he felt they resolutely ignored the data to the point of their complaints being implausible. At another level his optimistic temperament meant that despite plentiful evidence to the contrary, in the agonies of the war that had just ended, he had an unbreakable sense of the universe being ultimately 'on our side'. His optimism and his sense of destiny were not naïve. He knew perfectly well that villains as well as saints had had similar convictions. In his autobiography he quoted the following example drawn from the archives of the Religious Experience Research Unit he founded in 1969 because he felt the account closely paralleled his own experience:

> When I was about 16, or perhaps a little earlier, I began to have what I call 'a sense of destiny'. It was only long afterwards that I realised that Napoleon and Hitler were the supreme examples of 'men of destiny' and that no good came of it. Though it explains nothing, I consoled myself with the thought that this was an example of the polarities of life. This sense of destiny is still with me. I suppose some people would call it 'guidance', but that implies a personal guide which is no part of the experience.[39]

It was with this burning conviction at the centre of his awareness that Alister returned to Oxford to study zoology under the care of T. H. Huxley's grandson, yet fully committed to his vocation to 'devote his life to reconciling the theory of evolution and the spiritual nature of man'.

CHAPTER FOUR

Returning to Academic Life

Honour is flashed off exploit, so we say;
And those strokes once that gashed flesh or galled shield
Should tongue that time now, trumpet now that field,
And on the fighter, forge his glorious day.
On Christ they do and on the martyr may;
But be the war within, the brand we wield
Unseen, the heroic breast not outward-steeled,
Earth hears no hurtle then from fiercest fray.

Gerard Manley Hopkins[1]

Alister came back to an Oxford that was short of money, short of
staff and crowded with ex-servicemen. In addition, there were
disadvantages in the arrangements he had made for his return to
Exeter College. The college agreed to his homecoming, but he was
not given the excellent rooms he had occupied in his first term.
More annoyingly, after only one term he was required to move out
into lodgings, and so he spent the rest of his undergraduate days at
6 Parks Road (now demolished to make way for the New Bodleian
Library). Then there was the matter of the puny size of the zoology
department, for in terms of numbers it was one of the smallest
academic units in Oxford University. In his book *Science at
Oxford, 1914–1939: Transforming an Arts University*,[2] Jack
Morrell notes the minor role of science in pre-twentieth century
Oxford. Compared with Cambridge, and even more so with some
of the newer institutions of tertiary education, Oxford had a strong
bias in favour of the arts, a situation which did not begin to change
greatly until after the disruption of university life caused by the War.
The practical impact of this on Alister was that he found himself a
member of a very small class, with just two other members;
someone called Heath-Gray, of whom he tells us nothing more than

71

his surname, and Sylvia Garstang. Perhaps Heath-Gray faded into the background because of Alister's preoccupation with Sylvia, who was eventually to become his wife.[3] She was the daughter of the marine biologist Walter Garstang, Professor of Zoology at the University of Leeds, and this connection certainly played a part in Alister's increasing interest in fisheries and the sea.

Since he had already completed a term in the Forestry Department, he was allowed to proceed directly onto the final honours course in zoology. As an ex-serviceman, he was also able to benefit from a special arrangement by which people returning from the Forces followed a shorter curriculum than that taken by other students. In fact he felt sufficiently uncomfortable about the gaps in his elementary zoological education to arrange to sit in with the first year medics' introductory zoology classes. The situation was admittedly messy but Alister was not altogether disappointed with his foreshortened course. As he remarks in his autobiography, he was a man in a hurry for he had a Vow to fulfil.

In other ways the disadvantages of studying zoology in Oxford were far outweighed by the benefits. The Zoology Department had a prominence out of proportion to its numbers of staff and students. In part this was due to the size and controversial history of the building in which it was housed, the Oxford Museum on Parks Road, quite close to where Alister had his lodgings. It was the brainchild of the professor of medicine, Sir Henry Ackland, with the support of the eminent art critic, John Ruskin, and it had made a significant contribution to the Gothic Revival.[4] The building was erected between 1858 and 1860, and could be thought of as a distant precursor of the scientific growth in the university that was to commence half a century later. There was a degree of controversy over its financing, evidence of which can still be seen on the exterior fabric to this day. When Alister – the son of an architect – first walked up to the entrance of the museum he probably thought it looked very grand, but closer inspection would have revealed to him that the decorative carving was unfinished. This is still the case, and is most obvious on the archway that forms the main entrance. The work was done by two talented Irish sculptors, the O'Shea brothers, who managed to get into a dispute with the university and were dismissed with the result that the decoration was never completed.[5]

Alister was of course already aware of the other reason for the fame of the museum, its use as the venue for the meeting of the British Association in 1860 when T. H. Huxley and Bishop Wilberforce begged to differ on the plausibility of natural selection. But quite apart from the building in which it was housed, the Zoology Department had a first class reputation as a centre for the study of comparative anatomy. Anatomy was a discipline seen as necessary for a detailed understanding of the processes of evolution. Darwin himself had underlined this requirement when he undertook his laborious study of the *Cirripedia* (barnacles), between 1846 and 1854, to teach himself the principles of classification. Hence, when Alister arrived, the heart of the Oxford degree course was based on a systematic practical study of the evolution of anatomical structure (in so far as it was known) with the animal kingdom divided into two parts, invertebrates and vertebrates. Each of the parts took a year to complete and, to economise with staff time, invertebrate and vertebrate systematics were taught alternately, year by year. Alister remembered with annoyance that the timing of his release from the army meant that he arrived to find the vertebrate course in mid-session, having already reached the mammals. Thus, the logic of the programme was destroyed, for as far as he was concerned all the vertebrate stages leading up to the mammals were a blank.

The head of the zoology department when Alister arrived was Professor Gilbert Bourne. Bourne came from the landed gentry, having been educated at Eton and Oxford, and was reaching the end of his career. Most subsequent opinions of his academic standing judge him as a competent though not outstanding scientist, but his importance was ensured by his two volume text *An Introduction to the Study of the Comparative Anatomy of Animals*, published in 1900 by George Bell and running to six editions, the last in 1919. Bourne was also a rowing blue, having been a member of the winning Oxford crew in the annual boat race against Cambridge University on two occasions. He was later appointed coach to the Oxford University Rowing Club and wrote a highly successful manual, *A Textbook of Oarsmanship*. The book was republished in 1987 with an endorsement from Allen Rosenberg (formerly coach to the American Olympic rowing squad) who judged it to be the finest book ever written about rowing.[6]

With this background, it was hardly surprising that Bourne had the reputation of caring more about rowing than he did about zoology. His colleague, E. S. Goodrich was a very different sort of man, with certain parallels to Hardy in his early life. He spent his childhood in France where he developed a great interest in natural history and had the artistic ability to make extremely good quality paintings of the animals and plants he had collected. It was therefore no surprise that in 1888 when it was time to further his education, his parents sent him to the Slade School of Art in London. The Slade was adjacent to (and is now formally part of) University College and this circumstance led to the young Goodrich's career change. In his spare time he took the opportunity to attend a series of public lectures on evolution which were given in the evenings by the Professor of Zoology at University College, Ray Lancaster. After listening to a particularly inspiring lecture he approached Lancaster and asked if there was any way he could become a member of Lancaster's zoology class. Lancaster was impressed by the enthusiasm of the young man and agreed to arrange for his entrance to University College. In 1891 Lancaster was appointed to the Chair of Zoology and Comparative Anatomy in Oxford and he brought Goodrich with him.

In 1921, Goodrich was appointed to the Linacre Chair when Bourne retired. The common opinion was that he was a good deal more outstanding as a comparative anatomist than his predecessor.[7] His master work, *Studies in the Structure and Development of Vertebrates*, was thought to be sufficiently important to be reprinted in 1958 with an introduction by Hardy, who by that time was himself the holder of the Linacre Chair.[8] Goodrich was in charge of the vertebrate systematics course that Alister entered when it was more than halfway towards completion. Not surprisingly, Hardy's experience of being taught by the two men differed greatly. Goodrich had one outstanding teaching skill in the blackboard illustrations which accompanied his lectures. His background as an artist enabled him to build up, layer by layer, the various systems of the vertebrate animal he was discussing. Hardy, himself no mean artist, modelled his own work on the blackboard after Goodrich.

In other ways Goodrich was limited as a communicator. He regularly took the students into the cathedral-like main hall of the museum where there was an exceptionally fine collection of preserved animal remains, sorted into phyla, orders, families and genera, according to the classification system of Linnaeus. The exhibition had been first laid out by Ray Lancaster and added to by subsequent heads of department, with a large proportion of the exhibits being the responsibility of Goodrich. It was technically accurate, but as Goodrich once snobbishly remarked, it made 'no concessions to the housemaid' or other casual visitors. His practice was to lead his tiny group of students round the exhibits, strictly according to the order in which they were laid out, and stopping and saying something about each one as if he were giving a public lecture. The students trailing after him with open notebooks and pencils spent their time desperately trying to make comprehensible notes while he droned on in a weak monotone that was boring to listen to and very difficult to hear. The best Hardy could say of it was: 'We managed, somehow.' Charles Elton, a near contemporary in the department with Hardy, said unkindly of Goodrich: 'He made the whole subject seem equally unimportant.'

Bourne was less of a scholar than Goodrich, but had a much more sparkling personal style and was accordingly admired for his teaching ability. He taught on the invertebrate year and early on encouraged his students to go out into the field, collecting specimens which were then brought to the lab and identified. Predictably, Alister responded eagerly to Bourne's suggestion and one day, soon after the course started, he went down to the great lily pond in the Oxford botanical gardens to look for protozoa (single-celled animals). He found that the water was richly populated with many different remarkable species. When Bourne saw what Alister had brought back he was astonished to hear where the specimens had come from, and admitted that several of them were new to him. Incidents like this meant that, early on, Alister was building up a reputation with Bourne as a good student, and subsequent events added to his status. One day during the following term Bourne asked the class to dissect a species of worm, *Acanthocephalus gigas*, an intestinal parasite of the pig:

> ... one of its features of interest is an extraordinary
> pulsating bell, with little openings in it for the extrusion of
> eggs, which acts as a kind of sieve, letting out eggs of a
> particular size that are ripe. Into this same external channel
> run these extraordinary excretory ducts called solenocytes.

> They form a ... bunch of organs, very spectacular to look
> at, and very difficult, apparently, to dissect; but by some
> stroke of luck, almost by accident, I found the whole
> system of the pulsating bell in the solenocytes had fallen
> out into my dissecting dish. I had been cutting round it with
> my scalpel, never expecting to get such a good dissection –
> it was really by accident. I mounted this on a slide and
> called to Professor Bourne. He was amazed. 'Look my
> boy, what a marvellous dissection you have made!'[9]

From now on, with mixed feelings of discomfort and gratification, Alister became the blue-eyed boy in the class. A few days later, any false pride he felt was dispelled by a laughable near-catastrophe. Bourne produced a preserved specimen of a giant earthworm from India, explaining that the department possessed a very small number of these animals, hence they could only afford to use one. Having decided that a student ought to do the dissection, he looked round the group and murmured audibly to himself: 'Who shall we have? ... Ah! Hardy.' Any schoolboy dissecting an earthworm in a biology class knows that you have to open it by cutting along the upper (dorsal) surface, to avoid damaging the nerve cord which runs along inside the lower (ventral) side of the body. A ventral nerve cord is a feature of all members of the phylum *Annelida* (earthworms). Alister knew this perfectly well, but the giant Indian worm had bristles arranged uniformly round its body, making it difficult to tell the dorsal from the ventral side, and he recalled:

> To my horror I suddenly realised I had cut it up the ventral
> surface ... so wrecking its nervous system. At that moment,
> by extraordinary luck, the head technician came in saying
> the professor was wanted by the boat club. Saying he
> wouldn't be long, he added: 'You get on with your
> dissection.' That allowed me time to remove all the pins,
> and I put the wretched worm in the drawer and got a
> second one, and to my horror there was nothing inside the
> second one at all. Something had gone wrong with it and
> it was quite obviously not the one that Bourne began to
> look at ... So I tore that one out and pushed it into a
> dissecting dish and took a third one, which I did dissect up

the right way and luckily managed to get it fairly well
displayed by the time Bourne returned. He asked for a
[dissecting] needle, so I gave him my needle. 'A needle!' he
said, 'That's a barge pole! Give me something respectable.'
I pulled out my drawer and to my horror realised I had
pushed it too with a great jerk, whereupon three worms
came out and hung over the edge of the drawer. I had my
back to the professor, so opened it again very quickly,
pushed them in and got out a more reasonable needle. But
it was a near shave.[10]

Towards the end of Bourne's classes on the Annelids, he dealt with
an odd collection of aberrant species, including *Priapulus*,[11] which
was believed to be very rare in England. One of the last specimens
to be found, Bourne told them, was in the mud of Scarborough
harbour. On hearing his boyhood holiday home mentioned, Alister
was caught up with the idea of going back and finding *Priapulus* for
himself. The last time it had been seen was in the 1880s and when
he followed up his idea and returned to Scarborough, he failed to
find any. He came to the conclusion that the advent of motor
vessels had destroyed the habitat by polluting it with oil. This was
unfortunate, but he refused to be beaten and returned to the search
at a later date and at another location.

In Alister's second year the little class was augmented. The people
who joined him in the advanced class included several who were to
become eminent members of the scientific profession. In a letter
written in 1972 to his old tutor Julian Huxley, he reminded him of
some of his fellow pupils. C. P. 'Pip' Blacker figured prominently, as
he and Alister formed a pair visiting Huxley in his rooms in New
College for their weekly tutorials. Arbitrary pairings like this are not
always successful and there was at first an uneasy relationship
between the two students, for Huxley's habit was to comment
briefly on their essays and then use the rest of the time conversing
on zoological topics in a free and exploratory manner, sometimes
wandering far away from the chosen subject. For instance, Alister
remembered a lengthy discussion of Wegener's theory of continental drift, following Huxley's attendance at some conference on the

subject. He thoroughly enjoyed conversations like this, which stimulated his imagination and deepened his thinking about the subject.
Blacker on the other hand was constantly annoyed by what he
considered was Huxley's offhand treatment of his essay, which he
had expected would be discussed in detail, point by point, to help
him prepare for the final exam. In spite of his annoyance Blacker
did very well in his finals and eventually became the director of the
British Eugenics Society, where he advanced views that were
controversial and considered by some critics to be morally unacceptable. Other Huxley pupils recalled by Alister included John
Baker, who for a time was paired with Sylvia Garstang for tutorial
meetings. He became Reader in Cytology in the Oxford Zoology
Department. Others who stayed in Oxford included Charles Elton,
ecologist and founder of the Oxford Animal Bureau, and E. B.
'Henry' Ford, who became Professor of Ecological Genetics. Alister
mentions the names of other fellow students in his autobiography,
including Gavin de Beer, Bernard Tucker and Tommy Barnard, all
of whom became well known in their fields. There is no doubt that
he had joined an elite – and he knew it.

It was an elite that, once a person had managed to break through
an invisible (and to an outsider a somewhat unfathomable) barrier,
allowed all sorts of intimacy between teacher and pupil in a way that
did not become widespread until the 1960s and beyond. In Hardy's
archive there is a tiny photograph, probably taken in 1921, of a
group of people capering wildly on the wooden bridge beside a
famous student watering hole, the Trout Inn at Wolvercote, on the
outskirts of Oxford. Using electronic technology it has been possible to enlarge the minute image to reveal that the wildest cavorter,
looking like a crazily dancing M. Hulot,[12] is Alister. De Beer, Tucker
and Barnard are also there, along with the population biologist Alec
Carr-Saunders who had recently been appointed to the staff of the
zoology department. There are also two young women in the
group, one of whom is Juliette, wife of Julian Huxley. Huxley
himself is not in the picture, possibly because he took the photograph. It has the feel of the high-spirited goings on in the
Bloomsbury Group,[13] perhaps not surprisingly, for Juliette had
worked as a governess for Lady Ottoline Morrell, whose salon was
central to the group's activities. In her autobiography, Juliette
describes similar prancing about among members of the Set on the
lawn at Garsington, Lady Ottoline's home near Oxford.[14] Alister

found Juliette enchanting and carried on a separate correspondence with her, written in a slightly flirtatious tone, quite distinct from the style he used in letters to Julian.

Alister's playful nature meant he thoroughly enjoyed being a part of these entertainments, but not enough to distract him from his Vow, which continued to govern every decision he made with regard to his biological career. He took additional opportunities to develop his theoretical and practical understanding of biology. One of the most attractive extras was attendance at the marine biology course that was laid on annually during the Easter vacation at Plymouth. The series had been inaugurated by Walter Garstang, who, it will be remembered, was the father of Alister's sweetheart, Sylvia, thus creating another small emotional link with her family.

Garstang had set up the course to last for a fortnight and much of the time was spent on the rocky shore collecting specimens from rock pools, or examining samples of sea water for the different species that made up the plankton. Garstang himself was an enthusiast for plankton, particularly the larval forms that made up part of the population. He wrote a number of mildly comic verses, well known to generations of zoology undergraduates, to illustrate his teaching, which were edited and published by Hardy in 1951.[15]

The outing to Plymouth was generally a light-hearted affair, remembered affectionately in later years by Alister. With his fellow students Pip Blacker, John Baker and Tommy Barnard he went on the course shortly before they had to face their final degree exams. They lodged together in a house near Plymouth Hoe, the spectacular greensward where according to legend Francis Drake played bowls while the Spanish Armada approached. In the evenings Alister and his colleagues wandered down to the Grand Hotel for a drink and passed the time away sitting in the main lounge, looking through past exam papers and speculating about the questions that were likely to turn up in the final honours examinations. In those days of prim rectitude, Alister recalled:

> ... discussing the various questions, many of which, I may say, were very anatomical. One of us would read out a question and the others would decide what was the appropriate answer. This had been going on for a little time when the head waiter came across rather nervously and coughed and said: 'Excuse me, gentlemen, the ladies

on the other side of the lounge request that you finish your stories in the smoke room.'[16]

Back from Plymouth after the Easter vacation, the class went through the systematics of the *Arthropoda* with Professor Bourne, finishing off with the *Insecta*. The regulations permitted Alister, as a returning serviceman, to sit his final examination at this point, having completed only four terms of the total honours course, a fact he liked to keep quiet about when qualifications were discussed. He chose to do this because of his strong wish to get on with the task of fulfilling his Vow, but he was aware of the incompleteness of his zoological education, so he attended Goodrich's classes on fish during the term after he graduated.

There were no classified degrees awarded to students who had followed the shortened degree course, but Alister was awarded his degree 'with distinction'. His ambition did not stop there, for he knew about the Christopher Welch Research Scholarship, which was offered to the most outstanding student in the year and entitled the winner to study marine biology in the *Stazione Zoologica* in Naples. He also knew that if he got there he wanted to investigate the marine worm *Priapulus*, but he needed to find out more about it before facing the examiners. He had to prepare carefully if he was to outdo his closest rival, Gavin de Beer, a brilliant man who was, according to Alister, 'irritatingly knowledgeable' on everything to do with zoology.

After writing about *Priapulus* to a number of people who might know where these rare animals could be found, almost at the last minute he received a message from Professor Arthur Dendy of King's College, London, advising him to try the outermost reaches of the muddy estuary of the Thames at Brightlingsea, near Colchester. On the day before the oral examination, Alister dashed down to Brightlingsea and spent fruitless hours sieving the black mud to the point where the last train to get him back to Oxford was about to leave. Feeling desperately that he might have made a foolish mistake, he decided to stay the night at Brightlingsea and, meanwhile, carry on searching for the worm. The tide was coming in, so he hired a boat and dragged mud from under the water with a bucket. The sun was just setting when he pulled in the bucket one last time, to find that it contained three specimens of *Priapulus*. Thrilled, he decided not to stop and went on to find two more.

Then, filling five of the glass jars he had brought with him, he put one specimen in each.

Now exhausted, he found a room in a local hotel, had supper, a glass of beer, and went to bed where he fell asleep almost at once. In the middle of the night he was awoken by a racket coming from the next room and:

> … to my surprise I saw what looked like little blue goblins dancing at the end of my bed. I thought, good gracious, I only had a beer last night. I had no bedside light, just a candle which I lit. I think this is an embroidery to the story: I imagined I was in a four-poster bed – it was a very old fashioned hotel – but I got out of bed, put the light on, and found that in my five jars that stood on the mantelpiece, level with the end of my bed, were very small jelly-fish-like creatures, Ctenophores, which were luminescent. When I turned the full light on they ceased to glow, and then I made a discovery without knowing it. Only two or three years later I came across a paper, by a Czech I think, showing that the effect of a bright light would (sic) cut off the luminosity of these Ctenophore animals.[17]

Next morning Alister hurried back to Oxford with his precious jars, arrived at the room where the examiners were waiting and left the jars outside while he went in to face some academic scrutiny from Bourne and the other examiners. He explained his intention to do research on *Priapulus* and waited for the inevitable scepticism. Sure enough, it came:

'This is all very well, Hardy; it's a splendid idea to think of taking up the study of *Priapulus* but you know it hasn't been seen for years. Your chance of getting it is almost nil.'

'Well, I have got some outside.'

'You've got some; what do you mean?'

'I've got some outside the door – may I bring them in?'[18]

When he came in with his five jars, they were 'absolutely astounded', 'and', said Alister with a flourish, 'that was how I beat Gavin de Beer for the Christopher Welch!'

Hardy's many-sided interests were illustrated around this period, when he patented the first of several inventions. By this time, he must have felt Oundle belonged to the remote past, but his inventions recalled aspects of his schooling that lingered on in a somewhat surprising way. It will be recalled that he had been particularly critical of Sanderson's innovation of workshops where boys could learn the practical skills of inventing and manufacturing a useful commercial product, good enough to be patented. Yet here in Oxford he got to the stage of making a practical model and patenting an idea that had been in his mind for several years. He called his new idea the Historiograph, consisting of a long sheet,

> ... arranged to wind from one roller on to another placed at a convenient distance. Along the top of the sheet is marked off a scale of dates; the left hand side is in a box, on the lid of which are headings such as: — sovereigns, politics, religion, war, literature, etc. Opposite and under their correct dates on the chart are marked by lines or points according to their duration. Thus the relation of one event to another may be seen at a glance. The left loader has a spring attached which will rewind the chart, and the right hand loader is fitted with a handle (and retaining catch); by turning the handle one may pass the whole of history from the earliest times to the present day before one's eyes.[19]

While not the most remarkable of innovations, it was to be the forerunner of his most famous invention, the Continuous Plankton Recorder (CPR; his invention of this will be described in Chapter Six). These two ideas give the impression of being variations on a theme, in this case flat sheets being automatically wound on and off a pair of rollers, as is the case with the CPR. The sequence is further evidence of two of Alister's salient talents, lateral thinking and his ability to persist enthusiastically with a task, well after others would have given up. He seems to have been proud of his first patent, since he wrote a letter to Sanderson, explaining it and hoping he would remember him. He may have found Sanderson's reply disappointing and a little hurtful. His old headmaster wrote to say that he remembered Alister 'quite well' while adding polite congratulations on his successes. This to Alister, Bourne's blue-eyed boy and the Welch Memorial Prizeman, must have felt like faint praise and added emotional strength to his critical attitude to Oundle. Certainly his son and daughter could not remember any occasion when from his own initiative he had returned to the school; a lack of enthusiasm in marked contrast to his devotion to the old cyclist's battalion.

The most important support for Alister during his time as an undergraduate came from his friendship with Julian Huxley, who could hardly fail to have been bowled over by the young man's enthusiasm and creative imagination. Alister in turn continued to find Huxley inspiring and always in touch with the latest developments in zoological theorising and research. He was soon a member of the coterie of clever students and family friends that surrounded Huxley, visited him at home and went on holiday with him. He thus created social and political alliances that were to prove invaluable in the making of a career. In the summer vacation after he graduated Alister went down to the West Country to stay with Julian and his wife Juliette, in the house they occupied in the village of Cawsand, on the Cornish side of Plymouth Sound. By this time Alister had pinpointed a spot in the mud at Brightlingsea where he could be sure to find specimens of *Priapulus* and he brought a supply with him to work on. Huxley was studying phases in the growth of the shore crab and had invited another promising young man to join them for a time. This was James Gray, who was also researching in Plymouth, and who some years later became head of the zoology department in Cambridge. Each morning they would walk over the hill out of Cawsand, past the splendid Tudor mansion at Mount Edgecumbe and down to the pier at Cremyll Ferry, where they crossed the Sound and caught a tram into Plymouth. The combination of ecstatic landscape, novel research and stimulating talk ensured that the personal bonds between the members of the group became greatly strengthened. Clearly, Alister was now one of the in-crowd. He came back to Oxford in the autumn to attend the remaining lectures on fish given by Goodrich, before going off to Naples. Realising that the Welch Prize would not cover all his costs, he also entered and won the competition for the Oxford Biological scholarship to Naples. All was now in place, and he set out for what he hoped would be an enchanting adventure in Italy.

There is an archetypal story that most English people visiting Naples have heard, especially those who can afford to stay at Parker's Hotel, near the *Stazione Zoologica:*

> One morning in 1889 bailiffs came to confiscate the
> Grand Hotel in Naples for the owner's gambling debts.
> One of the guests was George Parker-Bidder, a wealthy
> Englishman who was studying at the marine laboratory
> nearby. It was about ten o'clock and Parker-Bidder was as
> usual sleeping late. The bailiffs knocked several times and
> Parker finally responded in an annoyed but courteous
> voice. Remaining outside the door the bailiffs explained
> what was happening and, without getting out of bed,
> Parker sleepily asked them to tell the owner to add the
> cost of the Hotel to his bill. From that day on, the Hotel
> was known as Hotel Parker's–Tramontano.[20]

The story conjures up images of wealthy young men from Oxford and Cambridge on a version of the grand tour, indolently passing the time away with a little light biological research, while their thoughts are taken up with the perfumed air of Naples and its romantic history. When he first arrived, Hardy blew a considerable sum of money living the dream for a few nights in Parker's, before moving to rather less expensive lodgings near the laboratory. This was after an enjoyable visit to Rome, about which he wrote at considerable length in his journal, and a journey down the coast to Naples. His senses and imagination were overwhelmed by the romantic nature of the place; its colourful squalor, and the fact that ordinary workmen in the street could be heard singing arias from grand opera. Life in the *Stazione* was at first surprisingly positive. Though it had not yet recovered from the austerities forced upon it by the war, Alister was given an attractive room above the entrance to the *Stazione.* The members of the Italian staff appeared surprised to see him, but at once were very solicitous, even on the first day providing him with embarrassingly large amounts of research material before he had got himself sufficiently organised to start work on it.

Life was also made more entertaining by an ongoing colourful and impenetrable wrangle over ownership of the building which was well under way before Alister arrived. He was not sure that he fully understood what was going on but it seemed that Reinhard Dohrn, German born and the son of the founder of the lab, Anton Dohrn, was about to return to his directorship and take over from Montecelli, the Italian currently in charge. Apparently the Italian government began to feel uneasy about local reaction to the forthcoming change, and sent an official down from Rome to take over the *Stazione* while they awaited the arrival of Dohrn. This action triggered the municipal authority into deciding that the building actually belonged to Naples; a local councillor grabbed the keys and refused to hand them over to the government. Just to add to the confusion, a crowd of local university students held a protest meeting at which it was decided that should Dohrn reach the point of taking up his post, they would burn down the *Stazione*. This caused the alarmed authorities to place an armed guard round the building until tempers calmed.

Behind this conflict lay a long story of international hostility, principally involving the well-funded British scientific community, which therefore had a strong hand in determining who the director was to be. In a letter to Huxley dated 9 January 1921, Hardy presented his excited picture of the complex power struggle for control of the *Stazione* involving Italian, German, British, French and even American interested parties. At the end of his lengthy and repetitive message, Alister wondered whether a way out of this morass would be to form an international marine biological association, along the lines of the British Marine Biological Association. He saw this as a way of transcending the politics of nationalism, which had deeply unpleasant and irrational aspects to it, for example the spreading of false rumours of Italian inadequacy, or hostility to German leadership based on prejudice deriving from the recently concluded war.

The excitable tone of Hardy's letter was somewhat out of keeping with his normal writing style, which while enthusiastic was usually in a calmer mode. Was it perhaps because as a newly graduated zoologist and thus possibly the most junior member of the community at the *Stazione*, he was nervous least he was seen as straying beyond his legitimate concerns? It may be significant that these thoughts were put first to his tutor, Julian Huxley, who at that time was a similarly junior member of staff, back in Oxford. Hardy says explicitly that he is turning to Huxley rather than to Bourne or Goodrich, on the grounds that the last two would think it a cheek to make such a proposal. With Huxley he was on safer ground, though even here he followed up with another letter a few days afterwards, apologising for his foolish outburst and presenting his argument more calmly. Then, discovering from Huxley's response that he was being taken seriously, his subsequent letters are level-headed and more confidently expressed. Whether fully conscious of it or not, it seems that already as a new graduate he was implicitly teaching himself the skills of diplomacy and higher level policy making; competences that would recommend him when it came to seeking advancement in his career. It is also noteworthy that, in line with his Vow to reconcile science and religion, his preferred solution to the problems at the *Stazione* was a practice run in the art of bringing about reconciliation.

In another way, Hardy's maturing relationship with his tutor was to prove crucial in the handling of a personal crisis that blew up after he had been a few months in his lonely laboratory. He found himself beginning to be bored by what he was doing and wishing he had never won the Welch Scholarship. In part this was due to loneliness, for there often seemed to be nobody else in the building and Alister wrote of the depressing effect of coming in every morning to work and hearing his footsteps echoing along the deserted corridors. However, he struggled on with the work on his chosen research topic, expanding it to include a study of the parasitic relatives of *Priapulus* found in Mediterranean fish. Meanwhile, and most significantly in view of his subsequent career, he found he was becoming interested in the marine plankton of the region.

It so happened around that time that Hardy heard from Professor Stanley Gardiner of Cambridge University that he was recruiting staff for a new fisheries laboratory. It was being set up by the Department of Agriculture and Fisheries to study the conditions in the North Sea as they affected the commercial fishing industry. Gardiner and Hardy had met each other briefly when Julian Huxley introduced them and Gardiner took the opportunity to write to enquire whether Alister might be interested. Hardy's response was positive, even to the extent of specifying the area of research he wished to take up, if offered a job. He stated that he had recently become fascinated by plankton and that he would love to have the opportunity to investigate the relationship between plankton distribution and the life cycle of the herring or mackerel. Gardiner arranged to meet Alister back in England after he had completed the first six months of his programme in Naples.

Away from the laboratory, life was taking a turn for the better. People started arriving to work in the *Stazione*, including Armand Denis, an undergraduate in the chemistry department in Oxford who was also very interested in natural history. Among other things, he was collecting reptiles for Antwerp Zoo and Alister accompanied him on several of his expeditions which sometimes ended with a few too many glasses of wine, out in the glorious countryside surrounding Naples. The two men cemented a lifelong friendship and some years later Armand and his wife Michaela were to become popular television presenters of natural history programmes.

Meanwhile, inside the lab, Alister's misery was getting out of hand and in his alarm he decided to confide in Julian Huxley. It must have taken courage to write so frankly about his problems, but he felt forced to do something drastic about his plight. This becomes clear in the 12-page letter he sent to Huxley on 27 April, which reveals that things were starting to go seriously wrong in his personal life. After a few inconsequential opening remarks about being invited to tea with Reinhard Dohrn, who was by this time back in post, he launched into the real purpose of his letter:

> I have been through a most critical period in my zoological career – a period of being absolutely 'fed up'. I never thought I should get like this, but perhaps most people pass through such a phase, but perhaps not so acutely as I have done recently.[21]

Apparently taken aback by the temerity of his self-revelation, Alister avoided the subject for the next five pages, before his distress welled up again:

> Things were not going at all well and it was then that I began to get so fed up. I nearly wrote to Bourne and asked if I should return and get on with my *Priapulus* work … I passed through a phase when I never wanted to see a microscope or solenocyte again – and could do nothing but walk up and down my room thinking of matters social, political, religious even – anything but science.[22]

He managed to break out of his misery temporarily by taking a few days holiday in Florence, where he wrote a moving description of the beauties of the city and wondered to himself whether he had made a mistake in taking up a scientific career. He at first avoided mentioning this particular uncertainty:

> I bathed myself in Renaissance art, went crazed over Donatello's and Michelangelo's sculpture and have returned full of beans and am now getting ahead with my work quite well ...[23]

But the unhappiness through which he went, wrought a change of mood with regard to his future career:

> You will think I am quite mad, I know – I probably am – but I am seriously thinking of taking a post in the fisheries – rather than a university post – in fact I have already filled in a preliminary application form. Firstly, I do not think I shall ever be keen on demonstrating, lecturing or tutoring. I should take a university post for the opportunities for research and the long vacations ... Secondly, regarding research in pure science – I shall always be keen on it – but I have begun to hate the feeling of being expected to turn out research. As a hobby it is delightful, but to feel as one does when one holds a scholarship, or as one would at a university, that one has to produce something, robs the work of all its fascination. I have decided that I shall never work at pure science in the future for money. And again I have asked myself if a lot of the work I am doing or thinking of doing is really worth it, or rather the best that I can make of my time. I shall certainly not do much morphological work in the future. At the present time I am sure there is more valuable work to be done. I feel I want to be working – really working at something directly useful to the community. The Fisheries attract me for this reason, also for the many fascinating oceanographical problems, and also the sea life ... There are many things I do not like about a university life. I mentioned some of these on my last walk with you at Oxford in the Botanical Gardens. I hate the petty jealousy and backbiting that goes on in

donnish circles; I dislike the unreality of the whole life … a life which during term one never gets away from. Senior Common Rooms would drive me mad in a very short time! All this is between ourselves. I have not definitely made up my mind – but that is how I feel – I may perhaps go to Leeds – I have been waiting to hear from Professor Garstang for some time.[24]

This remarkably frank letter nevertheless conceals matters that were of crucial concern to Alister. For example, when he was walking up and down in his room, unable to work, and found himself absorbed by social and political issues, he added, almost as an afterthought, 'religion even'. Considering that elsewhere, Alister tells us that his entire life is dedicated to the investigation of the boundary between religion and science, the throwaway quality of the afterthought strikes one as ingenuous; an illustration of how sensitive Alister felt about mentioning his religious preoccupations. Similarly, his remark that he might go to Leeds to see Walter Garstang is overtly to do with sorting out his professional future. What is missing from that statement is the fact that the solution to his loneliness, and the emotional refuge from his disturbance, also lived in Leeds: Walter's daughter Sylvia.

Huxley was greatly alarmed when he received Alister's news and replied on 12 May in a similarly long letter. To begin with he sympathised with him over the issue of trying to work in an empty building and lacking companions with whom to discuss his work. Then he moved on to Alister's proposed change of vocation:

> I am also very sorry to hear that you are thinking of putting in for the Fisheries. That is not your line, I am quite convinced. In any case – I say it with (?) intention – you *ought* not to make up your mind out there where you have just been passing, obviously, through rather a mental crisis, and where you have no-one to discuss pros and cons with.[25]

Setting aside Huxley's startling misjudgement about Alister's future, his letter is a deeply moving act of self-revelation written with the purpose of assisting his former pupil to move out of the darkness. The Huxley family, including Julian's eminent grandfather, tended to suffer from depression and Julian had had to face the tragedy of his brother Trevenen's suicide. It made him particularly sensitive to problems of this type and perhaps inclined to project his own experience onto other people's somewhat less troubled situations. At any rate, few university tutors can have gone to such lengths on behalf of their pupils as he did for Alister, and it is an example of care that surely contributed to shaping Hardy's treatment of his own students.

For Huxley shared with Hardy his own frustrations with his research failures when he himself was working in Naples and his sense of uselessness; how hard he found it to understand physiology when he first began to study; how when people praised him for his high intelligence he inwardly dismissed them as mistaken fools; and how in the past his unhappiness was such that he was plagued with thoughts of suicide. Then he turned to the joys of university life, and made Alister an offer:

> If you come back *here* for a year to demonstrate – simply a probationary job – I will undertake to find you research abundantly that will interest you and occupy you ... For your own sake come back; don't go into the Fisheries.[26]

On 16 May Alister replied and began by thanking Huxley effusively for his letter:

> I had not the slightest idea you had been through anything like this. How awful it must have been. I have tasted a little of it, but to have endured it for 10 years and to have then triumphed. Your letter is the most remarkable document I have ever read – I return it at once because it is so sacredly private. I could not destroy it, yet dare not keep it lest it should fall into other hands.[27]

With all his respect for his tutor, Alister knew that he could not at this juncture in his life turn in the direction advocated by Huxley. He wrote more openly than before about the sequence of events when he came to Naples:

> I became for the time being really excited by such things as nephridia – coelomoducts – etc. and hitting a

comparatively unworked beast like *Priapulus* stimulated
this interest still further, so that when I came here I had
hoped to work on similar problems in *Echinorynchus* –
Sipunculus etc. But when I found myself alone here and
work not going well, I had time to think of things in their
true proportions. The wider interests, the interests which
first took me to Biology, the desire to understand better
the meaning of Life – rushed back and I found myself
working at things which I began to realise I didn't care a
button about. I frankly now do not care whether *Priapulus*
or any other animal excretes by solenocytes, open
nephridia or coelomoducts any more than I care whether a
motorcycle has one or other type of valve, carburettor or
magneto. I admit that collectively all these are of great
interest to the student of evolution – but isolated I find
them in themselves dull and I find I have not the
temperament for such work.[28]

And later in the same letter:

Now with these wider interests which have returned to me,
there have returned also interests which are not Biological
at all. Interests which during my time at Oxford I succeeded
in repressing as much as I could but which have now
reacted with great force. Strong interests which I don't
think I have ever revealed to you, of a religious and
socialistic nature, and although I realise the danger of this
uncertain ground I sometimes believe it will predominate in
my life's work.[29]

Having almost revealed his hand ('I *sometimes* believe' suggests
slight self-protection, though he may of course have had doubts
about his Vow from time to time) he then entered the diplomatically
difficult task of insisting on his decision to apply for a post with the
fisheries. He pointed out that he would be starting as a Probationer
('If I am no good they can kick me out and if I don't like it I can
withdraw I presume') and he heavily underlined the date when the
selection committee met to decide who to appoint, which was just
ten days away. If Julian got the letter in time and had a moment to
spare, would he kindly write a short testimonial for him and address

it to the appropriate official in the Ministry of Agriculture and Fisheries in London?

CHAPTER FIVE

Hunting the Silver Darlings

There is no record of Julian Huxley's feelings when he received Alister's letter. But at least he did not stand in the way of Hardy's longing to escape from the work that had become repugnant to him in the laboratory in Naples. Hardy wrote to Professor Goodrich in Oxford about the dilemma in which he found himself and asked for permission to renounce his Welch Prize and return home. In the event a somewhat uncomfortable compromise solution was arrived at; Alister would complete the first six months of the normal two year period in Naples, and would then return to England, but would continue the work begun in the *Stazione*, part-time, to bring it to completion and thus not lose the results of his studies.[1]

Alister's cry from the heart was to be involved in some enterprise that was of practical use to humankind. Whether he was fully conscious of it or not, in selecting the fisheries he chose wisely, for the industry was facing increasingly serious problems that would eventually affect the livelihoods of many thousands of people in the British Isles. Doubts about the abundance of the fish stocks in the oceans became a matter of public concern in 1854 when the scholarly John Cleghorn introduced the term 'overfishing' in a paper given at a meeting of the British Association.[2] Cleghorn lived in Wick on the coast of the far north of Scotland, where herring fishing was a vital source of income. He had noticed a falling off of the catches of herring over the years, in spite of the greatly increased number of nets in use. His advocacy of a close season to help preserve the stocks of fish was met with great hostility by the local fishermen. They could foresee a loss of income, and Cleghorn was persecuted unmercifully, being insulted and having the windows of his house regularly smashed.

At the time, detailed evidence on the levels of the stocks of fish in the North Sea were almost non-existent. There were heated and unsubstantiated arguments over the possibility that commercial fishing had a significant effect on the numbers of fish in the sea. By coincidence, two of the most prominent participants in the dispute provoked by Cleghorn were T. H. Huxley and Alister Hardy's future father-in-law, Walter Garstang. Huxley made a public statement of his views when he gave the opening speech at the International Fisheries Exhibition, held in London in 1883. He took the opportunity to insist that 'with current fishing methods',

> I believe that it may be affirmed with confidence that, in relation to our present modes of fishing, a number of the most important sea fisheries, such as the cod fishery, the herring fishery, and the mackerel fishery, are inexhaustible. And I base this conviction on two grounds, first, that the multitude of these fishes is so inconceivably great that the number we catch is relatively insignificant; and, secondly, that the magnitude of the destructive agencies at work upon them is so prodigious, that the destruction effected by the fisherman cannot sensibly increase the death-rate.[3]

Huxley gave the following startling example of abundance:

> At the great cod-fishery of the Lofoden Islands, the fish approach the shore in the form of what the natives call 'cod mountains' – vast shoals of densely packed fish, 120 to 180 feet in vertical thickness. The cod are so close together that Professor Sars tells us 'the fishermen, who use lines, can notice how the weight, before it reaches the bottom, is constantly knocking against the fish.' And these shoals keep coming in one after another for two months, all along the coast.[4]

On the other side of the argument was Garstang, whose major statement was a 69-page essay entitled *The Impoverishment of the Sea*, published in 1900, 17 years after Huxley's assertions.[5] Referring to the first passage just quoted, Garstang noted that the crucial phrase was 'In relation to our present modes of fishing', for with the arrival of new types of fishing gear and the introduction of the steam trawler, the percentage of total stocks caught annually began to encompass a much higher proportion of the fish population. Drawing upon statistics for the fishing ports of Grimsby and Lowestoft, he concluded:

> The results obtained from all these various independent sources of information display a melancholy unanimity … the bottom fisheries are not only not exhaustible, but in a rapid and continuous process of exhaustion … the rate at which sea fishes multiply and grow … is exceeded by the rate of capture.[6]

The figures quoted by Garstang were impressive, but referred to only two English fishing ports. The available statistical data were still not much better than in Cleghorn's day, which meant that the arguments continued to become heated and unproductive. Since these uncertainties applied to all the other European countries with large fishing fleets, attempts were made to secure cooperation at a number of conferences during the latter part of the nineteenth century. The first truly significant international meeting at governmental level was the second conference held in Christiana (now Oslo) in Norway in 1901, and among the British delegation was Garstang, representing the Marine Biological Association. Four major decisions were made which eventually were to influence the direction of Alister Hardy's research work:

1. To obtain an accurate knowledge of the serial and periodic changes in the waters of the North Sea, the Baltic Sea, the Norwegian Sea and the south-eastern Barents Sea and of their causes.
2. To determine the amount of variation in the character and abundance of the food supply of the food fishes, whether it be planktonic or benthic.
3. To determine the variations in the abundance of the food fishes at all stages of their life history.

4. To determine the extent to which those variations were due, either to natural physical causes acting directly on the fish or indirectly through their food supply, or to the operations of fishing vessels in modifying the conditions of reproduction and growth of the fish.[7]

In the report of the British delegation to the Foreign Secretary, Garstang recommended that the programme be adopted by the United Kingdom. Following a discussion in the Cabinet, the decision was taken to accept the recommendation and to allocate the necessary funding to implement it, once the costs were known. No doubt the fact that two members of the cabinet were Vice-Presidents of the Marine Biological Association (Arthur Balfour, First Lord of the Treasury and later Prime Minister, and Joseph Chamberlain, who was the Colonial Secretary) helped them to come to this decision. Garstang was appointed convenor of a committee that would be responsible for co-ordinating and studying these questions as they applied to the English fishing industry. In September 1902, as part of its brief, the committee set up a small fisheries laboratory in Lowestoft and, as the obvious choice, Garstang was appointed its first director.

Arthur Lee, who was director of the Lowestoft laboratory between 1974 and 1980, identifies Garstang as the founding father of modern English fisheries research.[8] His leadership left him very vulnerable, in a situation where there was a great deal of dispute and he was often under attack from opponents of the hypothesis of overfishing. Frustrated by the hostility and obstruction, he eventually resigned as director to take up the post of Professor of Zoology at the University of Leeds. His leadership nevertheless had a strong influence on the development of the laboratory and he continued to be a well known figure in the town. One familiar story shows this. He regularly had samples of fish sent to the laboratory from other parts of the country for investigation. The parcels often took several days to arrive at the central sorting department of the Post Office in Lowestoft, with the result that they stank, and became known as 'Garstangs' by the sorting staff. The name was applied from then on to any strongly smelling package arriving in the sorting office, a custom that continued for many years after he had left Lowestoft.

It was in the context of this history that Alister Hardy entered the scene, bringing with him the political advantage of a growing personal relationship with Garstang, via his daughter Sylvia. Two years after the ending of the Great War, Stanley Gardiner was appointed by the Ministry of Agriculture and Fisheries as part-time director at Lowestoft while retaining his Cambridge Chair. His primary task was to identify and recruit staff to undertake an increased programme of research in the fisheries and the letter of invitation that Alister received while he was in Naples was part of that recruitment drive. He was only one of a group of talented young men appointed to the staff during this period. At much the same time, E. S. Russell took over from Gardiner as the new full-time director, a post which he held until 1945. The building in which they operated was adapted from two large boarding houses knocked together to form the fisheries laboratory, situated near the Claremont pier.

The arrangement was unpretentious but comfortable and Alister recalled his years in Lowestoft as one of the happiest times in his life. It is easy to see why. Most obviously, he had found employment that had practical relevance to human wellbeing, which is what he craved. In addition he had requested, and was granted, the opportunity to take up the interest in plankton which had been triggered while he was in Naples. The relaxed style of Russell's direction and his dislike of mechanistic approaches to science made him an attractive leader, on a wavelength similar to Alister. At the personal level it brought him closer to the Garstang family, thus strengthening the bond that had developed between himself and Sylvia, who liked to recall how their romance was sparked off over a dissecting dish in the Zoology Department in Oxford. Career-wise, through his personal relationship with Walter Garstang and his informal knowledge of the latter's negotiations with the government, he was given a privileged insight into the power-broking of the Whitehall bureaucracy. For all these reasons, along with the firm and long-lasting friendships he made with many of the Lowestoft fishermen, to whom he came to be known as 'MacAlister', or simply 'Mac',[9] he felt he was at home among congenial companions. By this time Alister was 25 years old. Undoubtedly ambitious, his thoughts of fame were as yet no more than daydreams. Distinction was a world away and he was getting used to his first job, which had the humble and delightfully old fashioned title of 'Assistant Naturalist'.

The memories of Lowestoft recorded in Alister's autobiography reflect as much on carefree youthful escapades as on the important scientific work he did. His years there had a slightly chaotic beginning. Having been told to report to the laboratory on 1 August 1921 he turned up to find it completely closed and deserted because it was Bank Holiday Monday. 'Typical', he thought to himself. Subsequently, matters took a livelier turn and very shortly after he arrived he was pitched into an exciting opportunity to exercise his enthusiasm for flight. A question had been asked in the House of Commons about the French, who had begun spotting fish from the air. Why, asked a patriotic MP, weren't we doing the same? The Ministry responded by requesting that someone from Lowestoft Laboratory should undertake investigations using one of the seaplanes operating from an air base in near-by Felixstowe. Alister was familiar with these large biplanes, powered by two Rolls-Royce engines and with an open observer's cockpit right out in front to make it easier to observe. He volunteered at once, citing his experience during the war as an aerial observer on the look out for enemy camouflage work.

To his delight he was selected and he made arrangements to lodge temporarily in Felixstowe. After delays due to bad weather, eventually a plane piloted by Flight Lieutenant Modin was able to take off on 19 August, not quite three weeks after Alister had first arrived in Lowestoft. They flew up past Smith's Knoll[10] to where the herring fleet was fishing in the North Sea, but after repeatedly circling round them, Alister had to admit that he could see nothing. The strong tides running in that part of the sea stirred up a great deal of mud so that any herring shoals that might be there were hidden. In any case herring tend to come to the surface at night, which might be another reason for drawing a blank. These fruitless attempts at shoal spotting and further unsuccessful flights undertaken with the same purpose, in the area of the western mackerel fishery off Cornwall, constituted Alister's first formal investigation on behalf of the Ministry of Agriculture and Fisheries. The pamphlet, *Fishery Investigations* Series II, Vol. VII, No. 5, 'Report on the Possibilities of Aerial Spotting of Fish', by A. C. Hardy, MA, was eventually published in 1924 in London by His Majesty's Stationery Office, and looked impressive, but it did not tell the whole story.

Flight Lieut. Modin, who had been a taxi driver before joining the Air Force, was a lively character. The first search had taken nearly four hours without success, and, feeling bored, he suggested to Alister that they should have a bit of fun. Then, diving down towards the herring fleet, he started leapfrogging over the drifters, dipping very near the sea, then rising and dropping over each one, causing outrage and consternation among the skippers, but excitement in Alister. More thrills were to follow. Although the flight had been fruitless, Alister decided to repeat the exercise in the hope of better luck and this led to an incident that remained particularly vivid in his memory. It had occurred to him that he could avoid having to stay in Felixstowe by requiring the pilot to fly the seaplane north and land in the water at Lowestoft. He was told that landing there was very dangerous because of the strong tides, but Modin had already shown that he liked a challenge and he acceded to Alister's request. There was one proviso; that a motor boat must be made available to take the aeroplane in tow as soon as it landed on the water, thus preventing it from crashing into Claremont Pier, one of the two long pleasure piers with which the Victorians had endowed Lowestoft. Alister arranged for the harbourmaster to have his motorboat at the ready on the morning that the plane was due.

All seemed to be well, the aircraft took off from Felixstowe and Alister cycled to the harbour to meet the motorboat. But then, crisis! He was told: 'Oh, the engine has been taken out of the motorboat, but we have a couple of very good men who will take you out and land you at the flying boat as soon as it comes down.'[11]

Aghast, Alister almost shouted: 'That isn't the point at all! We need a powerful motorboat to take the machine in tow before it drifts on to the Claremont Pier.'[12]

He rushed frantically around, trying to get hold of an alternative vessel, but none was to be had. As a desperate last resort he got the men to row him out of the harbour as quickly as possible. Already he could hear the drone of the approaching plane. Then it began to descend. He stood up in the rowing boat, waving his arms in an attempt to warn the pilot to abort his landing. No good. Alister couldn't remember a time when he had been so frightened, or felt so guilty for letting someone down. Then what seemed like a miracle happened. About half a mile off, in a great sheet of spray, none other than Malcolm Campbell's speedboat *Bluebird II*[13] was hurtling across the water towards them. Alister had no time to wonder if he was dreaming. He told his oarsmen to row out into the path of the oncoming vessel, forcing it to stop. While he was jabbing his finger upwards like a madman to indicate the oncoming plane, the people aboard the *Bluebird II* were becoming enraged, for they were in the middle of a time trial. Running the gauntlet of their anger, Alister yelled: 'For God's sake take this plane in tow before it hits the Claremont Pier, and get me on board.' The crew of the *Bluebird II* realised there was an emergency and thus it came about that Hardy was ferried out to his seaplane aboard the fastest racing vessel in Britain, which then towed it safely out of danger.

Undeterred by this drama, Alister and his pilot took off again to look for herring, but with no more success than before. The weather began to deteriorate, first into drizzle, then into thick fog, so that the pilot had to come down very low, with the waves visible just below the floats as they flew towards the shore. Eventually, the beach became visible and they turned south for Felixstowe, still in solid fog. Suddenly Alister got a shock, for he saw through the mist, 'flicking below the wings', one after another, the tops of the promenade lampstands. His heart was in his mouth, but at last the hanger came into view and they landed safely in a clear space in an expanse of water that was otherwise crowded with vessels. Very relieved to have got down safely, Alister congratulated the pilot on his skilful flying, but he was assured this was standard practice in foggy weather, for which all the seaplane pilots at Felixstowe were trained.

In retrospect, apart from escapades, the two and a half years Hardy spent at the Lowestoft lab gave him a unique opportunity to build up his reputation in marine biology. Since he had no formal ties, he had freedom to follow up the subject of research into plankton he had requested, and Russell put no barrier in his way. The work assigned to Alister was a study of the feeding of the herring from its youngest stages to its adult condition, in relation to the plankton of the North Sea. Around him were fellow scientists working on related subjects – William Wallace on the distribution of the young herring, Hugo Buchanan-Willeston investigating the accuracy of judging the age of a herring by the number of rings on its scales, Billy Hodgson on the different races of herring to be found in the North Sea, and finally R. E. Savage who was studying plankton and with whom Alister was paired when he first arrived at the laboratory. The sense of being a part of a team, co-operating together with the joint purpose of understanding the life of the herring, was immensely stimulating to him, with the result that he, like the rest of the team, worked with great commitment at his assigned task.

A further aid to their social cohesion was the practice of going to sea as a group aboard the research vessel belonging to the lab, *RRS George Bligh*. Sometimes the socialising extended beyond immediate colleagues. For example the ship made several courtesy visits to Norway while Alister was on the staff and he recalled how they spent delightful days in Bergen as guests of their fellow Norwegian scientists. At other times, Alister needed the solitude he had known on his boyhood country walks. When the *George Bligh* was out in heavy weather, he would get dressed in a thick oilskin coat and sou'wester and make his way right up into the bows, confronting the great waves crashing against the ship and breaking over him in liquid shards that made him gasp with delight. Later, he drew an affectionate cartoon of the *Bligh*, liberally sprinkled with caricatures of many of his colleagues, which at the time of writing hangs framed in the library of the modern and very much larger laboratory in Lowestoft.

In the joyful working atmosphere aboard the *Bligh*, Alister made his first discovery relating to plankton. The research vessel worked to a set grid pattern on the North Sea, taking regular samples of fish, plankton and water, as it sailed back and forth from one grid point to the next. By examining the samples he had been collecting, he had noticed an influx of oceanic plankton organisms into the North Sea, particularly a pteropod,[14] *Limocina leseuri*, which was normally only present in the North Atlantic ocean. He found he was able to chart how these and some other species were distributed in patches in the middle of the North Sea. The publication resulting from his observations[15] was of relatively minor importance, but it alerted Alister to the potential of plankton sampling as a way of monitoring the dynamic changes that are always happening in the marine environment. It also crossed a barrier that many young research workers find difficult, being his first scientific research article to appear in a professional journal, since it preceded the paper on aerial spotting of fish.

Alister made his first truly important scientific breakthrough in response to a request to unravel the complex relationship between the feeding habits of the herring and the distribution of plankton in the North Sea. His approach to the task was formidably ambitious. He wrote:

> I went out a great deal in the herring drifters, collecting plankton and taking samples of the herring guts as the fish were prepared for breakfast on the boat. Among my equipment was a collection of jars of formalin, which were issued to a great many different drifters so that the herring stomachs could be preserved for me, each jar bearing a label giving the position, date and so on. So gradually I was able to work through the food of many thousands of herring. I also studied the food eaten at all the different stages, from the young herring hatching from their eggs which fed on the plant life of the sea.[16]

Simply to read this description evokes the tedium that most people would experience in completing such repetitive work, but Alister had a quite unique capacity to take infinite pains. His enthusiasm and burning desire to succeed carried him through this and many such potentially wearisome tasks The diagram he produced of the network of feeding relationships in the herring was soon recognised as a masterpiece, the result of his sustained research. To this day it is reproduced in textbooks and is familiar to most students of ecology. However, it was not this particular piece of research that marked a radical shift in his career.

Arguably the most important of Alister's early investigations was begun in 1922. He remembered the very day, 31 March, when he made a discovery that changed the direction of his scientific work and set his foot on a ladder that would lead to eminence. He and his colleague William Wallace were due to go out in the *George Bligh* as part of an investigation of the distribution of young herring in the Southern Bight of the North Sea. The constraints of time and the limitations of the equipment meant that it was impossible to stop at more than a small number of regularly spaced grid points if the whole area was to be covered. At each station they used trawl nets at the surface, at mid-water and near the bottom to sample young fish. On this particular day, Wallace fell ill at the last moment and

Alister found himself in charge of the expedition – the first time he had been in such a responsible position:

> The weather was unusually kind so that we had no delays and I found that I could finish the cruise in six days instead of the seven allowed. I was at this time making a special study of the food and feeding habits of the young herring and, as they were so plentiful at one station, I decided to spend a day in one place devising a way of catching them unhurt, so as to watch them feeding upon plankton in tanks on deck. I also thought that at the same time I would repeat the whole routine of the station at four different times during the twenty-four hours: partly as a check on the validity of the methods and partly to see if there was much difference between the vertical distribution of the young fish and plankton at different times of the day. We had arrived at this station and begun our first observations at 7 o'clock in the evening. I repeated the whole set of sampling again at 7 o'clock the next morning, at 2.30 in the afternoon and again at 7 o'clock the next evening ... The numbers of young (post-larval) herring taken respectively at the four times of sampling were: 2,448; 24; 7 and 341. The range of difference between these numbers taken at one station was greater than that between the largest and the smallest numbers taken at any of the other stations on the cruise ... It showed ... that the figures representing the numbers of young herring present at all the other stations of the cruise – and upon a number of similar previous cruises – were quite valueless.[17]

Hardy realised that something drastic had to be done if the samples collected were to be meaningful and this problem set him thinking about how to create an apparatus that would provide a continuous record, 'mile by mile as it crossed the area, of variations both in the young fish and plankton.'[18] What was to come was the Continuous Plankton Recorder (CPR) but, prior to this, he devised what he called a 'Plankton Indicator', a simple device to help skippers in their hunt for fish. It consisted of a metal tube, shaped like a torpedo with a small opening at the front and carrying at the back a removable disc of fine gauze. The idea was to tow the plankton indicator behind the fishing vessel so that water passed through the tube and any plankton organisms would be caught in the netting. After towing the indicator for a mile, the skipper could bring it back on board and have a look at the organisms that had been caught. If there was a considerable amount of plankton on the discs and the species corresponded with those that were commonly found in the herrings' stomachs, it would suggest that this was a good place to fish. Alister managed to persuade several local skippers to try out his indicator and he attempted to popularise it by getting them to write short articles in fisheries magazines and newspapers.[19] The development of radar as a means of detecting shoals of fish superseded the use of Hardy's device by commercial fisheries, but the indicator is still employed in research.

Testing the effectiveness of his plankton indicator required Alister once again to spend a great deal of time gathering thousands of samples, for which he needed to encourage the enthusiastic co-operation of many drifter skippers. He became a familiar sight in the fish dock at Lowestoft, chatting to the fishermen in the easy way he had learned with his men when he was in charge of C Company in the cyclists' battalion. As a result, he got plenty of assistance and received large numbers of discs, preserved in formalin in preparation for examination in the laboratory. He quite often followed up his requests for help by going to sea in one of the drifters, to observe how the indicator operated in everyday working conditions. On the whole, those conditions were not good. Many drifters were little better than floating slums. After a night's sleep on board he would go ashore itching and with red rings round his neck and wrists where he had been bitten by bed bugs. The herring fleet in those days was nevertheless an impressive sight.[20] At the height of the season it was made up of as many as 2,000 steam powered drifters. Each vessel was capable of letting out between a mile and a mile and a half of net, made up of possibly ninety smaller nets, strung together and hanging vertically in the water, ready to trap the herring when they moved to the surface at night.[21] With such a large fleet following the herring, there might be a total of over 2,000 miles of net in wait for the 'silver darlings', which when caught in this part of the North Sea were landed in either Lowestoft or Yarmouth. It was perhaps not surprising that there were fears of overfishing.

Eventually the time came for Hardy to give the first account of his stewardship. The occasion was a meeting of the Challenger Society[22] in Lowestoft, attended by numerous senior figures in the zoological world, including Professor d'Arcy Thompson from St Andrews, Stanley Gardiner from Cambridge and others of similar ilk. Alister had to be in good form, for he was due to present his plankton work to the august audience as well as the beginnings of his studies of the herring. This was to be the focus of another near-disaster that he could not resist recalling in his autobiography.

On the evening prior to the meeting, Alister went to a pre-conference dinner at the home of a colleague, where the good company and the conversation rolled heedlessly on to a point where he had missed the last bus. The only solution was to make his way on foot to his lodgings on the other side of Lowestoft. Unfortunately, having walked all the way and reached the annexe of the hotel where his room was, he suddenly realised that he had left his latch-key back at his friend's house. Not wishing to disturb anyone, he walked round the building looking for a way in and, with what seemed like good fortune, noticed that there was a stout creeper growing up the wall to his bedroom window. It looked strong enough, so he decided he could climb up to his room. He had almost reached the window sill when an appalling realisation was borne in on him; the creeper was coming away from the wall. It swung outwards and deposited Alister with a sickening crash in a chicken run.

Altogether too embarrassed to try waking someone in the small hotel, he walked down the esplanade to the only place he knew would be open, the much grander Royal Hotel. With as much dignity as he could muster in his torn and stained evening clothes, he managed to hire a room and arrange to be called early so that he would have time to tidy himself up. Next morning, still in his dishevelled clothing he was about to leave the hotel, only to remember that he had no money to pay the bill, so he left his silver cigarette case plus his watch with the hotel manager, dashed back to his lodgings to change and just made it in time to give his presentation to the Challenger Society. In spite of the circumstances his talk seemed to go well, though he ruefully reflected on another narrow escape.

Stories of near disaster, 'larking about', and playing tricks on one another was natural among the group of lively young men that

Professor Gardiner had assembled in the Lowestoft laboratory. One example of a silly jape is surely in a series of telegrams sent to Alister, one after the other, on the same day in January 1922 when he was away from the lab on a visit to Brightlingsea (still looking for *Priapulus*, but without any luck on this visit):

> *My cupboard lost. Suspect you. Police on track. Sending false nose.*
> *Signed: Limauna*
> *All discovered. Fly at once.*
> *Signed Osmic Jones*
> *Attendance book missing. Have you got it? Plank also missing from plankton.*
> *Signed Coreyeaus*
> *Notice you have not signed off for Challenger Reports. Are they with you?*
> *Signed Librarian*
> *One of my cylinders is missing. Have you got it?*
> *Signed Hiawatha*
> *Have accidentally liberated drift bottle from Claremont Pier. Try to intercept.*
> *Signed —*

These messages were obviously sent by a colleague who knew Hardy very well. The signature on the second message, 'Osmic Jones', must have come from someone who was aware that Alister was making attempts at short story writing, since this is the title he gave to the (unfinished) longest and most ambitious of his stories. The final telegram reads like a friendly dig at Alister following his *Bluebird II* adventure.

The heedlessness of youth fell away over the years, but Alister's combination of boisterous charm, enthusiasm and meticulously detailed scientific observation stayed with him and marked his personal style through the rest of his career, even into old age. It was a potent mix and an outside observer could be forgiven for thinking that these attributes represented the whole story of his life, when in reality they were the tip of an iceberg. The part of Alister's life that was of greatest importance to him was in none of these events and all but invisible to the casual observer, as we shall see.

Alister had by no means forgotten his Vow, and he continued to give a major part of his emotional and intellectual energy to thinking about the science/religion boundary. The evidence confirming the importance of this dimension of his life is to be found in a collection of proposed book outlines and chapter headings, along with several poems and short stories, mostly handwritten and held in Hardy's archive in the Bodleian Library in Oxford. Some are dated, and combining this information with clues that are internal to the texts, it can be deduced with a fair degree of confidence that they were mainly written between 1917 and 1923. That is, they come from the period covered by Hardy's military service, his undergraduate years in Oxford, his six months in Naples, and his employment at the Lowestoft laboratory.

Alister's attempts at planning a book seem to have been triggered by disillusionment with the inequalities and injustices he encountered after leaving the protected environment of Oundle. By the early years of the twentieth century many political radicals had discarded their faith and identified institutional religion as a major factor in the maintenance of this unjust state of affairs. Hardy wanted to get a clear understanding of the sceptical critique of religion and he got in touch with the Rationalist Press Association[23] for advice. Guided by the recommendations of the RPA he found he agreed wholeheartedly with its critique of the Church as complicit in maintaining the status quo, thus protecting the establishment and blocking scientific enquiry. The traditional view of the relation between science and religion was to delegate the investigation of the 'How?' of reality to science and the 'Why?' to religion. But if religion was as nonsensical as the rationalists claimed, it was ridiculous to imagine a meaningful dialogue with empirical science. Here Alister parted company with the RPA. His conviction of the reality of his own spiritual experience meant that he rejected the sceptical dismissal of religious belief as based on an illusion.[24] Indeed he attributed the social deterioration he saw around him to a loss of religious faith, and the manuscripts referred to, give considerable insight into Alister's youthful struggles to deal with these issues.

Probably the earliest of the manuscripts to survive from this period is a poem and commentary set in Durham. It was written in

1917 when he was a young officer in charge of his beloved Northumberland and Durham miners and while he was still looking at these matters through the eyes of a confirmed member of the Church of England. His literary inspiration seems to have been someone we met in Chapter Three, G. A. Studdert Kennedy ('Woodbine Willie'), who referred to some of his own verses as 'Rough Poetry'.[25] Accordingly, Alister's piece is subtitled 'A rough rhyme':

Impressions of a Visit to Durham
The dying sun with trust out throws
And tints the noble turrets gold and rose;
His arm is straight, he cannot reach the base
Where deeper shades the softer shadows chase.
The organ from within now softly swells
In contrast to the music of the bells,
A melody that wafts my soul along
As I go striding into Evensong
A moment's hesitation to exchange
A glance with that old knocker's face so strange
That stares out, hollow eyed, at passers by
Reminding them of days of Sanctuary;
Then on into the still Cathedral air
To seek the peace of spirit that lies there
And rest of body too – in air so cool
Like floating naked in a crystal pool.
So high the lofty vaulted ceiling sweeps:
That slowly over me a feeling creeps
That I'm so small in this the House of God
The stones of which could crush me at his nod.
The sunlight though, from somewhere up above
Says, this is not God's will – his will is Love
For on my head a coloured sunbeam streams
From where Christ's figure in a window gleams.
The white robed 'crocodile' now makes its way
From under Norman arches, dark and grey
As on with measured tread each body sways
And flings out loudly noble hymns of praise.
The silence reigns; and priests begin to pray;
Lord can it be to thee their prayers they say?

To thee, who bids't us praying, not to use
Vain repetition as the heathens choose.

These verses are followed by a heated diatribe against empty
religion, which has caved in before 'industrial materialism' and shut
out the light. Alister prays that some great prophet will arise who
will denounce the Pharisees of the Church as well as the Sadducees,
by whom he means 'those materialistic scientists who believe not in
the survival of the soul'. The retreat into the archaic syntax of
'scientists who believe not ...' suggests that Alister is beginning to
get carried away by his own rhetoric, but it is nevertheless very clear
who his targets are. He ends with three more verses in the form of a
prayer:

All grand impressions fly before this thought
Has all thy teaching to the Church meant naught?
Are not these Pharisees, who lead our way
And thy Great Prayer in twenty seconds say?
Are we much better as we silent kneel
Than the Tibetan heathen with his wheel?
Oh Lord, I pray thee help us as we grope
In darkness, back to thy pure words of Hope.
Why should this great Cathedral be confined
To please the highly educated mind
To the minority, a class apart,
Instead of to the humble – pure in heart?
In place of doubting few – let's have it filled
Each day by congregations that are thrilled
Oh Lord – by thine own simple prayer and word
Which babes and poor in Capernaum heard

As stars creep out at eve, when daylight's done
So shine the lamps that once but faintly shone.
Round shadowed walls and chapels dark, echoes
Amen, bringing the service to a close.
Out in the evening air once more – we gaze
At Durham – now bathed in a moonlit haze;
As – Lord – this is repaired to make it last
May religion no longer be
but a ruin from the past.

It is not great poetry, but it is heartfelt and makes Hardy's commitments clear. At this early stage he expresses himself unequivocally in Christian language and can be seen as an internal critic with a stance not too distant from radical Anglican clergy like Studdert Kennedy.

Alister's single most important question is preserved on an isolated sheet of paper in his archive. The context is a conversation, somewhat in the manner of a fragment from David Hume's *Dialogues*, but without accepting Hume's sceptical conclusion:

> Three men stood together in a garden. Said the parson to the materialist as if to convince him, 'Ah! But who designed and gave us all these beautiful flowers?'

'The Laws of evolution by natural selection', replied the scientist dryly.

'Tell me – what is it within us that appreciates their beauty?' asked the third man who had long been silent. The parson smiled weakly and the materialist looked uneasy.

It is a question that has often been asked and answered in different ways, and Hardy too poses it repeatedly in different forms (including verse), because while he accepted the Darwinian theory completely, the materialist's account failed to convince him. The young Hardy was not equipped to debate with sceptical philosophers but he had sufficient confidence in the reality of his own spiritual experience to reject their conclusions on empirical grounds. The analogy would be to a lay person who hears a professional philosopher presenting an apparently convincing argument for solipsism, but refuses to accept it because it violates common sense. Still, Hardy knew perfectly well that if he was to get a hearing he would have to construct a logical case that was sufficiently strong to stand up to the materialism that dominated (and still dominates) the outlook of many scientists. He made repeated attempts to outline a convincing argument in the form of chapter headings for books, which in most cases turned into rehashes of familiar ground, as can be seen from the following outline:

The Guiding Force of Future Evolution is intended as a seven chapter work 'by an Englishman who chooses not to give his name'. The chapter headings are:

Ch. I: The accepted fact of organic evolution and man's animal origins. The forces that have influenced Historic Man – Religious Movements

Ch. II: The position of religion today:
1. The doubts of the Free Thinkers
2. The effect of Higher Criticism
3. The conflicting views of Christ and Paul and later followers
4. The conscience as the balance point of instincts

Ch III: What is left of religion?
The spirit of fellowship and love
The outcry for the Kingdom of Heaven on Earth
The doctrine of the Gospels
(The spread of Spiritualism)

Ch IV: The Purpose of Life and the World
Striving after perfection – the making of Ideals – Real Evolution a process of unfolding
The new teaching: Not the Fall, but the rising from the Jungle to the Garden of Eden

Ch V: The new outcry for the Preachers
Let everyone work for the future
The meaning of Prayer
Prayer the factor in further evolution

Ch VI: Sin. Morality, Sex and Religion
The results of Psychoanalysis

Ch VII: What are we to think of God – and the divinity of Christ
The future race of Christian men

In these chapters Alister claims to speak for the nation. Regarding himself as stereotypically English, he continues:

Call me for convenience John Smith ... if anyone here
knows my name, I charge him on his honour to tell no one
– I address this particularly to members of the press ... It is
a cheek that I as an individual should get up and say what I
am going to say – but someone must speak out ... I call
upon parliament as representing England to break down
that which is useless to the community and place in its
stead something which will unite the country together in a
spirit of goodwill and endeavour. I refer to the Church.

The grandiose naïvety of Alister's rhetoric is recognisable as the
work of a young man not yet in touch with the background of
learning necessary to enter convincingly into this debate. He was
still disentangling the notion of religiousness as a human attribute,
contrasted with membership of a specific religion. We have seen
that he often found the practical life of the Christian institution
abhorrent, but his perspective at this period of his life was that of
someone deeply immersed to the point of being trapped in its
assumptions and therefore with the reflexes of a confirmed member of the Church of England. The reasonableness of the doctrines
of any particular religious culture, whether it is Christianity, Islam,
or some totally obscure religious sect, is a matter for philosophical
and theological investigation. Alister on the other hand, as an
empirical scientist, was feeling his way towards a generic view of
religion, the idea that the species *Homo sapiens* is also *Homo
religiosus*. Empirical science deals with universals, in this case a
hypothesised, physically based, phenomenon believed to be common to all members of the species. This view is often referred to as
the 'common core' hypothesis, and assumes that all religions share
this core. Many students of religion dispute the reality of such a
core, but if biology has anything of value to contribute to the
understanding of religion, it is most likely to be in testing the
plausibility of this conjecture.

Those in the know about Alister's ability to persist with a task and
learn from his mistakes would also know that it would be short-
sighted to dismiss what he says because of the overblown rhetoric.
In an undated, but certainly later, set of chapter outlines he has
moved on to a much more ambitious 'Scientific Theology', given
the title: *At the Top of the Ladder – What?* The manuscript has an
introductory diagram of the enlightened pilgrim's progress up a

ladder which begins with a series of rungs labelled: motion – heat – light – electricity – electrons – atoms – molecules – compounds – protoplasm – plant life – protozoa – invertebrates – etc., and ending at the top with the human mind. The sides of the ladder are made up of the scientific disciplines, beginning with physics and ending with scientific theology as the highest (perhaps the Queen of the Sciences?). A dazzling cloud, bearing a 'what next' question mark, floats above the top of the ladder, and below is the naked figure of an aspiring pilgrim, who is discarding sheets of paper labelled 'worn out creeds', 'dogma', 'superstition' and 'idol worship' as he climbs toward the cloud. There were to be seventeen chapters, advancing the view that scientific information and knowledge of evolution makes the existence of God more probable than before.

At this stage Alister thought that there is a discernible teleology in the process of evolution. Thus he refers to evidence of a movement from simple to complex organisms, and from organic structure to mental structure, with the human mind at the highest level. With the arrival of mind, social evolution becomes dominant and along with it an increasingly greater outreach from the mind, leading first to conscious co-operation between individuals and groups, and eventually to government at national and international level. Here, we can suspect the influence of Alister's conversations with Julian Huxley, who was greatly interested in the increased role of social evolution in the human species. Alister concludes with two further chapters on the controversial evidence for psychic phenomena, which will eventually play an important part in his mature view of the biologically inbuilt nature of religious experience.

A third and even longer effort at developing a rational scientific defence of religion (again undated and anonymous) begins by asking how his (presumed) readers feel about the rationality of the Rationalist Press Association. Hardy gives several pages to expounding their views, without attempting to refute them, and then turns to the question of how we can find God in the current world. He repeats the adage that if God is truth and science seeks the truth, the religious person must give a major place to science and God must be discoverable there. He suggests that by analogy with the term 'geologist', perhaps the term 'theologist' is a more appropriate noun than 'theologian' to describe someone who attempts in this way to create a scientific theology. He contrasts this with what he had to say about his visit to Durham Cathedral, noting how he was swept away on a tide of emotion by the beauty of the place – but was appalled by what he saw as the hypocrisy of the establishment, lacking commitment to the poor in the mean streets of working class Durham, the empty repetitiousness of the prayers (the 'vain repetition' condemned by Jesus) and the blind adherence to theological doctrines which are in Alister's eyes nonsensical. The statistical evidence, he claimed, was that most people agree with his critical remarks, and here he gave figures about declining church membership. For Alister, to come out of a service, held even in a masterpiece of religious architecture like Durham Cathedral, is nevertheless to return to the real God in nature and in the streets and alleys where the poor live. He is now seeing religion much more generically and closely associated with an ethical sense that is primordial and which underpins our theoretical moral systems.

There is one last, teasingly inexplicit list, scribbled on a piece of writing paper borrowed from the Queen's Hotel, Newton Abbot in Devon, dated 25 September 1925. It was written aboard ship the day after the *Discovery* finally set sail for the Antarctic. On the sheet he has scrawled a potential book title as *The Weaving* and notes that it will be a natural history of Life, considered as a web of relationships. It is only a scrap, but it is in tune with Alister's emphasis on the importance of ecology, and in later years his colleagues would use the notion of relationship as a key concept for understanding the nature of spirituality. At this stage, Alister was primarily looking for a convincing way to present his ideas on evolution and religion to the general public. His numerous attempts, which were then abandoned, show how unsure he was of his ground. Though there were hints of things to come it must be admitted that these early efforts were not particularly original, being personal statements on matters that had already been thoroughly discussed by other writers. It is obvious that he is feeling his way, and is not yet particularly impressed by what he has produced. A short verse preceding one of his attempts expresses his frustration at the difficulty of going beyond what has already been said:

> Oh Stranger! Look not here within
> It is my soul on paper thin!
> (But thinner are my thoughts alas
> Reflecting others like a glass!)

Nevertheless, some of the ideas that were beginning to emerge were sufficiently resilient to find expression in Hardy's most important theoretical statement, the Gifford Lectures delivered at Aberdeen University during the sessions of 1963–64 and 1964–65.[26]

Alister also turned to a rather surprising alternative approach to fulfilling his Vow. This was by writing stories in a fantastic, science fiction mode, but with an underlying religious theme. The intensity of Alister's feelings about this realm have been made abundantly clear in previous chapters, but once he became aware of how widespread the sceptical view of religion was among his fellow scientists, he realised the need to be prudent in the expression of his opinions. Consequently his ideas were frequently veiled, as in these dreamlike narratives, written either under a pseudonym, or with no attribution. Sometimes he distances himself still further by reporting the story as told to him by a third party. He is inclined to do this when he discusses ideas that are likely to be thought particularly outlandish by his readers, as in the references to clairvoyance and the ability to turn oneself into an animal in *The Whincroft Mystery*. There are nevertheless numerous self-references in the stories that are clear to anyone who knows Alister's life in detail. In an incomplete ghost story entitled *The Thing In The Wall* the narrator is revealed to be Alister, for in the course of the dialogue he mentions his childhood fear of 'floor ghosts'. In another story he writes of man-made caves that eventually link up with a vast network of naturally-formed caves deep below the surface. This has reference to Alister's knowledge of Nottingham as a city riddled with caves and underground passages and also to an implied link between the given (the natural caves) and the socially-constructed (the man-made caves), which is a vital distinction Alister made in his later writing.

The bout of unhappiness he experienced in Naples appears to coincide in time with some of the story writing, suggesting that they may have been written in part as an exercise in self-therapy. As compared with his book proposals, the allegorical and allusive aspects of the stories of necessity require the use of more generic language than in his book proposals, thus pushing him in the direction of thinking of religion, not so much with reference to a specific faith (e.g. Christianity, Judaism or Buddhism) but more as a human universal. Here we can once again detect the influence of his Oxford tutor, Julian Huxley, who himself took a considerable interest in these themes as instanced by his book *Religion Without Revelation*[27] and by his promotion of the work of the French Jesuit scientist-theologian, Pierre Teilhard de Chardin.[28]

Alister was by this time aware of Huxley's interest and talked to him about his stories while they were on a walking holiday in the Lake District in September of 1923:

> I was at the time amusing myself by trying to write short stories rather on the lines of those of H. G. Wells, part science fiction, part mystery. I told them to Julian as we walked and they amused him very much and he encouraged me to go on and publish them, but I never did.

It is true that his stories were never published, but two years after showing them to Huxley he did get round to trying out a sample of five of them on the London publishing firm of A. P. Watt & Sons. Watts published some of Huxley's books on religious and philosophical themes, so it is likely that Alister took advice from him as to where to send his writing. Watts' reader, a kindly soul who congratulated Alister on his style, nevertheless deemed the stories unsuitable for publication. In a letter dated 12 September 1925, one of the directors at Watts sent him a copy of the report, from which the following comments are taken:

> The author has failed to grip the reader's attention in the present cases ... it is difficult to be helpful in a case like this – one only knows that these stories leave one cold, and that they will not appeal to editors. Personally I think a fantastic story gains a great deal by being brief, with no suspicion of padding, or long-drawn-out detail, and written with delicacy and at the same time a certain pungency.

Alister may have felt crestfallen, but nevertheless he did not throw away his stories. Reading them through in later years, he agreed with the publisher and dismissed them as immature. They do have a naïve youthful quality, but for anyone who wishes to know something of Hardy's 'inner weather', they are more than that. They are self-revealing in a way not found in the rest of his writing, for he puts his own words into the mouths of his characters.

One of the five stories sent to Watts is entitled *The Alchemist* and will serve as an illustration of Alister's style. We are introduced to Sir Henry Braintree who after spending a fortune on restoring Chaines Castle in France, suddenly gave up and 'left it half finished – a more fantastic ruin than it had been before'. After stopping work, Sir Henry had suffered a nervous breakdown and it was rumoured that he had 'seen something' in the castle. He explains to his visitor what happened. During the initial clearing of the rubble, he had been surprised to come across an old passage, with a door at the end of it standing half open. He was intrigued and nervously walked down the passage to find out what lay behind the door. When he pushed open the door and entered, he discovered that he was in a dimly lit room, filled with ancient apparatus, bottles, flasks, and parchment scrolls, on one of which was written the Latin inscription:

QVI FVLVVM ILLVM VAPOREM
DEGOYNIO VIRO DOCTISSIMO
INVENTUM EXCITARE VVLT
CVIVS A AFFLATV OMNIA
IN AETERNITATEM CONSERVANTUR
HINC ARCANAM FORMULAM ACCIPIAT

[He who would make that yellow vapour, invented by the learned Degoynius, by the breath of which all things are preserved for ever, let him learn from this secret formula.]

Sir Henry realised that the room had belonged to an alchemist, whose vocation according to medieval tradition was to search for the secret of changing base metal into gold. For some reason, Sir Henry felt quite uneasy as he continued examining the room and slowly it dawned upon him that there was someone else already there. Turning round he saw the mummified body of an old man, 'almost bald, with a ragged fringe of snow white hair and a great white beard', seated on an oak chair. He wore huge spectacles with lenses made of horn and almost opaque. Sir Henry was petrified with fright, for it seemed to him that the old man might possibly come to life. Meanwhile he also became aware that everything in the room, including the old man, was covered with a layer of yellow dust. Sir Henry knew something about alchemy and realised that the dust was gold, suggesting that the old man had succeeded in finding the philosopher's stone and had used it to transmute base metal. Sir Henry was becoming more and more agitated, both repelled and attracted by the sight of the old man, whom he began to feel was looking at him through the obscured lenses of his glasses. To his horror he felt himself drawn towards the body until, pushing aside the spectacles, he found he was staring into the empty sockets of the dead man's skull. At this point Sir Henry's fear became uncontrollable and he ran from the room, never to return. He gave orders for the passage to be closed off and filled up with impassable rubble. In due course, with the fading of memory, there came a time when it was as if it had never existed.[29]

In this and some other stories, Alister uses the language of psychotherapy to represent the movement from conscious to unconscious thought, in this case via the imagery of passing through a corridor.[30] He wanted to make the point that the spiritual dimension of human experience had become repressed in our western culture. That he was using imagery in a way that was benevolently disposed to spirituality is shown by the centrality of alchemy to the story, reminding the reader of C. G. Jung, who was deeply interested in the subject. The medieval belief that base metals could be turned into gold is used here to represent the validity of spiritual wisdom, for the petrified figure of the old man and his surroundings are covered with a golden dust. But like alchemy, spirituality has been ignored for many generations, and if stumbled upon by chance, it is fled from, blocked off and excised from the memory as no more than a frightening legend.

Echoes of Hardy's life are to be seen repeatedly through all his stories, often with reference to his father who, it will be recalled, died when Alister was eight years old. Thus, in *Scrooby's Hole*, Scrooby is described as 'the rare combination of the successful businessman and naturalist', an inveterate collector, not of the more showy forms of life – beetles, butterflies or moths – but of those lowly creatures: centipedes or their kin. When the story begins Scrooby is complaining of the habit of professional naturalists, who resemble Alister in rushing abroad 'to collect either marine worms from the coasts of Brittany or birds eggs from Northern Siberia'.

In all Alister's stories the imagery he uses is multi-levelled and the associations he makes are intuitive rather than rational. This makes for obscurity, but in the manner of poetry, it uncovers surprising connections. For example, the repeated use of physical ruins as symbolic of a badly damaged spiritual culture connects with the well known story of the beginning of the religious vocation of St Francis of Assisi. Francis was praying in the ruins of a small chapel when he heard the voice of God lamenting the (similarly) ruinous state of the Church and asking him to rebuild it. Though in many ways Alister Hardy was a modest man, he felt he was similarly commissioned, with the same uncertainty about what that might mean in practice, but driven by an unshakable conviction of the importance of the task. He certainly believed that a recovered spirituality had extremely valuable positive implications for the social and political health of the nation.

In another story, *George and the Dragon*, the main character is obviously a reference to Hardy himself. The narrator meets some-one called Arling, whom he had known twenty years ago at Oxford. Arling was 'a big fellow with a pale complexion, tousled fair hair and *pince-nez* sitting very crookedly upon his sharply pointed nose'. Arling had been 'peculiar', coming up to Oxford from the hands of a private tutor, not participating in games, and he had been ragged a bit at first, but soon left alone once they realised he was 'not quite right'. Alister knew that such accusations of 'oddity' came his way. This was another reason for presenting his ideas in these obscure stories. He feared that he would undergo professional death if it became widely known that he, a supposedly responsible empirical scientist, took religious experience seriously.

The stories contained in Hardy's archive are fanciful, allusive and quite often do not hold together logically. Although Alister came to share the publisher's view that they were a failure, the ideas concealed within them would eventually prove to be in some cases more durable than his consciously constructed plans for book chapters. They also give fascinating insights into the interior life of a young man who to all intents and purposes had no such preoccupa-tions and was enjoying a carefree life.

But Alister's life was about to undergo a dramatic change. It would take him far from home, down to the 'great waters' of the Antarctic, aboard Scott of the Antarctic's old ship, the *Discovery*, and separate him from his beloved Sylvia for two long years. How this came about will be made apparent in the next chapter. Meanwhile he celebrated the end of his time at the Lowestoft laboratory with a riotous farewell party that went on well into the night. The revelry concluded with a very happy Alister being carried in triumph around the Imperial Hotel in a huge plant pot, from which the palm tree had temporarily been removed.

CHAPTER SIX

Deep Waters

They that ... do business in great waters;
These see the works of the Lord,
And his wonders in the deep.
Psalm 107:23–24[1]

In early 1923 Alister had been working at the Lowestoft laboratory for a year and a half. He had thoroughly enjoyed himself, but in spite of his pleasure in the job he began to have occasional surges of world weariness, triggered by the recognition that time was passing. In February of that year, when he was just 24, he wrote to an unidentified friend:

> I often think that far far greater than death in human lives is the dying of a hope – an ambition – an ideal. Isn't it awful how time rushes you along, years come and go – and how very little nearer is one, if any – to doing the things one swears to oneself one could do? Whatever happened? It is awful.[2]

In the back of his mind was his Vow, and in spite of the stories, poems and plans for books that he had created, he felt that somehow he had reached a dead end. Assessing himself soberly, he was a junior civil servant, stuck in a laboratory in a small provincial town. Admittedly his early researches showed great promise, but living as he did in the company of highly able scientific colleagues, perhaps he was not fully aware of his own competence.

Meanwhile his pledge had created an intense ambition that had contradictory effects on his state of mind. On the one hand his religious commitment led him to consider working for the Church, perhaps to become a clergyman. On the other hand, his intention

121

to reconcile science and religion might imply that the best strategy would be to make himself as successful as possible in the world of science. In that way he would maximise the chance of gaining respectful attention for his religious views from his fellow scientists. An equally important factor pushing him in the latter direction was his relationship with Sylvia Garstang. Sylvia and he were becoming closer, to the point that he had begun to speculate on the possibility of marriage. Walter Garstang, Sylvia's father, had by this time been Professor of Zoology at the University of Leeds for 16 years and had an international reputation among his fellow marine biologists. If the romance unfolded traditionally, Alister would have to consider how best to keep Sylvia in the manner to which she was accustomed.

It was at this point that Alister's life changed radically. The trigger came from something he happened to read in *The Nineteenth Century*[3] magazine for May 1923. Entitled 'A New Antarctic Expedition' the article was written by Rowland Darnley, who chaired a committee set up by the Colonial Office to consider the whaling industry. Darnley's article sketched out the tragic history of European whaling from the seventeenth century onwards. Britain played a leading part in the story, which was first fully recorded in Captain William Scoresby's treatise on the northern whales, published in 1820.[4] In the early days the industry had been extraordinarily successful but, Darnley pointed out, 'the glory has departed, "right"[5] whales are nearly extinct'[6] due to overfishing. Subsequently the whalers turned their attention to the abundance of great whales in the distant oceans surrounding the Antarctic continent, where once again they were very successful. But would their efforts bring about the same catastrophe as happened in the north?

Mindful of the pitiful end of the industry in the northern hemisphere, the committee decided to finance an investigation of the natural history of the southern whales, with the intention of creating a policy to conserve the animals. Data were to be collected on the numbers of whales, their distribution, their anatomy, their life-histories, breeding habits, feeding and lifespan. Previous attempts to examine the situation had petered out from lack of adequate funding. This expedition was not likely to founder, for it would be financed from the so-called 'oil tax' levied on the highly profitable whaling industry itself. The committee was therefore able to purchase two ships for the project, the first of which was the

Discovery, built in Dundee in 1901 for the Scott Expedition to the South Pole. It was a sailing ship, a three-masted barque equipped with a coal-fired back-up engine and with a hull designed to prevent it being crushed when it was caught in pack ice.[7] The second ship was a motor vessel, specially built for the expedition by Cook, Welton & Gemmell Ltd, of Grovehill Shipyard, Beverley, near Hull, and appropriately named the *William Scoresby*.

In addition to E. R. Darnley, the members of the Discovery Committee included: Sir Sidney Harmer, Director of the Museum of Natural History in London, J. O. Borley, deputy director of the Lowestoft laboratory as well as representing the Agriculture and Fisheries Board, H. T. Allen, from the Colonial Office with responsibility for financial matters, Rear-Admiral H. P. Douglas from the Admiralty, Sir J. Fortescue-Flannery, a Consulting Naval Architect, H. G. Maurice of the Ministry of Agriculture and Fisheries and J. M. Wordie of the Royal Geographical Society. The impressive and many-sided membership of the committee indicates the importance given to the enterprise by the Colonial Office. The expedition was the most ambitious attempt at marine exploration since Charles Wyville-Thomson of Edinburgh University had led the *HMS Challenger* programme of marine exploration from 1872–76 and laid the foundation for modern marine science.[8]

Darnley made this same comparison with the *Challenger* expedition and added some remarks about adventure, reminding his readers of the dangers of tidal waves caused by underwater volcanic eruptions, and of the unpredictability and power of whales. As to the latter, he gave the example of an attack on a ship by an enraged sperm whale with enough force to spring sixty rivets and allow water to pour into the forecastle. Following these seductive warnings he ended with a reassurance and a prediction:[9]

> The safety of the ship will be the first consideration, and, although physical adventures will probably not be lacking, they will, as far as possible, be avoided. But it would be hard to overrate the splendour of the opportunity for spiritual adventure which will be afforded to fresh minds eager to penetrate into the unknown, and we can confidently anticipate that it will develop men not unworthy to be mentioned in such company as that of Darwin and Hooker,[10] Ross[11] and Nares[12], Murray[13] and Bruce.[14]

The description of the expedition corresponded so closely with Alister's boyhood dreams that he was thrilled by the thought of being a part of such an adventure. He kept a lookout, and at the beginning of August 1923 the secretary of the Discovery Committee placed an advert in the national press:

DIRECTOR of RESEARCH REQUIRED for FALKLAND ISLANDS GOVERNMENT SHIP 'DISCOVERY' now fitting out for marine research in Antarctic and other waters, mainly in connection with whales and whaling. Applicants should preferably be graduates in natural science with a record of research work in biology and experience in the execution of scientific work at sea, and must be qualified to coordinate and control the work of a scientific staff.[15]

The salary offered was £1,000 per annum, which was approximately three times the amount Alister was paid as an assistant naturalist. He realised that an application from a junior civil servant for the post of Research Director might be seen as impertinent, but it was too good an opportunity to miss. Julian Huxley agreed to be his academic referee and among additional referees or providers of testimonials he named Professors Bourne and Goodrich from Oxford, Walter Garstang and F.W. Sanderson, his old headmaster at Oundle. Alister's completed application form makes an impressive read. Considering the briefness of his time at Lowestoft, his track record of research was notable, with his accomplished study of the feeding habits of the herring and his innovations in the investigation of plankton being highly relevant to the purposes of the Discovery Expedition. Alister wrote with refreshing frankness about some minor weaknesses. He responded to a question about languages by acknowledging that he was no linguist – but adding that he had enough French and Italian to get him down the street and that he was currently studying German. He also admitted that he had no athletic distinctions, though he was a good swimmer and had qualified as a physical training instructor at Aldershot while he was in the army. Here in addition he made mention of his interest in boxing, perhaps triggered by tales told him by his father of Bendigo, the Nottingham-born bare knuckle fighter. Sadly, his forthrightness deserted him at the end of his answer to the sport question, for the importance given in England to team games led him to make the misleading, if self-protective, remark that he 'played of course rugby and cricket at school'.

When he looked through the completed form, Alister probably felt uncertain about sending it off – Was it sensible? Was it good enough? – for he left it until the last minute before finally signing it on Tuesday, 28 August. He posted the application just in time to be sure of its arrival by the closing date of Friday the same week.

The applications received by the committee were first whittled down to nine (thus excluding one by a proud mother on behalf of her son, though no approach had been made by the man himself!). Then the list was shortened to four, including Hardy and his colleague in the Lowestoft laboratory, Michael Graham, who later became the director of fisheries research for the Ministry of Agriculture, Fisheries and Food. Some members of the committee were disappointed with the short list, for the candidates seemed too young or too inexperienced to lead a great venture. One of the critics was Sir Sidney Harmer who, after some amateur head-hunting, announced to the committee that he had reason to believe that Stanley Kemp, superintendent of the Zoological Survey of India was currently at home in Britain. Via Harmer, Kemp let it be known that he was willing to be considered for the directorship,[16] provided the financial arrangements permitted his salary to be raised to £1,500. The committee recognised his excellent qualifications and he was added to the list of four.

The five were interviewed and after much wrangling the choice seemed to be between Hardy and Kemp. To try to ease the difficulty E. J. Allen, of the Plymouth Marine Laboratory, and Professor McBride, of Imperial College, were temporarily co-opted as advisers to the committee. The other Allen, H. T. Allen, who represented the Colonial Office (the paymasters), was unable to attend the discussion of the appointment. He sent a letter to Howard Darnley that is revealing of the conflict in the committee. He strongly supported Hardy and was annoyed by what he saw as Kemp's unwarranted financial demands. Hardy, he wrote, was recognised as exceptionally talented and in addition the nature of his research at Lowestoft was particularly apt for the work to be done on the *Discovery*. The fact that Hardy had been nervous at the interview was due to his youth and should not count against him. He pointed out that the other Allen on the committee supported Hardy, as did Professor McBride, hence there was no reason to give in to Kemp. Borley supported Hardy; not surprisingly, for Hardy was his subordinate in the fisheries laboratory in Lowestoft, and Borley knew Hardy was good. Similarly, Michael Graham, Alister's colleague and fellow candidate for the job had indicated that he was happy to work with him. Alister also received glowing testimonials from his old professors at Oxford, Goodrich assuring the committee that 'he is a very pleasant fellow, and was and I believe still is extremely popular among his associates and friends',[17] adding that he was 'full of energy and go' and 'particularly well fitted to undertake the leadership of the expedition you mention'. Walter Garstang confirmed Goodrich's high regard for Hardy in a testimonial ending with the statement:

> Of his inventiveness and resource I probably need say nothing, as this must have shown itself to his colleagues at Lowestoft. His chief faults – if they are not additional virtues – are his youth and modesty. Personally I should regard his appointment as a guarantee of the expedition's greatest likelihood of success.[18]

Alister came away from his interview worried that he had not given a good account of himself. He agonised about it for several days, then sent off a letter to the committee, apologising for what might have been seen as a wrong emphasis in what he said.[19] Professor McBride had asked so many questions about his plankton recorder that he may have been thought to hold the view that the prime purpose of the expedition was purely scientific. That was far from the case; he was quite clear that the objectives were economic. The investigation was analogous to an attempt to conquer the debilitating effects of tropical disease on the economics of a country. Scientific facts might well come out, but only as a bi-product of the main economic purpose. Alister had realised that political expediency invariably forces governments to take the economic outcomes of their decisions seriously. In addition it seems that he was still in rebellion against the deadening research in which he became trapped when he was in Naples.

The arguments continued to drag on until the spring of 1924. There was uncertainty about whether Stanley Kemp could get away, but in the end he negotiated his release from his job in India. Hardy didn't get the Director's post, in spite of the weight of support for him on the committee. Harmer was a man who got his way and Kemp was appointed in March on the grounds of his excellent track record and seniority. Whatever the infighting and private bargaining, in hindsight, it seems to have been the right decision.

> A man of great physical stature, Kemp was modest, beloved of his staff, whom he was able to inspire, and sometimes exasperate, through his own devotion to the task, in the often trying conditions of the ever rolling ship.[20]

Kemp's leadership made a very strong impression on Hardy, who wrote of him in an obituary:

> Future generations might wonder at his outstanding position; his scientific publications were in the main in a somewhat restricted field of zoology, he was not a writer of books and he shunned publicity. We his contemporaries ... know what it was: it was not an autocratic power but an exceptional capacity for a most energetic devotion to the task in hand, the example of which compelled all his followers to action ... How in his modesty he would hate to hear all this said! I can almost hear him now replying to a speech I made in his praise at a dinner when he left the *Discovery* directorship to become director at Plymouth [Marine Laboratory]; instead of the thanks I had expected for my words, with a pretence at scorn but with a twinkle in his eye for my benefit, he dismissed them as: 'This nauseating eulogy'.[21]

Alister's good showing in the competition for the directorship gave him a head start on the other candidates for jobs as members of Kemp's staff. It was therefore no great surprise that he was appointed Chief Zoologist to the Discovery Expedition. He had done well to get this less prestigious post, for the field included several men who subsequently became eminent biologists in their own right.[22] Apart from Kemp and Hardy, three other scientific staff were appointed to work in the laboratory aboard ship: Rolfe Gunther, who had special responsibility for plankton studies and therefore would be working closely with Hardy for much of the expedition, J. E. Hamilton, who was delegated to study the seal populations, and H. F. P. Herdman, who was a hydrologist. These five shared one laboratory aboard the *Discovery* and were due to get to know each other very well.

Alongside the scientific staff were the navigation staff under the command of the previously appointed Captain Joseph Stenhouse,[23] a Scotsman, described as 'a burly sea dog and romantic from the heroic age of Antarctic exploration',[24] even though he was still only 35. He was sail trained and had been Master of the *Aurora* on Shackleton's Imperial Trans-Arctic Expedition, as well as sailing with the British Expeditionary Force sent by Winston Churchill to North Russia shortly after the Revolution. He was notably brave, having been awarded the DSO, DSC and the Croix de Guerre. According to the reference supplied by James Wordie, who had been with him on the Shackleton expedition, he was head and shoulders above all other applicants for the post of skipper of the *Discovery*.[25] Wordie assessed Stenhouse's two closest competitors as fine seamen, but 'out for themselves', whereas Stenhouse was 'utterly loyal.'

The influence of Kemp and Stenhouse on the 28-year-old Chief Zoologist was profound. Whilst retaining his boyish enthusiasm, in their company Alister Hardy became a man. In one way Hardy's maturing as a leader was forced upon him because Kemp was not able to withdraw from his previous post on the Zoological Survey of India until June of 1924. After a series of planning meetings held as soon as the two men were appointed, he had to return to India for three months, leaving Alister in temporary charge of the scientific preparations, although he too did not finish formally at Lowestoft until May.

He found himself on a steep learning curve. The first worry was the condition of the timber in the *Discovery*. After the Scott expedition in 1901–3 she had been sold to the Hudson Bay Company for use in the fur trade and was eventually re-acquired for the new mission. Hardy remembered the shock he got when he visited Portsmouth to assess how the refit was progressing and saw the gaunt skeleton of the *Discovery* in dry dock. It reminded him of the remains of a Viking long ship, dug up by archaeologists. He could see that setting out in 1924 was out of the question and he even began to wonder if the ship would be ready for service in 1925.

During the hold-up Hardy busied himself with innumerable preparatory tasks.[26] He designed the laboratory and living quarters for the scientific staff who would be resident ashore in Grytviken, the whaling station on the island of South Georgia. Their task would be to make anatomical and embryological studies of the whales. Alister, the architect's son, tried to imagine himself working in the laboratory and made detailed sketches of what it would look like, along with plans and elevations for the builders. The sections of the buildings were manufactured in Britain to exacting standards and shipped out to Grytviken, where they were fitted together in time for the arrival of the scientific staff[27] in 1925. The success of this prefabrication depended on the great attention to detail insisted on by Kemp. His firmness about meticulous care over the smallest tasks struck Hardy forcibly when he started working with Kemp full-time:

> The many new devices of plankton net design, the various
> mechanisms for opening and closing nets at different
> depths below the surface (to ensure that they only took
> samples from the required levels and not on the way up or
> down) and numerous other gadgets, including depth gauges
> and my continuous plankton recorder, were all invented in
> that room. Each was drawn to scale on squared paper,
> discussed, redesigned and redrawn perhaps several times
> before finally being passed for construction. Then during
> their manufacture there were many visits to be made to the
> various engineering firms carrying our ideas into effect ...
> All the different kinds of log books with their various
> headings and columns for the entry of hydrological and
> plankton data, also the many kinds of labels to go in the
> specimen jars, were evolved after much deliberation and
> the testing of various label papers in sea water. Nothing
> was left to chance. It was this attention to small but vital
> points that contributed so much to the subsequent success
> in the field.[28]

In spite of the care taken, not all preparations proceeded smoothly. One of the most important tasks was to study the migration patterns of the whales. Alister was well aware of the problem in relation to fish, for similar research had already been done on the major species of fish in the North Sea, by marking them and seeing where they were subsequently caught. If the same method were to be used with whales, a reliable way of marking them had to be found. The problem was to create a missile which could be fired from a weapon into the whale's blubber with sufficient force to stay in place, without seriously injuring the animal. A version of a harpoon gun seemed the most obvious tool for the job, but at least for a time the committee went along with an alternative idea suggested by Sidney Harmer, that a silent weapon was needed so as not to frighten the whale.

Harmer got his friend Professor C. V. Boys, a Cambridge physicist, to design a crossbow that would fire a marker at a whale with the same force as a gun. It looked extremely dangerous and Alister remembered with amusement testing the weapon under the supervision of Harmer in an open space behind the Natural History Museum in London.[29] Alister deemed it necessary to take cover in case the metal 'string' snapped while it was being cranked back into the firing position and hit him with lethal force. He thought the idea was ridiculous. Nevertheless as has been noted, Harmer was a man who tended to get his way, so it was persevered with until finally abandoned after an embarrassing demonstration of its uselessness in the presence of the great Norwegian oceanographer, Johan Hjort. Hardy had gone to Norway to inspect the equipment used aboard the Norwegian research vessel, the *Michael Sars,* where it so happened that Hjort was testing a method of marking whales with a hand-held harpoon gun. Hardy also tried out a version of a harpoon gun quite successfully, but:

> With the crossbow I never succeeded in dispatching an
> arrow at all, for it was much too cumbersome; the whale
> never came up in just the right place and by the time I had
> got the bow on its tripod mounting into position the whale
> was well below the surface again! ... Sir Sidney Harmer
> had two cross bows made, one of which I took with me on
> the *Michael Sars* and had instructions to present it to
> Hjort. After the way he laughed when he first saw it I

found it a little difficult to break the news that I had brought it specially for him; however, we both saw the funny side of it and when I left I expect it was quietly dropped over the side![30]

Eventually after months of mishaps and tedious hold-ups the *Discovery* set sail from Portsmouth for the Antarctic in July 1925, only to be frustrated yet again. The ship encountered a storm in the Bay of Biscay that exposed the weaknesses of the hurried job done in Portsmouth, causing numerous leaks and revealing dangerously faulty equipment. Captain Stenhouse turned the ship around and headed for the river Dart in the English West Country where she lay for a further two months being made seaworthy. To occupy the time the scientific staff turned their hands to making small items of equipment out of spare pieces of teak, such as racks for test tubes and bottles. Kemp was a very good woodworker, producing beautifully dovetailed joints, while Alister sadly had to admit that the best that could be said of his products was that they had 'a certain rustic charm'.

At long last the *Discovery* was finally ready to go and on the evening of 24 September 1925, with sails furled, she slowly steamed down the beautiful tree-edged estuary of the Dart, heading for the Antarctic. Even after all the delays, the sheer romance of the trip appealed to Hardy from the moment when they reached the open sea and the sails were set:

No one who has not experienced it can appreciate the full attraction of seeing – and *hearing* – square-rig sails set. Gradually, one after another, they are unfurled and the yards raised; they are raised to the chorus of some old sea-shanty – 'Blow the Man Down', 'Whiskey Johnnie', or 'Roll the Cotton Home', as all hands heave on the long rope stretching away aft. We all give a hand at it, or in the case of the lighter fore-topgallant sail, we run aft with the rope. A number of our crew have been specially selected for their experience in square-rig; and old sails himself (sailmaker Jimmy Forbes) in his younger days, had made a number of voyages in the old Dundee whaler days. To anyone who has only heard sea shanties sung in drawing rooms, or from the concert platform, it is indeed impressive to hear them used *functionally:* to lighten the labour of heaving and to keep all hands pulling together.[31]

There is no substitute for reading *Great Waters*, Hardy's wonderful account of the expedition, illustrated by his watercolours and drawings. He carries the reader through adventure after adventure: the horse play involved in crossing the Equator, a visit to Ascension Island and the pause in Cape Town. Then leaving Table Bay for the Antarctic, they called in at Tristan da Cunha, where lived possibly the most remote community of all European colonists. Hardy noticed that prolonged isolation had produced small but detectable changes in speech, with the islanders talking in curiously high pitched tones. On again into Antarctic waters, Hardy delights with his descriptions, ranging from the tiny plants and animals that make up the plankton to the largest animals that have ever existed, the great whales. When eventually the *Discovery* made her landfall at Grytviken in South Georgia, Alister got his first, and to him a very shocking, view of a southern Atlantic whaling centre:

> Before us is the flensing [Hardy's footnote: Removal of the blubber, the thick layer of fat that lies under the skin of the great whales.] platform or 'plan'; a scene of great activity for the fishing just now is exceptionally heavy. Floating in the water, belly-upwards are many fin and blue whales, blown up like balloons waiting to be dealt with ... it is a fantastic scene. The water in which the whales float and on which we too are riding is blood red. On the platform itself there are whales in all stages of dismemberment. Little figures busy with long handled knives like hockey sticks look like flies as they work upon the huge carcasses.[32]

Alister was both fascinated and horrified by the extent of the slaughter of the giant animals and one of his more dramatic watercolours illustrating *Great Waters* is of the bloodbath at Grytviken.[33] Along with that grim scene, in the many months to come he would face the bitter cold, the storms, the icebergs and the pack ice. Through all these changing conditions the survey work had to go on, very often bringing Alister and his colleagues to a state of extreme exhaustion. Though even here his boyish sense of humour did not desert him, as on one occasion:

I cannot resist recording that as the trawl was emptied on to the deck … with a big catch of fish, I introduced, unobserved, a life-size papier mâché model of a flat fish – a dab – most realistically coloured. It had been given me, full of chocolates, before I left and I had kept it for just such an occasion. From its top side it looked perfect. I slipped it under a pile of fish and waited whilst my colleagues began to sort out the catch. Such a flat-fish from the Antarctic would indeed be a remarkable discovery. Yes – sure enough, the excitement was intense when it was seen – it even for the moment deceived our Director who cried 'Bless my Sam' as he pounced upon it! On turning it over the truth was seen; I had inscribed its white underside with the date: April the 1st![34]

Alongside the joking there was a heroic quality to what they were doing. In a talk given after his return, Hardy explained the work of the *Discovery* to a meeting of the Geographical Society in London in April 1928.[35] He was quick to point out that his excursion south was not comparable to the story of Scott of the Antarctic and by implication many of the other great voyages. Yet it is obvious that the two-year journey was an epic that *did* belong there, as becomes clear in *Great Waters*, which as a travel book is comparable in many ways to Darwin's *Voyage of the Beagle*. In his director's report, Kemp also recognised the significance of the venture when he described it as 'one of the most complex schemes of oceanographical work ever undertaken by any country in the world'.[36]

It was in this Antarctic environment that Hardy did much of the development work on the piece of apparatus that was to make him universally known in the field of marine biology. The Continuous Plankton Recorder (CPR) was based on the simple torpedo-like plankton indicator that Hardy had invented to help skippers locate areas in the North Sea that were likely to provide good fishing. Alister's earlier discovery of the patchiness of the distribution of plankton in the North Sea made him feel the need of a machine which, by giving a continuous record mile by mile, to scale, would enable him to study variations in size, density and frequency'[37] of the plankton over long distances. The importance of the CPR was emphasised by the fact that the huge whalebone whales feed entirely on creatures in the plankton. The CPR was used along with direct analysis of the contents of the stomachs of animals brought ashore for flensing, to provide a complete picture of the feeding habits of the whalebone whales. Blue whales for example feed exclusively by straining vast amounts of sea water through the whalebone in their mouths to gather a single species of shrimp-like plankton animal, *Euphausia superba*.

The first model of the CPR had a cylindrical body with fins and a buoyancy chamber enabling it to remain stable while being towed at speeds of up to 16 knots. Water flowed in through a circular four-inch opening at the front, and out of a similar-sized opening at the back, en route encountering a nine-inch wide strip of silk netting gradually unwinding from a roller to one side of the main body of the CPR. The netting passed across the stream of water and was picked up by another set of rollers. The whole system was connected to a propeller which rotated as the CPR was towed through the water, causing the silk to move from one roller to the other. The incoming silk was drawn together with another roll of formalin-impregnated silk and collected on a storage roller, thus preserving and separating the layers of plankton organisms. The result was the accumulation of a continuous sample of plankton across many miles of the ocean, enabling suitably trained technicians to interpret the gathered material.

This remarkable, yet fundamentally simple, machine became a reality via two aspects of Hardy's personality that we have seen were already there in early childhood: his imagination, and his ability to persist with a task long after most people would have given up. The basic idea was fairly obviously the outcome of lateral thinking about the invention he patented when he was an undergraduate, the Historiograph. A sheet of paper that had the purpose of unrolling a continuous record of historical events was now transformed by an imaginative leap into a band of silk for rolling up a continuous record of plankton distribution. The early versions of the contraption were very bulky and did not work well, but Alister's ability to persist meant that there was no question of giving up. He made (or rather, had manufactured according to his instructions) a multitude of adaptations until the machine was fully functional.[38]

The design of such a successful and unique machine required familiarity with the world of technology and confidence in the possibility of turning ideas in the head into working realities. These were competences given great importance by F. W. Sanderson at Oundle, and so although Alister was critical of the time and energy given to the workshops at school, it seems they influenced him more than he realised. Furthermore, as noted earlier, Alister was not particularly skilled with his hands so there was no question of him making the parts himself (perhaps this lay behind his dislike of the workshop system at Oundle). He had to present his ideas sufficiently clearly to make them comprehensible to the engineers he employed to manufacture the CPR. Again and again in his writing, Hardy paid tribute to the technical brilliance of the engineers, who also supplied suggestions for alterations to the original design. The production of the CPR eventually took on the look of a team effort, which in important ways it was, but with Alister at the centre, masterminding the process.

Apart from Stanley Kemp, the person most closely associated with Hardy in his work on the plankton was Rolfe Gunther, who was 23 and had recently graduated in zoology from Cambridge. In spite of his name, Gunther was thoroughly English. His father was a don at Merton College, Oxford, and he himself was educated at the Dragon School in Oxford and Winchester College, before going up to Cambridge. Like Hardy, he kept a diary-journal throughout the expedition, and three lengthy extracts from it were published in successive issues of the *Draconian,* the magazine of the Dragon School.[39] His writing style is usually light and amusing and he had a skill for overhearing oddly comical remarks made by his colleagues. In heavy weather, as the ship was making for Cape Town and rolling badly, Captain Stenhouse, who liked to sing hymns at the top of his voice, remarked: 'When advising your sons on a career, remember that the pulpit does not roll'. Gunther was amused on another occasion by Hardy's description of the regular replacement of plankton nets, torn by the atrocious weather, as 'changing tyres'.

Gunther had little time for the social niceties of class distinction, and wrote critically of those around him who made much of such matters. At one point he was particularly scathing when Second Officer J. M. Chaplin put down a junior officer for not addressing him by his proper title.[40] Subsequently there are further digs at Chaplin in the journal. Perhaps because he was the youngest member of the scientific staff, Gunter was alert to bullying talk. He felt that at times he himself was being slighted, particularly by the wit of Kemp and Stenhouse, both of whom could be bitingly sarcastic.

Though Gunther made sharp remarks about several of his colleagues, one person who never appeared in his journal in anything but a good light was Alister Hardy, whom he quite obviously saw as a friend and an ally. He took a genuine interest in the development of 'Hardy's Baby', the plankton recorder (usually shortened to 'H. B.'), and felt that Alister allowed himself to be put upon by others. He disliked the way one of their colleagues (Chaplin again) implied that Alister did no work because he happened to see him in his cabin, lying on his bunk reading a book. Gunther even enjoyed receiving friendly insults from Hardy. When the *Discovery* was visiting the Falkland Islands, Gunther advised a local woman in charge of a group of young children that Alister could entertain them by doing magic tricks. When Hardy admitted that he did a few conjuring tricks that were astonishing only 'to those under ten and to Mr Gunther', he took no offence and interpreted the remark as a sign of affectionate teasing.[41]

Rolfe Gunther was a thoughtful man, hard working and meticulous in his attention to detail. He was a competent amateur watercolourist and sketched in pen and ink, was interested in the philosophy of religion and though not formally religious, he was sensitive to the spiritual dimension of human experience.[42] Like Hardy, he was moved by the beauty of the whales and shared his horror at the slaughter. In spite of these indications of the likelihood of close friendship, it did not happen and Gunther felt that 'one does not get far with Hardy at the best of times'.[43] In later years the feeling of distance turned to bitterness, for reasons that will become clear in the next chapter.

Gunther's sense of a boundary in Alister's otherwise outgoing and friendly style was perceptive. It brings up the necessity to consider some painful disjunctions in Hardy's inner world that caused him considerable personal disturbance at that time. The barrier that Gunther detected is most easily seen in the journal Hardy kept throughout the 1925–27 Discovery Expedition and which provided the text of much of *Great Waters*. The journal is contained in two stiff-covered ledgers clearly marked in block capitals 'PRIVATE'. In truth they need not have been, for there is virtually nothing in them about his intimate personal concerns, almost certainly because for most of the time they were too anxiety-provoking to be written down.

Before Alister left England he and Sylvia had agreed to get married, though keeping it a secret for the time being. It might seem a little surprising that he had chosen to go for two years to the other side of the world just after declaring his love for Sylvia and his desire never to be parted from her. On the other hand he could be forgiven for taking a unique opportunity, for it was the chance of a lifetime. In a letter written to Sylvia while the *Discovery* was sailing towards Cape Town in December 1925 his inner ambivalence came into the open and perhaps explains his need to keep his distance. This strange and at times laughter-provoking letter is very long, to the point that when he had completed its 43 pages, Alister thought it necessary to provide Sylvia with advice on the content:

> I said at the beginning of my letter that it would almost make a book and on finishing I find that it has nearly too! So here is a preface or guide: From p. 29 onwards it is mere narrative. Pp. 21–29 are the most important, but pp. 1–21 should be read first.[44]

Following Alister's advice and turning first to pages 1–21, is to find that they are in the form of an essay on his developing understanding of his intensely religious nature:

> I have made more progress, I believe, in sorting and rearranging my mental confusion, in the last two months, particularly in the last week or two, than I have made in the last two or three years … It is amazing that I have not been able to sort out these simple things before – but there is a world of difference between being able to sit alone on the ship's rail with nothing but sea and sky and trying to think amid the hectic rattle and rush of London life.[45]

Here he quoted from Samuel Butler's semi-autobiography *The Way of All Flesh*:

Everyone has a mass of bad work within him which he will have to work off and get rid off before he can do better – and the more lasting a man's ultimate good work is, the more sure he is to pass through a time, perhaps a very long one, in which there seems to be very little hope for him at all. We must all sow our spiritual wild oats.[46]

Presumably Hardy had a copy of *The Way of All Flesh* and other books with him since he often gives the page from which he drew a reference, as in this case, while urging Sylvia to turn to the original and read it. If she did, wrote Alister, she would learn about him too, for he could not think of another literary work that gave a portrait of life so similar to his own:

For years I have been floundering round trying to fit my religious feelings into my scientific conceptions of the universe, but never quite succeeding, blowing bubble after bubble only to burst them again and again. At times I could feel that my religious side was an undesirable complex to be repressed and that I should confine my self solely towards material science and at others I would fly to the opposite extreme and feel that the religious experience was all that mattered and that sooner or later I should throw over my science entirely and plunge wholeheartedly into my religion without attempting to connect it with my science. This unsettlement has been frightful.[47]

Alister continued with the information that he was reading as many of the Rationalist Press Association pamphlets as he could get hold of, but the most useful guide he had come across was his own former tutor, Julian Huxley. When he read Julian's *Essays of a Biologist*, first published in 1923, he realised that during his undergraduate days he had been almost completely blind to Huxley's deep interest in religion. It is a measure of the importance for Alister of the final essay in the book, 'Religion and Science: Old Wine in New Bottles', that he makes an almost peremptory remark to Sylvia: 'If you have not read this essay I do wish you would'. Helpfully he provides extensive quotations and, as usual, the relevant page numbers to enable her to follow the topic further.

The aspect of Huxley's essay that made the strongest impression upon Alister was what he had to say about sexuality and the concept of sublimation. He quoted with approval the following paragraphs from Huxley:

> There is another process at work in the human mind, which is of utmost importance for our problem. I mean the process of sublimation ... [the] sexual instinct may find an outlet at higher levels and contribute to the driving force of adventurous living, of art, or as we may see in many mystics – St Teresa[48] for example – of religious ecstasy. It is as if a swift stream were falling into underground channels below the mill of our being, where it could churn and roar away to waste. But some of it is led off at a higher level and we can learn to lead off still more; and we can make an installation of pipes whereby it can be taken up to the original level, and made to fall through new machines and do any work we may ask of it.[49]

> ... sublimation involves not the suppression or repression of instincts and emotional experiences ... When the sex instinct is repressed, the emotional and religious life is meagre, though often violent. When the sex instinct and religious feeling exist side by side, without conflict but without union, you have the 'natural man' of St Paul; but when religious ideals are dominant, and can catch up the sex instinct into themselves, and in so doing give it a new form and a new direction, then you get one of the highest types of emotional lives ...[50]

Huxley's argument led Alister to the hypothesis that spiritual experience is based on a natural faculty common to all members of the human species. This is a more important breakthrough than it at first appears, for much of Hardy's previous confusion was focused on the impossibility of making a logical connection between what he conceived as the natural and supernatural dimensions of human experience. He now became convinced that the mediation of all primordial experience, from whatever source it emanated, natural or 'transcendent' (preferable to the word 'supernatural'), must be via the body.

Alister felt he knew this embodied experience in himself and was convinced that the evidence for it lay all around him as a contemporary reality that was not confined to formally religious believers. One vivid example that came to his mind occurs in Shackleton's *South* where the great explorer recalls the heroic trek across South Georgia to save his men:

> When I look back on those days I have no doubt that Providence guided us, not only across the snowfields, but across the storm-white sea that separated Elephant Island from our landing place on South Georgia. I know that during that long and racking march of thirty six hours over the unnamed mountains and glaciers of South Georgia it seemed to me often that we were four, not three. I said nothing to my companions on the point, but afterwards Worsley said to me, 'Boss, I had a curious feeling on the march that there was another person with us'. Crean confessed to the same idea. One feels the dearth of human words, the roughness of mortal speech' in trying to describe things intangible, but a record of our journeys would be incomplete without a reference to a subject very near our hearts.[51]

Shackleton had been a hero to Alister since the day he had sought his autograph as a schoolboy in Harrogate, and the context of Shackleton and his companions' experience was spectacular. But Alister felt that the vast majority of such experiences were to be found in the everyday lives of ordinary people. Here he was thinking especially of the young men belonging to the cyclists' battalion, or the many fishermen and their families he had befriended in Lowestoft.

Alister wanted to get beyond assertion and provide empirical data to support his conjecture. He had been pondering how to identify and collect the evidence even before coming across Huxley's essay, and had made a start in that direction just before setting out on the *Discovery*. He approached a press-cutting agency with a request to collect all references to practical religion (i.e. experience), that appeared in the British press while he was away in the Antarctic. The information he collected was still at second hand, but already, fifty years before he founded the Religious Experience Research

Unit, he was feeling his way towards a method of testing his hypothesis.

Eventually, after 21 pages of his letter spent explaining his passionately held religious beliefs to Sylvia, Alister finally turned to speak of their personal relationship. Obviously his beliefs were of great importance to him, but it seems likely that while he was writing the first part of his letter he was working up the courage to address some very difficult and sensitive personal issues that never appear in his journal. He wrote that he supposed he ought not to say what follows, or at least not yet. This part of the letter is deeply moving, for Alister finally bares his soul to Sylvia, specifically in relation to his sexuality and how it connects with his religion.

This section refers back to a previous letter Alister had sent from Norway while he was visiting Johan Hjort. In that letter, Alister made a proposal about the form of their relationship that was not to Sylvia's liking. Since the letter has not survived we are left to conjecture about the exact nature of his suggestion, which he now said he greatly regretted. The impression one gets is that he was wondering whether, if they were to marry, their relationship could remain Platonic, or to put the point directly, could they live their lives out as a celibate couple. Naturally enough Sylvia objected, pointing out that there must be more in a marriage than friendship. Behind Alister's curious idea was his awareness that his sexual development had been very slow, affected, he thought, perhaps by the war. He did not believe that he was without a sexual instinct, nor had he consciously repressed it, but he was quite deeply disturbed by the thought that there was something abnormal about his situation.

It was here that Huxley's views on sublimation gave him a way of making sense of the connection between his own sexuality and his religious preoccupations. It also relieved him of an anxiety that hovered in the back of his mind that his condition may have been because he was homosexual:

> I have not consciously repressed it – but have diverted it – sublimated it unknowingly into this longing for some kind of religion and I suppose have had real 'religious

experience' of a kind. I have had the greatest joys in my
wild indescribable pantheism. A certain amount of feeling
too may have gone in the joy of getting to know my miner
friends. I have sometimes had the horrible feeling that I
might be unconsciously homosexual – a horrible
abnormality – but thank heavens it has not been so[52].

Popular notions of psychological defence mechanisms were quite
well established in public awareness by the 1920s,[53] but Alister
does not seem to have been fully aware of the sceptical implications
of this sphere of thought. Huxley discussed sublimation with only a
fleeting mention of the familiar corollary that it was a defence
mechanism concealing an unacceptable truth, in this instance that
religious or spiritual experience was 'nothing but' concealed sexuality. Consequently, when he read Huxley's essay it enabled him to
interpret sublimation entirely positively.

   The unusually slow emergence of sexual feelings in Alister, taken
along with the idea of sublimation, seemed to him to offer a
plausible explanation for the strength of his interest in religion in
comparison to most of his contemporaries. It also gave him a
reason to reject the possibility that he was homosexual. With regard
to what many people would feel was his illiberal attitude to homo-
sexuality, it needs to be said that he had the prejudices of his time,
when homosexual acts were officially regarded as criminal and
severely punishable by law. Indeed sharing these difficult matters
with Sylvia required considerable courage and in entrusting his
thoughts to her, he showed his confidence in the depth of their
relationship.

   In the last part of his letter Alister turned to more mundane
practicalities. The question of finance came up and he pointed out
that while his salary was currently providing him with £700 per
annum, his income was likely to drop to £350 when he left his post
with the *Discovery*. He then rather surprisingly suggested as a
solution that he might join another two-year long government
sponsored expedition, ostensibly because he would be better paid.
Alister would thereby increase his separation from Sylvia to a
period of four years. He tried to soften the blow by pointing out that
she could live in Cape Town and would see him from time to time
when the ship called in for a refit. It is not known what Sylvia
thought of this proposal, but she can hardly have applauded the

idea. At any rate her reply, which again has not survived, must have shown sensitivity and great good sense, for it thrilled and relieved Alister.

On 28 July 1926, Alister wrote what amounts to a follow-up letter to his future father-in-law, beginning rather too gushingly: 'My dear Professor Garstang, (I long for the day when I may call you Father)'.[54] He told Garstang how much he and Sylvia loved each other, and that he had cleared up the intellectual difficulties that had threatened to be a barrier to their marriage. He named a number of books that he had been reading that had been helpful in resolving the problems, including Huxley's essays and another collection of essays entitled *Science, Religion and Reality*, edited by Joseph Needham.[55] Somewhat ingenuously he added that he assumed Garstang had read these, perhaps as an encouragement to investigate Alister's perspectives if in fact he had not already done so. As reassurance that the material security and stability of life of his daughter was not in jeopardy he affirmed to Garstang, once and for all, that he had decided against professional work for the Church, which would have meant going along an intellectual path that Sylvia would not have been able to share. Instead he would throw himself wholeheartedly into the life of a zoologist.

Turning to the arrangements for announcing the engagement, Alister asked Garstang to take a look at the rough draft of an engagement announcement he had sent to Sylvia and alter it in any way he thought fit. Alister's brother Vernon would arrange to have the announcement placed in *The Times* and *Morning Post*, or other papers Garstang might suggest, as for example the *Daily Telegraph*. Alister then moved on to the question of an engagement ring. Since he professed to be entirely ignorant of rings or precious stones, he suggested that Sylvia chose one herself. He would be sending Garstang a cheque for £20 and would be grateful if he would accompany her and assist in the choice of a suitable ring. He would have liked to have spent more, but he was saving prudently for their future.

The private turmoil of Alister's inner life could not have been other than very painful to him, to the extent that one might expect there to be evidence of distraction and anxiety in his everyday relationships. On the contrary, to those outside his immediate circle his most striking characteristics were steadfastness, along with his infectious enthusiasm, energy and mischievous good humour. A party at the Marine station in South Georgia on Christmas Eve 1926 was the occasion of a memorable display of Alister's exuberance. Drawing upon a misspent youth in the music halls of Nottingham, he presented a nonsensical parody of the Edwardian musical comedy song *Yip-I-Addy-I-Ay*. Singing badly out of tune and with wild lunging kicks, he launched himself into:

Doctor Kemp our Director, world famous dissector,
Collector of all forms of life,
Led a great expedition, to put down sedition,
'Mongst whales where 'twas said to be rife
With high nets and low nets and all kinds of tow-nets
He fished up the life of the sea
But when someone below, sang this song that you know,
He flung it all back in his glee!
(as if he would!)
Yip-i-addy-i-ay, Yip-i-addy-i-ay!
I don't care what becomes of me,
When you play me that sweet melody,
Yip-i-addy-i-ay!
My heart wants to shout 'Hooray'
Sing of joy, sing of bliss
Home was never like this,
Yip-i-addy-i-ay!
Now Stenhouse our skipper, a hard case old ripper
Since he was a nipper of nine,
Took command of this barque, 'Cutty Sark' of an ark,
And sailed her far over the brine.
He'd coal short and pack-ice, and fog that was not nice,
Conditions most sure to annoy
But when the chief at the keys, played with such breezy ease,
He set the wheel spinning with joy!
Yip-i-addy-i-ay, Yip-i-addy-i-ay! [56]

And so on ... *Yip-I-Addy-I-Ay* continued to be Alister's party piece for the rest of his life. He had a naturally sunny temperament, as we have seen, but his good humour also related to his unshakeable conviction that he was being guided along a divinely ordained path.

Hardy needed his tranquil temperament, for the expedition was plagued by quarrels and complaints among both the scientific and the naval staff, though with one exception the severe difficulties (at least of those recorded) concerned the latter group. Among the more significant of these disturbances was the dismissal of Stenhouse's chief officer, W. H. O'Connor in August 1926 on the grounds of unreliability and his complete inability to get on with his fellow officers. Captain Mercer, Stenhouse's opposite number as master of the *William Scoresby*, ran into similarly serious trouble with his officers, who complained of his critical and overbearing nature. Eventually, early in 1927, Stenhouse received a joint letter of resignation from the chief officer and second officer, and the chief engineer and second engineer, giving as their reason Mercer's overbearing behaviour. Rather than losing four senior officers, Mercer had to go.

The most significant breakdown of relationships was between Stenhouse and Stanley Kemp. Their mutual antipathy was sufficient to cause Kemp to inform the Discovery Committee in October 1927 that he was not prepared to work with Stenhouse again. Rosalind Marsden[57] has noted that tensions between navigational and scientific staff had caused problems at least since the voyages of Captain Cook. No doubt this was in part due to the cramped conditions and lack of privacy aboard a small ship over a prolonged period. Possibly of equal importance was the dual command – navigational and scientific – triggering hostility because of a failure to set clear boundaries to each of the two roles. Resentment arose over perceived trespasses into each others' territory, as was the case with Kemp and Stenhouse.

The Discovery Committee decided to have the matter brought into the open, after the expedition came to an end. A meeting was arranged between the two men at the Colonial Office in London, along with three witnesses, including Alister Hardy. In *Ice Captain*, Stephen Haddelsey's biography of Stenhouse, Hardy's contribution is summarised:

> Of the three witnesses Alister Hardy was perhaps the most reluctant, knowing that his remarks must contribute to one man or the other losing his job. He believed himself to be,

he said, the friend of both men and had the greatest respect for each. Fundamentally he thought the problems encountered had arisen through incompatibility of temperament. 'Kemp was a man' he stated 'who did not like any show or fuss and perhaps he could have done more to awaken the interest of the marine staff, who had never had the importance of the work made clear to them'. Stenhouse, on the other hand, 'had not the scientific temperament. He has tried his best, but has sometimes appeared tired and disappointed ... [Hardy] thought that the ship would be better under a Captain with a scientific interest, rather than under one of the 'dashing explorer' type. Kemp's quiet temperament simply did not fit in with that of the Captain. He also thought that Stenhouse was inclined to 'spend too much time on the bridge' and became overtired; this exhaustion, in turn, may have contributed to making him increasingly cautious and this propensity retarded the progress of the scientific work.[58]

Hardy's measured judgement did not save Stenhouse. The difficulty of replacing a person of the academic standing of Stanley Kemp meant that the captain was sacrificed.[59] The outcome was upsetting to Hardy, who was moved to make his opinion of the two men absolutely clear when *Great Waters* was published in 1967. Following the title page there is a page left blank apart from the dedication:

TO THE MEMORY OF
Dr Stanley Kemp, F.R.S.
Leader of the1925–27 'Discovery' and the 1929–31
'Discovery II' Expeditions and Director of Research
for the 'Discovery Investigations' 1924–36
AND OF
Comdr. J. R. Stenhouse, D.S.O., O.B.E., D.S.C., R.N.R.
Captain of the R.R.S. Discovery 1923–28

When the *Discovery* finally came home, almost exactly two years after she had started out from the estuary of the river Dart, the painful conflicts were forgotten and very different feelings gripped Alister's heart:

> We had expected to sail into Falmouth Bay on the afternoon of 29th September. Mrs Kemp and Sylvia had come to meet us, and were watching from the cliffs; a change of wind, however, delayed us and robbed them of the sight of our sails appearing over the horizon – it was dark before we got in. I shall never forget the excitement of dropping anchor, going ashore with Kemp in the ship's boat, and meeting my wife-to-be for the first time since we were actually engaged – meeting her on the steps of the quay on a dark and windy night. For me it was a fitting end to one voyage and the beginning of another.[60]

CHAPTER SEVEN

In the Grip of Ambition

Alister must have been mightily reassured to meet Sylvia's welcoming embrace on the shadowed quayside in Falmouth. The anxieties that had occupied him aboard the *Discovery* were replaced by the reality that he was in her arms and soon to be married. He still felt the need for a good friend with whom he could share his private thoughts, and for this reason he approached Geoffrey Vickers, someone it will be recalled he had known since childhood, to be his best man. Like Alister, Geoffrey was sent to Bramcote School in Scarborough, followed by Oundle, and then proceeded to Oxford a year before his friend, in 1913.[1] There is little evidence that Hardy had much direct contact with Vickers[2], who seems to have been the kind of soul mate one seldom sees, yet with whom one is immediately at ease. The easefulness that comes from a shared life history and set of values meant that Vickers was not only one of Alister's oldest friends, but also someone to be trusted with intimate matters.

Vickers knew Alister well enough to be aware of his habitual silence on subjects of personal concern. At the same time he, Geoffrey, was able to cross that boundary and smilingly complained when Alister gave him the news about his engagement:

> You hadn't told me anything about the lady though you frequently wasted a hell of a lot of time being silent on the subject.[3]

Alister had explained in a long letter to Geoffrey[4] that he had fixed on his thirtieth birthday (10 February 1926) as the day by which he decided on his life-plan. It was on that same day that he was down in the southern ocean, perched on the bowsprit of the *Discovery*, with his marker gun cocked, in pursuit of a whale he had sighted earlier. In that moment he made his personal decision and chose to take the 'daring route':

> Everything hung on this solution – I would not even face married life happily until it was arrived at. Had I not seen clearly by the time of my thirtieth birthday – I should have concluded that I was not fit to take it – I should have settled down to be a 'disillusioned' economic biologist – leading a dull yet perhaps mildly useful life.

But what did Alister mean by the 'daring route'? He began unpacking the implications of this phrase by making an explicit link between spiritual insight and the common good of society:

> You will realise that the mystical side of life has always been real to me. I have always felt the need of an Idealism. I use Idealism in preference to Religion. I realised too that every community must have some form of mysticism if it is to survive, and that the real cause of unrest in the modern industrial world, whilst expressed in material wants, is actually the pressure on this potential idealism [of?] active materialism which dominates and stifles it. My contacts and friendships with working men, miners, fishermen, sailors, soldiers – even professional boxers! – has strengthened this view. I saw early on that there was nothing in the world I wanted to do more than to help – be it ever so little – the bringing of this idealism into the world – or rather increasing the little that exists. How to set about it? Equally competing with this intuitive realisation of the mystical or ideal – was the faith in the scientific method.

At this point in his life Alister reinterpreted his unhappiness in Naples and made a second important statement, this time about the relationship between spirituality and the scientific method:

I had a sort of intellectual breakdown – I was not yet strong enough – I ran away from zoology and jumped into economic fisheries as a means of subsistence to give me time to get my mind straight. I floundered about in the dark with utterly false and muddled philosophical conceptions; my intuition and emotions quite outstripping my poorly equipped reasoning powers. Can you believe it – Plato was but a name to me! As were most philosophers (Damn the modern education which calls itself scientific and is really technical) ... Through the little philosophy I have now read I have realised that the antagonism I had supposed to exist between science and the mystical is not real. I have a long way to go, I have much philosophy and psychiatry to master yet – but the whole time now I feel I am building, if slowly, solidly. I am now coming back to biology ... for I believe it is through science and from an established position in the scientific world that I can do most.

It was in reading William James[5] that Alister became convinced that there is a way of investigating at least certain aspects of the spiritual life by empirical methods:

I believe that before long the reality of the mystical world will be as well established as the physical world of sun, moon and stars (what a wonderful [intimation?] of this is William James' *Varieties of Religious Experience*).[6] The essential truth of Platonism will be established by Aristotelian methods! ... It will be necessary to gather a body of evidence as great or greater than that which has convinced the world of the reality of evolution.

Reflecting on his own experience and its possible association with sexuality, Alister conjectured that 'perhaps sex has some deeper function than the mechanical use attributed to it by biology'. Returning to his reading of Julian Huxley's ideas on sublimation, and by now more aware of the sceptical critique of religion, he found the assertions of some psychologists – that mystical/religious experience was 'nothing but' disguised sexuality – too simplistic and implausible.

There is no record of what Geoffrey Vickers thought of the opinions expressed in Alister's letter, but it is highly probable that he was sympathetic, for his own views on self-transcendence were in tune with them. At any rate he agreed to be Alister's best man at the wedding ceremony in Leeds Parish Church on 3 December 1927, where the approval of the Garstang family was evident. Sylvia was given away by her father, her attendant was her sister Muriel and after the ceremony Mrs Garstang held a reception for the happy couple in her home.[7] The occasion was marked by a report in the local press accompanied by a photograph of the pair coming down a flight of steps after the service, with the caption 'Marriage of Antarctic Explorer'. Sylvia is in her 'travelling costume' of a beige gown with coat and hat to match and Alister is in tailed coat, striped trousers, wing collar and spats. The bride and groom left for their honeymoon in Tunis and Algeria, returning to take up residence in 28 Collingham Place, London SW7.

In the days immediately after the return of the *Discovery* and before his wedding day, Alister had been aware that his short term contract with the Colonial Office was due to run out and he had no idea how he was going to make a living.[8] In choosing to go to the Antarctic with the Discovery Expedition he had given up an enjoyable job and a civil service pension in exchange for the thrill of a lifetime. At the time, more timid souls among his colleagues in Lowestoft had thought him mad to throw away such security. And it was true; soon he had to find a way of providing a stable income to support a young wife, and no doubt children in due course.

It was at this moment that a remarkable piece of synchronicity occurred. Alister thought of it as a miracle. Just when he needed a job, exactly the right one was more or less pushed under his nose and brought him to the city of Hull. The immediate coincidence between Alister's needs and the ambitions of a civic authority had quite a long prehistory. For many years the city fathers of Hull had desired to set up an institution of higher education but were unable to fund it. The only way that it was likely to come to pass was via a windfall from some wealthy individual who had a commitment to education. It seemed improbable, though there were pre-existing parallels in other English towns – for example Reading, Bristol and

Nottingham[9] – where a local philanthropist had decided to have his name remembered by providing the means to found or support a university. Eventually, in 1925, Thomas Ferens, one of the originators of Reckitt and Sons (manufacturers of domestic supplies), and previously MP for Hull East, wrote to the Lord Mayor with the news that he was about to give £250,000 towards the foundation of a university college. Ferens had already donated an eighteen-and-a-half-acre site in Cottingham on the eastern side of Hull for use as the campus of the new institution, which began life as an extension college of London University.

The first Principal was Eustace Morgan, who had been professor of English at Sheffield University. Morgan's task was to create the new university, starting with 16 staff and, as it turned out on opening day, just 39 students.[10] He had the vision to look well beyond the minuscule beginnings and, in particular, took seriously the university's role in the local affairs of the city of Hull. Along with Grimsby on the opposite side of the Humber estuary, the two ports formed the biggest commercial fishery in the world. For that reason Morgan decided that the first full professorship in the new University College would be in zoology, with a special interest in marine biology. During his search for a suitable person to take up the chair, Morgan got to hear on the grapevine that an able young man called Alister Hardy had those interests but was currently away on the *Discovery* in the Antarctic:

> … so I waited until Hardy had come back, and as soon as he was back in London I saw him, I talked to him about things, he was willing to become a candidate and with very little difficulty he was appointed.[11]

This same event looked rather different from Alister Hardy's side of the fence. When he came home he was contacted by two important but unnamed members of the scientific establishment; perhaps people with whom Morgan had spoken. Both of then urged him to submit an application for the Hull job; the position was as if tailor-made for him (could one of these people have been Walter Garstang?). Alister felt appalled by the thought of applying for a Chair. It was several years since he had finished his degree, and had he not burned his boats with respect to the academic life after his experiences in Naples? How could a young man who had spent just four terms as an undergraduate in Oxford, who had never given a lecture, never held any kind of university post, not even that of demonstrator, have the cheek to apply for a Chair? Yet in other ways Alister was highly qualified for the job. His practical experience with the commercial fishing industry was as great if not greater than any other likely candidate for the post. His work in Antarctica had equipped him with a unique understanding of the plankton. As a winner of the Welch Memorial Prize his intellectual competence was not in doubt and he had the guaranteed testimony of a group of the most senior figures in the zoological world. With mixed feelings he put in an application for the job.

Principal Morgan invited Alister to meet him at his London club for a preliminary conversation. Hardy was surprised by how much Morgan already knew about him, including the fact of his limited experience of university life. The talk instead was about the richness of Alister's practical knowledge of the fishing industry. Morgan was impressed by what he saw and wrote to him asking him to attend a meeting in Hull with the members of the university council. The fact that he was invited to stay at Morgan's home the night before the meeting can hardly have escaped Alister's notice; the signs were that the job was his for the taking. Nevertheless when he sat down before the council next morning and it dawned on him that they were not interviewing him but offering him the job, he could not help feeling a pang of fear. He stammered out some remarks about his shortcomings, only to have them brushed aside; the principal had already told them all they needed to know. Alister informed them of another snag; his heavy obligation to the Discovery Committee to write up his report on the plankton of the Antarctic. This would take up a great deal of time until the university was due to open at the beginning of the next academic year. Might this disqualify him? The council assured him that there was no problem over his attention to these responsibilities. After some further desultory interchanges he walked out of the room in a daze, with the realisation that he had just been appointed the first Professor of Zoology at Hull University. He was 31.

Alister's conviction that his vocation was divinely inspired had the contradictory effect of turning the next 15 years of his life into a

single-minded drive for worldly achievement. This he did and for all
that time there was to be very little observable evidence of his true
religious motive. The first step was daunting, for how do you set
about founding a new university department in a new university?
Alister had been allocated the top floor of what was then called the
Science Building. Again recalling his father's profession, he decided
to begin by looking at the allotted space along with the plans for the
alterations proposed by the architects. He made pencil sketches of
the rooms and started imagining what they could become, with full
details of the benches, cupboards, shelves and scientific apparatus.
The perspectives of his drawings were automatically accurate, for it
will be recalled that Alister's strabismus caused his eyes to operate
like a *camera lucida*, projecting an image of what he saw onto the
paper in front of him. The architects were impressed by the near
professional quality of his draughtsmanship and the suggestions he
made were gladly incorporated, but the building was obviously not
going to be ready for occupation on 11 October 1928, when the
first batch of students were due to arrive. They would have to be
accommodated temporarily and most inconveniently in huts.

That was a disappointment. On the other hand Alister had been
reassured that none of the new arrivals would be doing an honours
course in zoology, thus giving him time to prepare a lecture series
and to attend to two other basic requirements – creating a museum
of specimens to support a systematics course; and the provision of
literature – books and academic journals. He was therefore horrified to find, standing before him on day one, a boy from Hull
Grammar School who had taken the external London University
preliminary examination while in the Sixth form. His name was
Cyril Lucas. Lucas came to the department expecting to enter the
honours course in zoology – which he assumed would commence
on the following morning. Alister thought about turning him away,
but Cyril had refused offers from Leeds and other established
universities in order to come to Hull. How could he reject him?

The academic staff in the zoology department consisted of one
person – Alister himself. That meant he had to sit down on the
evening of Day One in the existence of the University of Hull and
write his first honours lecture for the benefit of Lucas. For the rest of
that year he felt honour-bound to spend every night during term
time preparing lectures. This usually entailed struggling on until half
past two in the morning, fortified with a plentiful supply of whisky.

Then, after a short night's sleep and gulping down a hurried breakfast, the young professor, all six feet three of him, pedalled madly from his house at 32 Park Avenue,

> ... up Newland Avenue where there was Jackson's grocer's
> shop at the corner of a side street, with a large clock
> above its doorway facing towards me as I approached. The
> daily passing of that clock became a never-to-be-forgotten
> memory of my early days in Hull. Would I arrive in time
> for my lecture at 9 o'clock? I was often peddling [sic] hard
> against a strong north wind.[12]

It was fortunate that Alister seemed to like last-minute dashes. Providentially he had been able to employ a first class technician, Hugh Steedman, who made excellent microscopic preparations for use in teaching.[13] With the help of Steedman he was just about able to keep in step with the requirements of the systematics course on the vertebrate and invertebrate animals that he had copied from the Oxford lectures of Goodrich and Bourne.

Meanwhile, Hardy went on a desperate search for other kinds of material to back up the course. He began by approaching museums, asking their curators if they had spare duplicate specimens. In particular he put pressure on the Natural History Museum in South Kensington. At the time he was going down to the museum once a month to work with Rolfe Gunther on the study of the plankton material they had brought back from the Antarctic. Alister took the opportunity to give lists of the specimens he wanted to the staff at South Kensington. He found them very willing to help, to the extent of passing on his requests to colleagues in other museums.

Alister backed up his trawl through the museums with occasional lucky finds. For example he discovered a dealer in furs who bought up the bodies of animals that had died at circuses and menageries. He managed to persuade him to sell the skulls of lions, tigers, sea lions, camels and the like, for a few pence each. Another source of help was Tommy Sheppard, an eccentric museum director in Hull, who owned an excellent exhibition of items connected with the whaling and fishing industries. Alister remembered him as 'the most acquisitive of men', filling his museum to overflowing with whatever he could lay his hands on. Tommy had a star exhibit, the skeleton of a blue whale or, as it was called in those days, Sibbald's rorqual. It had been washed up on the Yorkshire coast many years previously and was what is called a 'type specimen', that is, it was used to compare with other specimens for identification purposes. For some time the British Museum had wanted to acquire the skeleton but Tommy was unwilling to part with it, until Hardy's negotiating skills prevailed. He managed to persuade Tommy to change his mind and in return the Natural History Museum gave Alister numerous specimens directly related to his systematics course. As a result, for several months during 1929 an observant passer-by would have been puzzled by numbers of large furniture vans, mysteriously coming and going, carrying a succession of huge whale skeletons through the streets of Hull, at the behest of Hardy.

Apart from specimen collection, the other major task that Alister set himself was to create a comprehensive zoology library, including complete sets of the most important academic journals, especially those concerned with marine biology. Some were the result of Alister's raids on second-hand book shops in the Charing Cross Road in London. Other sources turned up, more randomly. One example that caught his eye was an advert in the personal column of *The Times*:

> Lady who has a complete set of the *Journal of the Zoological Society of London* since its foundation in 1826, would be prepared to present them to a deserving zoologist or zoological institute, who is prepared to pay their carriage.[14]

He sent a telegram immediately, followed by a letter, and was astonished to receive a reply with a ducal coronet on the envelope. It was from the Duchess of Bedford, who told him his application was one of 60, and she had selected it as the most courteous reply she had received. She refused to accept payment for carriage and guaranteed to keep him supplied with the latest issues as they came out, as long as she was alive.

In this matter of putting together a library, once again Tommy Sheppard proved to be of major importance, for alongside his exhibits he had built up a very extensive collection of books connected with fishing. They included the complete set of over fifty volumes of monographs produced from the results of the Challenger Expedition. The books were – or so Tommy claimed –

available for loan to the public, but when Hardy asked to see them Tommy was reluctant, for they were stored out of sight, in cabinets with the covers screwed down. None the less, he did allow some of the books to be on loan, which gave Hardy an idea for a strategy. He began by saying how unfortunate it was that the books were shut away; they would be invaluable to the university. As usual Tommy wouldn't budge, so Hardy took to sending Cyril Lucas along to borrow books every few weeks, after the storage cabinets had been screwed shut. Again and again Tommy had to unscrew the cases, until one day he could stand it no longer and said 'Damn it, you've won' and the entire set of books was given to the university library on permanent loan.

In spite of his efforts, the shortage of specimens often required Alister to rely on drawings on the blackboard, which he did with considerable skill, copying the method of Professor Goodrich in building up the various systems of the body in different coloured chalk. At times, he admitted, his lecture notes were somewhat thin:

> Sometimes, I am ashamed to say, as I was approaching
> the end of the lecture and felt I was running dry, I would
> say, 'Well, now that we have looked at the material in
> longitudinal and transverse sections, it will help in the
> understanding of it if we look at it from a dorsal or ventral
> view'. I believe it did help, but whether Cyril Lucas realised
> it was a dodge to fill up the full hour, I never really knew.[15]

Whatever Lucas thought about the 'cobbled together' tuition he was receiving from his novice professor, he certainly profited by it, not least because he was the sole beneficiary. Looking back in old age, Hardy judged Lucas to be one of the brightest students he ever taught. The young undergraduate fulfilled his promise. He went on to become director of the marine laboratories in Aberdeen and was himself knighted for his contribution to oceanography.

Apart from formal duties in his department, Alister had to deal with other pressures. Principal Morgan was very keen on building links between the university and the surrounding community and urged his staff to undertake extramural teaching. Hardy tried to comply with this by giving lectures to all sorts of local clubs: Soroptimists, Rotarians, the City Businessmen's Club and others. Those that took place within Hull itself were easy to deal with. He simply had to speak off the cuff about his experiences in the Antarctic to be applauded and praised for his teaching. More distant extramural ventures were another matter. He quite often had to cross the Humber into north Lincolnshire, which was a trial, as it took much more time. In those days the only way to get to the other side of the estuary was to go by ferry. It would be many years before the Humber Suspension Bridge was built.

One evening, much against his will, Alister was called upon to make the crossing and it led to what he remembered as the most embarrassing occasion of his life. He was to be met on the opposite side of the estuary at Barton-on-Humber, somewhat to the west of Hull, but as the ferry moved off a thick fog came down and surrounded the vessel. His description of what happened is both amusing and evocative of a 1920s England that has long gone. It merits quotation at length:

> Presently we were stuck in the middle of the Humber, sounding our fog horn and listening to the horns of trawlers going up and down the [estuary] on either side of us ... to and from the fish dock. We arrived at Barton over an hour late. There I was met by two, I am sure charming, old ladies, but to me they appeared dragons. 'Oh, Professor Hardy', they excitedly exclaimed, 'we are sorry you are late but you have no idea how much my sister and I have been looking forward to your visit and now you are really here.' They led the way to a large Rolls Royce limousine and said, 'We have a twenty mile journey and in this fog it is going to take quite a time, but never mind, you can come and sit between us – there are so many, many questions we want to ask you'. My heart sank. 'You will know dear Lord Grey, of course.' I had to disclaim that privilege. 'Oh, really, I thought all bird experts knew Lord Grey.' I protested that I was only an expert on the birds of the Antarctic. 'Never mind', they said, 'a professor of Zoology must know a great deal about our own birds I am sure.' They began the questions. 'Now what do you think', one said, 'of these rumours reporting a whimbrel

being seen on the Yorkshire moors?' A whimbrel, I thought
– what is a whimbrel? I had a vague idea it was something
like a curlew. I, chancing my luck, said 'Don't you think it
might have been a young curlew?' 'Ah, Agatha,' she cried,
I knew I was right!'

I was almost exhausted when we arrived at the village hall ...
[it] was an old army Nissen hut with a gangway down the middle and an entrance at the back. As we went down between
the crowded seats towards the platform at the other end, we
passed the most antiquated magic lantern I have ever seen. It
stood on a great tripod and had a funnel like a puffing billy
and the operator, a fairly elderly man, was frantically pumping as if he was working a primus stove, and I realised it was
an old fashioned lime light, but he seemed to be having some
difficulty in getting the flame to make it glow sufficiently.
There was a wonderful gradation of society; in the front rows
of course, there was the local parson, the doctor and other
dignitaries, going back to the farm yokels towards the back.
The two old ladies took their seats in the front row and I was
escorted to the platform where there was a large sheet for the
slides.

'Ladies and Gentlemen,' I said, after the introduction, 'I
have many, many slides to show you of the birds of the
south and as we are already late I will begin with them
straight away. May I have the first slide please?' But the
operator was still frantically pumping at the machine below
the lime light. For a moment the image of a king penguin
appeared on the screen ... then suddenly the whole lantern
burst into flames. I must say the operator was a hero ... he
picked up the tripod with the flaming lantern on the top of
it and ran with it down the gangway to the door at the
back, and there he just threw it out – bang, crash. I looked
at my watch; 55 minutes to go ...[16]

Left with an informational vacuum, Alister did the only thing he
could think of. All these penguins he was going to show them feed
off fish, and the fish feed off plankton, so now he was going to tell
them about that ...

Even in the packed first year, Alister's priorities meant that he managed to set aside time to make improvements to the Continuous Plankton Recorder. Although he had been able to gather uninterrupted samples of plankton over 10,000 miles of the southern ocean, the first CPR was very large and clumsy and broke down too often for comfort. Alister had the ambition to extend the coverage of his plankton investigations by persuading shipping companies to allow their vessels to tow a CPR routinely along their commercial routes. He realised that if busy shipmasters were to agree to participate in this programme he needed a lighter, more compact and reliable machine that was simple and relatively foolproof in use. With the help of an excellent technical superintendent, A. W. Hawkins, and his staff, he was able to modify the CPR and test it by having it towed behind a fishing vessel he had previously used and which came up from Lowestoft for the purpose:

> She called in at Bridlington late one evening, where I had the new machine waiting on the harbour quay in a large box. I vividly remember when the ship's boat came in to collect it and me for its trials, as the box, long and rather coffin-like was being loaded into the boat, I heard two figures on the steps above in the rapidly darkening night, saying one to the other, 'Mark my words, they are taking a body off to dump it somewhere'.[17]

The success of the trials meant that he could start to make his ambition to reach the heights of his profession a reality. In October 1929, the municipal authorities in Hull launched a Civic Week to publicise the life of the city. It coincided with the official opening of the University College by the Duke of York, later to become George VI. As part of the celebration, on 16 October Alister gave a public lecture on 'Science and the Fishing Industry' and began by repeating Eustace Morgan's point:

> There is no other University or University College that is so well placed, or, indeed, can be so well placed, in relation to the fishing industry as this. This is no brag; it is a measure of our responsibility. We have upon our arms

the lily of Lincolnshire as well as the white rose of York; the two great Humber ports of Great Grimsby and Kingston upon Hull form together the most important fishing centre in the whole world.[18]

At the end of his talk he explained his plan:

The experiment I want to make from this College consists in running a number of these instruments [CPRs] on definite steamship routes across the North Sea, such as from Newcastle to Bergen, Hull to Oslo, Hull to Hamburg, etc., at definite monthly intervals. The instruments will be little trouble to run from the ships, and I am sure that the hearty cooperation of ships' officers would be readily obtained. The rolls [rolled up silk with the plankton preserved on it] would be worked up here, and charts made from the results. The experiment must be carried out over at least five years before we can hope for any economic result. When these charts are examined and the results compared with the position of herring shoals from year to year, we shall know whether or not we can forecast the position of the fish from the distribution of the plankton. I do not want to *promise* the trade any economic result. I would say to them that it was a gamble, but I believe it is economically worth trying, that it is worth the money invested ... I have said that this experiment may have a wider bearing than upon the herring trade only. The instrument records not only the ordinary plankton organisms, but also the eggs and young stages of many fish. By charting the relative abundance and positions of these from year to year we may learn a great deal about the movements and relative strengths of the present and future stocks of fish.[19]

Ambitious words, but Hardy's enthusiasm was dampened when he approached a major shipping company in Hull. The vessels owned by the firm used several routes to the continent that were suitable for Alister's purpose and he tried to convince them of the value of helping with his programme. He got the brush-off: 'A most interesting device, I am sure, but we are a commercial company and we cannot be concerned with running such experimental devices'.

Now he needed a stroke of luck. He got it via the Professor of Physics at Hull, Leo Palmer, who happened to be friendly with the director of the German-Anglo Line which had routes between Hull and Hamburg and Bremerhaven. This man was very interested in science and was delighted to help, with the consequence that the first plankton survey using a commercial vessel was in 1931 by a German ship running between Hull and Bremerhaven. Hardy went personally on that initial trip and was wined and dined in Bremerhaven by the senior director of the Hamburg Line.[20] Returning to England he revisited the company that had been so discouraging and made the point that it looked bad if the only companies willing to help a British scientist were German. They were surprised by the news, but they got the point and became much more cooperative. By 1939 he had managed to persuade eight shipping companies to take part in the experiment.

The excitement Alister felt about the progress of these developments kept him going when he had become seriously exhausted. At the end of the first year in Hull he was in a state of near breakdown. He and Sylvia fled to a small mountain village in Switzerland and did nothing but doze in the flower-filled meadows for days on end, and gradually he began to feel fit again. When the new academic year began in October 1929 he was relieved further, when he was joined by a second member of the academic staff, Paul Espinasse, who took over some of the teaching and enabled Alister to move more easily beyond survival mode.

The relief was temporary, for it served to highlight the fact that there were many other professional and family matters crying out for attention. The most obvious professional discomfort was the unfinished business left over from the Discovery Expedition. Having made himself ill with overwork in his new job Hardy could not, or would not, permit himself more than one visit per month to work with Rolfe Gunther on the plankton data in the Natural History Museum in London, and it was not enough. The Discovery Expedition as a whole had been the subject of criticism, with some individuals holding the view that it had been a long-winded and fruitless waste of money. There was therefore a degree of urgency, not just about completing the reports, but also in letting the general public know about the importance of what had been achieved. The situation was not helped by the fact that Stanley Kemp was by temperament a retiring man, uninterested in publicity. In any case he, like Hardy, had partly removed himself from the scene by taking up the directorship of the Plymouth Marine Laboratory.

The result was that almost the full weight of responsibility for working on the plankton data fell on Gunther, who found the task extremely burdensome, perhaps because he was isolated in a way rather like Hardy had been in Naples. There are hints of this in his correspondence. In a friendly note to Alister, sent from Caius College, Cambridge and dated 5 December 1928,[21] he intimated that he might be crossing London on the seventeenth or eighteenth of the month (and hence could call in on Alister at his London address), '*and am returning to slavery at the Museum on January 2nd*' [my italics]. The impression given is that Gunther is politely but desperately hinting that he needs to have a face-to-face talk with Hardy to try to improve matters. There were other outside pressures, for Gunther was aware that not everyone felt that the expedition had been a success. In her interesting paper on the work of the Discovery Committee, published in 1999, Rosalind Marsden (who is Rolfe Gunther's daughter) describes how matters came to a head:

> H. H. R. Gresham, of the Falklands Islands Company, criticised the work on plankton.[22] Fifty-seven of the reports are on plankton and invertebrates and Hardy and Gunther collected plankton from early 1926. Back in London, with an enormous number of samples to analyse, Gunther spent three years counting and sorting. Kemp grew very dissatisfied at the rate of progress, and, exasperated, said that at Gunther's rate of progress it wouldn't be completed until 1954, so in 1930 Gunther was taken off the work and sent south for two years. The work on the plankton of the South Georgia whaling grounds was published in 1935 (Hardy and Gunther, 1935). They had a lengthy argument by correspondence about this volume. Gunther, disagreeing with Hardy, complained that the hypothesis of animal exclusion should not be publicised until after the publication

of their paper. His notes say 'and recommend that you
don't explain the data by your principle. That is putting the
cart before the horse. But you show how the data supports
the principle'.[23]

Hardy's hypothesis about animal exclusion, to which Gunther
referred, was based on the fact that phytoplankton (microscopic
plants) and zooplankton (animals) were never found together. He
believed that in some way the animals were actively excluded from
the areas of dense phytoplankton. Gunther felt that the evidence
for this conjecture was not particularly strong and that Hardy was
allowing an unproven idea too much space. To be frank, he felt that
Hardy either misunderstood or was distorting the scientific
method.[24]

There was also a dispute between the two men about precedence, that is to say, whose name should go first on the title of the
paper. Questions about intellectual property are among the commonest causes of bitterness in academic life, and in this case the
argument was between two stances: the view that the director of a
project has automatic precedence and alternatively that the person
who has done most work should be placed first. In this case Hardy
won out, but only after an argument that ended in a shouting
match,[25] for Gunther felt aggrieved at being, as he saw it, left in the
lurch to do years of tedious hack work for minimal reward. Hardy
on the other hand saw the CPR as his invention and the true source
of the data, so that apart from his role of chief zoologist he was also
the instigator of the work.

It was so unusual for Hardy to become involved in a heated
argument that one must ask why it had erupted in this case. In part
it was certainly due to the very considerable pressures felt by both
men in their professional situations. It may also have been generated by Alister's assurance that he was on a God-given path that
brooked no interruption. Hardy and Gunther's paper eventually
appeared in 1935 as a 456-page report in Volume XI of the
Discovery Reports. It was, at that time, by far the most substantial
publication of either man, uniquely relevant to the purposes of the
Discovery Expedition and the summation of many hundreds of
hours of practical research in the most difficult conditions. It had the
potential to establish their names as leaders in their field and indeed
in Hardy's case his subsequent career bears witness to that fact.

Hardy himself was aware that not all convictions of divine guidance lead to admirable behaviour and perhaps his belief in his mission tempted him to force his point of view on this occasion. Gunther's caution about the plausibility of Hardy's animal exclusion hypothesis and his resentment at being left on his own at the Natural History Museum was enough to trigger an explosion of irritation, not unmixed with guilt on Hardy's part.

Yet other interests filled the few spaces in Hardy's life. In parallel with his important marine research, Alister returned to studying insects, an interest that had filled his life as a small boy. His imagination had been triggered aboard the *Discovery* when it was in tropical waters. He had been testing the working of a type of plankton net that could be used to collect specimens from a particular depth in the ocean, while not being contaminated by organisms from other layers of the water. This was done by having a remotely controlled system of opening and closing the net, so that it could be lowered into the water closed, then when the appropriate depth was reached it was opened to collect plankton, then closed while it was brought to the surface.

At the time that this programme of testing was going on, the *Discovery* was about 200 miles from the coast of West Africa, with a hot offshore wind blowing from the land. The effect of the wind was to cover the ship with hundreds of insects, mostly small, but not all. For example, Alister noticed some butterflies and even a hawk moth. He remembered his enthusiasm for kite flying when he was a schoolboy and the realisation struck him that he could use a system of nets like those he was testing, to collect samples of insects in the air. The nets could be attached to the cord of a kite and carried upwards until they reached what Alister judged was an appropriate height, and then opened. Along with his research student Philip Milne he tried out the idea. He bought two very large kites and then an old Morris car from a scrap yard for £5. Removing the tyre from one of the driving wheels of the car, he could use it as a winch to let out a reel of very fine piano wire into the atmosphere, carried upwards by the kites. Alister found that with this system he could lift the wire to a height of 2,000 feet:

Putting the clutch into free wheel and keeping a check with
the brake we were able to control the ascent to whatever
height we wished, having made allowances for the timing
of the device for opening the net at the desired height and
then closing it again – after a period of one, two or
perhaps three hours collecting. What fun it all was.[26]

By analogy with his marine research, Hardy referred to the insects
as 'aerial plankton' and started applying the idea more widely in
other parts of the country. Once, he and Milne took the battered
Morris down to the cliffs of Dover to monitor the insects being
blown across the Channel from continental Europe. As was the
norm for most of Alister's exploits there were also hilarious misad-
ventures. Occasionally as they were working, the wind would
suddenly drop so that the kites fell out of the sky, bringing the piano
wire with them. One day when this happened, the wire draped itself
across two other overhead wires supplying power to the Hull
tramways, fusing a large part of the system and bringing the trams
to a halt. There is no report of how annoyed the passengers were.
When a similar drop in the wind caused the piano wire to cut off the
telephone connection of a Hull stockbroker as he was making an
important deal, he threatened to sue the university. Naturally, with
his interests Alister insisted that he couldn't be held responsible, for,
'legally a sudden fall in wind must be regarded as an act of God'.

In 1931 two events occurred which brought Alister to a realisation
that his priorities were affecting the lives of those nearest and
dearest to him. Sylvia's first child was born on 24 August and given
the name Michael Garstang Hardy. Up until Michael's arrival Sylvia
was able to give practical support to Alister in his work. For
example, she assisted him with a new study of *Priapulus*, the
notorious marine worm that had helped Alister to win the Welch
Prize and then brought him low in Naples. An amateur naturalist, F.
J. Lambert, who lived at Leigh-on-Sea on the Thames estuary, was
able to help in finding specimens of the supposedly rare animal, to
the point that Sylvia had more than she needed. Now the joyful
burden of caring for a newborn infant brought that activity to a halt.

The other event concerned Alister's mother. She was still living in
Harrogate and naturally enough wanted to come over to stay in Hull

Richard Hardy, Alister's father

Elizabeth Hardy, Alister's mother

Alister's father, Richard Hardy, c. 1901, with fellow officers of the Robin Hood Rifles

Richard and Elizabeth Hardy,
with Jack, Alister's older brother

Alister, aged 7

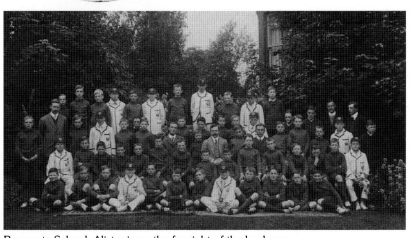

Bramcote School. Alister is on the far right of the back row

Oundle School. Alister is second from the left, second row from the back

Alister in penguin fancy dress

Hardy as a young officer in the Cyclists' Battalion, practising his Donatello stance

Thrills from Leeds to Bradford

PE in the army at Aldershot, 1915. Alister is on the first row, second in from the right

With the old pals in the Cyclists' Battalion

Oxford undergraduate days –
with illustrious friends. Alister is
second from the left, with
Gavin de Beer to his left

At work in Hull

Lowestoft: at sea in the early 1920s with Jack Lumby (left) and E.S. Russell (right)

On board the *Discovery* with an early version of the CPR

Sylvia and Alister's wedding,
3rd December 1927,
at Leeds Parish Church

Testing out the aerial plankton recorder,
© The Yorkshire Post

Hardy's diagram of
'The Ladder of Evolution'

Kite flying in 1946

Cottingham, Hull, 1939, with his
children, Michael and Belinda

Eccentric work in Hull

The Department of Zoology, Oxford, 1954. Hardy is in the centre of the second row, and Desmond Morris appears just above him in the third row. Michael Hardy is third from left in the back row

Is a 'Kinsey report' on religion possible?

Sir Alister Hardy has already spent a lifetime of scientific inquiry into conscious behaviour and into ecology (such as blue tits learning to raid milk bottles). Now retired from his career as an eminent biologist, he is applying similar scientific techniques to the mystery of unconscious behaviour and spiritual experience.
PETER LEWIS reports.

A newspaper article from c. 1969 on the setting up of the Religious Experience Research Unit

Alister, with Sylvia and Belinda, receiving his knighthood in 1957

for a few days and see her new grandson. This seems to have caused some consternation at the Hull end of the family, and eventually sadness. By this time Mrs Hardy senior was in her seventies, and was living up to her 'cantankerous and difficult' reputation within the family.[27] It seems that either Sylvia did not get on with her mother-in-law, or possibly the house was too crowded because the nurse who looked after Michael took up the spare room. At any rate, Sylvia and Alister decided that they could not have Mrs Hardy as a guest at 23 Park Avenue. Instead they arranged for her to be put up in a small hotel further along the avenue. Most unfortunately, while she was there Elizabeth Hardy suffered a cerebral haemorrhage and died on 23 October 1931. The death certificate states that Alister was present at the death, so presumably a member of staff in the guest house saw that the old lady was ill and got in touch with the family. In any case the event was a source of much self-searching and embarrassment on the part of Alister and Sylvia.[28] They brought her body back to Nottingham and buried her beside her husband, 27 years after Richard had been laid to rest.

When parents die and there is a realisation that one is now a member of the senior generation, the pressure of one's responsibilities can sometimes seem much heavier than in more carefree days. With so much work and little leisure, Alister began to be concerned about his health and he turned to the idea of boxing as a way to keep fit. There is no documentary evidence, but hearsay suggests that he had done some sparring in the back room of a pub when he was working in Lowestoft. In Hull he advertised in a local newspaper for a sparring partner to visit him weekly at home for boxing practice. A young man named Cyril Buck answered the advertisement and thus began a relationship which lasted for many years and led Alister to meet Buck's wife and family, and even for a short time have them living with him in his house at Cottingham. Hardy's daughter Belinda remembered how when she was a small child, Buck would arrive on Wednesday afternoons and he and Alister went out to the garage which was the scene of their pugilism. Belinda was given a stern warning that she was not to try to witness their sparring, but being a normally curious little girl, she used to creep up to the garage door where she could peer through a crack and see the action.

Why boxing appealed so much to Alister is something of a mystery, though as I said previously, it was possibly triggered by his harking back to his father's tales of Bendigo. Surely his lack of stereoscopic vision should have handicapped him in the same way that it prevented him from participating successfully in ball games? But there is no doubt that he persevered and was committed to the noble art, for in his wallet along with the other mementoes of matters close to his heart, there is a photograph of him stripped to the waist, wearing boxing gloves and with fists in the appropriate stance for sparring. There may also have been an association in his mind with his often repeated desire to transcend the social divisions in class society. In his reminiscences of his time in Hull, written for the University archive department, he describes Cyril Buck as living in a slum in a poor part of Hull. Hence the friendship with Buck served his persistent and nagging social ambition to get to know members of the 'working class'; to be able to call them real friends. We have already seen that Alister's desire to cross the barriers of social class was a repeated motif, met first in the cyclists' battalion, then in relation to the fishermen and laboratory maintenance staff at Lowestoft, and now in Hull.

The question of how successfully Alister transcended class boundaries cannot be answered simply. The mental subdivisions with which we split up the world are not as easily brushed aside as physical blockages. Quite often there seems to have been an unconsciously collusive aspect to the relationships that Alister formed. That is to say, both he and the person he was attempting to befriend, behaved in such a way that they perpetuated the barrier they were attempting to transcend. For anyone who knew the man, there is no doubting Alister's intense and genuine desire to befriend others, yet his attempts could sound patronising. One suspects that it was an annoying conditioned reflex, left over from his upbringing. As we have seen, the story of the social emancipation of the Hardys went back for several generations. In particular his own father Richard had spent his childhood within touching distance of the miseries of the Nottingham slums and had taken steps to isolate himself from them. The behavioural, and perhaps verbal lesson to be learned from this was 'those people are not like us, and we should have nothing to do with them'. Alister profoundly disagreed, but even if he was right, socially-constructed differences in upbringing and personal style sometimes interfered with his attempts to redress the wrong.

Equally, the socially-constructed attitudes of those people who were the objects of Alister's bids for friendship influenced the nature of the relationship. At one extreme were people who saw Hardy's attempts to befriend them with a cynical eye, as due to naïvety, and therefore realised that he could be swindled. There is no doubt that he was at times trusting when suspicion would have been more appropriate. There are records in the Bodleian Library that illustrate such cases. He arranged for one woman who was in financial difficulty to receive regular sums of money to help her to pay her rent. After a time she began begging for more money to buy necessities for her children, and Alister gave her more help. When one of the woman's children found out what his mother was doing, he rather liked the idea and wrote his own letter to Hardy, requesting him to buy toys for him. Even Alister felt this was going too far and he replied to the boy with some stern words about the error of his ways. Eventually the woman's game was exposed when Alister discovered that the money was being used to finance an affair, while her husband was abroad on military service.

Mercifully, such behaviour by people to whom Alister had offered friendship seems to have been very infrequent. But once again, class barriers were still liable to cause a different, more obscure problem in relationships. On the occasions when Alister's attempt at friendship across class boundaries collapsed, it may have been in part due to his failure to take account of economic disparities. He seems to have been somewhat blind to the power relationship between himself and other people, in a way that another son of a well-to-do family, Karl Marx, was not. The commonest difficult case was where those coming from the humbler strata of society found it hard to respond to Hardy in any other way than with deference. They instinctively recognised the authority of a university professor, were overwhelmed by his aristocratic appearance, and experienced Alister's attempts at boundary breaking as a charade, a pretence that the boundary was crossable when it was not. Still others took Alister at face value and it would be true to say that real friendship developed between them. With all his simplicity and straightforwardness, Alister was utterly genuine in his wish to abolish social division at the level of personal relationship and this meant that as trust developed the association between the two was dynamic rather than static. When someone fell into this last category, the friendship quite often moved across the generations to the children and grandchildren. It was here that Alister found refreshment and where he was known by endearments like 'Uncle Prof', 'Mac' and 'Clarence'.

Questions about social power and economics arose quickly in the story of the growth of Hardy's influence in the University of Hull. In this area he was anything but naïve. Between the years of 1928 and 1942 when he left Hull, Hardy oversaw a remarkable expansion from that first year when Cyril Lucas was his single honours student. Over the five years from 1931 – the first year of his scheme to investigate the whole of the North Sea using the CPR – until 1937, oceanographical research came to dominate not only the zoology department, but overshadowed the other science departments. This development led to the alteration of his title and the position now became that of Professor of Zoology and Oceanography. In a report published in 1937, Alister summarised the progress:

> In August 1931, the scheme came into operation and the Department of Zoology was enlarged to one of Zoology and Oceanography. The college provided laboratories, a £1,000 capital expenditure on equipment and an annual contribution towards the research expenses. His Majesty's Treasury on the recommendation of the Development Commissioners, made a substantial grant which has been maintained at an average of £1,067 over the five years. Annual grants have also been received from the Leverhulme Trustees, the Hull Fishing Vessel Owners Association and the Fishmongers Company of £250, £100 and £50 respectively ... It is gratifying to record that the Development Commission, after examination by their Advisory Committee on Fishery Research of the results of this trial period, have recommended to His Majesty's Treasury not only that the grant should be continued for another five years, but that it should be increased so as to add greatly to the scope and extent of the plankton

recorder survey. The college council having generously agreed to make a further increase in its contributions, His Majesty's Treasury has now given its approval to an extended scheme which will cover the whole of the North Sea, including a traverse between the North of Scotland and Norway.[29]

In referring to the Development Commission Hardy was speaking about an institution that lay very close to the financial heart of the national government. Probably through his relationship to Walter Garstang, Alister was more aware than most of his colleagues of the existence and power of the Commission. It had its origins in the Development and Road Improvement Fund Acts of 1909 and 1910 and, according to the Act, the Commission's responsibility was to carry out specified measures for the economic development of Great Britain. In order to fulfil that brief, the Commission set up a number of bodies of experts to whom they could turn for advice, including the Advisory Committee on Fishery Research which began work in 1919. Members of the committee who served continuously from the date of its foundation included Walter Garstang, E. W. MacBride, and, as chairman from 1931, Gilbert Bourne; then, in 1935, they were joined by Stanley Kemp and James Gray. With a membership as packed as this was with supporters of Hardy, it is perhaps no surprise that they were happy to grant substantial sums of money to support the work at Hull.

Neither was it a surprise when Hardy's successes were derided by some and by others were a cause of jealousy. T. W. Bamford, the historian of Hull University, reported one typical piece of gossip, when it was alleged that:

> ... Hardy's Department was a waste of money. The finding of the feeding ground of fish was Professor Garstang's hobby and should be kept as a hobby. The important thing was not to find their food but to find fish. Hellyer Bros. had succeeded in doing this in their own boats in the Davis Strait and the Arctic ... the Government Research Department has never done anything for the [fishing] industry – they are a quarter of a century behind the industry.[30]

Others made a joke out of Hardy's interest in herring. Hull was a deep sea port which concentrated on catching Arctic cod. Alister, they said, is looking for the wrong fish in the wrong waters. In spite of the gossip, the oceanography research continued to grow and eventually, in 1937, needed to expand to take account of the increasing use of the CPR. Cyril Lucas was invited to open a branch in Leith, which he did, initially in the humblest of circumstances, in a room over a pub, but soon to expand.

Alister prospered in other ways during the years at Hull. In 1938 he was awarded the degree of DSc by Oxford University and the following year, while Julian Huxley was the Secretary of the Zoological Society of London, Hardy became the first recipient of a new prize, the Scientific Medal of the Zoological Society of London. This was to be awarded for the excellence of work done by a zoologist under the age of 45, and Alister was pleased to note that the medal was inscribed: 'FOR HIS WORK ON MARINE AND AERIAL PLANKTON'. He felt that the inscription summarised accurately the main direction of his zoological research while he had been in Hull. Finally, in 1940, Hardy was elected a Fellow of the Royal Society.

With these accolades it was not surprising that he was sought after by other institutions. Indeed, two years after he arrived in University College, Hull, and thus before any one of these honours was awarded, he was invited – and declined – to take up the post of Director of a large Marine Biological Station in Bermuda. In 1936 he was offered the prestigious Chair of Natural History at Marischal College in Aberdeen University. Hardy was tempted, but in the end he stayed on in Hull, helped by an anonymous grant of money to continue the plankton research.[31] In 1941 Aberdeen tried to obtain his services again, and this time, encouraged by a promise by the Aberdeen authorities that he could retain his directorship of oceanography in Hull while holding a professorship in Aberdeen, he succumbed and left Hull in 1942.

Meanwhile the Second World War had arrived and it affected Hardy in two ways. He was invited to become an ARP officer and he also became, temporarily, the warden of the men's residence on the Hull campus, Needler Hall. In addition the women's hall, which was called Thwaites, was soon to be requisitioned as a base for military personnel, in this case, French Colonial troops. The women were shifted to Needler, thus making Hardy, for a short time, the warden of the first mixed sex student residence in the United Kingdom.

The war was the trigger for one last piece of work begun by Hardy before he left Hull. It is important because of its disastrous consequences. German action against the North Atlantic convoys bringing food to a beleaguered Britain made it a priority to hunt for alternative ways of supplying nutrition. Alister became involved very directly because of his expertise in the study of plankton. The story began when an MP, Sir John Graham Kerr, asked a series of questions in parliament about the possibility of using plankton as food, then wrote a letter to *The Times* of 6 May on the same theme. [32] This was followed up by an article by Hardy in the prestigious scientific journal *Nature*[33] in which he reminded his readers that the whalebone whales were both the largest animals that had ever existed, yet lived by feeding on plankton. The real needs of the time, plus Hardy's burgeoning reputation, led to the success of a research proposal to the Agricultural Research Council and work began in 1941.

The safest place to find out if it was feasible to harvest plankton from the sea was thought to be in the sea lochs on the west coast of Scotland. They were away from large scale naval installations and from the part of the coastline facing the enemy. Under the direction of Hardy and Cyril Lucas the work was proceeding satisfactorily. That was, until one morning when they set out from their overnight anchorage in Loch Caolisport, an indent in the mainland looking out towards the Hebridean islands of Islay and Jura. The scientists and crew had spent the night sleeping aboard the *Christine Rose*, the vessel they were using for the research. It was time to move off, but suddenly and shockingly, as the skipper steered them out of the loch, the bow struck a submerged reef and the vessel was held fast. They waited, and the changing tide eventually began to free it up, only for it to spin round and be caught on rocks again, this time by the stern. As the tide went down, the vessel began to list to port and the skipper ordered the lifeboat to be lowered, as a precaution. The tide continued to go down and suddenly the vessel keeled over, trapping the lifeboat under it.

Hardy had hurried below to gather up his research papers and when he came on deck, he found that Lucas, who could not swim, had been sitting in the lifeboat and was being dragged under water. Somehow Lucas got free and came to the surface where Hardy, who was a strong swimmer, supported him until he found a lifebelt. As they fought to keep their heads above water and looked round, the full extent of the tragedy began to be clear. Several members of the crew were bobbing around in the water, but in spite of their struggles the current was carrying some of them out to sea. Eventually the wreck was noticed by a passing plane and then, after a tedious and terrifying wait, the rescuers arrived and help them to a place of shelter. The skipper and four members of the crew were missing and the following morning when Alister returned to the shore to look for them, he found their bodies washed up on the beach, and ironically, his brief-case with the papers intact. Sylvia sent Alister a telegram from Oxford, where she happened to be staying, probably with her parents. The message read:

> WHAT A TRAGIC BUSINESS. IF YOU ARE NOT WELL ENOUGH TO TRAVEL YOU MUST WIRE AND I WILL COME TO ARRAN. HOWEVER HOPE TO SEE YOU HERE ON MONDAY.

Alister was very badly shocked, much more than he realised, and he had to go into a nursing home where he had a prolonged complete mental and physical rest. Since he was one of the initiators of the research he felt partly responsible for the catastrophe. Deeply distressed by what had happened to his companions he wrote personal letters to the relatives of all five dead men. He also sent money where he could, usually £5, the equivalent today of approximately £200. Would it be right to call his gifts patronising? Possibly. The fact remains that he received letters from the widows, thanking him for his help. The following, from Mrs McIntosh, the wife of one of the drowned men, is fairly typical in tone:

> … I must say it was ever so good and kind of you to send me that £5 which I have kept. I cashed it and put it into P.O. savings book. I will have to be desperate before I spend it for I felt for you very much. You are a perfect gentleman and I just can't thank you enough for writing to me.

Alister also received a reply from the skipper's wife:

… it has meant a great deal to me to know that you held my husband in such esteem and it is a consolation to know that he gave his life in such a splendid cause.

I am grateful for your gift of five pounds.

May you gain considerable success in your future experiments.

This was probably the most tragic event to befall Alister in his entire adult life. The drowned men had died doing their duty, but it also seemed they had been dutiful for nothing. The project did not even have the redeeming feature of having found a way to feed the people. The supply of plankton was too variable and its nutritional content too unsuitable to use it for human consumption. At best it might have been turned into cattle food.

What Alister made of this disaster in religious terms is unknown and in general he seems to have set spiritual matters to one side during his time in Hull, or at least he gave very little evidence of his interests. There is no doubt that at some level, they were still there, He had shared his thoughts about spirituality with Geoffrey Vickers prior to his wedding, and was impressed by the synchronicity associated with getting his professorship, but after that there was almost nothing. Certainly that is true of his writing and, as far as can be ascertained, also of his public statements. Sheer overwork partially explains the silence. For a great part of the time he was run off his feet in the chase to fulfil his ambition and there is no doubt that other parts of his life were shelved or neglected. Probably of greater importance was his strategy mentioned earlier, to achieve eminence in the scientific profession before turning openly to the fulfilment of his Vow.

Nevertheless it is disconcerting to find that his silence on these matters extended to his home life. Alister's daughter Belinda was born on 26 August 1934, and he greatly enjoyed being with the two children. Their recollection of their early years includes memories of delightful companionship with their father, though often he was 'too busy' to take part in their games.[34] When he was with them, one might assume that Alister, with his strong interest in religion, would have spent much time sharing his thoughts on the matter with Michael and Belinda. The reality is surprising. Both his children were baptised, which symbolises at least some concern for religion, at the level of conforming to the *status quo* as it was at that time. On the other hand, as to religious education at home, they had none. Neither of them can ever remember going to church, or being sent to Sunday School, or being spoken to by their parents about the subject of religion, or even overhearing their parents discussing religious topics. Michael reported that the first time he fully realised his father was interested in religion was when Alister gave the Gifford Lectures in Aberdeen University in 1963. By that time Michael was a man of 32.

Behind this wall of silence, it is occasionally possible to detect the motivation for Alister's huge professional efforts. One small hint in 1935 was when he wrote to a press cutting agency and asked them to do a repeat of his 1925 collection of cuttings from a wide range of newspapers on religious and spiritual matters. Then in 1937 the Bishop of Hull wrote to Hardy to invite him to participate in a small informal conference on the state of the world; where it was going and what should good people be doing about it. In his courteous initial refusal, Alister let drop the remark that he had 'always been much more interested in religion than science', but could not abide the doctrinal side of the Christianity in which he had been raised. Subsequently he relented from his decision and participated in one or two of the meetings. The silence continued until the end of his service in the University of Hull. In 1941 he applied for – or rather was offered – the Regius Chair of Natural History in the University of Aberdeen. He was appointed, and took up his post in the autumn of 1942.

CHAPTER EIGHT

Walking a Tightrope

The Granite City of Aberdeen lies four hundred miles north of Hull, facing the North Sea, on the boundary of the great elbow of mountains and farmland that forms the Grampian region of Scotland. Aberdeen resembles Hull in having a long history as a major fishing port. Like Hull it is also a university town but here the contrast is considerable. Alister had been present at the birth of a brand new academic institution in Hull, starting out with a mere handful of staff and students. When he came to Aberdeen he entered a university founded before the Reformation, by Bishop William Elphinstone in 1495, on the strength of a Papal Bull from Alexander VI in Rome. As one of the four ancient universities in Scotland it had a number of senior Chairs that were in the gift of the monarch, including Natural History. It was therefore a 'Regius Chair', and claimed to be the oldest department of biological science in Britain, with its origins traced back to 1543. When Hardy was appointed, the department was sited in Marischal College, a multi-pinnacled neo-Gothic edifice reputed to be one of the largest granite buildings in the world.[1]

There were other contrasts to which Alister had to adjust. The students differed in age from those in England, for the Scots normally go up to university at the age of 17, a year younger than the English. Students can opt for a three-year Ordinary Degree or, if they are sufficiently able, they can continue for a fourth Honours year. At the time of Hardy's move to Scotland there was a popular stereotype, not entirely dead even now, of Oxford and Cambridge as finishing schools for the well-to-do. In Scotland it was much more common to picture students as coming from humble backgrounds. The mythical hero was a 'Lad o' pairts', that is to say, a peasant boy, walking many miles into Aberdeen from his croft out in the hills, carrying a bag of oatmeal to enable him to live frugally in some garret by the docks. By diligence and a sharp intellect he contended against dire poverty to gain a degree.[2] There were in those days no residents in colleges or halls. In this respect the Scottish university system resembled the universities on the continent of Europe, rather than those in England. It was normal for most students to attend their local university and, if close enough, to live at home. Others were in lodgings where they had to contend with the oftentimes stern authority of the Aberdeen landlady.

When it came to the fishing industry, Alister was on relatively familiar ground. At the time he arrived in Aberdeen from Hull, both towns still depended heavily on the industry as a source of employment and income. Not unexpectedly, Aberdeen University was a pioneer in fishery research. James Cossor Ewart, Professor of Natural History, with his colleague G. J. Romanes, opened the first marine research station in Britain in 1879 just outside the small town of Stonehaven, approximately fifteen miles south of Aberdeen. Back in the city, on the other side of the river Dee from Marischal College, government-funded fisheries research got under way in 1923 when what is now the Scottish Fisheries Research Services Marine Laboratory was opened.[3]

Aberdeen differed from Hull in that the methods of fishing were more varied. Hull skippers specialised in deep sea trawling for cod and travelling long distances to find their prey, for example up in the Barents Sea between Spitzbergen and Novaya Zemlya, north of Russia. Hardy's detractors in Hull had been happy to point out that his interest in the herring was of minor concern to them. Here in Aberdeen and in the fishing towns and villages spreading north and all the way along the Moray Firth – like Peterhead, Fraserburgh, Banff and Buckie – as well as trawler-men, there was a large fleet of vessels built for catching herring in the North Sea with drift nets. There were also 'long line' fishermen specialising in catching large flatfish like turbot and brill.

At the beginning of 1942, when the Second World War was at its height, the Hardy family came north and settled in a pleasant terraced house in Albert Street in the west end of Aberdeen. Michael was sent off to Lathallan Preparatory School in St Andrews[4] in anticipation of going to public school at Marlborough (for Alister had not changed his mind about the weaknesses of Oundle, his own *alma mater*). Belinda stayed at home in Aberdeen and attended the nearby Albyn School, a polite establishment for young ladies, not entirely remote in style from the Marcia Blaine Academy in Edinburgh, where Miss Jean Brodie was in her prime.[5]

Very little written evidence survives from this period in Alister's life, but what there is suggests the continuation of a familiar enthusiastic pattern. His initial assessment of his new department led him to take particular interest in the museum which had been founded in the 1840s by one of the most eminent of his predecessors, the ornithologist William McGillivray.[6] The museum had an unusually rich collection of specimens, but one obvious lack to someone interested in whales was the absence of a blue whale skeleton. Was there an alternative? During his initial rooting around, Hardy found a length of old gas piping stored in a cupboard and was about to throw it out when it occurred to him that it had this other use. He shaped it into the outline of the whale, painted it red and attached it to the ceiling of the museum hall. What was particularly impressive about the outline was that it was too big to fit the hall, so had to be bent back on itself.[7] He also used his artistic skills to paint a mural on one wall representing an extinct Pterodactyl and on another wall an extinct Moa, the giant flightless bird from New Zealand.

Hardy had taken over the Chair of Natural History from Lancelot Hogben (best known as author of *Mathematics for the Million*), who moved on to become Professor of Zoology in Birmingham.[8] Hogben's education had many parallels with Hardy's, though unlike Hardy, Hogben's experience of childhood was not a happy one. The opening paragraph of his autobiography contains the arresting remark: 'I came of poor but intellectually dishonest parents'.[9] He was the son of strongly committed fundamentalist Christians with strict ideas about children's upbringing. The ironic way he describes his religious education gives the strongest evidence of his anger with this aspect of his childhood. He steadily repudiated his religious beliefs so that they had been entirely removed by the time he finished his degree. He had become a humanist and a socialist, scornful of religion, though because of his childhood he was biblically highly literate. Having done very well at school, he went on to win a scholarship, taking him to Trinity College in Cambridge. He continued to shine, and like Alister, won the prize for the best student of his year. As a result he came to the attention of practically the same list of senior figures in biology as Hardy, including Julian Huxley. He had courage and was willing to stand alone, for he had been a pacifist during the First World War, and in his implacable hostility to eugenics he differed from many senior biologists, who at that time were its enthusiastic supporters.

Alongside these attributes Hogben was an intellectual snob and his cutting dismissal of his colleagues could be severe. One of those censured was the eminent population biologist, Alexander Carr-Saunders, a member of the group photographed cavorting (though Carr-Saunders is not joining in) on a bridge at Wolvercote with Alister Hardy in his undergraduate days. Hogben said of Carr-Saunders that he was 'an intellectually second rate bore, whom I had met in the early twenties when staying with Julian Huxley'. Hogben may have mistaken diffidence for dullness, for others who knew the man were aware of his temperament and indignantly denied the assertion.[10] Hogben was rather free with frankly-stated estimates of others as boring or stupid, which did little to endear him to those in danger of his censure. Consequently, when he left Aberdeen, apart from the few people he admired and thought of as friends – for example Sir John Boyd Orr[11] and the Principal, Sir William Hamilton-Fyfe – he also left a fair number of enemies.

After Hogben, Alister was a complete change. In his inaugural lecture, delivered on 28 April 1942, he explained how he saw the work of the Natural History Department developing. The lecture was entitled 'Natural History – Old and New', and in it he deliberately distanced himself from Hogben:

> I believe what Professor Joad said the other day to be
> profoundly true: that the unconsciously frustrated desire for
> spiritual experience is no less important than the
> unconsciously frustrated sex upon which the
> psycho-analysts have laid so much stress. My colleagues
> must forgive me if I dissociate myself from the
> philosophical standpoint of my immediate predecessor; but

it is only right that at the outset I should say where I stand.[12]

The strength of Hardy's conviction comes across in the following confession and *Credo*:

Perhaps I may make a confession. I have worked hard at marine ecology, but I have done so only partly because I have had a desire to benefit the fishing industry. I have this desire most sincerely, but I also have felt that I have been working towards a better understanding of animal relationships and making contributions to the development of general principles in ecology ... I will go further – I will confess that perhaps my main interest in ecology is the conviction that this science of Interrelationships of animals and their environment will eventually have a reaction for the benefit of mankind quite apart from any intermediate economic one.

I believe that the only true science of politics is that of human ecology – a quantitative science which will take in not only the economic and nutritional needs of man, but one which will include his emotional side as well, including the recognition of his spiritual as well as his physical behaviour.

I believe that the dogmatic assertions of the mechanistic biologists, put forward with such confidence as if they were the voice of true science, where they are in reality the blind acceptance of an unproven hypothesis, are as damaging to the peace of mind of humanity as was the belief in everyday miracles in the middle ages.[13]

It was possibly the first time that he had been publicly so open about his concern for spirituality, and by doing so in his inaugural lecture, he underlined its centrality in his interpretation of our biological nature. Having become the holder of a Regius Chair, he was beginning to feel that he had the authority to be explicit on this point, but within the larger context of contemporary scientific culture, he knew that from the perspective of career advancement he was treading a questionable and dangerous path.

Alister felt he had done well to achieve the Aberdeen professorship, and there is no doubt that, in turn, he was seen as a considerable catch by Aberdeen. His self-belief was greatly enhanced by an incident some two years after he arrived in Marischal College. He received a letter dated 30 March 1944,[14] and marked 'Confidential', sent to him by Sir Hector Hetherington, at that time Principal of Glasgow University. Although Hetherington stated that he had also sent a copy of his letter to Sir William Hamilton-Fyfe, it has the tone of a somewhat shady piece of headhunting. Hetherington had been searching for someone suitable to take over the vacant Chair of Zoology in Glasgow, and the authorities he had consulted had advised him that the ideal appointment would be Hardy. Sir Hector hoped to be able to spirit him away to Glasgow with the inducements of a larger department and a substantial increase in salary.

Alister immediately scribbled out a brief reply to Hetherington. He explained politely that he was gratified by the news that his colleagues had a high opinion of his ability:

> ... it is very kind of you, yourself, to extend me such a friendly invitation. I do thank you sincerely, but as you thought probable, I could not think of accepting. I have three reasons: firstly I would not dream of leaving here so soon after my arrival, secondly I have become an Aberdonian, and thirdly the future scientific man-power argument does not appeal to me – I intend to make this the largest Scottish Department! [I would not accept?] even [if] I should be invited to Oxford at Goodrich's retirement ...[15]

Hardy showed Hetherington's letter to Hamilton-Fyfe, along with his reply. The Principal was greatly relieved and said so in a hand written note:

> My dear Hardy,
> Many thanks for letting me see Hector's letter (damn him!) and your admirable reply, to which I hope you will consent to add the postscript I have suggested. It is quite true. It was – after reading the Glasgow epistle a vast relief to read your reply. Thank you. Thank you. If Oxford does [invite

you] – well, as a loyal Oxonian, I should have to applaud – with tears in my eyes.[16]

After signing the letter Alister added,

P.S. The Principal asks me to add that if I had given any other answer he would have committed hari-kari on your doorstep.[17]

The letter is a good example of Hardy's skill at administering a reprimand in a civilised manner. He was very rarely sharp-tongued, but he *was* extremely single minded and his associates could sometimes find this disconcerting.[18] In spite of this resolute aspect of his nature, Alister took time off to be unusually solicitous for the welfare of his students and he in turn was much loved by them. A retired medical consultant who still remembered the care he took of him wrote, sixty years after graduating:

I was "up" to the University of Aberdeen from 1943–1949, graduating then in Medicine. I did not do too well in my first term exam in zoology. We were all interviewed by [Hardy]; he was more than kindly and gave me every encouragement to do better in my next term. Unfortunately, I fell ill with Rheumatic Fever and was admitted to the Aberdeen Royal Infirmary for treatment – for the next fifteen weeks. Professor Hardy made it his business to find out about any illness suffered by his students – he then visited them – in my case, every Sunday evening, bringing me interesting books from his library to keep me occupied, also little games for my amusement.[19]

Hardy made himself thoroughly at home in the North East. The same former student remembers chancing upon him with his family on the shore at Cullen, a fishing village on the Moray Firth, and being invited to join them for tea. As a marine biologist with a special interest in the herring industry the string of fishing villages stretching along the Firth fascinated him. But he was not to remain in Scotland for much longer.

Alister's self-righteous tone when he turned down the offer from Glasgow had an embarrassing sequel. Just over a year after Hetherington's attempted seduction, the eventuality that Hamilton-Fyfe had feared came to pass. There had been rumours that E. S. Goodrich, Hardy's teacher at Oxford, was thinking of giving up his Chair. Like other professors at that time, Goodrich had no official retirement age but in 1945, when he was approaching 78, he had become very tired and the department was in the doldrums. Hardy was urged by his friends to prepare himself to apply for Goodrich's post, the full title of which was the Linacre Chair of Zoology and Comparative Anatomy. The ornithologist Bernard Tucker, who was on Goodrich's staff, wrote to Alister on 17 February of that year to alert him to the probability of an impending retirement:

> Dear Hardy,
> Now that the German part of the war seems to be within measurable distance of its end and Goodrich is beginning to talk (unofficially) about retiring I have decided to write and ask you without any beating about the bush whether you have considered putting in for the Linacre Professorship when the time comes ... The future of the Linacre Professorship is (as I'm sure you will agree) a matter of such importance in British Zoology that I would like to commend it to you as almost a duty to put in for it. The possible field does not seem to me large and I cannot see anyone so well qualified as yourself, while it seems to me that there are at any rate one or two other 'possibles' with a certain following whose appointment would not be at all to the advantage of Oxford zoology.[20]

Tucker pointed out that the Cambridge department, under James Gray, was fully committed to the experimental side, and perhaps Oxford could contribute to the growth of biological science by taking an interest in ecology. Alister's work was along this line and he would be an ideal leader of a department with such a bias. In his note of thanks, Hardy admitted that he had thought about applying for the Chair, but doubted that he was the right person for the job. Oxford's reputation was for comparative anatomy and he was a marine biologist with strong interests in ecology. But on the other hand, perhaps he could maintain the anatomical side while developing ecological research. As he thought about it, the prospect of going back to Oxford seemed more and more delightful. Warming to his subject, Alister imagined the staff of the department as a united team, combining experimental and observational zoology, to the extent that ecology would come to have the status currently enjoyed by physiology. The staff included John Young and Peter Medawar who, as committed physiologists, would ensure that the latter was not ignored.

The mention of the name John Young (best known by his initials 'J. Z.') brought Alister face to face with the uncomfortable fact that Young was almost certain to apply for the same vacant post. Young was clever, fiercely ambitious and had a very short fuse, making Alister quail at the thought of rivalling him. In a second letter, dated 10 March, Tucker confirmed that Young was indeed a candidate. He was apprehensive about the possibility of Young being appointed, and while hastening to reassure Alister that he was a candidate on merit, added that it would be fortunate if his application had the effect of blocking Young:

> ... I can assure you ... that the whole staff are in varying degrees, and several of them strongly, opposed to the idea of appointing Young ... He is, I agree, very able in many ways, but he is also not mature enough to have control of a big department like this, with others on the staff who are leading experts in their own lines and older than he is ... he is intolerant and peevish with those with whom he doesn't see eye-to-eye and selfish with regard to his own particular resources.[21]

Hardy's old friend the cytologist John R. Baker also wrote to him, asking him if he was applying for the Chair. Baker admitted that he himself was also putting in an application, and hoping against hope that the department did not get landed with another ill-suited candidate:

> I am going to apply myself, though I suppose it is a waste of ink – that is, I am going to apply if one is permitted to apply, but the appointment may be made in the secret method, as is sometimes done. The only other member of staff who is applying is J. Z. Young. It would be fun to

have you here as Professor. The staff is in consternation at the thought that Hogben might be appointed. It would be a catastrophe.[22]

What would happen if Alister were to be appointed? Young and Hogben would have been kept out, but would Young as an internal candidate be able to overcome his resentment and co-operate with his erstwhile competitor? Another possible competitor might have been Alister's old rival for the Welch Prize, Gavin de Beer, but Tucker had news that he was definitely not applying. Then there was the embarrassment of leaving Aberdeen after a mere four years. It made Alister's pious rejection of Hector Hetherington's mischievous invitation to leave Aberdeen seem hypocritical. It might help if Goodrich could be persuaded to stay on for one more year. This would give Alister an extra spell in Aberdeen and make his departure look less indecently hasty.

No such luck. Alister had to submit an application, or risk losing the opportunity. His submission was very brief, consisting of a three page personal statement followed by his C.V. on a single page. His opening pages are the production of a confident man, an insider who knows what he wants to do, very unlike the surprised young adventurer newly back from Antarctica, who applied for his first professorship in Hull. The statement is full of Alister's exuberance and creativity and is an expansion of the remarks he made to Tucker. His perspective implied a radical change in the objectives of the zoology department:

> Although my lines of research have been far removed from the grand tradition of Oxonian Comparative Anatomy, I venture to offer myself as a candidate in the belief that I could help to maintain the spirit of Oxford scholarship, for which I have an abounding admiration, and at the same time throw myself into the development of the department as a centre for the study of the living animal under natural conditions.[23]

He had obviously made a careful study of the interests of the staff in Oxford for he adds:

> If I could join my marine ecological interests with Elton's mammalian work, Ford's entomological evolutionary

studies, Baker's interest in climate and breeding seasons, Tucker's field bird observations, and Professor Hale Carpenter's work at the Hope Department,[24] I believe we could, working together, build up a strong school of experimental and observational research; one that would help to place the study of living animals in the field on the road to gaining equality with physiology in biological prestige. That would be my aim. It would be a centre for research but essentially a school as well. There is a growing need for marine ecologists throughout the Empire: for men fired with the spirit of the old field naturalists, yet equipped with the training for a quantitative and experimental attack. Such men must have first a thorough grounding in pure zoology, and then the stimulus of being in a department in which field research is being actively pursued.[25]

Hardy's stated objective was the creation of a new centre of energy in zoology, sufficiently focused to rival and contrast with the marked emphasis on the laboratory in Cambridge:

I believe that since Cambridge has developed so much on the side of laboratory experiment, it would be well for Oxford to follow for a time a different but equally important line.[26]

For all the reasons mentioned, he was appointed.

Alister left Aberdeen to prepare himself for his new job which was due to commence in January 1946. The family settled in Oxford in a house in Belbroughton Road, selected for them by Walter Garstang. It was very smart but the rates were prohibitive and after a few years they moved to a less pretentious house in Woodstock Road. Michael was by this time a boarder at Marlborough and Belinda started at the Oxford High School, but then was sent to Downe House School,[27] near Newbury in Berkshire. At this point Alister could finally and rightfully congratulate himself on achieving one of the major components of his ambition – to be the Head of the Zoology Department in one of the truly great universities of the world.

Triumphant beginnings can sometimes end in tears. Alister's first months in Oxford turned out to be far from happy, for in January 1946, just after Hardy had arrived, and three months after he stated that he was going to retire, Goodrich collapsed and died, leaving the Zoology Department without a leader. Alister had assumed that he would have plenty of time to ease into the job, supported by the knowledge and wise advice of Goodrich: so to speak, an apprentice professor under his old teacher. Goodrich's sudden demise left Alister feeling very vulnerable and he did indeed have to run the gauntlet of hostility from his colleagues. On many occasions during those early weeks his family noticed that when he came home from his office in the Oxford Museum on Parks Road he was unusually quiet, seemingly deeply preoccupied. His mood was sufficiently apparent for his 12-year-old daughter Belinda to recall that she felt something was different from normal.

Alister must have expected that he would be tested by a group of strong-minded colleagues with very different points of view. He would therefore have considered quite carefully how he stood, personally, with his fellow members of staff. For example, he would have felt confident that he could count on support from Tucker and Baker, since they had asked him to apply for the job. Charles Elton was an old friend and as a pioneer ecologist had much to gain from Alister's interest in the subject, so he was most probably on side. But what was the likely stance of the gifted entomologist and geneticist E. B. ('Henry') Ford, of Wadham College, and eventually to become a Fellow of All Souls? He had a reputation as a misogynist, and was alleged by some to have a cruel streak. He was one of the best-known eccentrics in Oxford, whose oddities had given amusement to generations of students. The most familiar story about him refers to:

> ... a time when progressively declining numbers of male undergraduates attended his lectures ... the numbers of men went down until there was only one, when Ford replaced his customary greeting 'Gentlemen!' by 'Sir!' Eventually, even the single male failed to turn up, and Henry entered the lecture room to find only women. 'How extraordinary', he said 'there is no one here', and he left the room.[28]

Then there were J. Z. Young and Peter Medawar, neither of whom were ecologists, hence they were unlikely to have sympathy with Hardy's aims and indeed both left the department. Perhaps fortunately for Alister's peace of mind, at the same time as he applied for the Oxford Chair, Young went after a Chair in London. He succeeded in the latter attempt and was appointed Professor of Anatomy at London University, resigning from his Oxford post in December 1945, before Alister arrived. Peter Medawar stayed on in Oxford, but left at the end of the session in 1947 to take up the Chair of Zoology in Birmingham University.

No doubt Alister would have made similar appraisals of everyone on the staff before taking up his Oxford post. The personal statement in his job application job implies as much. Unfortunately the two problems that he met were a good deal more unpleasant than he could have predicted. The first difficulty was self-inflicted and meant that he got off on the wrong foot even prior to his arrival. The trigger was a circular he sent in advance to all the staff, which was meant to introduce them to his point of view and how he hoped to run the department. But he had badly miscalculated the feelings of his colleagues about their new Professor. He seemed to have forgotten that this was Oxford.

He soon realised he had made a mistake, for John Baker confronted him with it after he had been a short time in Oxford. Baker was as annoyed with Alister as anyone else, but his long-standing friendship enabled him to transcend the mood of hostility. John pointed out the misgivings people had when they received a duplicated message that asked them, as university dons, to see themselves as a 'crew', under the 'captaincy' of Alister Hardy. Nor was it wise of Alister to keep referring to 'my' department, as if he owned the place. Baker let him know how the old hands on the staff felt – some of them already world leaders in their field. The 'crew' in general were men who either had, or would soon have, outstanding reputations, to the extent that most undergraduate zoologists in university departments anywhere would have come across their work. They felt demeaned and anonymised by the circular.

We may wonder what possessed Alister to express himself this way. It was a surprising *faux pas* for an Oxford man who had spent a great deal of time thinking about leadership and who claimed to have egalitarian views. Perhaps he was harking back to his days as an army officer. The language he used was reminiscent of the way he had spoken to the young miners under his command in the cyclists' battalion. Another possible explanation of Alister's behaviour is that he was somewhat overawed by his appointment and was very well aware of the reputation of several members of the staff and the likelihood of resentment. With their academic status, these men saw themselves as autonomous, and resented the newcomer appearing to throw his weight around. One way for Alister to cope with the resulting anxiety would be to regress to the apparent safety of a hierarchical model of management, in which the leader is accepted without question.[29] In the event such a move was only likely to create more turmoil.

In ordinary circumstances, given time, this mistake by Hardy would probably have been forgotten, but the situation was made worse by a still more serious difficulty. The zoology department had a loose and unclear connection with two other organisations, the Bureau of Animal Populations and the Edward Grey Institute of Field Ornithology. The registrar of the university wanted the uncertainty of the relationships tidied up and asked Hardy to take both organisations fully into the zoology department. This move would have added seven senior researchers to the staff, all with a bias towards ecology. The physiologists and other non-ecologists felt they were unfairly discriminated against, particularly because of the amount of scarce resources they would consume. Then there was the vexed question of the ambitions of Charles Elton, director of the Bureau of Animal Population. He certainly did support what Alister was trying to do. But Elton wanted the Bureau to be upgraded to the status of a sub-department and his assistants promoted to the rank of Demonstrator. Did this mean that almost as much funding would go to the Animal Ecology people, as to all the other units in the Zoology Department put together? The tension aroused by the situation is well summarised in Richard Burkhardt's scholarly book on the founders of ethology:[30]

> This plan astonished and displeased the other
> demonstrators in zoology (John R. Baker, E. B. Ford, Peter
> Medawar, H. K. Pusey, and Bernard Tucker). They were
> outraged to hear that the university was being asked to
> spend almost as much on the sub-department of animal
> population as 'on the whole of the rest of zoology'. Tucker,
> the ornithologist of the group, had himself been hoping for

the establishment of a sub-department of ornithology, but Ford, Medawar, Pusey and Baker persuaded him to withdraw his proposal and not to ask the university for more than a small annual subsidy of two hundred pounds for ornithological studies. Tucker then agreed to go along with the others in opposing the foundation of a sub-department of animal population.[31]

John Baker again took it upon himself to tell Alister that the department was seething with anger in a way that he had never seen before during his twenty-five years in Oxford. Hardy must have felt abandoned when even Tucker and Baker, who had begged him to apply for the Chair, seemed to have turned against him.

Alister survived. Gradually, his openness, his honesty and kindness, allied to his overwhelming enthusiasm, began to change the mood. He continued to make mistakes, one of the most painful being his judgment to allow his son Michael to enter the Oxford Zoology Department as an undergraduate. A departmental photograph of the time gives a hint of the tension resulting from this decision; Professor Hardy is seated centrally on the front row, while his son Michael is as far away as possible, on the back row, near one end. Known as 'Mick' to his companions, he did very well in his studies, as befitted his competence, and along with his friend Quentin Bone[32] and two other students, achieved a First Class degree. Any man placed in such a position has a life-long burden to carry, aware of the unspoken question when the source of his degree comes up in conversation. Why did Alister do it? Again there is no answer, but one can speculate that taking his son into his own department was perhaps an attempt at reparation for being absent from the father role so often during his son's childhood.

Alister went on to do more than survive. As he gained confidence he managed to correct many of his mistakes through diplomacy and good humour. His style in meetings at first seemed disorganised; to the extent that one former member of staff said of him: 'Alister gave the impression that he couldn't administer himself out of a paper bag'.[33] Yet it was his administrative skill that brought about the resolution of the 'fragmented department' issue, by joining together the Bureau of Animal Population and the Edward Grey Institute to form a new Department of Field Studies. His diplomatic ability to unite and energise this talented group of men suggests that his management skill was of a high order.[34]

Above all, what he inspired was deep affection. Over and over again he was described by former colleagues of all ranks, from senior academic to junior technician, as well as by his former students, as a 'very lovable man'. During these years he accumulated a fund of stories relating to his exploits, many of them relating to his intellectual openness and schoolboyish enthusiasms, some of them bizarre enough to make onlookers laugh out loud. One of the most celebrated incidents involved a speculation about night flying moths. He and E. B. 'Henry' Ford wondered if the well-known propensity of moths to fly towards a light meant that at the time of the full moon they would attempt to fly towards it. So on one or two nights in 1947 and 1948, Alister and Henry were to be seen hovering high above the little village of Weston-on-the-Green near Oxford, suspended in a basket beneath a floodlit balloon, on the look-out for ambitious moths making their way upwards.

This playful feature of his personality, allied to his fairness and intellectual competence, meant that in a remarkably short time he was able to create a happy department, and in due course one that was academically good enough to rival any in the world. Desmond Morris remembered being charmed when he arrived there as a research student:

> Although he made his scientific reputation as a brilliant marine biologist, he was at heart a wide-ranging Victorian naturalist, fascinated by a much broader spectrum. This, combined with a natural warmth and energy, made him the perfect professor for those of us lucky enough to be members of his department. He literally brought the old zoology department to life by filling it with living animals, tanks of fish in the corridors, a huge aviary of birds covering the roof and even a complete termites' nest, full of termites, carefully shipped in from abroad to grace the central courtyard. Compared with Hardy's animated domain, other zoology departments always seemed boringly clinical and unstimulating.[35]

The rapidly growing reputation of the department enabled him to attract people of the highest calibre to join him. The most remarkable *tour de force* was undoubtedly in 1950, when he persuaded the brilliant Dutch ethologist, Niko Tinbergen, to leave the University of Leiden and join him in Oxford, rather than accepting an invitation to the United States where he would have been financially rewarded much more handsomely.[36]

Hardy's achievement was acknowledged by Peter Medawar in a letter dated 9 March 1949. It purported to be a note of thanks to Alister for promoting the cause of Medawar's membership of the Royal Society, but Peter had something else on his mind. Very movingly, the letter turned into an expression of his feelings of remorse about the treatment meted out to Alister when he first took over the Chair in Oxford. Medawar wanted to apologise,

> ... for the really contemptible behaviour of the resident staff on your first arrival in Oxford. It was not until I had a bit of responsibility of my own here, that I realised with horror and regret just how badly we had behaved and how upset you must have been by it ... Incidentally, wherever I go now the Oxford zoology department is being spoken of in a way that is altogether quite novel – as the leading department in the country. To have achieved this stature in 3–4 years is something you ought to be jolly proud of ...[37]

Hardy produced a short annual report for every year that he was head of department. These summaries show how the department grew and provide data on lectures delivered and research carried out. In the first report, Alister noted a good deal more sincerely than is often the case at such times, his great regret at the loss of Goodrich and how it deprived him of advice about the running of the department. John Baker stood in as deputy to the Linacre Professor and consequently the series of lectures for that year simply followed the pattern set by Goodrich and was overwhelmingly taken up with invertebrate systematics. There were no formal lectures on evolution and there were 22 people on the Advanced Course.

The subsequent radical alterations to the lecture curriculum in Oxford cannot be understood fully without a consideration of Alister's Vow. When he was in Aberdeen, he had felt able to lay bare his life's agenda in his Inaugural Lecture. We can see that the act of self-revelation was intensely meaningful to him, for in 1982, 40 years after he gave the lecture, he asked for copies to be distributed to the five copyright libraries in Britain and Ireland other than the Bodleian in Oxford, which already had a copy.[38] We can therefore give the Aberdeen Inaugural the status of a major statement of his core commitments.

But what happened to Alister's Vow during the 18 years that he spent as a university don in Oxford? During his turbulent settling-in period, and for many years afterwards, there is, to the casual glance, very little sign of him remembering the depth of his religious pledge. He did publish pieces on the subject during that time, but they were few in number and small in scale. One or two meetings, together with these publications, complete the brief record of Hardy's work in the field of religion and spirituality. This paucity of material naturally gives rise to the suspicion that, being caught into the excitement of building a zoology department worthy of a great university, he had become bored with, or lost his religious beliefs.

The truth is quite to the contrary. He had by no means lost his convictions and was following a consciously planned strategy to achieve his spiritual ambition. To make sense of what was happening it is necessary to be aware of the surrounding academic context, or to put it biologically, the way in which Alister adapted his behaviour to increase his chances of survival in his ecological niche. He could safely give his inaugural lecture in Aberdeen because he knew that it was politically opportune, following the departure of the unpopular and sceptical Lancelot Hogben. Sir William Hamilton-Fyfe was deeply interested in the philosophy of religion and had been headmaster of a famous religious foundation, Christ's Hospital School in Horsham, Surrey. His successor, Sir Thomas Taylor, who became Principal during Hardy's second year in Aberdeen, was recognised as a committed Christian, and fortunately, from Hardy's point of view, his religious opinions were very liberal.[39]

When he came to Oxford, Alister felt that he needed to be much more circumspect, since he was well aware that some of his colleagues were extremely dismissive of religious beliefs as wrong-headed or infantile. The wholesale rejection of the religious dimension of life was something he had noticed in a significant proportion of population in Oxford when he was a student; indeed it was the

major reason for his youthful vow. The hostility made him create –
for most of the time – a sharp boundary between his work as an
empirical scientist and the religious preoccupations that lay behind
his scientific ambitions. The boundary was sufficiently impenetrable
for many students to have studied in his department for three years
and come out with a degree, without realising that he had the
slightest interest in religion.[40] Hardy maintained this split rigidly,
although from the point of view of his ultimate aim to bring about a
reconciliation between science and religion, it was paradoxical.

With this in mind it is revealing to examine how the changes in
the curriculum in the Oxford department have a direct logical
bearing on the unfolding of Hardy's religious ambitions. By 1959
the emphasis of the teaching had changed radically in the ecological
direction, as outlined by him in his original application for the
professorship. Most obvious among the innovations was the revised
lecture programme. There were new lectures on Animal Behaviour
given by Niko Tinbergen and on Zoogeography by Charles Elton.
Hardy added lectures on Marine Biology and, most significantly of
all, 15 lectures on Evolution given by himself. Towards the end of
his time in the department he wondered briefly about increasing the
numbers of lectures on evolution to 20, as can be seen from
scribbled notes preserved in the Bodleian Library.[41] The number
stayed at 15, perhaps due to constraints on the timetable. Nevertheless, the intended increase underlines the importance Hardy
gave to a detailed understanding of natural selection.

Laying claim to evolution as his special area was for Alister a way
of opening up a route to get a hearing for his views on spirituality. It
hardly needs saying that all members of the zoology staff would
have given their lectures and tutorials in at least an implicit context
of Darwinism. That was axiomatic. But by making himself the sole
member of staff lecturing explicitly on evolution, he, above all, had
to ensure that he understood the subject thoroughly and was up to
date with the latest thinking. Taking on the sole responsibility for
the evolution programme had the implicit function of training him
intellectually for the presentation of his hypothesis on the evolution
of spiritual awareness. At the level of popular feeling it also helped
to strengthen Alister's reputation as an expert at the heart of the
Darwinian tradition, that he was teaching evolution theory in the
University Museum, where the famous battle between Huxley and
Wilberforce had taken place.

His expertise was recognised by Julian Huxley, who had published *Evolution: the Modern Synthesis*, in 1942. This famous textbook was accepted as the standard account of the synthesis that began to take place between evolution theory and genetics, following the rescue of the researches of Gregor Mendel from obscurity. The final assurance of Alister's Darwinian orthodoxy came about when Huxley invited him, as one of nine senior biologists, to contribute to the Introduction of the 1974 (third) edition of this standard text.[42] Hardy's topic in the book was 'behavioural selection'. This is an idea that he employed in his argument for the biological reality of spiritual experience and will be discussed more fully in the next chapter. He was aware that putting forward this conjecture would elicit severe criticism from some other biologists. In those circumstances it was handy to have a reputation that made it highly implausible for his critics to accuse him of ignorance.

During Hardy's last few years as Linacre Professor, the Zoology Department was increasingly experiencing both the drawbacks and the exhilaration of success. By 1959 one of the drawbacks, overcrowding, was becoming intolerable. In the advanced class lecture room there were 76 people packed into the restricted teaching space available in the University Museum. That is to say that there were nearly four times the number of students in the class compared to when Alister first arrived. Postgraduate studies had to be restricted for the same reason, though extra accommodation was found in a nearby house. On the positive side, relatively large sums of money were beginning to come in, including support from the Nuffield Foundation for E. B. Ford's work on the evolution and genetics of wild populations, Niko Tinbergen's research[43] on animal behaviour and Arthur Cain's work on polymorphism. The Department of Scientific and Industrial Research funded Bernard Kettlewell's famous and controversial studies of industrial melanism in *Biston betularia*, the Peppered Moth.[44] The general feeling of the staff was by this time full of life, fizzing with energy and highly competitive. Soon there would have to be a new building to house zoology. Past students spoke of the excitement, the atmosphere of infectious enthusiasm and particularly the welcome given by the Hardy household. This had been a feature from the early days.

Desmond Morris remembered being entertained there, shortly after arriving as a new research student:

> I was invited to take tea with him in his North Oxford house. There, I and several other newcomers were regaled with amazing anecdotes, full of impish humour, culminating in his famous 'mermaid story'. It began with a description of a stuffed mermaid which an old sailor had brought to England from some faraway island and continued with details of how this sailor and all subsequent owners of the mermaid had suffered terrible and inexplicable misfortunes. Then, with a melodramatic flourish, a beaming Hardy plunged his arm behind his chair and held the mummified mermaid aloft in front of us. 'Now it is in my hands', he cried, defying the fates to do him harm. It was a fascinating object, fashioned long ago from the front end of a monkey and the rear end of a large fish ...[45]

Fellow members of staff felt the same delight in Hardy as a naturalist and raconteur. One of them wrote:

> Hardy brought with him a whiff of the great oceans, and the emphasis on teaching was tipped from comparative anatomy towards general zoology. His lectures were anecdotal and amusing and gave the impression that he really had witnessed what goes on outside the confines of the laboratory. His lecture on *Amphioxus* became famous and was illustrated by mime. He was very tall and thin, and all the while his substantial whiskers twitched like buccal cirri, as he drew his jacket round his shoulders to illustrate the relationship of the atrium to the rest of the body.[46]

There were other enjoyable rewards arising throughout his career from Alister's success as a biologist. In 1953 he had a ship named after him. The *Alister Hardy* research trawler was built for Hong Kong University which paid for Sylvia and him to travel to the Far East for the launching. Another of Alister's sources of pride was the number of items named in honour of him. His philosopher friend J. R. Lucas who, like Alister, was a Fellow of Merton College recalled:

> A fellow once asked him how many things were named
> after him. There was a boat in Hong Kong, an octopus, a
> squid, an island in the Antarctic and – he would add,
> lowering his voice in a tone of comic embarrassment – two
> worms.[47]

It needs to be added that the love and respect felt by almost all who
met Alister did not prevent at least some of them from having their
criticisms. The same member of staff who enjoyed Hardy's mime of
Amphioxus, tempered his praise when assessing his interest in
biochemistry and physiology:

> He was above all a naturalist and was at his best as an
> observer: he encouraged observation rather than analysis.
> The hypothesis and the testing of it was not for him; but if
> there was something inherently interesting out there, in
> Nature, then the taking of notes would necessarily be a
> justifiable activity and might prove profitable; the
> explanation it provided should not, however, go too deep,
> it should only disturb the surface and leave plenty of room
> for awe: the mystical side of life must not be sullied.
> Evolution fascinated him because there were no techniques
> at the time that would disturb more than its surface. He
> developed an interest in behaviour because analysis still left
> a big magma of unknown – 'drive' was a fine idea because
> it rested on an unexplained neurological foundation.
> Behaviour was safe, but biochemistry and physiology were
> suspect as they came nearer to an explanation in
> physico-chemical terms, and he had no stomach for this.[48]

This criticism perhaps represents those members of staff whose
cast of mind was more analytically inclined than Hardy. Alister was
always drawn by holistic ideas that synthesised and provided overarching interpretations of empirical data, and we have seen that the
split between the two ways of thinking was the cause of tension
between ecologists and others when Alister first arrived.

Given the reality of these differences of intellectual stance,
Hardy's status as an academic was not in doubt, and was recognised
in the form of public accolade. During his time as, successively, a
Professor in Hull, Aberdeen and Oxford, he managed to accumu-

late enough academic and other trophies to more than fill his mantelpiece. They suggest a picture of a man greatly admired by the academy:[49]

First recipient, Scientific Medal of Zoological Society of London, 1939

Elected a Fellow of the Royal Society, 1940

DSc, Oxford University, 1948

Honorary Fellowship, Zoological Society of India, 1956

Knighthood for services to the fishing industry, 1957

Honorary Life Member, New York Academy of Sciences, 1961

Honorary LLD, University of Aberdeen, 1961

Honorary DSc, University of Southampton, 1962

Honorary DSc, University of Hull, 1963

Appointed Gifford Lecturer, University of Aberdeen, 1963

Honorary Membership, British Ecological Society, 1963

Honorary Fellowship, Merton College, Oxford, 1964

Lecompte du Nouy Prize for *The Living Stream*, 1968

Phi Beta Kappa Prize for *Great Waters*, 1961

Vice-Presidency, World Congress of Faiths, 1979

Vice-Presidency, Scottish Marine Biological Association, 1984

Templeton Prize, 1985

However eminent a person is deemed to be by their peers, any inner uncertainties they may have about personal commitments that diverge from those of the surrounding majority, are not easily brushed aside. Apart from his remarkably outspoken inaugural lecture in Aberdeen University, and quite separate from matters of strategy, Alister's shyness about his central pledge when addressing a professional audience remained with him all his life. The paucity of his writing and speaking on religious matters has been remarked upon, but once in a while, where it seemed prudent, Alister spoke directly of his beliefs. An early opportunity came when he was invited to give an address[50] on *The Faith of a Scientist* in the Priestley Hall in Leeds in December 1948, as part of the celebrations for the centenary of the building of the Mill Hill Chapel. The lecture was given on behalf of the Unitarian Church, for by this time Hardy had allied himself to Unitarianism. Then in 1951 Hardy was invited to give the annual Essex Hall Lecture. This Lecture was sponsored by the British and Foreign Unitarian Association and given the title *Science and the Quest for God.*[51] In both these papers there is evidence of Hardy's thought moving towards a coherent, empirically based, hypothesis about the nature of human spirituality. In his Essex Hall lecture he appeals to theologians:

> I do not wish to disturb or hurt the feelings of those who have certain fixed convictions, nor to try to convert them to a different point of view. I cannot, however, help feeling that it is likely to be more important for religion in the future to have a theology that is founded on the reality of religious experience, than to have one that builds its doctrines on supposed events in the past: supposed events which some of the best scholars of history are unable to establish beyond doubt by the rules of evidence accepted in other fields of historical research.[52]

In both cases he was preaching to the converted, but in between these two meetings, in 1949 there was an annual assembly in Newcastle of the British Association for the Advancement of Science. At that time Hardy was the President of Section D, which was concerned with Zoology, and as part of his presidency he was required to give an address. The mode of the address tells us something of his stance when talking to fellow professional biologists. The theme he chose was 'Zoology outside the laboratory', and his major objective was to persuade people that field work could be, and ought to be, as scientific as work in the laboratory. He urged on his audience the necessity to get out of the laboratory and into the field to study the whole animal, in its environment. This, he believed, would soon convince them that mechanistic biology gave an inadequate and misleading account of the real life of animals operating in their normal lives. He illustrated the point with a summary of his work as a marine biologist. Towards the end of his talk he introduced the idea of 'behavioural selection'[53] and in the final few minutes he raised the issue of telepathy, briefly and apologetically:

> There has appeared over the horizon something that many of us do not like to look at. If it is pointed out to us we say 'No, it cannot be there, our doctrines say it is impossible'. I

refer to telepathy – the communication of one mind with another by means other than by ordinary senses. I believe that no one who examines the evidence with an unbiased mind can reject it, particularly the evidence of the vast number of experiments of the last twenty-five years and of the group of them which has passed successfully the statistical tests regarded as decisive when applied to normal scientific techniques ... our ideas on evolution may be altered if something akin to telepathy – unconscious no doubt – was found to be a factor in moulding the patterns of behaviour among members of a species ... If there was such a non-conscious group behaviour plan, distributed between and linking the members of the race, we might find ourselves coming back to something like those ideas of subconscious racial memory of Samuel Butler, but on a group rather than on an individual basis ...

If I appear to be ending in fantasy or in the spirit of harlequinade, I do so only to emphasise my conviction that we fool ourselves if we imagine that our present ideas are more than a tiny fraction of the truth yet to be discovered ... [54]

His thoughts about how to win over his listeners began by presupposing that many were dismissive of religious ideas as fantasy. In that case, perhaps he could convince them of the reality of practical reports of telepathy that apparently transcend the currently standard scientific picture of reality. From a purely biological perspective, studying experience of this kind, if the methodology and results proved to be reliable, would go some way towards understanding the remarkable communication abilities of many social animals. Taking his speculations still further, perhaps these researches might also contribute to a scientific understanding of religious experience, conceived of in Hardy's words as 'awareness of being influenced by a presence or a power, whether called God or not, that is different from one's everyday self'. Ecological ideas, with their emphasis on interrelationship and community, stand logically much closer to the 'relational consciousness'[55] that appears to characterise the spiritual realm, than the analytical approach common to more traditional empirical science. But if Alister thought he could help the members of his audience to become more open to the possibility of these phenomena, he was sadly mistaken. With one or two exceptions, at best his words were taken as the amiable eccentricities of an otherwise brilliant man, and hence they were tolerated, then ignored.

No wonder that Alister kept silent on these matters when at work. But his stubborn and, as he felt, empirically-based belief, showed no signs of being destroyed. As a tailpiece to this chapter it seems appropriate to refer to one touching and fragile clue to the persistence of Hardy's convictions, in spite of ridicule. Buried in his archive in the Bodleian Library are a few tattered sheets of paper bearing a record of a series of annual payments, starting at £10 but rising to £25 in later years, for the restoration fund of St Giles Church in Oxford. These donations, unknown to either his colleagues or his family, are accompanied by a letter to the vicar, Canon Diggle, dated 16 October 1956:

> I was so glad I happened to meet you this morning, for as I told you, I had been meaning to come and see you for some time. I enclose my cheque for £10, a little subscription towards the upkeep and renovation of your beautiful old church – this is for 1956; I will send you another subscription in January for 1957. I call whenever I can on my way to work in the mornings for a few minutes in your little side chapel. It is very good of you not to mind my telling you that I do this without coming to any of your regular services.[56]

CHAPTER NINE

The Gifford Lectures

Sincere lovers of and earnest inquirers after truth.
Lord Gifford's requirement of his lecturers[1]

Hardy retired from the Linacre Chair in 1961, though he continued for a further two years as Professor and Head of the Department of Zoological Field Studies. What immediately precipitated his decision was the move of the Zoology Department to new premises. His complaints about the overcrowding amidst the Victorian splendour of the University Museum finally persuaded the authorities to build a replacement round the corner in South Parks Road. The person appointed to succeed him was J. W. S. Pringle, an insect physiologist who had a perspective on his task that was different from Alister's. The latter therefore took the opportunity to withdraw from the scene so as not to interfere with Pringle's oversight of the building programme. Peter Medawar, perhaps with lingering regrets about Alister's rough welcome in the early days at Oxford, tried to dissuade him.[2] He reminded him of the way he had lifted the place from a state of torpor to become one of the premier zoology departments in the world. But Alister was resolute; he had other plans.

While this was going on, Alister, who had a habit of getting his name in the press, found himself once more flung into the news. He had, without seriously considering the outcome, published a two-part article in the *New Scientist*, based on a talk he gave to the British Sub-Aqua Club in Brighton. It was about his conjecture that, at some period in its evolution, the human species had returned to living in the water. Hardy first got the idea back in the 1930s from reading Frederick Wood Jones' book *Man's Place Among the Mammals*.[3] Wood Jones had remarked that, among the primates, the layer of fat we have under the skin is unique to our species. It

203

reminded Alister, recently returned from the Antarctic, of the whale blubber he had seen on the flensing platforms of South Georgia. Did it imply a similar purpose, insulating the body from cold water? Along with this feature, human hair tracts – the directions in which the small hairs on the surface of the body lie – are not the same as in the apes. Especially on the back, the hairs lie in streamlined fashion following the line of the water over the body when someone swims forwards. This arrangement, thought Alister, might have been a first step in adaptation to an aquatic environment, before the eventual disappearance of substantial body hair.

Alister supposed that environmental pressures such as overpopulation and food shortages had forced our early ancestors to return to the sea. In this they were not unique, for something similar had happened to other water-living mammals like the whales and seals. Here is Alister, letting his imagination run freely:

> I am imagining this happening in the warmer parts of the world, in the tropical seas where Man could stand being in the water for relatively long periods, that is, several hours at a stretch. I imagine him wading, perhaps still crouching, almost on all fours, groping about in the water, digging for shell fish, but gradually becoming more adept at swimming. Then, in time, I see him becoming more and more of an aquatic animal going farther out from the shore; I see him diving for shell fish, prising out worms, burrowing-crabs and bivalves from the sands at the bottom of shallow seas, and then breaking open sea-urchins, and then, with increasing skill, capturing fish with his hands.[4]

From the nature of his audience and knowing Alister, it can be surmised that he gave his talk ever so slightly tongue-in-cheek, but the story was picked up by the popular media and taken much more seriously than he originally expected. Most notably, the Welsh broadcaster and writer, Elaine Morgan, used his idea in her highly successful book *The Descent of Woman*.[5] Alister and his former student Desmond Morris intended to write another book about the speculation, but were forestalled by Elaine, who returned to the hypothesis, with *The Aquatic Ape*, in 1982,[6] going into much more detail on the evidence in support of the idea. Hardy's conjecture continues to generate controversy today, particularly on the Internet. At the time, Desmond recalled, some of Alister's friends were alarmed at the way he had gone out on a limb:

> ... [It] earned him a stern rebuke from his old friend, the great anatomist Le Gros Clark, who telephoned him and pleaded with him to abandon the idea, exclaiming: 'Alister! Alister! Think of your reputation!' This only slightly subdued his enthusiasm, because, try as he might, he could think of no good argument against his theory. His great quality was (and still is – for in his mid-eighties he still has the fresh, open mind of a twenty-year-old) an ability to relish the outlandish that marks the brain of the true explorer. The scientist in him brings caution to bear at a certain point, but not too soon – not before he has had time to savour and consider some new thought and give it the chance to breathe a little. All too often today, research scientists clamp down too soon with an iron self censorship that stifles rebellious ideas at birth.[7]

It was perhaps the recognition of this original quality of mind that led to him receiving a surprising letter[8] from the Principal of Aberdeen University, Sir Thomas Taylor, dated 29 May 1962. On behalf of the Gifford Lecture appointing committee, it invited Alister to give two annual sets of lectures in the university as soon as convenient. This was no ordinary invitation, for the Gifford Lectures are a unique feature of Scottish academic life. They were initiated in 1885 by the will of Adam, Lord Gifford, a wealthy Edinburgh lawyer. He provided a legacy to each of the ancient Scottish Universities (Aberdeen, Edinburgh, Glasgow and St Andrews) to finance a lectureship 'for promoting, advancing and diffusing the study of Natural Theology'. The Lectures are remarkable because of the extremely liberal terms governing the appointment of the lecturers. Lord Gifford made a number of provisos in his will, the fourth one of which states that:

> The lecturers appointed shall be subjected to no test of any kind, and shall not be required to take any oath, or to emit or subscribe any declaration of belief, or to make any

promise of any kind; they may be of any denomination whatever, or of no denomination at all (and many earnest and high-minded men prefer to belong to no ecclesiastical denomination); they may be of any religion or way of thinking, or as is sometimes said, they may be of no religion, or they may be so-called sceptics or agnostics or freethinkers, provided only that the 'patrons' will use diligence to secure that they be able, reverent men, true thinkers, sincere lovers of and earnest inquirers after truth.[9]

One consequence of this freedom is that from 1887, when the first Gifford lectures were delivered, the list of scholarly presenters has included many of the greatest and most original thinkers on these matters, not merely in Scotland, but in the world-wide academic community. The educator and historian Jacques Barzun accurately described the Gifford Lectures as 'virtuoso performances and the highest honour in a philosopher's career'. [10]

No wonder then, that Alister replied to Taylor's letter by return, on 31 May:

> My dear Taylor,
> Few things have excited me more than your letter which I received this morning. There is no honour I would rather have than this: being invited to be a Gifford Lecturer, if only I can produce lectures that will be worthy of the great tradition before me. ... It has always been a secret ambition that one day I might try my hand at such a book; you and your committee have given me a wonderful opportunity for which I am deeply grateful. I cannot do other than proudly accept, though my gladness is tempered with an apprehension of the gravity of what I am agreeing to undertake. It is just wonderful to contemplate that I shall be coming back to Aberdeen to lecture – and to lecture on what is dearest to my heart ... I cannot tell you how thrilled I am by this opportunity.[11]

The prestige of the lectures was of course important to Hardy, but the other more concealed reason for his excitement was that the invitation brought him very much closer to fulfilling the Vow he had made half a century ago.

To outsiders unaware of Hardy's religious preoccupations, he must have seemed an odd choice for the Gifford lectureship. He had made his reputation as a marine biologist, not as a student of spirituality. It is true that he had intimated his view of the importance of spirituality in his Inaugural Lecture as Professor of Natural History in Aberdeen in 1942, but as noted in the previous chapter, Alister had published very little more on the subject. Such knowledge as there was about his interests must have come from the members of the appointing committee. Tantalisingly, it is not known who the members of the Gifford Committee were, for they kept no records, but it must be assumed that Hardy was in personal contact with one or more of its members, perhaps Sir Thomas Taylor himself. This eventuality is quite likely, since Taylor followed Hamilton-Fyfe as Principal during Hardy's time as professor in Aberdeen. All that is known for sure is that the committee was unanimous in its endorsement of the invitation and a stipend of £2,000 per annum was agreed. Arrangements were made for Sir Alister and Lady Hardy to stay in Crombie Hall, the recently opened first student residence, which was just across the road from King's College in Old Aberdeen. Whatever lay behind the option to appoint Hardy, it was a courageous and innovative decision because his views on the biological basis of religion were both radical and little known at that time.

In one important respect Alister was certainly an appropriate choice, since he had made it clear that his perspective on religion was that of an empirical scientist. Lord Gifford had made as his fifth proviso:

> I wish the lecturers to treat their subject [natural theology] as a strictly natural science, the greatest of all possible sciences, indeed, in one sense, the only science, that of Infinite Being, without reference to or reliance upon any supposed special, exceptional or so called miraculous revelation. I wish it considered just as astronomy or chemistry is ...[12]

Gifford spoke as a man of his time. In a more recent series of Gifford lectures in Edinburgh University in 1988, the philosopher Alasdair MacIntyre questioned whether it is possible for a well-informed contemporary lecturer to fulfil these conditions,[13] for ways of understanding the relationship between religion and science had changed radically since the nineteenth century. If anyone could still approach Gifford's ideal in the second half of the twentieth century, it would be someone like Alister Hardy. He held to the critical realist position typical of most empirical scientists and was firmly convinced of the applicability of the scientific method, not to the essence of religion, but certainly to all the surrounding phenomena.

Both in his determination to fulfil his boyhood Vow, and as a convinced Darwinian, Hardy wished to approach religion from the perspective of evolutionary science. He saw himself as following very directly in the footsteps of that earlier celebrated Gifford lecturer, William James, who in Edinburgh in the sessions 1901 and 1902 had given a pragmatist's account of religious experience.[14] Hardy consulted Principal Taylor[15] about his strategy and Taylor concurred. This meant that although he was lodging just across the road from the Divinity Faculty in King's College, he was adamant that the lectures should take place in the Natural History Department, which was a bus ride away in Marischal College.

Taylor had requested that the lectures were to be given as far as possible in straightforward language, avoiding academic jargon, in keeping with Gifford's desire that they should be directed towards the general public. Hardy was a master of popular communication and as a result his talks attracted a large audience. The lectures were delivered in the old First Year lecture theatre on the first floor of the Natural History Department.[16] Fred Holliday,[17] at that time a lecturer in Zoology in Aberdeen University, was present at many of the lectures and remembers one of the meetings when the room was so packed that the heat became intolerable. A member of the audience fainted, causing the temporary abandonment of the session while the unfortunate individual was carried outside and revived.

In keeping with his estimate of the importance of this unique opportunity to fulfil his most pressing personal ambition, Hardy prepared meticulously for his presentations. He had organised a syllabus of the lectures in advance, with extended summaries of what he intended to say in each session provided for his audience. Alongside the lectures he held a series of seminars, in the main chaired by the Aberdeen geneticist, Michael Begg,[18] in which the general public were invited to offer their comments and criticisms of what Hardy had said in his previous lecture. These meetings were also well attended and generated a number of developments of his ideas that were incorporated into the published version of his talks.

The task he set himself was to present plausible, empirically-based reasons for thinking that the religious or spiritual dimension of our human experience is not a fantasy, but a reality based on our biological make-up. In doing so, he was contradicting a reductionist tradition which first took its modern form in the work of the nineteenth-century German philosopher Ludwig Feuerbach. Feuerbach was a member of a politically radical group in Berlin, *Die Freien*, which included among its members Karl Marx. Their philosophical stance was broadly a borrowing, and then radical reversal, of the views of the dominant philosopher in Berlin at that time, the idealist, G. F. W. Hegel. For this reason they were called neo-Hegelians. A familiar summarising slogan about their difference is that whereas for Hegel, 'Man is an idea in the mind of God', for the neo-Hegelians, 'God is an idea in the mind of Man'. This thesis is worked out in Feuerbach's best known book, *The Essence of Christianity*, published in 1841.[19] There he made his famous assertion that God is nothing but a projection of the virtues of humankind onto an imaginary figure in the heavens. During a lecture series, given at the invitation of a group of radical students in Heidelberg in 1848,[20] he took this point further. Turning a critical eye on the view that spirituality is innate, he scornfully denied the possibility 'that man has a special organ of religion, a specific religious feeling':

> We should be more justified in assuming the existence of a specific organ of superstition. Religion, that is, the belief in gods, in spirits, in so-called higher invisible beings who rule over man, has been said to be as innate in man as his other senses. Translated into the language of honesty and reason, this would only mean that ... superstition is innate in man. But the source and strength of superstition are the power of ignorance and stupidity.[21]

Feuerbach's interpretation of religion has been highly influential in shaping subsequent expressions of sceptical opinion. This is directly acknowledged by both Marx and Freud, and is implicitly the default position of most contemporary critics of religion, even those who have never read Feuerbach. It is thus clear that Hardy was taking on an opposition that continues to be formidably powerful in the academic world.

He went about it in two stages. The first series of lectures was delivered in the session of 1963–64 and published as *The Living Stream: A Restatement of Evolution Theory and its Relation to the Spirit of Man.*[22] His purpose was to offer a new kind of basis for natural theology, not dependent on the philosophical 'argument from design' which claims to deduce the existence of God from the patterns we observe in the natural world. Within Christian culture, the most distinguished exponent of the design argument was the thirteenth-century Dominican friar, Thomas Aquinas. However, it must be emphasised that Aquinas' faith was not based on this argument: he did not think that religious belief was the result of a logical argument; rather it was the outcome of one's own experience.[23] The philosophical process was simply to demonstrate, in the context of faith, that religious belief did not run contrary to reason.

Six hundred years later, in nineteenth-century England, the argument was still in vogue. The authority on the subject was the Reverend William Paley, the Dean of Carlisle, well known at the University of Cambridge because his book, *Natural Theology,*[24] was required reading for all undergraduates. Most significantly from Hardy's point of view, Charles Darwin had read Paley while he was a theology student at Christ's College, Cambridge.[25]

The subtitle of the book is *Evidence of the Existence and Attributes of the Deity, Collected from the Appearances of Nature.* Paley's famous opening analogy is to compare the pattern apparent in nature with the design of a watch. He asks his readers to imagine someone walking across a heath, when they happen to strike their foot against a stone. Apart from a momentary jolt, the act means nothing to the walker. But suppose instead, the object was a watch. This evidence of contrivance would more likely make the walker stop short, perhaps bend down and pick up the watch. Who made it? And so, by analogy, as the existence of a watch implies a watchmaker, so the adaptations of animals and plants to their environment require the existence of a divine designer. As a student, Darwin was impressed by Paley's argument,[26] but as is well known, he himself brought about the downfall of Paley's elegant line of reasoning with the publication of *The Origin of Species* in

1859. His proposal that natural selection is the driving force in the production of adaptations to their environment in living things, dispensed with the necessity of a 'divine watchmaker', or, as Richard Dawkins bluntly put it in 1986, the watchmaker is blind.[27]

The common assumption of many eminent biologists was, and continues to be, similar to Dawkins' belief. Hardy quoted one of the world's leading authorities on evolution, George Gaylord Simpson, who was director of the American Museum of Natural History, to illustrate the standard view:

> It would be brash, indeed, to claim complete understanding of this extraordinarily intricate process, but it does seem that the problem is now essentially solved and that the mechanism of adaptation is known. It turns out to be basically materialistic, with no sign of purpose as a working variable in life history, and with any possible Purposer pushed back to the incomprehensible position of First Cause.[28]

As an illustration of this blind procedure, school children are often told a 'just-so' story of how the giraffe got its long neck. Giraffes have necks like this so that they can feed off the leaves of tall trees. If there is a bad season and the leaves are in short supply those giraffes with longer necks will be able to reach the leaves higher up the tree. In very difficult feeding conditions these animals are more likely to endure the famine than giraffes with shorter necks, and thus survive and pass on the genes for long necks to their offspring. On this thesis, the process of natural selection is directed entirely by mechanical factors outside the control of the animal.[29]

Hardy agreed with this model of selection, as far as it goes. The major thrust of his 1963–64 lecture series was to question whether the empirical evidence really supports this assumption as an exhaustive account of natural selection. His purpose in the first four talks was to exhibit what was known in the early 1960s about this process, in a form accessible to the general public. It was an orthodox presentation, in which he was at pains to emphasise his complete acceptance of the mechanistic aspects of the selective process, and the fundamental importance of the chemical properties of DNA, the complex molecule of which genes are composed.

But Hardy went on to demonstrate that impersonal mechanism by no means tells the whole story of evolution.

Therefore in the fifth lecture he began to give a series of examples of the creativity of natural selection in animals concealing themselves so that it is difficult for their predators to find them. This was a return to his expertise as a young Captain in the First World War, when he taught camouflage to army officers. He pointed out that the disguises seen in animals are far superior to the achievements of human experts. A commonplace example is the countershading exhibited by most daylight-living animals, so that they are dark on the upper surface of their bodies, merging into a paler shade on the under-surface. The adaptation makes it more difficult for a predator to see its prey, for the countershading destroys the solid appearance of the body. The importance of this as a mode of concealment is underlined in animals that, for good reason, have their countershading reversed, i.e. their upper surface is pale and their under-surface is dark. Alister gave the eccentric example of the Nile Catfish which, rather oddly, habitually swims upside down.

There is another form of concealment involving imitation or mimicry. Some of the most remarkable examples are in insects which imitate leaves, twigs and other parts of plants, to the extent of deceiving even the most careful observer. Thus the grasshopper species *Cycloptera excellens* reproduces not only the shape and veining of a leaf, it even copies the blotched appearance of a leaf infected by a fungus. Another kind of mimicry is widely used in insects as a form of protection, in which an animal masquerades as a member of another species that is dangerous or noxious to eat. Commonly in Britain, predators learn to avoid stinging insects like wasps and bees, and they also steer clear of the flies that mimic them. The mimicry can be so accurate that human beings are also deceived, as was the case of an expert beekeeper known to Hardy, who admitted that he sometimes mistook drone flies for his bees.

A still more remarkable example given by Hardy refers to what are called the Heliconid species of South American butterflies, studied by the nineteenth-century German naturalist Johann Friedrich 'Fritz' Müller. Müller had collected a large number of Heliconius butterflies with identical and very distinctive patterns of veining and orange, yellow and black colours on their wings. One day he decided to examine these specimens in more detail. To his utter astonishment, a close study of the anatomy of the butterflies made it obvious that while their wing patterns were identical, other details revealed that they belonged not merely to two different species, but were not even of the same biological family. Hardy continued the story:

> The former Heliconidae he now found to be made up of two quite distinct families ... the Heliconiinae and the Ithomiinae. He went on to show that in different parts of South America there were members of these two families having almost identical colour patterns and, further, that associated with them were often found many other butterflies and even day-flying moths having the same type of colouration. Now the Heliconiinae and the Ithomiinae are both characterised by noxious qualities and so avoided by vertebrate predators, birds, monkeys and lizards. Müller spoke of what he called a mimicry ring in which a number of species, speaking again in metaphor, clubbed together to adopt the same warning pattern, such a ring made up of noxious kinds, but also a smaller number of harmless ones.[30]

Hardy's purpose in discussing mimicry in such detail was to emphasise the fact that the selecting agent in all cases was not impersonal, but a living and conscious animal (e.g. a monkey, lizard or bird) hunting for food and therefore making choices. In these examples, natural selection is the result of a conscious selection process of extraordinary refinement, with the predator choosing which butterflies to eat and which to avoid, on the basis of small differences in the wing pattern. Because they look exactly like the nauseous species, harmless ones are left alone and thus survive. Therefore, said Hardy, to concentrate on the *inorganic* or *impersonal* environment as the main agent of selection was to ignore this much more significant evolutionary dynamic, especially in the higher mammals, including *Homo sapiens*.

In the examples mentioned, the selecting agent is the predator. But the centrepiece of Hardy's argument is the proposal that most animals *themselves* play a major part in their own evolution via their ability to change their habits. Hardy illustrated this idea by giving a practical example of the selective power of choice that happened to be in the news shortly before he gave his Gifford

Lectures. During the 1950s a new habit began appearing among Blue Tits – the opening of milk bottles, first the cardboard tops, then the metal tops – spreading, apparently by copying, right through the tit populations of Europe. Given the permanence of this change of habit, he suggested, in due course any members of the tit population with a gene complex giving a beak slightly better adapted to 'milk bottle top pecking' would have a better chance of reproducing than those less well equipped. When he presented this idea at a meeting of the Linnaean Society in London, some wit reflected on what might happen if the metal tops were made thicker, in order to combat the birds. Would they develop beaks shaped like tin openers? Exactly right, said Hardy. Active choice (and in the case of the human species, conscious choice) is, he claimed, in a majority of cases the directing agent and precursor of natural selection, certainly in higher animals. Since those days the understanding of the interaction of behaviour and biological evolution has been dramatically developed, one early example being William Durham's magisterial book, *Co-Evolution*.[31]

But here we need to be cautious. At one time it was thought that bodily changes caused by an alteration of behaviour could be passed on genetically to the next generation. For example, a seven-stone weakling who gets sand kicked in his face by bullies on the beach might decide to undertake a course of strenuous exercises to make himself into a muscle man that others would think twice about attacking. He might think his muscle-bound body would now be passed on to his offspring, enabling them to avoid the seven-stone weakling stage. This 'inheritance of acquired characteristics' was how the French biologist Jean-Baptiste Lamarck[32] explained evolutionary change, but we now know that (in general) acquired characteristics are not passed on from generation to generation. The children of the transformed weakling will not inherit his big muscles.

The interaction between (changed) behaviour and natural selection is what Hardy called 'behavioural selection'. The idea is not original to him. It is a variant of what is often called the Baldwin Effect,[33] after James Mark Baldwin, an American child psychologist, who first wrote about it in 1895. Baldwin was attempting to explain how relatively rapid bodily and behavioural adaptations could occur in animals.[34] His explanation of rapid evolutionary change looks perilously close to Lamarckism, so it is important to be clear about the difference. Take the case of a group of animals

that change their behaviour. Any random genetic variations
enhancing the survival of animals that have chosen the new behaviour will be selected for in the normal process of evolution. In other
words, behavioural change precedes genetic change. Hardy asks us
to imagine the case of a land-living animal that changes its behaviour and takes to the water, perhaps because the pressure of
growing population forces it out of its normal habitat. Is it more
likely that the appearance of a genetic variant causing webbed feet
would be selected before or after a choice to take to the water?
Surely the latter.

There have been several suggestions of examples of the Baldwin
Effect in the human species. One possible illustration concerns how
certain adult human populations have evolved a tolerance of lactose, the sugar in milk. The enzyme lactase gives infants the ability
to digest lactose, but normally the enzyme is not produced by the
body after early childhood. Consequently most adults have lost this
ability, but in some cultures where milk is drunk in large quantities
throughout life, a mutation seems to have occurred and been
selected for, which allows lactase production to continue into adult
life.[35] If indeed it is an example of the Baldwin effect, the way it has
operated is to transform the choice to make milk the staple diet in
some herding tribes between 3,000 and 8,000 years ago, so that
lactase production continuing into adult life becomes a genetically-
determined biological attribute. There is no question of the inheritance of a Lamarckian acquired characteristic, though it looks very
like it. The conscious human choice to take up milk drinking is here
the source of an evolutionary change. Changed habit supports the
natural selection of a mutation or re-assortment of genetic material
that in other circumstances would have been eliminated.

Hardy's belief that conscious choice was the most important
factor in the evolution of the higher animals, including *Homo
sapiens*, has consequences for his interpretation of spiritual awareness. Alister was convinced, on the basis of his own experience,
that members of the human species have the potential to become
aware that they are in the presence of a transcendent reality. This
turning towards transcendence is highly rewarding because along
with the awareness there is a strengthening of a sense of relationship with the rest of reality. It becomes self-evident that the
'psychological distance' between one's self and the rest of reality is
much shorter than was hitherto assumed. The primordial or instinc-

tive awareness expresses itself socially in different ways, determined by the local religious culture. In atheistic belief systems, such as the Hinayana in Buddhism, Enlightenment brings with it the realisation that separation into this or that, you or me, is an illusion, for all is One. In the Monotheist, direct experience of the presence of God, usually but not always as the result of contemplative prayer, brings about a similar realisation of unity. All things are the creation of the one God and therefore demand our equal respect.

One recent philosopher, Emmanuel Levinas, expresses this primordial sense of obligation when he speaks of 'ethics as first philosophy'.[36] Before any kind of extended thought whatsoever, be it scientific, religious or philosophical, thought Levinas, we find in the immediacy of our awareness an obligation to care for the Other, even to the extent of self-sacrifice. Levinas also spoke of the importance of the gaze, for according to him it is when I gaze, simply and unaffectedly, at another person, I find in myself a duty towards them. Since Levinas, who was Jewish, lost all his family in the Holocaust, it would seem that the horrific ending of his relatives' lives indicates that his philosophy was misplaced and hopelessly over-optimistic. His response was to assert that barbaric cruelty or plain blindness to the needs of the Other comes about when social evolution runs counter to the biological evolution of altruism, e.g. when a Nazi concentration camp guard is training for the task, he spends a great deal of time learning that Jews are not fellow human beings, so that the natural innocent gaze becomes blocked. A specific kind of socialisation blinds him to his primordially inbuilt ethics.

Hardy had most likely never heard of Emmanuel Levinas, but his insistence on the social and political importance of spirituality arises from an insight that is very like Levinas' realisation.[37] It has social implications of a highly positive kind. Hence the community is likely to benefit to the extent that its members persevere with what amounts to contemplative prayer or meditation. Given this choice on the part of the individual, genetic mutations or re-assortments that strengthen this dimension of awareness are selected for. What was originally a socially constructed choice turns into a biologically-determined reality, with the resulting accumulation of what is nowadays often referred to as 'social capital' or 'spiritual capital'.[38] A helpful comparison may be to consider 'instinct' in a similar way. What originally was a culturally-mediated choice becomes, through natural selection, a more and more automatic and biologically-determined process.

If, for the sake of following where Hardy's hypothesis leads us we assume (temporarily) that he is right, the next problem must concern the biological nature of the experience. Even to pose this query is to enter into very complex and difficult philosophical territory and to question commonly-held basic tenets of the post-Enlightenment picture of reality. As an empiricist, Alister had no doubts about the reality of his and others' reported experience and he chose not to go along with Feuerbach. This was new territory, hence proposed explanations must inevitably be highly speculative, and Alister chose to conjecture in terms drawn from psychical research, to the extent that he gave over the whole of his Ninth Lecture to the subject. Alister's view of such matters was extremely open – unusually so for an empirical scientist, for most of whom such alleged phenomena are dismissed as nonsensical because they conflict with the standard ontology of mainstream science.

There is of course a popular interest in psychic phenomena that has much to do with entertainment, laced with credulity. Alister's own mother was not averse to visiting fortune tellers and wrote to him in his teens, naïvely excited, when one of them predicted, as fortune tellers are inclined to do, that her son would have a successful career. His mother's credulity may have swayed Alister to the extent that he did not close his mind about psychic phenomena. Events that seem to defy the standard view of reality can be approached with varying degrees of naïvety or scepticism, with common sense lying somewhere between the extremes. Alister's attempts to grapple with the phenomenon were at the common sense point, and were triggered by a chance meeting during the First World War. A patriotic lady by the name of Mrs Wedgwood happened to be entertaining a party of young army officers in her home in Lincolnshire. Alister was one of the young men and, while he was there, she happened to mention that she was a spiritualist medium. At the request of her guests she demonstrated her clair-voyant ability. Hardy was sufficiently impressed to make it his business to befriend her, and her subsequent displays of clairvoy-ance continued to surprise him. The cases were in themselves trivial. One example was when she exclaimed suddenly to Alister at the dinner table: 'Oh, what have you been doing? I see a large pink square on the table in front of you.'[39]

That afternoon he had been painting a large piece of white cardboard with pink distemper. He had been repeatedly looking intently at the pink square to see if it was dry, because he was anxious to get on with his task, which involved cutting the square into smaller pieces. Puzzled by Mrs Wedgwood's abilities, Alister decided to make a thorough study of the literature on psychic phenomena. He came to the conclusion that there was a genuine reality there which ought to be amenable to scientific investigation, and he decided to join the Society for Psychical Research (SPR).[40]

However, when as Chairman of Section D he gave his British Association Lecture in 1949 to fellow zoologists, he made clear that this kind of explanation might prove to be futile:

> It may be that I am making a tactical, or even strategic, mistake in introducing the subject into this course of lectures. By so doing I may be diverting attention away from the main argument I have presented in support of habit and behaviour as important elements in orthodox evolution theory. I run the risk of perhaps making people believe that I regard something like telepathy as essential to this process; I must make it quite clear that I do *not* regard it as at all *essential* to the principle I have hitherto presented.[41]

In 1973, a decade after he retired, Hardy, along with Robert Harvie and Arthur Koestler, wrote *The Challenge of Chance*. It is about an experiment conducted in Caxton Hall, on seven consecutive Monday evenings in 1967, by Hardy with the help of Robert Harvie, a psychologist and statistician. The object of the experiment was to test the reality of extra-sensory perception using a group of approximately 200 volunteers drawn from the membership of the SPR acting as 'agents', seated round but not in visual contact with a small group of 'percipients'. The percipients were in booths which prevented them seeing the agents and each other. The agents were shown a succession of drawings or slides and the percipients were asked to guess what the picture showed. Hardy's notion was that having a large number of agents would multiply the effect of any telepathic phenomena that might be present.

The results illustrate the complexities associated with such research. Only a small percentage of direct hits were recorded, but there were quite a number of curious instances of coincident thoughts recorded by percipients sitting in adjacent booths. *The Challenge of Chance* gives a very detailed account of the methodology and results, along with speculation about the phenomena by the two researchers and the third author, Arthur Koestler. It cannot be said that the results demonstrate the existence of ESP in the way that Hardy might have wished, although the coincident thoughts on the part of some percipients seemed to suggest telepathy. The experiment was thus in some ways a disappointment, as is the book. Further doubt was cast on the validity of the conclusions in 1989, when two senior mathematicians at Harvard University, Persi Diaconis and Frederick Mosteller, published an influential paper on statistical methods for studying coincidences.[42] One of the examples they used to illustrate statistical inadequacy was *The Challenge of Chance* and it must be admitted that the questionable mathematics damaged Hardy's case for the reality of telepathy, at least as far as the findings reported in the book are concerned.

The existence of telepathy, as Alister had noted at the beginning of his British Association lecture, is not an essential part of his main argument. What the admittedly flawed book *The Challenge of Chance* does demonstrate is Hardy's determination to hold steadily to a scientific approach to reality, thus he did not shy away from experimental investigations in this difficult and controversial field. It also underlines his insistence that the avoidance of psychical phenomena by mainstream science was not entirely rational. He felt that the previously mentioned rebuff he received from his fellow scientists was based on a prior decision that the standard picture of reality inherited from the European Enlightenment was not open to question. Alister might have compared this rejection to the alleged refusal of the philosophy professors in Pisa to look through Galileo's telescope. Their knowledge of Aristotle's cosmology enabled them to dismiss his claims as nonsense so there was no need to check what was, to them, self-evident.

Hardy's final lecture in the first series is a plea for a scientific approach to the primary experience of a transcendent presence, an experience that he believed was everybody's birthright. Only in this way could religion be rationally restructured to take account of the realities of life in our time. Alister persisted to the end in labelling such experience 'religious', but his own claims for universality make this seem not quite right. People who reject religion are not thereby denied a universal part of human biology, therefore it is less confusing to refer to such experience as 'spiritual', with 'religious' experience as a sub-set within that category. This distinction cannot always be maintained when quoting from writings on the subject because they use the traditional nomenclature. Therefore when the term 'religious experience' is used it will often refer to the larger, spiritual category.

This leads us to a consideration of the second series of lectures, published as *The Divine Flame*.[43] In agreement with Edmund Burke, Hardy believed that we are *Homo religiosus*, 'religious animals'. As we have seen, in his view, as part of the process of consciously investigating their environment, the precursors of the human species discovered their relationship to a transcendent presence that met them in a different way from everyday phenomena. Throughout the second series Hardy is constantly attempting to convey the immediacy and intensity of the experience. In his fifth lecture he gives two significant examples of what he means.

The first example is borrowed from Rudolf Otto, a German philosopher/theologian who particularly impressed Alister. Otto's most important book is *Das Heilige,* translated as *The Idea of the Holy* for the English edition. The use of the word 'idea' in the translation is unfortunate, because Otto was attempting to get beyond concepts to reach towards what he conceived to be the primordial *mysterium tremendum.* To try to encompass this realm he invented the term *numinous* as a portmanteau word to refer to the experience of the sacred. In an appendix to *The Idea of the Holy*,[44] Otto reproduces a description of an ecstatic moment experienced by the English art critic, John Ruskin (it will be remembered that he had a hand in the building of the Oxford University Museum):

Lastly, although there was no definite religious sentiment mingled with it, there was a continual perception of Sanctity in the whole of nature, from the slightest thing to the vastest; an instinctive awe, mixed with delight; an indefinable thrill, such as we sometimes imagine to indicate the presence of a disembodied spirit. I could only feel this perfectly when I was alone; and then it would often make me shiver from head to foot with the joy and fear of it, when after being some time away from hills I first got to the shore of a mountain river, where the brown water circled among the pebbles, or when I first saw the swell of distant land against the sunset, or the first low broken wall, covered with mountain moss. I cannot in the least describe the feeling; but I do not think this is my fault or the fault of the English language, for I am afraid no feeling is describable. If we had to explain the feeling of bodily hunger to a person who had never felt it, we should be hard put to it for words; and the joy in nature seemed to me to come to a sort of heart hunger, satisfied with the presence of a Great and Holy Spirit ... these feelings remained in their full intensity till I was eighteen or twenty, and then, as the reflective and practical power increased, and the 'cares of this world' gained upon me, faded gradually away, in the manner described by Wordsworth in his 'Intimations of Immortality'.[45]

Ruskin was a religious believer, and since Alister was keen to emphasise spiritual awareness as a human universal, his second example is drawn from *The Story of My Heart* by the secular mystic Richard Jefferies. In Jefferies' case he retained his vision until the end of his short life (he died of tuberculosis at the age of 38):

I was not more than eighteen when an inner and esoteric meaning began to come to me from all the visible universe, and indefinable aspirations filled me. I found them in the grass fields, under the trees, on the hill tops, at sunrise, and in the night. There was a deep meaning everywhere. The sun burned with it, the broad front of morning beamed with it; a deep feeling entered me while gazing at the sky in the azure noon, and in the star-lit evening.[46]

In these examples it is important to emphasise that what Otto, Jefferies and Hardy are referring to is immediate, here-and-now practical experience and definitely not some kind of detached intellectual exercise. While there is no doubt that each account is pervaded by cultural presuppositions, these are implicit and not part of a discursive thinking process.

An illustration will help to clarify this important point. One of the letters sent in to Hardy's Religious Experience Research Unit[47] in Oxford is a recollection of a painful incident:

> The following occurred at a time when I had no feeling for religion. It was not the result of religious ecstasy or a joyous heightening of the spirit. A certain event had hurt and humiliated me. I rushed to my room in a state of despair, feeling as worthless as an empty shell. From this point of utter emptiness it was as though I were caught up in another dimension. My separate self ceased to exist and for a fraction of time I seemed part of a timeless immensity of power and joy and light. Something beyond this domain of life and death. My subjective and painful feelings vanished. The intensity of the vision faded, but it has remained as a vivid memory ever since. *Years later I read of Pascal's moment of illumination and was amazed at the similarity of mine.*[Italics added]

The final sentence in this quotation is a reference to the seventeenth-century French mathematician Blaise Pascal's 'second conversion', an experience that overwhelmed him on the night of 23 November 1654. It was so important to Pascal that he wrote a description on a piece of parchment and sewed into his clothing, where it was found after his death. It reads:

> FIRE,
> God of Abraham, God of Isaac, God of Jacob, not of the philosophers and savants.
> Certitude. Certitude. Feeling. Joy. Peace.
> God of Jesus Christ.

My God and thy God.

'Thy God shall be my God'

Forgetfulness of the world and of everything except God.

He is to be found only in the ways taught in the Gospel.

Grandeur of the human soul.

Righteous Father, the world hath not known Thee, but I have known Thee.

Joy, joy, joy, tears of joy.

I have fallen from Him.

'They have forsaken Me, the fountain of living waters.'

'My God wilt Thou forsake me?'

May I not fall from Him for ever.

This is life eternal, that they might know Thee, the only true God,

and Jesus Christ whom Thou has sent.

Jesus Christ.

Jesus Christ.

I have fallen away: I have fled from Him, denied Him, crucified Him.

May I not fall from Him for ever.

We hold him only by the ways taught in the Gospel.

Renunciation total and sweet.

Total submission to Jesus Christ and to my director.

Eternally in joy for a day's exercise on earth.

I will not forget thy word. Amen.[48]

When we compare these two texts, separated by more than three hundred years, it is quite obvious that at one level the modern description is not in the slightest bit like Pascal's account. Pascal's parchment is passionately Catholic and floridly devotional, mentioning the words 'God' or 'Jesus' more than twenty times. The modern account is spare, minimal and restrained and the writer positively denies that his experience has any reference to God or religious belief. So why does this correspondent say he was 'amazed at the similarity' between his experience and that of Pascal?

One published commentary on both these passages asserts explicitly that 'it is plain that Pascal is not trying to record the happening as it occurred, he is using it as a peg on which to hang an affirmation of Catholic loyalty.'[49] The commentary seems to be

asking 'What really happened, as opposed to what Pascal mislead-
ingly *tells* us happened?', with the implication that the modern
account is a good deal nearer the truth. The man who sent in the
modern narrative to the Religious Experience Research Unit
doesn't seem to be bothered by that question, and assumes that he
and Pascal are really talking about the same experience with
different words. This implies that he sees himself (and Pascal) as
having to use language, with all its cultural limitations to communicate something of a 'primordial' human experience, a bodily
awareness or 'felt sense' that is there before words or thinking
happens. Furthermore that awareness was already pregnant with
meaning before he opened his mouth or sat down to write a letter
about it to Hardy's Research Unit.

All human experience, secular as well as religious, is inevitably
theory-laden, because it is conveyed to us by some language or
other. It follows that the primordial basis of human universals like
tasting, seeing, touching, is creatively expressed in many different
and at times contradictory ways. Opinions about food for example
can be totally at odds, as in the case of the prohibition on eating
pork among Jewish people, whereas to others it may be a luxury.
No one, secular or religious, denies that we need food if we are to
stay alive. Religious experience is in Hardy's opinion like that. It
appears in a multitude of cultural forms, but wherever it is genuine,
it is based on a primordial biological reality, already there before
cultural expression.

Hardy turns for help to the philosopher-scientist Michael Polanyi,
whose Gifford Lectures were also given in Aberdeen University.
Published as *Personal Knowledge*, they introduce the notion of
preverbal knowing, or *tacit* knowledge, which we share with other
animals. As such it is primordial and, as Polanyi insists: 'We always
know more than we can say'. When we come out with words to
express our experience, we immediately restrict it to what can be
said in the culture to which we belong, as the person reporting the
'Pascal type' experience instinctively knew. Giving expression to
our personal knowingness is always at the mercy of the culture (or
cultures) in which we find ourselves. For Alister Hardy, spiritual or
religious awareness belongs in this realm of tacit knowing and
furthermore it has evolved by the process of natural selection. In
other words, it has been retained because it plays an essential part
in the survival of the animal.

How far back in evolutionary terms this consciousness might stretch is not clear, but Hardy certainly assumed that it was not confined to the human species. In other words he is thinking of a biological predisposition that is not a construction of language, though of course from his perspective, discourse about this consciousness is more or less universally manifested in the world's religions, great and small. At the same time it is important to emphasise that the religions of the world do not own spiritual awareness. There is such a thing as secular spirituality.[50] As we have seen, Alister believed the biological reason for the natural selection of this predisposition was that it has survival value to the individual.[51] One of the most convincing parts of the initial argument is Hardy's reference to social anthropology, possibly with advice from his friend E. E. Evans-Pritchard, who was Professor of Anthropology in Oxford and latterly an adviser to Hardy's Religious Experience Research Unit. Alister was particularly impressed by the work of the French scholar Émile Durkheim. Here he quotes from Durkheim's masterpiece on religion, the *Elementary Forms of the Religious Life*:

> The believer who has communicated with his god is not merely a man who sees new truths of which the unbeliever is ignorant; he is a man who is *stronger*. He feels within him more force, either to endure the trials of existence or to conquer them. It is as though he were raised above the miseries of the world, because he is raised above his condition as a mere man; he believes that he is saved from evil, under whatever form he may conceive this evil.[52]

And later:

> Our entire study rests upon this postulate that the unanimous sentiment of the believers of all times cannot be purely illusory. Together with a recent apologist of the faith [He is referring here to William James] we admit that these religious beliefs rest upon a specific experience whose demonstrative value is, in one sense, not one bit inferior to that of scientific experiments, though different from them.[53]

Hardy adds his view that an unfortunate 'materialist spin' is often put on Durkheim's interpretation of religion:

> Many, who perhaps have not read Durkheim sufficiently carefully, have thought, I believe, that his theory of religion is one linking it to a *mechanistic* interpretation of the evolution of man as a social animal. Nothing could be further from the truth, as is clearly shown when he says, 'it is necessary to avoid seeing in this theory of religion a simple restatement of historical materialism: that would be mistaking our thought to an extreme degree'.[54]

Hardy also refers to R. R. Marett, who preceded Evans-Pritchard as Professor of Anthropology in Oxford. Summarising his conclusions after a life dedicated to anthropology, Marett repeatedly stressed how in 'primitive' religion one always sees evidence of a living contact with a power that helps him in his life:

> It is the common experience of man that he can draw on a power that makes for, and in its most typical form wills, righteousness, the sole condition being that a certain fear, a certain shyness and humility accompany the effort so to do. That such a universal belief exists among all mankind, and that it is no less universally helpful in the highest degree, is the abiding impression left on my mind by the study of religion in its historico-scientific aspect.[55]

Alister turned especially to William James' masterpiece, *The Varieties of Religious Experience*, which is the published version of his Gifford Lectures, given in Edinburgh University in 1901–02. What interested Hardy was the pioneering empirical research conducted by James' doctoral student, Edwin Starbuck. James himself did no empirical research, but relied on Starbuck's investigations for many of his examples.

A couple of points need to be made in relation to Starbuck. He was a New Englander, studying theology in the Harvard Divinity School, who crossed an academic boundary to work with William James in the psychology department at Harvard. It is the general view that James was rather blind to the social dimension and, as one critic said, he had illegitimately gathered together a very mixed bag of experience and gave it the title 'religious'.[56] But in the case of Starbuck there was not a particular problem because the people he interviewed came from a relatively uniform religious background, that is to say, broadly they belonged to evangelical Protestantism, much preoccupied with salvation and the reassurance of religious experience.[57] This eased the way by reducing cross-cultural linguistic problems and as a result Starbuck was able to produce the first formal attempt to collect and classify religious experience, anywhere.

A curious historical sidelight is the fact that Estlin Carpenter, eventually Principal of Manchester College, Oxford spent a sabbatical as a chaplain in the Harvard Divinity School at the time when Starbuck was doing the fieldwork for his PhD. Starbuck gave Carpenter a pile of his questionnaires to take back to distribute to students in Manchester College and as far as we know they were the only set used outside New England. Hardy was unaware of this coincidence.

Although he was able to identify a number of precursors of his ideas, Hardy's Aberdeen lectures are in fact revolutionary in that they offer a testable naturalistic hypothesis about the nature and function of human spirituality that is not reductionist in intention. In this respect he is clearly at odds with major explanatory conjectures about religion that are currently dominant in the social sciences, that is to say, Marxist and Freudian hypotheses which, at least in their origins, were attempts to account for the phenomenon of religion conceived of as an almost universal human error. In spite of Hardy's remarks which were mentioned earlier, it is perhaps appropriate to include Durkheim as the third member of a reductionist triumvirate, perhaps not personally, but through many of his modern followers who do seem to interpret him in that way. Thus his statement that religious experience *is* the effervescence or excitement experienced in crowded religious gatherings has frequently attracted the prefix 'nothing but'.

Hardy's originality grew out of a stubborn empiricism, which refuses to bow down before the social constructions of our European history. Alister would not allow his own experience to be denied or reduced and in this respect he was less caught up in the presuppositions of post-Enlightenment culture than his reductionist predecessors. Paradoxically of course, in breaking free, he utilised the methodology of empirical science deriving from the Enlightenment to create a new kind of natural theology. Instead of coming at the sacred indirectly, by means of natural philosophy or the argument from design (as did Newton and Paley), he urged the necessity of looking directly at our religious experience.

On the whole the Aberdeen lectures received a remarkably positive critical response in the national media. In view of some criticisms of his understanding of the scientific method, it must have given Alister a boost to receive a letter from Karl Popper, already recognised as one of the finest living philosophers of science, praising *The Living Stream*. Popper continued to hold that view and in his autobiography, published in 1976, referred to it as 'Alister Hardy's great book'.[58] Hardy was also particularly fortunate that Arthur Koestler was invited to do the review of *The Divine Flame* for the *New Scientist*. In a letter to Hardy, dated 4 January 1967, Koestler wrote:

> I wonder what you thought of the review in the *New Scientist*. It was a kind of tightrope walk. There seems to be a change of heart in that paper, indicated *inter alia* by their printing Cyril Burt's long letter on ESP, and by the fact that instead of passing *The Divine Flame* in silence, or politely slaughtering it, they asked me to review it – knowing of course that the review would be favourable. (It was, incidentally, the first time that they asked me to review a book – after having my own last book reviewed by *Essence*, with foreseeable results). Given this background, I thought it advisable to tread cautiously and to avoid the atheists' delicate toes.[59]

The atheists' toes were not necessarily as delicate as Koestler assumed. The Aberdeen psychologist Margaret Knight had gained national notoriety in January 1955 for two talks she gave on the radio arguing the case for a morality that was not based on religion. She was headlined by one newspaper in two-inch-high capitals as the 'Unholy Mrs Knight'. The article went on to accuse the BBC of allowing 'a fanatic to rampage along the air lanes, beating up Christianity with a razor and bicycle chain'.[60] In spite of that, in a letter dated 2 August 1966, she wrote:

Dear Sir Alistair, … I have been reading *The Living Stream* with the greatest interest. I don't, of course, share your qualified theism, but I find your personal approach so much more congenial than what Sir Julian Huxley has called nothing buttery.[61]

Huxley himself was ambivalently amused by the lectures, remarking that Alister had begun by studying the plankton in the oceans, moved on to the plankton in the air, and it seemed that now he was investigating the plankton of the mind. Alister was undeterred, and, buoyed up by the success of the lectures, he felt ready to take on the next challenge: to found a research institution to investigate the plausibility and resilience to testing of his hypothesis about the nature of our religious or spiritual experience.

FULL MOON, MARISCHAL COLLEGE, UNIVERSITY OF ABERDEEN

CHAPTER TEN

The Religious Experience Research Unit

The success of the Gifford Lectures added fire to Alister's ambition to found an institution dedicated to testing his 'religious experience' hypothesis. He had often stated his belief that if even one-tenth of the financial support given to mainstream empirical science was made available for research into our spiritual nature, it would bring about a wholly benevolent revolution in the desperately impoverished spiritual life of the West. Now he discovered in himself an intense desire to convince the powers-that-be of the necessity for that change. The most immediate practical necessity was to identify a suitable location to house the new institute and attract enough financial backing to give it long-term stability. In many ways, it was to be the most difficult and taxing period of his life, for the effort exposed just how powerfully the surrounding culture was pulling in the opposite direction.

Hardy found himself in a radically weakened bargaining position when he withdrew from his Chair, where he was used to being listened to with respect. It is true that after his retirement his former status continued to function by opening doors that were closed to more anonymous scholars, but the political and financial muscle he had enjoyed as an Oxford don had largely evaporated. Now he was vulnerable to the cold winds of scepticism and a scientific establishment that at best gave little more than lip service to the spiritual life and at worst treated it with contempt. Representatives of scientifically-minded funding bodies were almost always polite to Alister because of his reputation, but indifferent to his requests for financial support. Subjectively, Alister's experience was of shifting from a position near the top of the scientific hierarchy, to finding himself beyond the pale, an outlaw.

Nor were his unorthodox theological opinions much more acceptable to the religious establishment. The result of his rejection of a great deal of orthodox religious doctrine meant that his proposed research into the biological basis of human spirituality made him equally an outsider from the main stream of religion. One outcome was his feeling that it was impossible for him to remain with integrity as a member of the Church of England. Eventually he found a home in the Unitarian Church,[1] which in Oxford meant attachment to Manchester College, though even here he was to find himself in difficulties.

To understand Alister's problems with the college, it is necessary to refer briefly to the history of Unitarianism in England. During the seventeenth century the Unitarians, who deny the divinity of Jesus, came to prominence as the result of discrimination against them by the national government. At that time religious dissent was a potential source of political instability and in an attempt to force dissenters to conform to the beliefs of the Established Church, an Act of Uniformity was passed in 1662. The Act disempowered members of non-conforming groups by requiring them to swear allegiance to the Church of England on entry to the grammar schools and universities. This was more than many of them were prepared to do. The Unitarians, along with other dissenters, responded by creating their own educational establishments, the first of which was opened in the village of Rathmell in the North Riding of Yorkshire, during 1669–70. In time these 'dissenting academies' prospered and came to offer an education that in many cases was at university level. Eventually in 1786 an academy was opened in Manchester, which after many ups and downs shifted to Oxford in 1889. The Unitarians were able to fund a building project and four years later, in 1893, Manchester College (now renamed Harris-Manchester College) opened its doors to students.

The record of their mistreatment by the Establishment meant that the original move to Oxford was not favoured by all Unitarians. Some felt that it amounted to a capitulation from the ideals of Unitarianism, for either the college would be swallowed up by the far larger and more powerful university, or, equally uncomfortably, it had the prospect of being ignored and frozen out.[2] Alister Hardy was largely oblivious of this history, but it was here, in Manchester College, that he came to worship, in the beautiful college chapel with its fine set of Burne-Jones stained glass windows. His presence did not go unnoticed. His congenial religious opinions and his acknowledged academic eminence within the university persuaded the college authorities that it would be an advantage to elect him its Honorary President, a position which he held from 1959 until 1975.

Now that he was an insider to Unitarianism (or so he believed), Alister realised that he might be able to persuade the college to help him in his attempt to set up his new research unit. He had been thinking about his strategy since 1966, but his campaign really began in earnest when he published an article entitled 'Science and an Experimental Faith' in the summer 1968 issue of *Faith and Freedom*. This journal had been founded by former students of Manchester College, and was directed specifically at a Unitarian audience. Alister's essay was a brief resumé of the main points of his Gifford Lectures, and was designed to make his co-religionists familiar with his ideas. The article also contained a thought-provoking question, which shifted the argument to a new level:

> Is it not possible that modern humanistic man, excited by the success of the scientific method, and exalted by a liberation from the absurdities of mediaeval thought, has been carried into a new realm of dogmatic folly only a little less absurd than that which preceded it? *Could he be making a gigantic mistake?* [Hardy's italics][3]

Hardy was certainly not consciously a postmodernist, but he did make the point that culturally-determined presuppositions could blind even the most brilliant minds. People of the stature of Dante, Milton and Michelangelo had a literal belief in what most educated people today would class as medieval mythology. But it is not only people from past ages who are trapped by mythology. All of us find ourselves situated within a culture which shapes our basic assumptions about the nature of reality. Alister felt that the materialist beliefs too dogmatically held by many contemporary scientists were without logical support and amounted to a superstition as unsupported as any medieval myth. He was inviting his readers to be flexible enough to make the difficult imaginative leap to a position where they could see the inevitable limitations of inflexible scientific orthodoxy, equally vulnerable to being trapped in logically unsustainable dogmatism (in this case, materialism) as were our medieval forebears.

No one is exempt from the processes of social construction, but critical realists like Hardy have the conviction that there are ways of questioning the adequacy of cultural myth and reaching towards the 'given' reality.[4] Alister was an empiricist who believed that the surest way out of the labyrinth was by direct examination of the phenomena, that is, reality as it presents itself to us in our immediate situation. This always requires the application of the methods of empirical science, but it would have to be a flexible science, untrammelled by materialist presuppositions, open to all aspects of what it is to be human, including those areas of experience that Hardy surmised to underlie religious belief. He hastened to add that even the scientific method had its limitations and that many forms of human experience – awareness of love, of beauty, of existence itself – were beyond its scope. In the same way, the essence of religion was beyond the purview of science, but what *was* investigable was the undeniable phenomenon of spiritual experience.

Hardy assumed that the lack of rigid dogmatism among Unitarians ought to imply sympathy with his cause, but would their religious openness extend to giving him practical help with the setting up of his new research unit? The next step was to approach the Manchester College Council and see if the members were willing to back his plan. In his initial proposal, Alister noted:

> Just as Nuffield College is a centre for research in social studies, I would like to see Manchester College, in addition to being a teaching institution, become a recognised centre into those fields which are fundamental to what a modern liberal religion is all about: religious experience, the nature of man's personality and his relation to divinity.[5]

Hardy had in mind some examples of the kind of investigations that he would like to see undertaken:[6]

> An extension and development of those pioneer studies by Professor E. D. Starbuck (*The Psychology of Religion: An*

Empirical Study of the Growth of Religious Consciousness, 1899)[7] and by William James (*The Varieties of Religious Experience: A Study in Human Nature,* 1902). These classics have never been added to in the same spirit in which they were undertaken, and they were confined to people (mainly university students) of a particular Protestant Christian community. As James says regarding Starbuck's work, 'the enquiry ought to be extended to other lands and to populations of other faiths' ... [Along with this programme there would be] surveys and analyses by questionnaire of other mystical experiences among different populations – on the lines of the agnostic author Marghanita Laski in her *Ecstasy: A Study of some Secular and Religious Experiences* (1961).[8]

The new centre would be called the Religious Experience Research Unit (RERU). At a meeting of the College Council he explained his basic needs for space and the necessary finance to give stability to the Unit. The sum he had in mind was at least £500,000 or more, perhaps as much as £1,000,000.[9] He hoped to accumulate this sum from a variety of sources, including the royalties accruing from *The Divine Flame*, fees from a forthcoming lecture tour in the United States, and donations and legacies from benevolently disposed individuals.[10]

Several members of Manchester College Council were more than a little alarmed by Alister's proposal. Behind their unease lay the long story of differing opinions about the wisdom of the move to Oxford. Most prominently among the doubters was the Principal of the college, H. L. Short. Short had at first been in sympathy with Hardy but, when practical measures were about to be taken to open the Unit, he began to feel worried about the weight of moral commitment being placed on the college. He sent round a circular, on 26 March 1969, to six senior members of the Council expressing his concern. Short explained that when he first heard of Alister's plan he assumed that it was on a small scale, but at the latest meeting (on 25 March, i.e. the day before he sent the circular) he realised that the project was much more ambitious. He felt that the Council had been somewhat naïve in letting Alister have the use of the cottage at 24 Holywell Street at a nominal rent. Now, in addition to the huge sum of money that Hardy intended to amass, he was already asking for the use of a second building, the old stables.[11]

Short felt that if Alister succeeded in fulfilling his ambitions, his new Unit would dominate the college to such an extent that it would destroy its Unitarian character. The endowments of Manchester College as a whole were only in the region of £250,000, a quarter of what Hardy was hoping to collect. Furthermore, Hardy also insisted that his Unit was to be completely independent of the college, as Short discovered when he asked whether one of Hardy's staff could be employed as a college tutor. The answer was 'No'. Another discomfort was Alister's desire to negotiate for the college to become a constituent member of the university, so that his research staff could work for a higher degree. This in itself would speed the loss of Unitarian influence. Finally, Short found Alister's repeated reference to his heart being in the Church of England, but his head with the Unitarians, irritating and somehow disloyal:

> ... he has also said that if the Church of England were to become more liberal he would rejoin it. Most of us whose heart is in the Unitarian cause find this attitude distasteful.[12]

Short was not alone. Another influential member of the Council was George Lee, the minister of the Unitarian Church in Exeter, and well-known for his agonised preaching style.[13] He too was disturbed by Alister's plans. He sent round his own circular to the Council members and wrote a long and heated letter of protest to Alister himself. He worried about the management of the boundary between the Unit and the college. Would the principal be a member of the governing body? What would happen if the new institution became very successful? Would it not flatten the college as a Unitarian community, built by the sacrifices of past generations of Unitarians? And what about the advisory committee that Alister had appointed? They were eminent scholars, but not one of them was a Unitarian.[14] The college was weak and Unitarianism itself in desperate straits. How was it that a minority of the members of the Council could bamboozle the rest into falling into this dangerously dependent state on outsiders who probably had no feel for the ideals of the Unitarians?

The suspicions surrounding Alister's typically vivacious personal presentation of his ideas were rooted in the Unitarian history described above, which was well-known to members of the Council. Alister was hurt by the fears and accusations, which he eventually got to hear about while he was on holiday in Malta in the summer of 1969. He wrote to George Lee, admitting that he now felt a sense of regret that in his enthusiasm he had ridden rough-shod over the sensitivities of the Council. He tried to reassure Lee about the panel of advisers, pointing out that the members were very unlikely to meet as a corporate body, they were simply a set of experts who could be called upon for advice. Consequently they would have no direct say in the life of Manchester College. He added that he believed the work of the Unit, far from undermining the Unitarian cause, would be of great service to that cause.

Despite the reservations of Short, George Lee and perhaps some others, Alister's disarming honesty and directness meant that he was able to get his way with the Council. But as subsequent events proved, the endorsement of his programme did not clear away all of the suspicions.[15] In October 1969 the Unit opened in the cottage at 24 Holywell Street, on the south east corner of the land owned by Manchester College. The cottage was very shabby but engagingly quaint. For all its discomforts, it was the sort of place that would be remembered affectionately as the starting point of the Unit. Hardy tried to civilise the rooms by laying down hardwearing carpets but could not disguise the dilapidation. He was now 73 but still full of enthusiasm and greatly excited by what he had begun. All of his resilience would be needed. The Unit continued to struggle financially, and until the very end of his life he never succeeded in getting anywhere near the level of funding that he felt was necessary. The extremely powerful cultural bias already referred to ruled that the field of his investigations was, at best, a curiosity of no social or political importance; at worst it was a delusion. Alister willingly, even joyfully accepted the strain of maintaining morale and good humour in this position, but it probably had a negative effect on his health.

Once he was established in the building, Alister wasted no time in getting started. Indeed he had advertised his work already, before he moved in. He was a naturalist by temperament and thought of his task as analogous to the work of the great Victorian naturalists. By their scouring of the globe in search of new and exotic animals and plants, they created the collections stored in the Natural History Museums that now dot the world. The next task of the biologists was the slow process of classifying these organisms. Alister felt he knew something of this from the painfully tedious labour of his colleague Rolfe Gunther on the material brought back from the *Discovery* expedition. It was toil of this kind that eventually provided the database from which Darwin derived the theory of natural selection. Therefore, by analogy, Alister's first intention was to gather many 'specimens' of spiritual/religious experience and then proceed to classify them. He went about this by soliciting responses from the general public to a question that he had devised, based on his own experience of transcendence:

> Have you ever been aware of, or influenced by a presence or a power, whether you call it God or not, that is different from your everyday self?

The question has been criticised by social scientists as having a vague meaning, and for being over-complex. Their criticisms are justifiable, but in spite of its portmanteau quality, in practice, people seemed to recognise the realm of experience to which Hardy was referring.[16] In his first attempt at specimen collection he used the question as the centrepiece of appeals in some 50 journals and newspapers associated with religion; for example, the *Catholic Herald*, the *Church Times* and the *Methodist Recorder*. Readers were asked to consider whether they were aware of any such experience in their own lives and if so, to write to Professor Hardy in Oxford describing their experience and its effects on them. He also asked for details of their age, sex, nationality, religious upbringing and any other factors that might be relevant.

It had seemed sensible to start by concentrating on religious publications, but the early response was thoroughly depressing. Following the nationwide publicity campaign, he received rather less than 250 replies and they were highly unrepresentative of the general population, being in the main from elderly women. The fact that most of them were obviously intelligent and articulate did little to assuage Alister's feeling that his Unit was, after all, chasing species of experience that were well on their way to becoming extinct.

Then Hardy had several strokes of luck. First the editor of the *Guardian* newspaper asked him if he would be prepared to be interviewed by Geoffrey Moorhouse for an article on the work of the Unit. He agreed on condition that he was permitted to publish an appeal for accounts of experience. Subsequently the same request was made by the editor of the *Guardian's* sister paper, the *Observer.* The journalist Peter Lewis did a feature article for the colour supplement, with the title: 'Is a Kinsey Report on Religion Possible?'[17] In a humorous reference to Hardy's views on behavioural selection, the article was accompanied by a caricature of him with his head shaped like a milk bottle with blue tits pecking at the top. Lewis emphasised Hardy's belief that the world he was studying was hidden from view, by quoting him:

> All my life I have sampled the sea, building up an
> ecological picture of a hidden world, which I could not
> examine at first hand, even with an aqualung. In a way, I
> am casting my nets into a different kind of ocean.

Hardy was aware that the political stance of the *Observer* meant that the article would likely be read by a substantial number of people who were sceptical of the claims of religion. Therefore he took the opportunity to point out that rigid adherence to particular mechanistic assumptions could be compared to the persecution of scientists like Galileo who took up a stance at odds with the dominant world picture in his day. Scientists who choose to examine experience which cannot be easily explained using contemporary scientific criteria are largely ignored, and publicising their openness to such phenomena could mean the death of their scientific career. Alister had in mind his own professional history. He had avoided serious disaster and managed to achieve a senior position at the heart of the scientific establishment, because he knew when to keep his mouth shut.

Peter Lewis pictured him as a new Darwin:

> The mediaeval and charming premises are [Hardy's]
> equivalent of Darwin's ship the *Beagle*. It doesn't matter

what the ship is like as long as the man on it is asking the right questions.

To receive such a positive accolade from Lewis was good fortune, and more was to follow. William Rees-Mogg, who was then editor of the London *Times*, invited him to write two articles for publication. Looking at the three national broadsheets that had advertised his work, Alister began to worry that his respondents were heavily drawn from the educated middle class. He was somewhat relieved when two more articles appeared in the *Daily Mail*. It had a broader social spread in its readership and yielded over a thousand records that were sent to the Unit. Subsequently the numbers of records in the archive of the Unit rose to more than 5,000. He was relieved that compared with his initial efforts in the religious press, the secular newspapers yielded a more representative spread of responses across the social classes, from both sexes and across the age range. It made him realise that by choosing to advertise first in the religious press, he had begun in the wrong place. Furthermore, it strengthened the plausibility of his conjecture that spiritual awareness is a human universal, not confined to formally religious people.

Apart from newspaper adverts, Hardy also solicited responses by distributing leaflets when he gave lectures. Their content helps to give a clearer understanding of the kinds of human experience in which he was interested. First, he used quotations from three of his contemporaries – highly competent people immersed in public life – who attested to the value of spirituality. One was Baroness Mary Stocks, Principal of Westfield College in London University, and the extract he used is from an address she gave to the World Congress of Faiths entitled 'The Religion of a Heretic':

> … Is there something that comes to meet us? Beatrice Webb's answer as recorded in her autobiography carries us straight into the realm of religious faith. 'For my own part', she writes, 'I find it best to live as if the soul of man were in communion with a superhuman force which makes for righteousness.' Beatrice Webb was conscious of experiencing a sense of reverence or awe – an apprehension of a power and purpose outside herself – which she called 'feeling' and which was sometimes induced by appreciation of great music or corporate

worship. But her experience went further than this nebulous fleeting 'feeling' – because as a result of it she achieved a religious interpretation of the universe which satisfied and upheld her and enabled her to seek continuous guidance in prayer – and this without compromising her intellectual integrity ... now that is a big step forward from rationalism, and once it is taken (as I take it, in company with Beatrice Webb) it opens up a great expanse of undiscovered country ...

Hardy's second example was taken from one of Estlin Carpenter's successors as Principal of Manchester College, L. P. Jacks. In his Hibbert Lecture in 1922 he had said:

All religious testimony, so far as I can interpret its meaning, converges towards a single point, namely this. There is that in the world, call it what you will, which responds to the confidence of those who trust it, declaring itself to them as a fellow worker in the pursuit of the Eternal Values, meeting their loyalty to it with reciprocal loyalty to them, and coming in at critical moments when the need of its sympathy is greatest: the conclusion being that wherever there is a soul in darkness, obstruction or misery, there also is a power which can help, deliver, illuminate and gladden that soul.

And thirdly, Alister quoted from a significant paragraph I have already used, written by the Oxford anthropologist, R. R. Marett:

It is the common experience of man that he can draw on a power that makes for, and in its most typical form wills, righteousness, the sole condition being that a certain fear, a certain shyness and humility, accompany the efforts so to do. That such a universal belief exists among all mankind, and that it is no less universally helpful in the highest degree, is the abiding impression left on my mind by the study of religion in its historico-scientific aspect.

The choice of examples is significant. In selecting these highly intelligent and independently-minded people, Alister was pointing out that the stereotype of religion as something clung to by weak and mentally limited people need not necessarily be correct. Those people he chose had both strength of character and shared a willingness to be quietly and undefensively open to their immediate experience of reality – which is almost a definition of meditation or contemplative prayer.

Once he had collected a substantial number of accounts from ordinary people he was able to give further help to potential respondents by giving a set of brief extracts of specific descriptions, demonstrating the variety of responses (the number at the start of each extract refers to its position in the archive, sequenced in the order of receipt by the Unit):[18]

(786) As far back as I can remember I have never had a sense of separation from the spiritual force I now choose to call God ... From the age of about 6 to 12 in places of quiet and desolation this feeling of 'oneness' often passed to a state of listening. I mean by 'listening' that I was suddenly alerted to something that was going to happen. What followed was a feeling of tremendous exaltation in which time stood still.

(183) I heard nothing, yet it was as if I were *surrounded by golden light* and as if I only had to reach out my hand to touch God himself who was so surrounding me with his compassion.

(651) I think from my childhood I have always had the feeling that the true reality is not to be found in the world as the average person sees it. There seems to be a constant force at work from the inside trying to push its way to the surface of consciousness. The mind is continually trying to create a symbol sufficiently comprehensive to contain it, but this always ends in failure. There are moments of pure joy with a heightened awareness of one's surroundings, as if a great truth had been passed across.

(854) About ten years later I began to pray for my children's safety, and this became a habit which I have never lost, and often the answer to such a prayer is

spectacular. Now I've evolved a belief which is identical with Beatrice Webb's: I find it best to live as if the soul of man were in communion with a superhuman force which makes for righteousness' ... May I add that since this belief grew in me I feel as if I had grown, as if my mind had stretched to take in the vast universe and be part of it.

(663) I find it difficult to describe my experience, only to say that it seems to be outside of me and enormous and yet at the same time I am part of it, everything is. It is purely personal and helps me to live and to love others. It is difficult to describe but in some way because of this feeling I feel united to all people, to all living things. Of recent years the feeling has become so strong that I am now training to become a social worker because I find that I must help people: in some way I feel their unhappiness as my own.

(712) It seemed to me, that in some way, I was extending into my surroundings and was becoming one with them. At the same time I felt a sense of lightness, exhilaration and power as if I was beginning to understand the whole universe.

(680) When I was on holiday, aged about 17, I glanced down and watched an ant striving to drag a bit of twig through a patch of sun on the wall of a graveyard in a Greek church, while chanting came from within the white building. The feeling aroused in me was quite unanticipated, welling up from some great depth, and essentially timeless. The concentration of simplicity and innocence was intensely of some vital present. I've had similar experiences on buses, suddenly watching people and being aware of how *right* everything essentially is.

(843) I have a growing sense of reality, and personal identity, which comes from being united to something more powerful than myself, something that is helping me to be what I want to be.

Following the accumulation of descriptions of experience, the next step was to think of a way of classifying them. There were some problems straight away. For one thing, there was a wide variation in the length of replies. Some people sent in a couple of sentences on the back of a postcard; others wrote long essays of twenty pages or more. Another very important source of variability was facility with language. Responses ranged from near illiterate statements to highly articulate accounts from people who were university-educated. A third source of difference was cultural background. On the one hand, most people who replied to Hardy were from a Western European background, which meant that, whatever their actual religious beliefs (or lack of them), the language they found themselves using was inevitably inherited from Christian culture. On the other hand, even within Christianity there are many varieties of language use.

An illustration of the difficulty arising from these cultural differences comes from some research done in the 1960s by two American sociologists of religion, Charles Glock and Rodney Stark; that is, in the same decade that Hardy began collecting his specimens. In their book *Religion and Society in Tension*[19] they described a study of religious experience in a large scale random sample of northern Californian church members. One of the questions they asked was worded: 'Have you ever had a sense of being saved in Christ?' Glock and Stark found that:

> Thirty-seven percent of Protestants were certain they'd had 'a sense of being saved in Christ' while only twenty-six percent of the Roman Catholics were certain they'd done so.

Rhetoric of the type 'Are you saved?' is characteristically the language of evangelical Protestants. It is alien to Catholics, who would be much more likely to talk about religious awareness at Mass, perhaps at the moment of consecration or when receiving Holy Communion. The finding that needs explaining is the fact that a quarter of the Catholic sample did claim that they had 'a sense of being saved in Christ'. It can perhaps be attributed to the multicultural nature of the population in Northern California. Catholics and others are likely to have been accosted on the streets by fundamentalist Protestants, seeking to find out if they have been 'saved'. Hence, though it is not part of their cultural upbringing, Californian Roman Catholics are perfectly familiar with the language.

The problems in comparing data from various social groups (in multicultural California or Britain) are very much more complex than that caused by differences in rhetoric between two kinds of Californian Christian. Dr Michael Mason, an Australian sociologist,[20] points out that even among the modern inheritors of Christendom there are many different symbolic universes, e.g. Roman Catholic, Anglican High Church, Low Church, Traditionalist, Modernist, Charismatic, Pantheist, Secularist, Marxist, Atheist, Parapsychologist, etc. To adherents of each of these universes the same questions about religious experience may have quite different meanings, or in some cases they may have no meaning or even seem repugnant. And then beyond believing or sceptical inheritors of Christian culture are all the people who have arrived as recent immigrants from completely different cultural backgrounds. Few members of these groups in fact responded to Hardy's invitation, but in the case of the United Kingdom these would be predominantly Muslim, but also include significant numbers of Sikhs and members of the Hindu community.

What are we to make of the huge array of cultural differences between human groups? Biologists as a breed are tempted to ascribe all characteristics of living organisms to genetics.[21] Sociologists on the other hand are tempted to overemphasise the effects of the environment. In Alister's case, his association with Julian Huxley made him more aware of social evolution than many of his zoologist colleagues. Nevertheless he was unprepared for its importance when it came to the task of classifying experiences. Hardy's biological hypothesis predicts that spiritual experience is common to all human beings, and that underlying the multitude of varied and sometimes contradictory cultural expressions, there is a common ground of genetically-inherited awareness. But how could one classify these cultural expressions? Surely what one would end up doing is to sort out differences in linguistic expression, rather than anything biologically innate. Alister had originally assumed that the accounts could be organised into hierarchical groups analogous to the taxonomies of living organisms introduced by Linnaeus. Thus there might be the equivalent of phyla, orders, families, genera and species of spiritual experience. This now seemed improbable.

The first serious attempt to tackle these problems within Hardy's Unit was made by Tim Beardsworth, a member of Bobby Wills' staff who was seconded to the Unit and paid by Wills to work there part-time. Beardsworth, whose training was in philosophy, began by reading through the first thousand accounts sent in to the Unit between June 1969 (that is, four months before the Unit was officially opened) and June 1970. He was supported in his work by regular discussions of the material with the other members of staff, including Hardy. Beardsworth's stance was phenomenological, meaning that he stood back from either a sceptical posture ('It's nothing but disguised sex!') or one of religious faith ('God moves in mysterious ways!') and attempted to remain descriptive. The classification he produced was nothing like the Linnaean system. The main headings were:

1. Sensory or quasi-sensory experience: visual
2. Sensory or quasi-sensory experience: auditory
3. Sensory or quasi-sensory experience: touch
4. Sensory or quasi-sensory experience: smell
5. Supposed extra-sensory perception
6. Behavioural changes: enhanced or superhuman power displayed by man
7. Cognitive and affective elements
8. Development of experience
9. Dynamic patterns in experience
10. Dream experiences
11. Antecedents or 'triggers' of experience
12. Consequences of experience

Beardsworth's first four categories have a directly biological aspect and probably Hardy would have argued that this is true of his fifth, ESP. Bearing in mind the insistence of the acknowledged experts in the spiritual life (in Western culture that would mean someone like St Teresa of Avila) that the profoundest and most reliable level of spiritual experience is without (conventional) sensory content, Beardsworth's first four categories are surely not exhaustive. However, by emphasising the senses, he was attempting to be respectful of the biological perspective. The remaining seven subdivisions fall more naturally into the sociological or psychological areas and the clarity of this division led to a shift in the direction of the research at the RERU. It had the advantage of broadening the approach to spirituality by recognising more fully the importance of the social dimension. It also emphasised that experience which stays at the level of an isolated 'oddity' without affecting a person's life can hardly be counted as religious. On the other hand, the temptation to turn away from the biological hypothesis towards other explanations of religious experience worried Hardy. It was eventually the cause of a quarrel that almost destroyed the Unit.

In addition to the above classification, Beardsworth came to the tentative conclusion that another way to handle the accounts would be to split them into two types. One group could be allocated to the category of 'numinous' experiences, that is, broadly speaking, experiences of the presence of God. The other category consisted of more 'mystical' experiences, where the writer is expressing something like the feeling of 'merging with the rest of reality', or losing the sense of self as over against everything else. It was clear that these two categories fitted rather well with the views of a number of Western philosophers of religion, returning Beardsworth to the same dilemma as before.[22] That is to say, Beardsworth and those who sent in their narratives came from a shared cultural background, that of Western Europe. Were these categories arrived at solely because both parties were shaped by a common culture? Or were these experiences, as Hardy believed, primarily due to a biologically-based awareness primordially present in all members of the species *Homo sapiens*?

The difficulties that emerged from Beardsworth's attempt at classification are formidable.[23] In a way this was the most valuable point to emerge from his efforts, because he identified the area of investigation that needed to be tackled if Hardy's idea was to be satisfactorily tested. If we ask what factors enter into the public expression of spiritual, or for that matter, any human experience, common sense suggests that both genetics and the environment play a part, but separating the two factors is not easy. At the time when Beardsworth was working on the archive, there was no way to make a direct investigation of the question, and thus assess the plausibility of Hardy's biological hypothesis. Research tools have improved greatly since then and new knowledge is accumulating very quickly, to the extent that the reference in the present text will certainly be out of date by the time it is published.[24]

There was another fundamental query raised by a few of the descriptions sent to Hardy. These came from what is unkindly and improperly called the 'lunatic fringe' and included some letters that were actually sent from mental hospitals. They required careful consideration because they fed a popular stereotype suggesting that people claiming religious experience are mentally disturbed. Hardy noted that accounts coming from people judged to be mentally ill were much less frequent than he had expected. Nevertheless, the fact that there *was* a category Z, made it look as if the mental imbalance theory might have a grain of truth in it. [25]

Towards the end of 1969, very shortly after the opening of the RERU, Alister received a letter from Edward Robinson, a lecturer in Divinity at Cheltenham College of Education. He was making an enquiry on behalf of one of his students who wanted to do some research on 'speaking in tongues' in the Christian Church. The student wanted to find out more about the psychological and theological angles on the subject and was very interested when Robinson told him what little he knew of Alister's Unit. Robinson asked if the young man could visit the unit and added: 'I should myself be grateful for any suggestions which you may be able to make'.

It is not known whether the student got what he wanted, but subsequent correspondence led to Alister's discovery that Edward was the brother of John Robinson, Bishop of Woolwich, author of the controversial book, *Honest to God.*[26] Edward had read Classical Mods and Greats at Oxford, which meant that during his first five terms he had studied Latin and Greek, followed by philosophy (Mods), and for the remaining seven terms he had gone on to study Greek and Roman history, along with ancient and modern philosophy. It is a four-year degree, thus longer than the normal three years required for a BA in Oxford, and clearly very remote from zoology. Nevertheless, in his subsequent career, Edward spent 15 years in Zambia and other central African countries, studying the plant life. On his return to England, he was employed at the Royal Botanic Gardens at Kew as a Senior Scientific Officer, working on the tropical flora of East Africa. Yet another interest was in the arts as they related to spirituality, and Edward himself was a talented sculptor.

Alister was impressed by him and kept in touch, though it was not clear how closely they had shared views on the nature of religious experience. In a letter written on 20 December 1969, Edward seemed to suggest that in some respects his personal views on the study of religion were different from Alister's:

> Inevitably I am more closely concerned than you are with the educational aspect of this kind of research. I become increasingly depressed at the impoverishment of our educational traditions and the once steady but now sudden decline into bankruptcy of our religious culture, to use a phrase I dislike. More influential I think than any other single cause has been an insistence, tacit or open, in the name of intellectual respectability on a distinction to be drawn between the objective and the subjective. An educational tradition which accepts this distinction is in danger of disinheriting the creative imagination. It then becomes infected with a pseudo-scientific spirit. The way is left open to the rationalisation of every impulse and intuition that does not fit into a recognisable category or conform to accepted ideas of what is beautiful, religious or even significant ... if one prefers to start by exploring the generally held ideas of what the majority of men would agree to call religious experience, even if one avoids the word 'normal', is one not in fact presupposing a norm, and indeed letting the tacit acceptance of that norm determine the direction of one's inquiry? This is a particularly critical question when one is considering a culture as sick as I believe ours to be today.[27]

Alister found the remarks in Edward's letter ambiguous. Was he agreeing or disagreeing with his point of view? Further interchanges took place and the two men finally decided that there was sufficient agreement between them to warrant increased co-operation in research. On 5 March 1970, Alister wrote to Edward at his home in Cheltenham, inviting him to become a member of his staff, in a senior post, with possible right of succession as director of the Unit. Edward accepted and joined RERU in 1970.[28]

After becoming a member of staff, Edward continued to be interested in education and his most enduring work while he was with the Unit was a study of the religious experience of children. When he went through the records, Robinson soon realised that a sizable proportion of the accounts were reminiscences of events occurring in childhood, sometimes in the very early years. As a result of pondering on these stories, Edward published an account of them in his book *The Original Vision*.[29] This was a pioneering attempt to question the application of Jean Piaget's developmental model of the intellect as it relates to religious understanding.[30] That is to say, Robinson's observations of the spirituality of childhood did not suggest that children gradually accumulated enough mental equipment to enable them to be spiritually aware. This would amount to saying that children are born spiritually ignorant and become less ignorant as they grow up. The evidence from the files in Oxford seemed to imply that, on the contrary, the reverse was true.

What first impressed Robinson was the way that these childhood experiences had remained vivid in the memories of his correspondents for the whole of their lives. People repeatedly spoke of them as having the greatest personal significance when they were contemplating their personal identity and the meaning of their existence. No doubt there had been a considerable development in the interpretation and perhaps embellishment of these experiences as the individuals thought about them over the years. Yet Edward found it hard to ignore the power of the initial impact of the event which had generated this wealth of reflection. Could it be that Ronald Goldman,[31] a leading figure in religious education in the United Kingdom, was giving a great deal of attention to the language and thought forms of religion, while ignoring the direct awareness out of which it grows? Robinson began to suspect, as had Wordsworth before him, that the vision of childhood could perhaps be locked out of awareness on entering the secularised world of adult life. The Orkney poet Edwin Muir, from whom Robinson drew the title of his book, also believed that the original vision could easily be crushed:

> A child has also a picture of human existence peculiar to himself, which he probably never remembers after he has

lost it: the original vision of the world. I think of this picture or vision as that of a state in which the earth, the houses on the earth, and the life of every human being are related to the sky overarching them; as if the sky fitted the earth and the earth the sky.[32]

Robinson's research movingly demonstrated that the vision was not always completely forgotten. But seemingly in most cases the vision had been lost for some time from conscious memory. Perhaps in the social circumstances of our time the dominant beliefs are such that the spiritual awareness with which we are born becomes suppressed or even repressed out of consciousness? Edward felt that the data he had gathered from the archive of accounts supported the plausibility of that hypothesis. Unfortunately there was a weakness in the data, for it depended on reminiscences of childhood by adults, some of whom were very elderly. There was no way to assess the reliability of such long-term memories, or to check up on the elaboration that must inevitably have gone on with repeated reflection upon the story over many years.

Edward was productive in other ways. He made an in-depth study of a limited number of cases, drawn from the archive, where people wrote about the growing influence of religious experience on them as their lives progressed. He felt that a shortcoming of *The Original Vision* was the absence of any account of the long-term effects of people's religious experience on their lives. Without such a practical follow-up the experience remained an isolated oddity, in which case Edward found it only dubiously categorised as religious. Inclined to be critical of a purely statistical approach which tended to apply external categories and rules of methodology which obscured the profuse varieties of religious experience, he turned strongly towards qualitative approaches. He selected 12 people from the records and in most cases arranged to have a conversation with them, attempting to draw from them the particularity of their religious life as it unfolded from their experience. To Edward the intention of his work was less to explain or measure experience but in a phrase which he took from Rainer-Maria Rilke, to 'live the questions'.[33] He wrote up the collected dialogues and comments in *Living the Questions,* published by RERU in 1978.

In the same year he produced another book, *This Time-Bound Ladder: Ten Dialogues on Religious Experience,* also published by the Unit. In this book, Robinson reported on conversations with ten people, eminent in some aspect of religion[34] with the purpose of exploring varieties of understanding what the term 'religious experience' might mean and what significance it had for humanity. In an important way, these conversations along with a careful study of the records could be a preparation for the next stage in Hardy's investigation, assessing the frequency of such experience in the general population. Edward was particularly aware that 'religious experience' is such a protean term that decisions about the kind of question one could legitimately ask in, for example, a large scale national survey, become problematical.

Meanwhile, behind the scenes Alister was engaged in lecture tours in the United Kingdom and North America with the purpose of raising money, but unfortunately without the success necessary to produce the financial stability he needed. Steady support came from a number of small trusts[35] and a surprisingly large body of individual donors, and Tim Beardsworth was paid by Bobby Wills. But the income for the Unit was still dangerously low. There were other worries. The Manchester College authorities seemed to be uninterested in the progress of the research, and Hardy began to wonder how securely the Unit was housed. He was right to be worried, for eventually the Unit would be asked to leave the college. Then there was anxiety about Sylvia, remembered by students who came to tea as vivacious and warm,[36] but now struck down with increasingly severe arthritis.

Not all was gloom for Alister during these admittedly difficult years. One day in 1974 he received a phone call from the BBC inviting him to take part in the radio programme *Desert Island Discs*. When they first rang, Alister – who had never listened to the programme – replied rather brusquely: 'You have made a mistake. This is Professor Hardy speaking; I think you want a disc jockey'. The BBC representative explained the guest each week was some-one well-known, who was asked to imagine being a castaway on a desert island. A gramophone had been washed ashore and eight recordings of favourite pieces of music could be chosen to entertain themselves on the island. The programme would consist of an interviewer, asking Alister about his life story and playing his choice of records. Supplied with the Bible and the works of Shakespeare, the castaway was allowed to specify one book and one luxury item. Alister said he would think about it and put the phone down. Sylvia overheard the conversation and told him he had been so rude that the caller would not get back to him.

The BBC did persist and Alister was interviewed for the programme by Roy Plomley. His first choice of music was familiar, a memory of his earliest days, the old music hall favourite 'You are the Honeysuckle, I am the Bee', and he continued with choices of popular music that marked the important points in his life.[37] For his special book he chose Wordsworth's *Prelude,* and as a luxury, paper, pencils and painting materials. The programme and the choices of music he made served to bring him into more conscious awareness of the unfolding pattern of his spiritual journey and, even in these difficult times, his sense of being somehow guided on the way. He became determined to write his autobiography, perhaps to reinforce his own sense of mission in the face of so many difficulties.

In January 1976 Alister was visited at the office in Holywell Street by the billionaire philanthropist, John M. Templeton, a man who was deeply interested in religious matters and who had created a Foundation specifically to promote research and debate at the religion/science boundary. Templeton noted that the Nobel Prize made no provision for an award in the field of religion. Since he, John Templeton, judged the religious dimension of life as the most important of all, he decided to rectify Nobel's omission by setting up an annual prize for 'Progress in Religion'. Moreover, because of the pre-eminence he gave to religion, he made it a rule that the monetary value of his prize would always be set at a level somewhat higher than the Nobel Prize. Templeton had been alerted to the work of the Unit in 1973 by Robin Woods, the Bishop of Worcester, who at the time was one of the judges for the Templeton Prize. Woods asked Alister to send him details about the work of RERU so that he could pass them on to Templeton. Naturally, Alister was thrilled, but was warned not to be too optimistic about a positive outcome, which could not be considered for the time being. Nevertheless, the judges were impressed by his Unit and appreciated what he was doing.

One of the most important unanswered questions to be faced by the Unit was the extent to which spiritual experience was manifested generally in the whole nation. It was at least possible to imagine that the 5,000 plus people who had written to Hardy were the small remnant of a dying culture, which no longer had much social reality for most of the millions who made up Britain's population. In the summer term of 1974, I had the idea of investigating the prevalence of spiritual experience in a random sample of 100 postgraduate students in my own workplace, the Department of Education at Nottingham University. Over several weeks in the summer I invited each of the hundred to come and have a private conversation with me in my office. During the chat, I asked Hardy's question: 'Have you ever been aware of or influenced by a presence or a power, whether you call it God or not, which is different from your everyday self?' To my considerable surprise, 65 per cent of the students responded positively to the question, and provided examples of what they meant.[38] This percentage seemed extraordinarily high, if only because of the small numbers of the students who belonged to any kind of religious organisation. I wrote to Hardy enclosing a draft list of the results of my small study. Hardy was interested and came up to Nottingham with the intention of persuading my head of department to let me go part-time to Oxford to work in the Unit. Alister, tall, elderly and aristocratic, had little trouble in getting his agreement. I knew it was in the bag when my head of department started calling Alister 'Sir'.

Translating the approach from a small-scale study such as mine in Nottingham University into a national survey was, for the time being, beyond our competence (Hardy and I were zoologists, not social scientists), so the next step was to employ a young sociologist, Ann Morisy, as a full-time research assistant. We decided on a two-pronged approach. The first part of the study would be a national survey of the frequency of report of experience in the adult population of the United Kingdom, and for this we needed to use one of the national surveying organisations. We approached National Opinion Polls Ltd (NOP) and worked out a set of questions to be asked as part of one of their regular Omnibus surveys covering the whole British mainland. This would be followed up by an in-depth study of the experiences of a random sample of Nottingham citizens, to provide a qualitative background to the national statistics. Ann Morisy and I were responsible for conducting the interviews in the follow-up stage. The project was costed and we produced a detailed research proposal to be submitted to appropriate funding bodies to be found in the Charities Aid Yearbook, as well as the national governmental funding agencies.

There are numerous handbooks on proposal writing which are helpful to a beginner, but the skills required in producing applications for research money can only be learned from experience. As novices, it is quite likely that our submission was not particularly good and for some time it failed to get a positive response. Nevertheless, during this time an incident in which I was involved revealed another major stumbling block. Hardy decided that it would be worthwhile making an approach to one of the major national funding bodies. He was used to such encounters being successful in the years when he was seeking backing for his marine research. So one morning in the 1970s I went along as junior partner to Alister on a trip to the London Headquarters of the funding agency, where he was to have a top-level meeting with the director. All went well and the proceedings were never less than courteous, but one significant moment stood out, when Alister enthusiastically banged his hand on the table in front of him and exclaimed: 'I know there's something there!' I groaned inwardly, for I could see a slight change in the director's face, representing a sudden distancing. Alister must have used that gesture successfully many times in his search for financial support for his zoological researches, but this was a different matter. Here two different ontologies were meeting, with disconcerting results. While Alister was sure there was something there, the director's contrary view about the nature of reality meant that a couple of days later we received confirmation that the application had been turned down.

In the event, the Unit was finally able to accumulate the funds to pay for a national survey in the United Kingdom, carried out for us by NOP in 1976.[39] The finding that 36 per cent of the national sample reported having had a religious experience, closely resembled the results of a similar nationwide survey run at approximately the same time in the United States by Professor Andrew Greeley at the University of Chicago.[40] The data gave Hardy greater confidence that he was dealing with a large-scale phenomenon, and this was further affirmed when the in-depth study done by Ann Morisy and myself in the city of Nottingham raised the figure to 65 per cent.[41] Since regular churchgoing in Britain has been at a very low level for many years, somewhere between 7–10 per cent, it was obvious that the great majority of these people were not formally religious. This discovery interested Hardy because it supported his view that spiritual awareness was likely to be a human universal and not the prerogative of churchgoers.

The other prominent finding we made was to do with the near doubling of the proportion of people responding positively to Hardy's question when the interview was more personal and longer than could be the case in a national poll.[42] Careful questioning during the Nottingham in-depth study showed that the major factor underlying the increase was the overcoming of shyness, born of a fear that other people would think the individual reporting their experience was either stupid or mad. The lengthier time taken to build up rapport in a small-scale investigation gave people time to make the judgement that the researcher was neither trying to evangelise them nor to sneer or laugh at their experience. We were encouraged in this interpretation by the findings of two American sociologists, Kurt Back and Linda Bourque. When they reviewed a sequence of national surveys of religious experience in the United States, they noticed an overall pattern of increase in successive years.[43] They, rather similarly to us, attributed the rise to improving interview skills being used successfully to overcome the shyness of the people being interviewed. Hardy himself was an example of this wariness, having concealed his profound spiritual experience from his colleagues in the Zoology Department, and even his own children. The strength of the taboo is striking evidence of the clash between what experiencers 'know' they have experienced and the orthodox post-Enlightenment scientific model of humanity, which rules out such experience as nonsense.

It is important to remember that during this time, even in retirement, Alister was maintaining his contact with mainstream zoology. In a previous chapter I mentioned that the third edition of Julian Huxley's book, *Evolution: The Modern Synthesis*, was published in 1974, containing as part of its lengthy introduction a section by Alister on behavioural selection. He must have felt a sense of convergence with his religious work, for in the same year he also published an account of the first year's work at the Unit, giving it the controversial title *The Biology of God: A Scientist's Study of Man the Religious Animal*.[44] Here too he talked about behavioural selection as crucial to the evolution of spiritual awareness.

But at last, in 1976, Alister felt it was time to retire as director of the Unit and hand on the directorship to Edward Robinson. He was approaching his eightieth birthday and in 1976 he withdrew, or, rather, he intended to withdraw. Alister found it impossible to relinquish the reins of the organisation he had dreamt of for so long, and to Edward's dismay he continued to intrude. Apart from personally attending to the day-to-day affairs of the Unit, Alister also appointed a new Advisory Research Council, chaired by himself. Quite clearly the Council had a major function in overseeing what Edward was doing and he did not particularly like it.

As so often is the case, the difficulties were aggravated by shortage of money. At a meeting of the Advisory Council at the beginning of 1979 the crisis was made plain. The Unit was in severe deficit and to clear it would require the withdrawal of over £11,564 from the already tiny reserves of approximately £17,487, leaving assets of only a meagre £5,923. Even making a guess that around £6,000 was likely to come in from the sale of RERU publications, royalties from Alister's latest book, *The Spiritual Nature of Man*, and donations, it was obvious that another year's programme could not be funded. In his alarm at the precarious position of the Unit, Edward decided, without consulting Alister, to call in the services of an organisation claiming to have expertise in raising funds. The consultant delegated to advise the Unit suggested that any appeal ought to be linked to a proposed programme of research, an opinion with which Edward agreed. Consequently, he decided to formulate a detailed plan for developing the work of the Unit. The proposal was entitled *Tradition and Experience* and emphasised his great interest in education and the arts, with much in it about young children. This was an appropriate enough expansion of the research programme, for, as Edward had pointed out, our knowledge of the spirituality of childhood depended too much on the long memories of elderly people.

It was here that serious disagreement arose between Edward and Alister, and the dispute very nearly brought RERU to an end. Alister wrote to Edward, hurt by the fact that he was making directorial decisions without discussing them. But quite apart from that, Alister made clear the other reasons for his disquiet. Firstly, he was unhappy about the (as he saw it) unilateral decision to hire a fundraising firm, which cost £500 of the Unit's tiny resources. Secondly, he disapproved of Edward's turn away from empirical science, by which he meant a purely biological approach backed up by statistical data. If in their initial enthusiasm the two men had paused to look more closely, they would have been warned of their differences of outlook, evident in their earliest meetings and exchanges of opinion. But all of that was suppressed by their common agreement about the importance of the investigation.

There then began a labyrinthine negotiation about the future of the Unit which it would be tedious to detail here, but it involved at different times: Alister's refusal to endorse the search for funds to mount Edward's programme, fears that the members of the Advisory Research Council might be held personally liable for the debts of the Unit, the dissolution of the Council by Alister, who took personal responsibility for any debts incurred, and eventually the resignation of Edward from the directorship when Alister died in 1985.

Both Alister and Edward were transparently men of good will, and both struggled to get beyond the feelings of anger and mistrust that resulted from their dispute. Alister wrote to Edward a moving and self-revelatory letter from which I quote to illustrate the depth of his religious commitment:

> Dear Edward,
> I have been thinking a great deal about the catastrophe
> that struck us last year, and also of the future of the RERU.
> I feel I am now beginning to see it in a new light and with
> greater understanding. I believe we have both been the
> victims of an extraordinary religious phenomenon, but I
> have not liked hitherto to admit it – a powerful form of
> what most people would call religious fanaticism.
> I am, as I think you have realised, a passionately religious
> person, and some, if they knew how I felt, would certainly
> call me a fanatic. I would however deny this; but others
> could well say that I myself cannot judge my own position
> in this regard.
> The *Concise Oxford Dictionary* defines the word 'fanatic'
> as: (Person) filled with excessive and mistaken enthusiasm,
> esp. in religion. I am extremely enthusiastic about the
> power I would call God and believe it can transform the
> world; but *is* this mistaken? I am *not* enthusiastic about any
> particular religious creed which could well be mistaken ...

There can be little doubt that fanaticism can become an exceedingly powerful force, one which can seize a person and drive him to actions which he would not believe himself capable. I remember your surprising me, when looking at a pencil portrait of myself (not a very good one I thought) in our hall at Capel Close, by saying that you saw in it a sign of ruthlessness; I was surprised because I had not thought of myself in that way, but I believe now that I am. I have secretly believed, but tried hard to hide it, that the RERU, if continued upon the course for which I had started it, would change the world, I still believe this to be so ...

It is difficult to see how Alister could have striven so hard to reach his goal, without the intensity that some would call fanaticism. But there is no neutral space here. The personal commitments are too strong and one's opinion of Alister's enthusiasm will to a large extent depend on one's own position on religious belief.

This was an unhappy period in the history of the Unit, which often seemed to be on the point of complete dissolution. For a time, in an attempt to save money, Edward had found himself living on half of the small salary provided by the Unit. Quite obviously things could not go on in such a fashion and it was at this time that Lord Bullock took a hand. Alan Bullock was the most senior figure in Oxford to become involved with the Unit. Famed as the author of the first important post-war biography of Adolf Hitler, founding Master of St Catherine's College and former Vice-Chancellor of Oxford University, Bullock was, like Hardy, a Unitarian. A straightforward Yorkshireman, the son of a self-educated Unitarian preacher in Bradford, Alan was the epitome of solid dependability. When Alister was in hospital, very near the end of his life and fearing that he would not survive, he begged his old friend to ensure the continuation of the Unit. Alan made a promise to do what he could, which was fortunate because the Unit was on the point of being asked to vacate the premises on Holywell Street and needed Bullock's skills and political influence to make a new start elsewhere.

Then, one day shortly afterwards, when Alister was in the midst of a sea of troubles, the telephone rang. It was his birthday, 10 February 1985, and on the line was Wilbert Forker, Vice-

President of the Templeton Foundation. He explained that he was ringing to congratulate Alister on reaching the age of 89. Then, after exchanging a few more pleasantries he revealed the main purpose of his call, which was to inform Alister that he had won the Templeton Prize.

Later that year, on Tuesday, 14 May, I sat with 700 other guests in the historic London Guildhall. Staring down at us with glaring eyes, as we came in, were the carved wooden effigies of the legendary ogres, Gog and Magog, protectors of the city. Though their names appear in both the Bible and the Qu'ran, the identity of the giants is totally obscure. While we waited, my imagination meandered away from Gog and Magog and drifted towards thoughts of ancient folk tales, about Robin Hood and the Merry Men, and about my own repeated feeling when I was with him, that Alister was an outlaw. He had gone against his own interests in struggling with the pervasive belief among the scientific aristocracy (of which he himself was a member) that wanted to impose a dogmatic material-ism on the rest of humankind. He strove as a Darwinian to give religion back to the spiritually-impoverished masses who, as he saw it, had their religion stolen from them. That was why we had assembled from all parts of the world. It was to celebrate the award of a prize to someone who was not prepared to give way to the dominating current in the stream.[45]

But where was the man of the hour? On the stage were Sir John Templeton, Wilbert Forker, the Templeton judges, Crawford Knox and Belinda Hardy, Alister's daughter. In the Chair was the Duke of Norfolk.[46] He rose to speak, paused, then announced the dramatic news that Sir Alister was unable to be present, for he had suffered a severe brain haemorrhage the day before the presentation. It was far too late to cancel the celebrations, so Hardy's daughter, Belinda, went to Buckingham Palace in the morning to accept the award from the Duke of Edinburgh, on behalf of her father. Sir Alister's speech, which just a few weeks previously he had been trying out on the elderly fellow inhabitants of his sheltered residence in Heading-ton, was read out on his behalf by Crawford Knox, who was then treasurer of RERU. As Crawford began reading the address in his polite Ulster accent, I could hear Alister's enthusiasm breaking through:

I am overwhelmed by the great honour that the judges of the Templeton Prize have bestowed upon me by electing me to be this year's winner; I hope they can imagine something of the great pleasure it gives me as well as my deep sense of gratitude. I am now 89 and I cannot but regard the award as the culmination of a long career.[47]

It was indeed the final accolade during Alister's lifetime, for a few days later, on 23 May, he died.

His passing released a host of expressions of love and gratitude, some of them preserved in the archive in the Bodleian Library.

Desmond Morris spoke for the very many people who had the good fortune to know him as a personal friend :

> We adored Alister and every time he touched our lives we felt the warmth of his personality.

A former student wrote:

> He was an enthusiast himself and with his highly innovative mind and kind disposition was an incomparable professor for any student to have.

Alister's care for even the most junior of his colleagues was remembered by a former Laboratory Technician for the way he kept up a correspondence with him throughout his National Service and came to his wedding in London.

A touching memory came from the daughter of a stoker on the *George Bligh*. As a child she had known him as 'Uncle Mac', and still with the third generation he was known by the same nickname:

> … he always made time to see us. It was an honour to know him, a great man, with humility, a Christian gentleman who cared about his fellow man. He has left a legacy to mankind with his books, watercolour illustrations and sketches. My daughter has some little drawings he done for her (sic) when she was a tiny tot. She is 27 now.

Others also remembered their childhood:

> … They still talk about him lying on the floor in front of
> the fire making paper aeroplanes and generally amusing
> them … a truly great gentleman whose equal I have yet to
> meet.

And an insightful comment from another former student:

> He could draw on the board with great speed and as his
> excitement grew and we were caught up in it, vivid sketch
> after vivid sketch was added to the picture he had already
> drawn … His greatness seems to me in some way linked
> with his child-like approach to life, his tremendous
> enthusiasm in exploring it and at the same time his deep
> respect for, and wonder at every tiny part. I wish I could
> have known him better, but I am very grateful for having
> known him at all.

Finally, words not drawn from a letter of condolence or an obituary,
but Richard Dawkins' blissful memory of Alister in full flood:[48]

> Nobody had a better feel for the great rolling pastures,
> sunlit green meadows and waving prairies of *The Open
> Sea* than Alister Hardy, my first professor. His paintings
> for that book still adorn the corridors of the Oxford
> Zoology Department, and the images seem to dance with
> enthusiasm, just as the old man himself danced boyishly
> round the lecture hall, a strabismically beaming cross
> between Peter Pan and the Ancient Mariner. Yea, slimy
> things did crawl with slimy legs upon the slimy sea – and
> across the blackboard in coloured chalk with Sir Alister
> bobbing and weaving in pursuit.

To read such rich and rewarding memories of Hardy's career as a
marine biologist is to be reminded that the concluding chapters of
Alister Hardy's life were paradoxical. Here was a man of exceptional ability, marked out and rewarded for worldly success, but who

had an invincible conviction that his true profession was to serve the cause of religion. This assurance is put absolutely explicitly in his unfinished autobiography, where he first publicly traced the origin of his vocation to the Vow made seventy years previously. It was thus virtually a lifelong feeling of certainty, repeatedly buoyed up by his experience of being given divine guidance, every step of the way. Moreover, the typescript of his autobiography, which it will be recalled he considered giving the title *For Fun and for Joy*, was written in his late eighties, after he had entered the struggle with his health and with anxieties for the future of RERU that marked the last part of his life.

To the eye of a sympathetic outside observer, Alister's story of his spiritual journey looks convincing up until the plaudits that greeted his successful Gifford Lectures in Aberdeen University. Thereafter the picture becomes darker. To summarise, for the period from 1969 when he founded the RERU, to 1985 when he died, Alister was faced by a whole string of troubles: repeated efforts to find even minimal finance to allow the project to continue, contending with the indifference and, in the end, a request to leave the premises by the Manchester College authorities, the painful conflict with Edward, his successor as director of the Unit and alongside all these difficulties, the battle against increasing physical frailty in both Sylvia and himself.[49] Lastly, when he did receive a substantial financial boost in the form of the Templeton Prize, he died before he could make use of it.

The trials Alister faced during this period of his life caused him a fair degree of anxiety, though probably more to Sylvia, who herself was not at all well, and one might be forgiven for supposing he died a disappointed man. There were certainly grave disappointments, but it would distort both Alister's joyful temperament and his deeply-held religious beliefs to think of this as the dominant story.[50] In the last two years of his life he was busy writing and publishing his book *Darwin and the Spirit of Man*[51] and in 1984 he also published *A Cotswold Sketchbook*,[52] a collection of pencil drawings and watercolours made over the years in the villages and little towns of the Cotswold hills. His life-long hobby of painting and sketching, especially in the Cotswolds, always lifted his spirits, to the extent that Sylvia called them his 'bottle of medicine'. As mentioned a moment ago, he was also part-way through drafting the chapters of his autobiography. In addition he was working on

Weekend with Willows, a small book on a ballooning trip he made with Ernest Willows, one weekend in 1924. The prevailing wind had determined the route of the flight, which was from London to Oxford, and the poetic language Alister used to unfold the story makes this one of the most magical and dreamlike of all his writings.[53] This was not the creation of a man in despair. Even the 'too late' award of the Templeton Prize, by far the biggest lump sum ever to come to him for his religious work, made his last few days of life bitter-sweet, and he willingly donated it to his successors in the Unit.

But quite apart from that merciful windfall, to ascribe the emotion of disappointment to him – as more than brief and passing – is to take an individualistic perspective on his life that is utterly contrary to Alister's holistic understanding of biology. He was an ecologist through and through. One only has to look at the opening chapters of his great book, *The Living Stream*, to be reminded of his vision of the human community, irrevocably bound together, for Alister firmly believed in John Donne's memorable epithet, 'No man is an island'. He had requested that after his death there was to be no funeral and no memorial service, ostensibly because the ceremonies would be too much for Sylvia in her very frail state. That may be true, for Alister was always courteous, but there seems to be a more profound meaning behind his request. He personally knew well the feeling of astonishment at having a body that initially is not separated from manifold reality by name, nationality or religious, political or scientific identities. On the other hand, he was certainly aware of being continuous with the great chain of God-given being, or to use his own more dynamic imagery, a vast, living stream. He needed no ritual or memorial.

Alister donated his body to medical research and it was taken to Addenbrookes Hospital in Cambridge. Without him, his beloved Sylvia did not stay for long. She died on 26 October in the same year. She had not been happy about Alister's decision to donate his body to science but, at her own cremation, the vicar of Headington was able to include him in the service without hypocrisy, for Alister knew the parish church and the vicar well. Until he was no longer able to walk the distance, Alister had the habit of making his way round the corner to the nearby church – not for services of course – but to sit quietly in the stillness for a few minutes, communing with the All. Seen from that perspective, any judgement we may wish to make on the life of Alister Hardy cannot be limited to an enumeration of his personal successes and failures. Rather, we need to ask how he, as part of the living stream, has influenced, and in the future will influence the dynamics of its evolutionary flow.

Still on two wheels you see !

1914-18

With best wishes for Christmas 1967 and the New Year from mac Hardy and family

7 CAPEL CLOSE , OXFORD

A Five-stage Model of the Growth of European Individualism[1]

It is not from the benevolence of the butcher, the brewer or the baker that we expect our dinner, but from their regard to their own interest. We address ourselves, not to their humanity but to their self-love, and never talk to them of our necessities but of their advantages.
Adam Smith, *The Wealth of Nations* (1776)[2]

The point is, ladies and gentleman, that greed – for lack of a better word – is good. Greed is right. Greed works. Greed clarifies, cuts through, and captures the essence of the evolutionary spirit.
Gordon Gekko in *Wall Street* (1987)[3]

We have to fight uphill to rediscover the obvious, to counteract the layers of suppression of the modern moral consciousness. It's a difficult thing to do.
Charles Taylor, *Sources of the Self* (1992)[4]

Alister Hardy experienced the greatest difficulty in getting a hearing from the scientific community for his application of its methods to the study of spiritual/religious experience. Behind this lay the almost axiomatic assumption, ultimately inherited from Feuerbach, that people cling to spirituality or religion out of stupidity or for psychologically defensive reasons. It is a prejudice that is particularly widely-diffused in the Western world and it has large-scale personal and social consequences.

Hardy's reasoned and empirically testable hypothesis about human spirituality as a biological phenomenon has often been rejected as irrational, when a careful look at the evidence suggests

265

that the boot is on the other foot. To put the matter clearly, amongst some secularist critics, there is a degree of irrationality, a refusal to look at the evidence that implies a closed mind, meaning that Hardy's ideas simply could not (and cannot) be heard. The remainder of this Postscript offers an outline of five stages in the social construction of the irrationality at the heart of western secularism in its dogmatic form.

I begin by noting that people, who on the basis of their own experience, are pretty sure that their spiritual experience is not a fantasy, learn to keep their opinions to themselves. The taboo can be extreme, as was vividly illustrated in much of the research that I directed on behalf of Hardy's Unit. One typical example is the responses to a question about religious experience that Ann Morisy and I asked everyone who took part in our in-depth study of a random sample of Nottingham citizens.[5] We became used to being told by our informants that 'I've never told anyone about this before', while they simultaneously asserted, sometimes in tears, how important their experience was to them. In all cases, the reasons given for reticence were either fear of being thought stupid or of being mentally ill; that is to say, they were frightened that their experience would be tossed aside as no more than a delusion.[6]

Hardy's view of the religious impulse as a human universal might itself seem delusory and to have its origins in irrational speculation that ignores the hard facts. When he first put forward his proposal, formal religious adherence had already been in steep decline in most of Western Europe for many years. By the year 2000, the statistics for the United Kingdom showed that less than 8 per cent of the population were regular attenders at a religious service.[7] It is therefore important to note the difference between adherence to a formal religion and personal spiritual awareness, a distinction about which Hardy was himself sometimes careless. What we find in the case of spirituality is a dramatic contrast to church attendance figures. National surveys of reports of spiritual/religious experience suggest that a large majority of adults in Britain claims such awareness, and the proportions have increased over time. Between 1987 and 2000 there was at least a 60 per cent rise in report of spiritual experience (from 48 per cent to 76 per cent of the adult population)[8] while over approximately the same period regular church attendance fell by more than 20 per cent.[9] Judging from data gathered by the European Study of Values (ESV)[10] there is a similar pattern of formal religious decline and increasing report of spiritual experience in much of Western Europe. The same phenomenon has been reported for Australia.[11] Even in the United States, which most obviously bucks the trend of institutional decline in Western countries, the work of Zinnbauer and others[12] suggests that there are parallels, with increasing numbers of young people claiming that they are spiritual but not religious.

The crucial question is what people mean when they talk about their spiritual life. 'Spirituality' is such a portmanteau word and people's stories are so varied that one begins to doubt that they have anything in common. A forceful response to the question arose, almost as a side issue, when I set up the Children's Spirituality Project in the Nottingham University during the mid 1990s. I reasoned that in a culture highly critical of religion, the place to find spiritual experience most easily – if Hardy was right – must be among children, because they have not yet assimilated the sceptical canons of the adult world. My then doctoral student, Rebecca Nye, and I chose to study the spiritual lives of six-year-old and ten-year-old children in primary schools in Nottingham and Birmingham, two large industrial cities in England. Prior to our research there had been some studies of children's spirituality, based in Europe and North America, but using the Christian terminology through which spirituality has traditionally been expressed in those regions. Such an assumption may be excluding, for if Hardy is right, spiritual awareness should be species-wide and affect all of us, whether or not we have religious beliefs. How in such circumstances does one recognise spirituality in a secularised culture? We needed to devise a research procedure that would allow us to leap over boundaries created by cultural construction.

At first, we attempted to produce a formal definition of spirituality by setting up a seminar group of theologians, philosophers and other specialists on the spiritual life. The seminar was a failure. There were profound disagreements between the experts about the subject under discussion. Furthermore the language they were using was very remote from the world of the child, partly because of its technical nature, but also because in secularised Britain religious language is alien to many children. Nevertheless, while the seminar group could not agree on a definition, all of them said that they recognised spiritual experience when they came across it, and could specify examples of the kinds of circumstances that were conducive to it.

Following that hint, we decided to focus our research on certain practical situations rather than theoretical definitions. We identified three types of commonplace situation where, if there is such a thing as spiritual experience, it will be likely to become manifest. At the time, we were thinking about children but, as the categories evolved, we realised that they applied to children and adults alike. The three are:

Awareness of the here-and-now. The Edinburgh developmental psychologist Margaret Donaldson reminds us that babies under eighteen months or so appear to have no memory of an extended past stretching out behind them. Nor, apart from the briefest anticipations, do they appear to have any conception of the future. Donaldson talks about this 'here-and-now' awareness as the 'point mode'. She identifies it as the most basic mode of the mind's operation and, as such, it continues to have prominence in children even when they have partly achieved the 'line mode'; that is, the ability to focus on the 'there and then' of the past and future.[13] This immediacy of awareness also lies at the heart of meditation and contemplative prayer. It is celebrated and taken to very high levels of sophistication in the practical life of religious cultures, both East and West. In the Christian tradition, this is most obviously seen in the practice of contemplation and those approaches to prayer that stress awareness of the presence of God in all things. The eighteenth-century French Jesuit, Jean Pierre de Caussade, speaks directly of the 'sacrament of the present moment':

> We are well instructed only by the words God speaks to us per-
> sonally. It is not by reading or historical study that we become
> wise in the science of God: such methods alone produce but a
> vain, confused and self-inflating science. What instructs us is
> what happens from moment to moment ...[14]

Awareness of mystery. There are aspects of our life experience that are *in principle* incomprehensible and about which we feel we can say nothing. To take the mystery that obsesses many a person lying sleepless in the middle of the night: 'Why is there something rather than nothing?' Another way mystery is brought to our attention is in occasional feelings of disorientation. 'Isn't life strange', we sometimes say, to which an appropriate reply might be 'Compared with what?' For young children the distinction between the commonplace and the profound may not yet have any meaning. Their sense of mystery can be awakened by down-to-earth and familiar phenomena, simple events such as the appearance of a flame when a match is struck, or a light coming on at the flick of a switch, or the operation of a tap producing water. In adult life, technical explanations learned in school obscure the underlying question of *Being* to the extent that it is forgotten, as pointed out by Martin Heidegger in *Sein und Zeit*.[15] I suggest that children's perceptions of mystery, in situations where from an adult perspective there is a simple explanation, arise from as profound an experience as those of the contemplative philosopher or the theologian.

Awareness of Value. Feeling is a measure of what we value. Those things that matter to us most are associated with feeling at its most profound. As someone trained in the methods of empirical science, I know that feeling, aroused by the intuition of emerging meaning, in fact drives the supposed objectivity of scientists. Children readily express their ideas of worth or value in the intensity of their everyday experience of delight or desolation. Much of this is connected with the endless curiosity and meaning-making of children. The following adult example seems to me to put explicitly what is implicit in childhood and is drawn from the archive of the Religious Experience Research Centre:

> One day years ago, I went for a walk in the fields with my dog. My mind suddenly started thinking about the beauty around me, and I considered the marvellous order and timing of the growth of each flower, herb and the abundance of all the visible growth going on around. I remember thinking 'Here is mind'. Then we had to get over a stile and suddenly I was confronted with a bramble bush, which was absolutely laden with black glistening fruit. And the impact of that, linked with my former reasoning, gave me a great feeling of ecstasy. For a few moments, I really did feel at one with the Universe or the Creative Power we recognise. I know it was a feeling of oneness with

something outside myself, and also within. I must have been confronted with the source of all being – whatever one should call it. I have often told my friends about it, though it seems too sacred to talk about. The experience has never been forgotten. It was quite electric and quite unsought.

Rebecca, who did all the fieldwork, spent many hours talking with the children individually, gently introducing the areas of our interest, yet without the use of religious language unless it appeared spontaneously. To avoid being directive in that way, she stimulated conversation with a set of photographs of children in situations akin to the three categories mentioned above:

- A little girl sitting gazing into the fire in the dark of the evening.
- A small boy sitting on his bed looking out of the window at a star-filled night.
- A girl crying as she looks at her dead pet gerbil in its cage.
- A boy looking skywards after dropping his packed lunch onto a wet pavement.
- A boy standing in a schoolyard alone, apparently ignored by other children.

Rebecca asked the children questions like 'What do you suppose the girl is thinking as she gazes into the fire?', or 'What is the boy thinking about as he looks up at the stars?' The children's replies showed that they were projecting themselves into the situation and offering their personal thoughts and experiences. Without exception, all the children with whom Rebecca spoke had what we recognised as a spiritual dimension to their experience, and over a thousand pages of transcribed research conversations resulted. She undertook a computer-assisted analysis of the units of meaning in the text, using the NUD*IST programme,[16] a forerunner of IN VIVO. The purpose was to use the programme's technical speed in producing a hierarchically-organised tree of meanings, to see if it was possible to identify an overall word or phrase that drew together what was common to all the spiritual talk of the children. As Rebecca's extremely laborious line-by-line analysis of the data developed, the phrase that increasingly dominated her awareness, and eventually mine, was 'relational consciousness'. By this we mean:

> A generalised awareness of intimate relationship to reality, whether other people, the environment, to the depths of ones' self or to God.

At first this finding disconcerted me, because I had a preconception of spiritual practice as an isolated, private matter and I thought there was scriptural warranty for it (cf. in the Gospels: 'When you pray, go to your private room and shut the door'; in the *Bhagavad-Gita*: 'Let the yogi find a secret place in the forest'; etc.). On thinking more deeply about the question, the primary purpose of physical privacy became clear: it is to cut down the tendency to be distracted from the here-and-now of the 'point mode' – closing the door behind you makes it easier to look directly looking directly at one's relationship with immediate reality – and avoid the temptation to posture or display oneself to people who may be observing one.

Rebecca's careful work caused me to change my understanding of spirituality and to propose that relational consciousness is the primordial, inbuilt precursor of publicly-expressed (and hence socially-constructed) spirituality. It is thus a biological reality and is the immediate source of the religious impulse. I therefore dissent from Feuerbach's repudiation of spiritual experience as delusory, and, during the past decade, empirical evidence has begun to accumulate that contradicts his assertion. Two areas of investigation are proving to be particularly interesting, neither of them available to the science of Feuerbach's day. I have in mind the use of twin studies to discriminate between genetically and environmentally mediated features of living organisms, and the development of scanning devices to investigate metabolic changes in soft tissue, especially in the field of neurology.[17]

Twin studies have been used for many years in helping to make a distinction between human characteristics that are inherited from those that are acquired from the environment. The methodology has only in the final years of the twentieth century been applied to the study of spirituality, presumably because the dominance of Feuerbach's assumptions made it seem a redundant exercise. The pioneering work of Lindon Eaves at the Virginia Institute for

Psychiatric and Behavioral Genetics is a particularly interesting example, especially the report published in 1999 on research done in cooperation with Katherine Kirk and Nicholas Martin at the University of Queensland.[18] The team examined more than 2,200 pairs of identical and non-identical twins. In assessing spiritual awareness, they were able to use a measure of self-transcendence devised by Robert Cloninger as one of the temperament dimensions in his Temperament and Character Inventory.[19] The twins also answered questions about church attendance and the data showed that while churchgoing had much more to do with upbringing than heredity, spiritual awareness was significantly linked to genetic inheritance, thus supporting Alister Hardy's contention that it is biologically inbuilt. In a subsequent twin study in Japan, Juko Ando and his colleagues[20] made a similar finding in relation to spiritual awareness, suggesting that biology transcends East/West cultural differences.

Scanning devices that can photograph events taking place in soft tissue in living organisms have been applied to the study of spiritual experience only since the end of the twentieth century. One of the more thoughtful applications of this technology is by the head of the Nuclear Medicine Department in the University of Pennsylvania, Andrew Newberg. Newberg used a SPECT scanner to measure the changes of blood flow in the brains of volunteers as they undertook the most characteristic religious activity, prayer or meditation. He began by studying experts in Tibetan Buddhist meditation and later repeated the investigation with Franciscan nuns who practised centring prayer.[21] In both cases, there were numerous alterations throughout the brain, but two stood out. In deep meditation and prayer, the flow of blood reduces in the left posterior parietal lobe of the cerebral cortex (the back of the brain). This is the part of the cerebrum that makes us aware of where the boundary of our body lies, or 'where we stop and the rest of the world starts'. At the same time, the flow of blood increases bilaterally in the parts of the frontal lobes that are concerned with awareness. The combined effect is to lose the distinction between the praying individual and their surroundings at the same time as raising the general level of awareness.

Newberg and his colleagues first reported these results in 2001. It must be stressed that the limited accuracy of measurement of images produced by SPECT scanners means that repetitions of

Newberg's work by other neurophysiologists are necessary to increase confidence in his methodology. Nevertheless parallel work at the University of Montreal is already supportive. In 2006 Mario Beauregard and Vincent Paquette[22] published the data from a study of a group of Carmelite nuns, for which they used an MRI scanner, which works on a different principle from the SPECT scanner. Their research method was also different from that used by Newberg, but they produced comparable data.[23] These findings potentially constitute a remarkable breakthrough, for the physiological data closely complement subjective accounts of mystical experience available in many religious traditions, including Christianity. Nor is this the prerogative only of 'professional' mystics, i.e. monks and nuns. Outside the monastery, many of the respondents to Hardy's appeals spoke of spontaneously experiencing a loss of self, of being immersed in a continuum accompanied by a sense of intense reality.

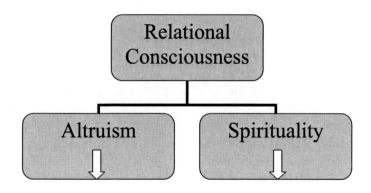

Ethics + Legal Systems   Theology + Religion

Figure 1.   **Key:** 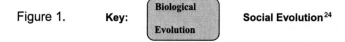   **Social Evolution**[24]

On this reading, spirituality and altruism are pre-discursive facets of biologically inbuilt relational consciousness. To get in touch with this primordium is to recover an awareness of the singularity of reality that we all had when we were infants. It brings with it the realisation that I am much closer to other people, the environment and the Transcendent than I had originally thought. In relation to other people and the environment I discover in myself an obligation to care for them, even to the point of self-sacrifice, perhaps equivalent to Emmanuel Levinas' account of ethics as 'first philosophy'.[25] Levinas is implying that before all extended discourse – religious, scientific, philosophical – there is a discovery of absolute obligation to the Other, and I take it that this is especially clear when we are in the 'point mode'. This may occur in the course of a disciplined life of meditation or contemplative prayer but also, as the empirical data demonstrate, it is reported very commonly in secularised cultures via spontaneous religious or spiritual experience. One important corollary is that socially constructed religion and altruism are independent of one another, though taking their origin from the same biological primordium. In other words, it is possible to be spiritually aware without being religious and religious without being spiritually aware. The model thus transcends a familiar argument about the link between ethics and religion. There is, or should be, a link between the two. However, people without religious belief are not necessarily out of touch with their relational consciousness and therefore have in them the same possibility of truly altruistic behaviour, though they will not attribute it to a religious source.

Given that relational consciousness underlies the ethical and religious impulses of the human species, we are in a position to understand why they are especially problematic for people who have absorbed the lessons of the European Enlightenment. The most obvious and important aspect of the Enlightenment that is at odds with relational consciousness is its Individualism. Returning for a moment to Fig. 1, it can be seen that the promotion of Individualism threatens not only relational consciousness, but also socially derived institutions including ethical and legal systems, and religious establishments. Europeans seem to have invented an extreme form of individualism – in a way that appears not to be duplicated in any other culture.[26] As such, I suggest that its development is an example of one kind of pathological social evolution described by William Durham, [27] that runs counter to natural selection and is damaging to the survival chances of a community. In what follows, my intention is to justify this claim by unpacking some of the factors lying behind the rise of Individualism and its negative effect on spirituality and altruism. Individualism has extremely complex roots in history[28] and, since we Westerners are ourselves immersed in this history, its assumptions are likely to be hidden from us.

Nevertheless it is possible to identify five major steps in its social evolution. Each of these steps has an ambivalent quality; that is to say, each is accompanied by both apparent gains and losses for our humanity.

Stage One: Coming to think of myself as 'I'. Some students of the origins of language argue that the skills necessary for the manufacture of stone tools imply being able to speak. If so, then this might apply to the human species *Homo habilis*, whose fossil remains in East Africa have been dated to two million years ago or, if recent evidence is to be believed, more than three million years.[29] Estimates that are more conservative confine language to our own species, *Homo sapiens*, in which case it cannot have its origins much before 200,000 years ago. Either way, the effect of language on the construction of the self is longstanding and universal, affecting all members of our own species.

Animals without language, although they are sensitive to their surroundings and relate to them in a knowing way, give at best only rather ambivalent indications of self-awareness.[30] While they quite clearly have a memory, they lack the verbal apparatus for reflecting upon their memories or for considering the fact of their own existence. Consequently they live almost entirely in the here-and-now of the immediate events around them, immersed in an unbroken continuum that includes themselves. The distinction between self and other, though it is acted out in the way animals manipulate their environment, is never clearly articulated. We saw earlier that the same is true of young infants. Adult observers of infants' behaviour can see quite easily that they operate in ways that implicitly recognise a distinction between self and other.[31] Putting it grammatically, they discriminate behaviourally between subject and object, but have little or no conscious awareness of the difference between the two. They are thus behaviourally strongly in touch with relational consciousness.

With the coming of language, a radical change occurs and, by the age of eighteen months, most healthy toddlers clearly and easily articulate the subject-object difference. When we are able to name the things around us it makes them stand out in contrast to their surroundings and we can also reflect on them remotely, at other times and in other places.[32] One of the most prominent objects that an infant learns about through language is its self, a fact that is drawn attention to constantly by the parents when they teach the baby to say 'You', 'Me' and 'I'. When 'I' becomes an object of consciousness, it can be thought about in the same way as any other object. 'I' begin to build up a set of memories and anticipations that make up a life history – and in the process, I become an individual. Nevertheless, it is important not to lose sight of the fact that the process of individualisation is not done in isolation; it is always done in the context of a culture and in intimate relationship to others.

Stage Two: Learning to read and write. Compared to the span of existence of the human species, literacy arrived almost yesterday. Most people for most of human history have been illiterate and this was true until little more than a century ago even in the industrialised West. For example, in Britain, it was not until the passing of the 1870 Education Act that a concerted effort was made to eliminate illiteracy – a task that is not yet complete. Human consciousness has therefore evolved over many millennia in the absence of the ability to read and write. In a fundamental way, becoming literate is a revolutionary move away from the longstanding natural and universal human condition.

Such a radical change is bound to have large-scale cognitive effects and these were first fully investigated by the Russian psychologist Alexander Luria. During the 1930s, the Soviet government under the leadership of Stalin decreed the forced collectivisation of agriculture throughout the vast republic. The decree was combined with a vigorous effort to teach the peasantry to read and write, for literacy was necessary if they were to be able to manage the complex work of the collective farms. Luria took the opportunity to study how the shift to literacy affected hitherto illiterate peasants living in a group of remote mountain villages and pasturelands in Uzbekistan and Kyrgyzstan.

In summary, Luria[33] showed that, compared with people who could read and write, the thinking of illiterates is much more tied to the immediate situation (that is, the here-and-now) than to abstract reflections on the past and future. This meant that intellectual tasks that were elementary for literate people, for example simple classification, were difficult or impossible for them. In one of Luria's experiments, semi-educated and only recently literate collective farm activists were easily able to sort skeins of wool in terms of category, shades of blue, red, yellow and so on. On the other hand, illiterate peasant women who, as expert embroiderers, were perfectly well aware of subtle variations of colour, when asked to classify a set of wools into shades of brown, would say things like: 'It can't be done, they're not at all alike; this is like calf's dung, this is like a peach.' Similarly, most men failed to complete simple syllogisms, such as: 'In the North, all bears are white. Novaya Zemlya is in the North. What colour are the bears there?' Many of the men were unable to give the correct answer, saying things like: 'How should I know, I've never been to the North. I've seen a black bear.' More crucially, people also seemed not to have much conception of themselves as individuals and, when invited to describe themselves, suggested to Luria and his assistants that they should ask someone else to answer for them.

Luria realised that such responses were due not to lack of intelligence, but to the structure imposed on thought by illiteracy. Literacy continues the process of individualisation initiated by the ability to speak, but with much greater impact. Literacy extends memory, permits us to classify and to generalise and gives us the ability to move in our imagination out of the concrete here-and-now and into lengthy abstraction. Above all, literacy opens the possibility of a private world and the ability to have a uniquely personal point of view, limited only by the size of one's library. In an important sense, literacy opens the door to personal freedom.

Complex modern society would be unable to operate without the skills that become possible with the ability to read and write. However, the construction of a vast private world also potentially creates blindness to our relationship with the here-and-now. Along with this loss, there is the likelihood of deterioration in our immediate sense of belonging to and being continuous with the surrounding community. In those traditional religious societies that are literate (Jews, Christians and Muslims are, after all, 'People of the Book'), this weakness is recognised and strategies have been created to counteract the loss of immediacy. Each of these cultures has developed a highly sophisticated set of practical exercises that help people to enter more and more deeply into holistic awareness of the here-and-now. I mean of course the skills of contemplative prayer (raising the heart and mind to God now, in this moment) or silent meditation (for example, maintaining awareness of the act of breathing) currently being investigated by Newberg and others. These practices are undertaken by the faithful as a structured routine, often attended to several times each day. Ultimately the aim is to remain in this state of alertness permanently, or as St Paul put it, to pray without ceasing.

Stage Three: Abandoning the holistic perspective. What happens to consciousness though, when these strategies for staying in touch holistically are largely ignored, or abandoned altogether, as is more often than not the case in contemporary Western society? This constitutes the third step towards the ideology of individualism. As literacy becomes more and more widespread it is more difficult, less natural, for people to enter the here-and-now awareness that is commonplace among members of primary oral cultures.[34] One effect on those who are highly literate is the increasing probability that they will acquire a disembodied, theoretical consciousness of the self, withdrawn from engagement in the surrounding environment.

The legacy in academic circles, perhaps especially in the field of empirical science, in which I was educated, is an admiration for detached objectivity as a necessary professional stance. Like every other beginner in the laboratory, I learned that the inconstant and emotionally labile 'me' never puts water in a test tube. In writing up experiments 'it was noted' that 'water was placed in a test tube' by an abstract, clinically detached being who had nothing to do with the scruffy bunch of schoolboys occupying the classroom. This cult gave the false impression that human factors like hesitancy, error and free-floating imagination do not enter into the properly conducted research act. Taken far enough, training in detachment can include a distancing from other people and a loss of awareness of one's own emotional state. Intellectuals are notorious for 'living in their heads', cut off from emotion, sometimes to the detriment of their health.[35]

Many conjectures have been made about both the timing and the historical and political aspects of this growing sense of personal isolation. The nineteenth-century Swiss historian, Jacob Burckhardt, was one of the first to suggest a specific period in which individualism began to become dominant in European history. In his pioneering study *The Civilization of the Renaissance in Italy,*[36] he identified the emergence of the 'free person' as occurring first in Italy, pre-eminently in renaissance Florence. Another suggested source of individualism is the Protestant branch of the Christian religion. Max Weber famously claimed that Protestantism, especially in its Calvinist form, created an inner isolation in the believer sufficiently powerful to change the entire economic and political structure of the countries of the Reformation during the sixteenth century. Calvin's emphasis on the doctrine of predestination faces anyone who takes this belief seriously with an unprecedented inner loneliness:

> No one could help him. No priest, for the chosen one can understand the word of God only in his own heart. No sacraments, for though the sacraments had been ordained by God for the increase of His glory, and must hence be scrupulously observed, they are not a means to the attainment of grace, but only the subjective *externa subsidia* of faith. No Church, for though it was held that *extra ecclesiam nulla salus* in the sense that whoever kept away from the true Church could never belong to God's chosen band, nevertheless the membership of the external Church included the doomed ... Finally, even no God. For even Christ had died only for the elect ...[37]

The mere appearance of goodness is no guarantee, since anyone can make a public pretence of virtue while being inwardly corrupt. Therefore, a robust doctrine of predestination encourages not only endless self-questioning, as Weber remarked, but also suspicion of the motives of others. A belief in predestination was not limited to Calvinism; it also appeared in certain seventeenth-century forms of Catholicism, especially Jansenism[38] In his essay *Of Charity and Self Love*, written in 1674, Pierre Nicole, Jansenist priest and friend of Blaise Pascal, explains how impersonation of virtue can be so accurate that it deceives everyone; hence it is not wise to trust anyone. It is deeply incongruous that a religious doctrine should have the effect of encouraging the erosion of the relational consciousness that, I take it, underpins spirituality.

The idea of 'man alone' also gained currency in seventeenth-century Europe through the influence of the two dominant and contrasting philosophical perspectives of that period. Two archetypal representatives are the idealist Descartes and the materialist Thomas Hobbes. In the case of Descartes, his decision to make the *Cogito* ('*I think*, therefore I am') the rock on which to build his philosophy had a devastating effect on the plausibility of relational consciousness. In the words of the Scottish twentieth-century philosopher John Macmurray:

> ... the adoption of the 'I think' as the centre of reference and starting-point of ... philosophy makes it formally impossible to do justice to religious experience. For thought is inherently private; and any philosophy which takes its stand on the primacy of thought, which defines the Self as the Thinker, is committed formally to an extreme logical individualism. It is necessarily egocentric.[39]

Thomas Hobbes' materialism was probably even more influential than Descartes' philosophy in promoting individualism. Hobbes was born in 1588 and lived through what historians see as one of the most violent periods of turmoil in European history. In particular, the Thirty Years War ravaged the continent throughout his early adult life. It is perhaps no surprise that he had a sceptical attitude towards the possibility of human benevolence. Most scholars believe he was a secret atheist at a time when publicly declared atheism would put a person in considerable personal danger.[40]

His materialist interpretation of human nature led him to the view that in the state of nature life is a warfare of all against all. If we co-operate with other people, it is only because we see these interactions as in our interest (in this sense he was a precursor of modern biological theorists of reciprocal altruism and kin selection).[41] His assumption that each of us is in a struggle for power against everyone else is based on a materialist metaphysics stating that 'minds never meet, that ideas are never really shared and that

each of us is always and finally isolated from every other individual'.[42] According to his most celebrated aphorism, life in the
state of nature is 'solitary, nasty, brutish and short'.

People who have not read Hobbes are not always aware of the
extreme violence he uses to describe the natural state of human
society – totally at odds with the insights provided by relational
consciousness. Thus:

> All men in the state of nature have a desire and will to
> hurt.[43]

In his masterwork *Leviathan,* Hobbes makes explicit the brutality
that people unleash upon each other in such a state:

> I put for a generall inclination of all mankind, a perpetuall
> and restlesse desire of Power after power, that ceaseth
> onely in Death ... The way of one Competitor, to the
> attaining of his desire, is to kill, subdue, supplant, or repell
> the other.[44]

Hence the need for Leviathan, a Sovereign to subdue the anarchy
and who himself gains that position through acts of terror or
outright warfare:

> The attaining to this Soveraigne Power is by two ways.
> One, by Natural force; as when a man maketh his children
> to submit themselves, and their children to his government,
> as being able to destroy them if they refuse; or by warre
> subdueth his enemies to his will, giving them their lives on
> that condition.[45]

*Stage Four: Individualism seen as the pivot of the market
economy.* The unbridled savagery that Hobbes loads onto human
nature is of much more than antiquarian interest. The Canadian
economic historian Brough Macpherson asserted that Hobbes'
account of society continues to dictate the organisation of the
modern bureaucratic state. It is based, in Macpherson's phrase, on
the doctrine of 'possessive individualism'.[46] The picture of human
beings that Hobbes came up with was not simply the result of his
free ranging scholarly reflection. It was conditioned by the social

order in which Hobbes was living; that is to say, seventeenth-century bourgeois society at the point where market forces first began to take on a dominant role. This is the fourth and most crucial step in the construction of European individualism because of its powerful economic impact.

Selfishness was not invented in the seventeenth century. What was new was the legitimation it gained at that point in time. Selfishness was to come to be seen as not merely acceptable, but a necessary expedient in the search for economic and political stability. The impassioned speech on behalf of 'greed as good' by the reptilian financier Gordon Gecko in the film *Wall Street* takes its justification from this belief. In his essay *The Passions and the Interests*,[47] the economic historian Albert Hirschman meditates on the remarkable metamorphosis of the mediaeval sin of avarice into a necessary economic virtue. Dante's *Divine Comedy*, completed at the beginning of the fourteenth century, had envisioned sins of avarice as sufficient to consign their perpetrator to the fourth level of Hell. By the end of the eighteenth century, avarice had come to be seen by economists as a virtue. Hirschman traces the evolution of this transformation in the first place to:

> ... a feeling [that] arose in the Renaissance and became firm conviction during the seventeenth century that moralising philosophy and religious precept could no longer be trusted with restraining the destructive passions of men.[48]

Hobbes' initial solution, the advocacy of the straightforward repression of uncontrolled passion, came to be seen as inadequate. His pessimism about human motivation was not sufficiently responded to by the mere existence of a sovereign power. Who can predict if the sovereign will truly guard the peace of society, when in reality he may himself be a cruel despot, heedless of the cries of the oppressed, or merely weak?

According to Hirschman, the answer that emerged was to harness one of the passions against the others. The key to this solution, according to a whole series of seventeenth- and eighteenth-century thinkers, was the unquenchable desire for personal gain. The term that came to be used for this particular lust for possessions and which sanitised and set it apart from the others was 'interests':

> Because of the semantic drift of the term 'interests', the opposition between interests and passions could also mean and convey a different thought, much more startling in view of traditional values: namely, that one set of passions, hitherto variously known as greed, avarice, or love of lucre, could be usefully employed to oppose and bridle such other passions as ambition, lust for power, or sexual lust.[49]

The effect of this semantic drift is important, because throughout the seventeenth century, outside the field of economic and political writing, ordinary popular tracts on virtue continued to refer to avarice as one of the most repulsive of sins. On the other hand, its synonym, 'interest', achieved a steadily enhanced status as the 'countervailing' passion. Finally, says Hirschman, it took on such a mantle of virtue, that in certain respects it was seen as more admirable, certainly more socially useful, than unselfishness. Thus in 1767 the Scottish economist Sir James Steuart could argue that in economic matters, self-interest is to be preferred to traditional virtue, *especially* a meddling concern for the public interest:

> ... were a people to become quite disinterested: there would be no possibility of governing them. Everyone might consider the interest of his country in a different light, and many might join in the ruin of it, by endeavouring to promote its advantages [quoted in Hirschman].[50]

The point was, as Steuart's colleague David Hume had also said of desire for gain, that it is a universal passion that operates at all times, in all places and upon everybody. It is thus much more predictable than other passions such as lust or revenge, which operate sporadically and are directed towards particular people. The very constancy of avarice had made it a virtue. Most famously, because of his influence on all subsequent economic thinking, in *The Wealth of Nations* published in 1776,[51] the Scottish philosopher Adam Smith gave a financial rather than a political or moral justification for the unrestricted pursuit of personal gain.[52] Individualist philosophy (whether materialist or idealist) and the promotion of self-interest as the necessary basis for a stable market economy were mutually and powerfully reinforcing. They could not fail to be severely damaging to any trust in relational consciousness, and hence to altruism. However, beyond the four steps leading up to this point there is a fifth and final step to go.

Stage Five: Relational consciousness totally repudiated. One might feel that Feuerbach's repudiation of religion was as extreme as it is possible to get. Not so. His opinion was to be violently rejected as incomplete atheism by Max Stirner,[53] a member of the neo-Hegelian group in Berlin to which Marx and Engels had once belonged. With Stirner, we see the final abandonment of any notion of relational consciousness, for he preached absolute egotism. Stirner concurred with the rejection of a relationship with God as fantasy, but felt that Feuerbach was a sentimentalist who had failed to see the full implications of his discovery. Feuerbach, though a convinced atheist, continued to hold to the moral ideals advocated by Christianity. To Stirner such ideals were also projections, no different in kind from belief in God. For him all ideals and moral laws, without exception, are simply religion by another name, since they imply an imaginary and enslaving obligation beyond the self.

Published in 1845, four years after Feuerbach's *Essence of Christianity*, Stirner's only major work is *The Ego and Its Own*.[54] Of all atheist writings, Stirner's is the most thoroughgoing in its uncompromising rejection of every philosophical, religious and political ideal, seen as nothing more than the depreciation of the individual:

> Away ... with every concern that is not altogether my concern! You think that at least the 'good cause' must be my concern? What's good? What's bad? Why I myself am my concern, and I am neither good nor bad. Neither has meaning for me. The divine is God's concern: the human, man's. My concern is neither the divine nor the human, not the true, good, just, free etc, but is – unique, as I am unique. Nothing is more to me than myself![55]

And, reminiscent of Hobbes:

> For me you are nothing but my food, even as I am fed
> upon and turned to use by you. We have only one relation
> to each other, that of *usableness,* of utility, of use.[56]

Stirner's biographer, R. W. K. Paterson,[57] comments:

> Whether owing to a failure of nerve, or to some basic
> astigmatism, the Feuerbachs and the Bauers[58] had all
> stopped short of the crucial point; at the last moment they
> had admitted the presence of some transcendental object in
> the scheme of things – not indeed a 'God' in the sense of
> a personal deity, but a 'Humanity', or a 'Society' or a
> 'Morality', all of which were as fictitious, and as autocratic
> in their claims upon the individual concrete human being,
> as any personal God had ever been; and thus the
> programme of atheism still remained to be carried through
> to its conclusion ...[59]

And with a brutality fully equal to Hobbes:

> *Nothing,* not even the primordial obligations not to lie,
> steal, kill etc. can induce the self-possessed egotist to take
> any step that is not in the fullest accord with his own
> distinct interests as he himself determines them ...[60]

Paterson sums up:

> Stirner's contribution to the German religious debate of the
> 1840s was to bring the whole debate to a momentary and
> stupefied halt. The full consequences of thoroughgoing
> atheism were now disclosed for all to see.[61]

Remarkably, Stirner's hero, the isolated self-sufficient individual,
had already been identified and attacked ferociously. He was none
other than the unencumbered entrepreneurial fat cat who is still
with us today in plentiful supply. He is:

> ... an individual separated from the community, withdrawn
> into himself, wholly preoccupied with his private interest
> and acting in accordance with his private caprice ... [For

him] the only bond between men is natural necessity, need, and private interest.[62]

Stirner's extreme individualism put into stark and uncompromising words what had been developing as an increasingly powerful, but muffled and disinfected assumption over the previous two centuries. Individualism encourages the complete suppression of relational consciousness and a consequent leeching away of ethical relations between the members of our modern commercial society. Once transcendence is abandoned (either belief in God or the kind of transcendental equivalent advocated by Feuerbach), morality becomes entirely subservient to what is financially prudent. In practice, Hobbes had already dispensed with all purposes apart from those that ensure the smooth working of the marketplace.[63] The binding obligation that remains in possessive market societies is to make sure the market does not collapse through financial mismanagement. In this circumstance, the difference between moral obligation and what is financially prudent becomes insignificant.

Where financial prudence is the arbiter of conduct, politeness and care for the other person become suspect as no more than a manoeuvre, an optional extra to smooth the path of a financial transaction. In other words, it is spiritually corrupt. Martin Buber makes the same point in his comments on Stirner:

> Responsibility presupposes one who addresses me
> primarily, that is, from a realm independent of myself, and
> to whom I am answerable. He addresses me about
> something that he has entrusted to me and that I am
> bound to take care of loyally. He addresses me from his
> trust and I respond in my loyalty or refuse to respond in
> my disloyalty, or I have fallen into disloyalty and wrestle
> free of it by the loyalty of the response ... Where no
> primary address and claim can touch me, for everything is
> 'My property', responsibility has become a phantom ...[64]

The difficulty for Stirner is that he has entirely lost touch with relational consciousness; hence, altruism is incredible to him. For Buber, he is a sociopath:

> He simply does not know what of elemental reality lies
> between life and life, he does not know the mysteries of
> address and answer, claim and disclaim, word and response
> ...[65]

Stirner and Hobbes between them bracket a period in European history when individualism led to the progressive and cumulative discrediting of what in my view is a fundamental aspect of our biological make-up, relational consciousness. The recent findings from twin studies and the exponential growth in the use of scanning devices to explore the physiology of the brain, give a degree of confidence to the assertion that Feuerbach was mistaken in his dismissal of spiritual experience. It is a dismissal that has been the default position for critics of religion over the past 150 years, and it continues to be almost axiomatic in sceptical rhetoric.

Neither of the types of finding exemplified above gets a mention in the most prominent critique of religion to emerge from the 'New Atheists', Richard Dawkins' *The God Delusion*. Though he never discusses the hypothesis of Alister Hardy, his old professor, Dawkins is nevertheless aware that a physiological basis for spiritual experience cannot be dismissed as easily as Feuerbach claimed. He responds by offering a radically modified hypothesis to explain spiritual experience, drawing his ideas from the fascinating speculations of the anthropologist Pascal Boyer[66] and the somewhat similar views of the American anthropologist Scott Atran. They move away from Feuerbach's outright denial of the biological reality underlying religion and accept that religious beliefs had survival value in the past and therefore were selected during the process of evolution. Whether such beliefs are thought to be merely the result of social evolution or have a deeper biological basis is not entirely clear, but in any case, Dawkins interprets this as a fortunate accident. That is to say, cognitive adaptations that have evolved for other purposes just happen to be available for the construction of what were once socially useful, but mistaken, religious ideas. Since we now 'know' that these ideas are delusory, they cease to have a function and become instead the source of fanaticisms and social divisions.

This is where Hardy and secular critics like Dawkins would certainly part company and where, in my view, Hardy's hypothesis is the more plausible. Dawkins' argument is flawed because it assumes as axiomatic that religious belief is erroneous and therefore he chooses to explain away the biological realities as accidental. That is to prejudge the issue within the sceptical canons of the European Enlightenment and to contort improperly the scientific method of which in other respects Dawkins is such an eminent defender. Science bases itself on empirical data and, following Occam's Razor, seeks the most straightforward and simplest interpretation of the facts. In this case, it is to say that there appears to be a transcendent dimension to human experience, universally found, associated with specific physiological states, and commonly but not exclusively associated with religious belief systems.

The resolution of this debate is of more than academic interest, since it has a bearing on a large group of social problems that arguably we have inherited from the Enlightenment. Several of the most important of these are comprehensively documented for the United States in Robert Putnam's study, *Bowling Alone.*[67] He provides statistics that show a collapse since the 1960s across almost all social behaviour. The loss of what Putnam calls 'social capital' and I identify as natural, unselfconscious altruism, is graphically illustrated in the contemporary urban environment: the ubiquitous deployment of the paraphernalia of surveillance (cameras, electronic tracking devices, alarm systems, databases) to discourage crime. At the same time, there is a considerable volume of recent legislation designed to protect innocent and vulnerable people from exploitation, either sexually or economically. No doubt such laws are needed, but they help to perpetuate and sediment a view of society as unfriendly and untrustworthy. They are a totalitarian means of controlling a society in which altruism has become suspect and virtue a fraud.

The history that I have outlined explains why it is no surprise that there are many doubts about the plausibility of religion. Nevertheless, the empirical evidence suggests that in investigating spiritual experience we are examining a biological constant that is not a delusion. The fact that human decency and mutual trust continue to be widespread is evidence of its resilience, even though severely constricted in its range by the straitjacket of individualism. Furthermore, since individualism is a socially constructed ideology, there is always the possibility of deconstruction.

Over the past four hundred years, religion has been under increasing attack in the western world. I have argued that commercial and intellectual pressures have forced us towards a heartless individualism that cancels relational consciousness/spiritual awareness out of the human equation. Until recently, spirituality has had a difficult time in the Western world, and along with it the plausibility of religious institutions. It is therefore no surprise that Alister Hardy had such difficulty in getting a hearing. Nevertheless, the empirical research that he initiated is becoming steadily more prominent. It has a major role to play in nudging our embodied relational consciousness into the foreground of our awareness, and the recovery of our spiritual health.

Appendix

The Religious Experience Research Centre, University of Wales at Lampeter

The following information was kindly provided by Professor Paul Badham, until 2010 the Director of the RERC.

The Religious Experience Research Centre moved to Lampeter in 2000. Since that time, the primary research activity has been 'A Global Study of Religious Experience'. The most important of these investigations was a four-year research programme, supported by a grant of £335,000 from the John Templeton Foundation, to study religious experience in China. In conjunction with seven Chinese Universities, a major survey was completed leading to three books and a succession of articles. This research has sparked off parallel surveys using the same questionnaire in Taiwan, Turkey and India. The results of such surveys appear to vindicate Sir Alister's conviction that, as the result of natural selection, human beings have evolved a biologically-based openness to a 'spiritual dimension' of experience that transcends differences in culture and religious tradition.

The ongoing research work of the Centre is largely carried out by doctoral students and typically there are about six PhD students working on different aspects of religious experience. The publication of their theses is one of the important ways in which the work of the Centre advances and is disseminated. In recent years five such doctoral publications have related to the study of near-death experiences.

Moving the Centre to Lampeter coincided with the decision of the four British Advanced Level examining boards to offer modules in Religious Experience drawing upon the work of Sir Alister and his successors. Since 2010 these modules have become increasingly popular. Modules in Religious Experience are characteristically taken in the second year of an A-level course and consequently carry half the marks in Year Two, on which the new 'A Star' Grade is based. The new A-level syllabuses refer directly to the work of the RERC, and the Centre has produced a number of publications to assist schools. In particular, past Associate Director, Dr Wendy Dossett, has published *Religious Experience: A Guide to A-level* (UWIC, 2006) and Marianne Rankin (formerly, Chair of the Hardy Society) has written a textbook entitled *An Introduction to Spiritual and Religious Experience* (Continuum, 2009).

The Research Centre offers a Master's degree in the Study of Religious Experience. This is primarily taught on a part-time external basis and is aimed in particular at RE Teachers wishing to equip themselves better for teaching about religious experience at Advanced Level in schools. The work of the Centre is also important for the 14–19 transformation agenda in educational establishments which stress the importance of developing 'spirituality' as a major aspect of personal growth. In connection with this work, the RERC frequently receives groups of visitors from schools and FE colleges and Dr Gregory A. Barker and the Research Centre team undertake visits to schools to speak on the work of the Centre.

Contacts:

The Alister Hardy Religious Experience Research Centre
Department of Theology, Religious Studies and Islamic Studies,
University of Wales Lampeter,
Ceredigion SA48 7ED
Tel: +44 (0)1570 424821
Fax: +44 (0)1570 423641
Email: ahardytrust@lamp.ac.uk
Website: www.alisterhardyreligiousexperience.co.uk

Directors: Dr Greg Barker, Dr. Bettina Schmidt (MA Religious Experience) and Sally Wilkinson (Learning Resources)

Tel: +44 (0)1570 422351
Email: c/o m.tobias@tsd.ac.uk

Administrator: David Greenwood
Tel: +44 (0)1570 422351 x 503
Fax: +44 (0)1570 423641
Email: d.greenwood@lamp.ac.uk

References

Allen, G. (1897/2007). *The Evolution of the Idea of God*, New York: Cosimo Books.

Ando, J. et al. (2004). 'Genetic and environmental structure of Cloninger's Temperament and Character Dimensions', *Journal of Personality Disorders*, 18 (4): 379–393.

Arnold, M. (1998). *Selected Poems*, London: Phoenix Press.

Atran, S. (2002). *In Gods we Trust: the Evolutionary Landscape of Religion*, New York: Oxford University Press.

Atran, S. & Norenzayan, A. (2004). 'Religion's evolutionary landscape: counterintuition, commitment, compassion, communion', *Behavioral and Brain Sciences*, 27 (6): 713–730.

Back, K. & Bourque, L. (1970). 'Can feelings be enumerated?', *Behavioral Science*, 15: 487–496.

Balls, R. (1934). 'A revolutionary development in herring fishing: the plankton recorder in commercial use', *The Fish Trades Gazette*, February 24.

Bamford, T. W. (1978). *The University of Hull: the First Fifty Years*, published for the University of Hull by Oxford University Press.

Bauman, Z. (1993). *Postmodern Ethics*, Oxford: Blackwell.

Beardsworth, T. (1977). *A Sense of Presence*, Oxford: RERU.

Beattie, Tina (2007). *The New Atheists*, London: Darton, Longman & Todd.

Beauregard, M. & Paquette, V. (2006). 'Neural correlates of a mystical experience in Carmelite nuns', *Neuroscience Letters*, 405 (3): 186–190.

Beckett, J. (1980). *The Book of Nottingham*, Buckingham: Barracuda Books.

Bekoff, M., Allen, C. & Burghardt, G. (2002). *The Cognitive Animal*, Cambridge, MA: The MIT Press.

Bentham, G. & Hooker, J. (1908). *Handbook of the British Flora* (6th edition), London: Lovell, Reeve & Co.

Berger, P. & Luckmann, T. (1967). *The Social Construction of Reality*, London: Allen Lane, The Penguin Press in 1967.

Berman, D. (1990). *A History of Atheism in Britain: From Hobbes to Russell*, London & New York: Routledge.

Blacker, C. P. (1967). 'Obituary: Alexander Carr-Saunders', *Population Studies*, 20 (3): 365–369.

Booth, W. (1890/2006). *In Darkest England and the Way Out*, Liskeard: Diggory Press.

Bourne, G. (1987). *Textbook of Oarsmanship: A Classic of Rowing Literature*, Toronto: Sport Book Publishers.

Boyer, P. (2001). *Religion Explained: The Evolutionary Origins of Religious Thought*, New York: Basic Books.

Brierley, P. (2000). *Religious Trends No. 1: 1999/2000*, London: Christian Research Association.

Brown, C. (2001). *The Death of Christian Britain: Understanding Secularisation 1800–2000*, London and New York: Routledge.

Browne, J. (2002). *Darwin* (2 vols.), London: Pimlico Press.

Bruce, G. (1982). *Kimberley Ale. The Story of Hardys & Hansons, Kimberley 1832–1982*, London: Henry Melland Ltd.

Bruce, S. (2002). *God is Dead: Secularization in the West*, Oxford: Blackwell Publishers.

Buber, M. (1961). *Between Man and Man*, (tr. by Ronald Gregor Smith), London: Fontana.

Buckley, M. (1987). *At the Origins of Modern Atheism*, New Haven and London: Yale University Press.

Buckley, M. (2004). *Denying and Disclosing God: the Ambiguous Progress of Modern Atheism*, New Haven and London: Yale University Press.

Burckhardt, J. (1860/2004). *The Civilisation of the Renaissance in Italy*, London: Penguin Classics.

Burkhardt, R. (2005) *Patterns of Behavior: Konrad Lorenz, Niko Tinbergen and the founding of Ethology*, University of Chicago Press.

Butler, S. (1903/2006). *The Way of All Flesh* (with an introduction by Richard Hoggart), Harmondsworth: Penguin Classics.

Cameron, E. Z. & du Toit, J.T. (2007). 'Winning by a neck: Tall giraffes avoid competing with shorter browsers', *American Naturalist*, 169 (1): 130–135.

Caussade, J-P. de (1933). *Self-Abandonment to Divine Providence*, (tr. by Algar Thorold), London: Burns & Oates.

References

Clark, K. (1950). *The Gothic Revival*, London: Constable.

Clarke, B. (1995). 'Edmund Brisco Ford', *Royal Society Biographical Memoirs*, 41: 145–168.

Clarke, B. (2003). 'Heredity – The art of innuendo', *Heredity*, 90: 279–280.

Cleghorn, J. (1854). 'On the fluctuations in the herring fisheries'. *British Association for the Advancement of Science*, 24: 124.

Cloninger, C. R. et al. (1994). *The Temperament and Character Inventory: A guide to its development and use.* St Louis, Missouri: Washington University Center for Psychology of Personality.

Cloninger, C. R. (2004). *Feeling Good: The Science of Wellbeing*, Oxford University Press.

Clydeside Cameos (n.d.). 'Uncle Tom', *Fairplay XIII*, 101–108.

Conan Doyle, A. (1909). 'Bendy's Sermon', *Strand Magazine*, April: 420–424.

Cohen, J. M. & Phipps, J-M. (1979). *The Common Experience*, London: Rider and Company.

Corfield, R. (2003). *The Silent Landscape: The Scientific Voyage of HMS Challenger*, London: Henry Joseph Press.

Damasio, A. (1994). *Descartes' Error: Emotion, Reason and the Human Brain*, New York: Putnam.

Damasio, A. (2000). *The Feeling of What Happens: Body, Emotion and the Making of Consciousness*, London: Vintage Books.

Dante Alighieri (1314/2006). *The Divine Comedy*, Lenox, MA: Hard Press.

Darlington, C. D. (1957). *The Evolution of Man and Society*, London: Allen & Unwin.

Darnley, R. (1923). 'A new Antarctic expedition', *The Nineteenth Century*, May.

Davie, G. (2002). *Europe – The Exceptional Case: Parameters of faith in the modern world*, London: Darton, Longman & Todd.

Davis, V. D. (1932). *A History of Manchester College from its Foundation in Manchester to its Establishment in Oxford*, London: George Allen & Unwin.

Dawkins, R. (1976). *The Selfish Gene*, Oxford University Press.

Dawkins, R. (1986). *The Blind Watchmaker*, London: Longman Scientific and Technical.

Dawkins, R. (2002). Article on F. W. Sanderson, *Guardian* July 6, archived on the Internet at www.guardian.co.uk/Archive/Article/0,4273,4455275,00.html

Dawkins, R. (2006). *The God Delusion*, London: Bantam Press.

Dawkins, R. (ed.) (2008). *The Oxford Book of Modern Science Writing*, Oxford University Press.

Defoe, D. (1724–26/1991). *A Tour of the Whole Island of Great Britain* (Abridged and Illustrated Edition) edited by P. N. Furbank, W. R. Owens & A. J. Coulson, New Haven & London: Yale University Press.

Desmond, A. & Moore, R. (1991). *Darwin*, London: Michael Joseph.

Diaconis, P. & Mosteller, F. (1989). 'Methods for Studying Coincidences', *Journal of the American Statistical Association*, 84 (408): 853–861.

Donaldson, M. (1992). *Human Minds*, London: Allen Lane.

Donne, J. (1623/1999). *Devotions upon Emergent Occasions/Death's Duel*, New York: Vintage Books.

Dossett, W. (2006). *Religious Experience: A Guide to A-level*, UWIC.

Dugatkin, L. E. (2006). *The Altruism Equation: Seven scientists search for the origins of goodness*, Princeton University Press.

Dumont, L. (1986). *Essays on Individualism*, Chicago University Press.

Durham, W. (1991). *Co-Evolution: Genes, Culture and Human Diversity*, Stanford University Press.

Durkheim, E. (1915). *The Elementary Forms of the Religious Life* (tr. J.W. Swain), London: George Allen & Unwin.

Ellegard, A. (1859–72/1990). *Darwin and the General Reader: The Reception of Darwin's Theory of Evolution in the British Periodical Press, 1859–72* (reprint edition), Chicago University Press.

Engels, F. (1845/1987). *The Condition of the Working Classes in England* (Penguin Classics Edition, edited by V. G. Kiernan), Harmondsworth: Penguin Books.

Feuerbach, L. (1841/1957). *The Essence of Christianity* (tr. George Eliot & intro. by Karl Barth), New York: Harper Torchbooks.

Feuerbach, L. (1851/1967). *Lectures on the Essence of Religion* (tr. Ralph Manheim), New York: Harper & Row.

Fodor, J. & Piatelli-Palmerini, M. (2010). *What Darwin Got Wrong*, London: Profile Books.

Franklin, J. (2006). *Exploration into the Spirit*, Lampeter: Alister Hardy Society.

Freud, S. (1900/1976). *The Interpretation of Dreams* (tr. James Strachey), Harmondsworth: Penguin Books.

Freud, S. (1928). *The Future of an Illusion*, London: The Hogarth Press.

Freud, S. (1916–17/1971). *Introductory Lectures on Psychoanalysis* (tr. James Strachey), Harmondsworth: Penguin Books.

Gadamer, H-G. (1975). *Truth and Method*, London: Sheed & Ward.

Gardner, W. H. (1953). *Gerard Manley Hopkins: A Selection of his Poems and Prose*, Harmondsworth: Penguin Books.

Garstang, W. (1900). 'The impoverishment of the sea', *Journal of the Marine Biological Association of the United Kingdom*, 6 (1): 1900, 1–69.

Garstang, W. (1951). *Larval Forms and Other Zoological Verses*, Oxford (with an introduction by Sir Alister C. Hardy), Oxford: Basil Blackwell.

Gendlin, E. (2003). *Focusing*, London: Rider.

References

Gendlin, E. (1997). *Experiencing and the Creation of Meaning*. Chicago: Northwestern University Press.

George, H. K. (1934). 'Science finds the best fishing grounds: no need now to take pot luck', *Fishing News,* June 16.

Glock, C. & Stark, R. (1965). *Religion and Society in Tension*, Chicago: Rand McNally.

Goldman, R. (1964). *Religious Thinking from Childhood to Adolescence*, London: Routledge & Kegan Paul.

Goodrich, E. S. (1930/1958). Studies on the structure and development of vertebrates (2 Volumes), New York: Dover Publications.

Graham, M. (1943). *The Fish Gate*, London: Faber & Faber.

Greeley, A. M. (1975). *The Sociology of the Paranormal: A reconnaissance*, Sage Research Papers in the Social Sciences.

Gunther, E. R. (1928). Extracts from Gunther's journal of the Discovery Expedition, *The Draconian*, January, 6703–6715; April, 6762–6777; August, 6874–6898.

Gurevich, A. (1995). *The Origins of European Individualism*, Oxford: Blackwell.

Haddelsey, S. (2008). *Ice Captain: The Life of J. R. Stenhouse*, Stroud: History Press.

Hampton, J. (1988). *Hobbes and the Social Contract Tradition*, Cambridge University Press.

Hand, S. (ed.) (1989). *The Levinas Reader*, Oxford: Blackwell.

Hankey, D. (1917/2008). *The Beloved Captain; The Honour of the Brigade; An Englishman Prays*, New York: republished by Kessinger Publishing.

Hardy, A. C. (ed.) (1920?). *'C' Company (Old 'F' & 'G' Coy's): A Memoir*, printed and published privately by A. C. Hardy.

Hardy, A. C. (n. d.). *An Apparatus for Displaying Historical Charts, etc.*, Patent applied for in the United Kingdom and other countries, by A. C. Hardy, Exeter College, Oxford.

Hardy, A. C. (1922). 'Notes on the Atlantic plankton taken off the east coast of England in 1921 and 1922', *Publications de Circonstance, Conseil International pour l'exploration de la mer, Copenhagen,* no. 78.

Hardy, A. C. (1926). 'The *Discovery* Expedition: a new method of plankton research,' *Nature*, October 30.

Hardy, A. C. (1928). 'The work of the Royal Research Ship "Discovery" in the dependencies of the Falkland Islands', *The Geographical Journal* LXXII (3): 209–234.

Hardy, A. C. (1939). 'Ecological investigations with the continuous plankton recorder: object, plan and methods', *Hull Bulletins of Marine Ecology* 1 (1): 1–57.

Hardy, A. C. (1941). 'Plankton as a source of food', *Nature* 147: 695–696.

Hardy, A. C. (1942). *Natural History: Old and New*. Inaugural lecture delivered in Marischal College, Aberdeen University on 28 April.

Hardy, A. C. (1949a). 'The faith of a scientist', *Faith and Freedom* 2 (2).

Hardy, A. C. (1949b). 'Zoology outside the laboratory', (Presidential address to Section D of the British Association), *Advancement of Science, London,* 6 (23): 213–223.

Hardy, A. C. (1951). *Science and the Quest for God*, London: Lindsey Press.

Hardy, A. C. (1956). *The Open Sea: Its Natural History*. Part I: *Plankton,* London: Collins.

Hardy, A. C. (1959). *The Open Sea: Its Natural History*. Part II: *Fish and Fisheries,* London: Collins.

Hardy, A. C. (1960a). 'Was man more aquatic in the past?', *New Scientist,* 7: 642–45.

Hardy, A. C. (1960b). 'Will man be more aquatic in the future?', *New Scientist,* 7: 730–33.

Hardy, A. C. (1965). *The Living Stream*, London: Collins.

Hardy, A. C. (1966). *The Divine Flame,* London: Collins.

Hardy, A. C. (1967). *Great Waters: A voyage of natural history to study whales, plankton and the waters of the Southern Ocean in the old Royal Research Ship*, London: Collins.

Hardy, A. C. (1968). 'Science and an experimental faith', *Faith and Freedom,* Summer 1968.

Hardy, A. C. (1975). *The Biology of God*, London: Jonathan Cape.

Hardy, A. C. (1979). *The Spiritual Nature of Man*, Oxford: Clarendon Press.

Hardy, A. C. (1984a). *Darwin and the Spirit of Man*, London: Collins.

Hardy, A. C. (1984b). *A Cotswold Sketchbook*, London: Collins.

Hardy, A. C. (1986). *Weekend with Willows*, Stroud: Sutton Publishing.

Hardy, A. C. (n.d.). Unpublished fragment of an autobiography, Bodleian Library, Oxford University.

Hardy, A. C. & Gunther, E. R. (1935). 'The plankton of the South Georgia whaling grounds and adjacent waters 1926–1927', *Discovery Reports*, XI: 1–456.

Hardy, A. C., Harvie, R. & Koestler, A. (1973). *The Challenge of Chance*, London: Hutchinson.

Hardy, A. C. & Milne, P. S. (1939). 'Studies in the distribution of insects by aerial currents: experiments in aerial tow-netting from kites', *Journal of Animal Ecology* 7 (2):199–229.

Harvey, E. N. (1925). Fluorescence and inhibition of luminescence in Ctenophores by ultra-violet light. J. Gen. Physiol. vol. 7: 331–339.

Hay, D. (1979). 'Religious experience amongst a group of postgraduate students: a qualitative study', *Journal for the Scientific Study of Religion*, 1164–182.

References

Hay, D. (1987c). *Exploring Inner Space* (revised edn.), London: Mowbray.

Hay, D. (1988). 'Asking questions about religious experience', *Religion*, 18: 217–229

Hay, D. (1990). *Religious Experience Today: Studying the Facts*, London: Cassell

Hay, D. (1994). ' "The biology of God": what is the current status of Hardy's hypothesis?', *International Journal for the Psychology of Religion*, 4 (1): 1–23.

Hay, D. (2006). *Something There: The Biology of the Human Spirit*, London: Darton, Longman & Todd.

Hay, D. (2007). *Why Spirituality is Difficult for Westerners*, Exeter: Imprint Academic.

Hay, D. (2011). 'Altruism and Spirituality as forms of Relational Consciousness and how culture inhibits them', in, R. W. Sussman and C. R. Cloninger (eds), *The Origins and Nature of Cooperation and Altruism in Non-Human and Human Primates*, New York: Springer [forthcoming].

Hay, D. & Heald, G. (1987). 'Religion is good for you', *New Society*, 17 April.

Hay, D. & Hunt, K. (2000). *The Spirituality of People who Don't go to Church*, Final Report, Adult Spirituality Project: Nottingham University.

Hay, D. & Morisy, A. (1985). 'Secular society/Religious meanings: a contemporary paradox', *Review of Religious Research*, 26: 213–227.

Hay, D. with Nye, R. (revised edition, 2006). *The Spirit of the Child,* London: Jessica Kingsley Publishers.

Hay, D. & Socha, P.M. (2005). 'Spirituality as a natural phenomenon: bringing biological and psychological perspectives together', *Zygon*, 49 (3): 589–612.

Heidegger, M. (1927/1962). *Being and Time* (tr. John Macquarrie & Edward Robinson), Oxford: Basil Blackwell.

Hirschman, A. (1997). *The Passions and the Interests: Political Arguments for Capitalism before its Triumph* (foreword by Amartya Sen), Princeton University Press.

Hobbes, T. (1651/1962). *Philosophical Rudiments concerning Government and Society*, Ch. 1, Section 4, 25–26, (quoted in MacPherson).

Hobbes, T. (1651/1962). *Leviathan* (ed. & intro. by C. B. Macpherson), London: Penguin Classics.

Hogben, L. (1936/1993). *Mathematics for the Million*, New York: W. W. Norton.

Hogben, L. (1998). *Lancelot Hogben, Scientific Humanism*, Woodbridge: Merlin Press.

Holden, C. & Mace, R. (1997). 'A phylogenetic analysis of the evolution of lactose digestion', *Human Biology*, 69, 605–628.

Hooper, J. (2002). *Of Moths and Men: Intrigue, Tragedy and the Peppered Moth*, London: Fourth Estate.

Houghton, W. (1877). *Sketches of British Insects: a Handbook for Beginners in the Study of Entomology,* London: Woodbridge & Sons.

Huxley, J. (1923). *Essays of a Biologist*, Harmondsworth: Penguin Books.

Huxley, J. (1945). *Religion Without Revelation*, London: A. P. Watts.

Huxley, J. (1974). *Evolution: The Modern Synthesis* (third edition), London: Allen & Unwin.

Huxley, Juliette. (1986). *Leaves of the Tulip Tree*, Oxford University Press.

Huxley, T. H. (1883). Speech given at the International Fisheries Exhibition, London 1883, Inaugural Meeting of the Congress, p. 14 Text available online at aleph0.clarku.edu/huxley/SM5/fish.html

James, W. (1902/1985). *The Varieties of Religious Experience*, Cambridge: Harvard University Press.

Jefferies, R. (1883/2002). *The Story of My Heart* (new edition), London: The Green Press.

Jones, S., Martin R. & Pilbeam, D. (eds.) (1994). *The Cambridge Encyclopaedia of Human Evolution*, Cambridge University Press.

Jung, C. G. (1973). *Synchronicity: An Acausal Connecting Principle*, Princeton: Bollingen Paperbacks.

Kant, E. (1793/1960). *Religion Within the Limits of Reason Alone* (tr. Theodore M Greene & Hoyt H. Hudson), New York: Harper & Row.

Kelly, T. M. (2002). *Theology at the Void: the Retrieval of Experience*, Notre Dame University Press.

Kinsey, A., Pomeroy, W., & Martin, C. (1948/1998). *Sexual Behavior in the Human Male*, Bloomington: Indiana University Press.

Kinsey, A., Pomeroy, W., Martin, C. & Gebhard, P. (1953/1998). *Sexual Behavior in the Human Female*, Bloomington: Indiana University Press.

Kirby, W. F. (1909). *Butterflies and Moths of Europe* (revised edition), London: Cassell.

Kirk, K., Martin, N. & Eaves, L. (1999). 'Self-transcendence as a measure of spirituality in a sample of older Australia twins', *Twin Research* 2 (2): 81–87.

Kissane, J. (2003). *Without Parade: The Life and Work of Donald Hankey, 'A Student In Arms'*, Sussex: The Book Guild Ltd.

Kruuk, H. (2003). *Niko's Nature: the Life of Niko Tinbergen and his Science of Animal Behaviour*, Oxford University Press.

Lambert, Y. (2004). 'A turning point in religious evolution in Europe', *Journal of Contemporary Religion*, 19 (1): 29–45.

References

Land, P. (1992). *Bramcote School: the First Hundred Years*, Edinburgh: The Pentland Press.

Laski, M. (1961). *Ecstasy: A Study of Some Secular and Religious Experiences,* London: Cresset Press.

Lee, A. J. (1992). *The Directorate of Fisheries Research: Its origins and development*, Lowestoft: Ministry of Agriculture, Fisheries and Food.

le Mahieu, D. L. (1976). *The Mind of William Paley*, Lincoln: University of Nebraska Press.

Lloyd Morgan, C. (1896). *Habit and Instinct*, London: Arnold.

Locke, J. L. (1998). *Why we Don't Talk to Each Other any More: The de-voicing of society*, New York: Simon & Schuster.

Long, A. (2000). *Unitarian Thought in the Twentieth Century*, Part II, www.unitarianhistory.org.uk/hsthought2.htm

Lukes, S. (1973). *Individualism*, Oxford: Basil Blackwell.

Luria, A. (1976). *Cognitive Development: Its cultural and social foundations.* (tr. Martin Lopez-Morillas & Lynn Solotaroff; ed. Michael Cole), Cambridge: Harvard University Press.

MacDonald, G. (2001). *At the Back of the North Wind*, London: Everyman's Library.

MacDonald, G. (2008). *Lilith*, Waking Lion Press.

McGilchrist, Iain (2009). *The Master and His Emissary: The divided brain and the making of the Western World*, New Haven and London: Yale University Press.

MacIntyre, A. (1990). *Three Rival Versions of Moral Enquiry: Encyclopaedia, Genealogy, and Tradition*, London: Gerald Duckworth & Co. Ltd.

Macmurray, J. (1957/1995). *The Self as Agent.* (introduced by Stanley M. Harrison), London: Faber & Faber.

Macpherson, C. B. (1962). *The Political Theory of Possessive Individualism*, Oxford University Press.

McCrone, J. (1990). *The Ape that Spoke: Language and the Evolution of the Human Mind*, London: Picador.

Marsden, R. (1999). 'The Discovery Committee – Motivation Means and Achievements', *The Scottish Naturalist* 111: 69–92.

Marsden, R. (2001). 'Expedition to investigation: the work of the Discovery Committee' in *Understanding the Oceans: a Century of Ocean Exploration*, edited by Margaret Deacon, Tony Rice and Colin Summerhayes. London/New York: UCL Press.

Martin, J. R. (1845) 'Report on the Sanitary Condition of Nottingham, Coventry, Leicester, Derby, Norwich, and Portsmouth', *Second Report of the Commissioners for inquiring into the State of Large Towns and Populous Districts*, Appendix Part II (610), XVIII.1.

Menzies, I. (1975). 'A case study in the functioning of social systems as a defence against anxiety' in Arthur D. Colman and W. Harold Bexton (eds.), *Group Relations Reader*, Sausalito: GREX.

Monroe, K. R. (1996). *The Heart of Altruism: Perceptions of a Common Humanity* Princeton University Press.

Morgan, E. (1972). *The Descent of Woman*, London: Souvenir Press.

Morgan, E. (1982). *The Aquatic Ape*, Souvenir Press.

Morgan Poll, (1983). 'Unpublished poll of reports of religious experience in Australia.'

Morrell, J. (2007). *Science at Oxford, 1914–1939: Transforming an Arts University*, Oxford: Clarendon Press.

Morris, C. (1972). *The Discovery of the Individual, 1050–1200*, London: SPCK.

Morris, D. (1979). *Animal Days*, London: Jonathan Cape.

Morris, D. (1985). 'Biologist with a broader outlook: an appreciation of Sir Alister Hardy', *Oxford Times*, May 31.

Muir, E. (1954). *An Autobiography*, London: Hogarth Press.

Nagy, E. & Molnar, P. (2004). 'Homo imitans or Homo provocans? Human imprinting model of neonatal imitation', *Infant Behavior and Development*, 27: 54–63.

Needham, J. (1925). *Science, Religion and Reality*, London: Sheldon Press.

Newberg, A., d'Aquili & Rause, W. (2001). *Why God Won't Go Away: Brain Science and the Biology of Belief*, New York: Ballantine Books.

Newcastle Illustrated Chronicle, Photographs of the Northern Cyclists Battalion in training. 6 March 1915.

Osborne, H. F. (1896). 'A mode of evolution requiring neither natural selection nor the inheritance of acquired characteristics', *Transactions of the New York Academy of Science*, 15: 1411–1418.

Otto, R. (1958). *The Idea of the Holy* (translated from the original German by J. W. Harvey), Oxford University Press.

Owen, W. (1994). *War Poems of Wilfred Owen*, London: Chatto & Windus.

Page, B. (ed.) (1993). *Marxism and Spirituality: An International Anthology*, Westport, Connecticut: Bergin & Garvey.

Paley, W. (1802/2006). *Evidence of the Existence and Attributes of the Deity, Collected from the Appearances of Nature*, Oxford University Press.

Pascal, B. (1660/1961). *Pensées*, (tr. J. M. Cohen), London: Penguin Classics.

Paterson, R. W. K. (1971). *The Nihilistic Egoist: Max Stirner* (published for the University of Hull), Oxford University Press.

Popper, K. (1976). *Unended Quest: An Intellectual Autobiography*, London: Fontana/Collins.

Port of Spain Gazette (1881). Leading articles on the Yellow Fever epidemic published in the issues of 20 and 27 August.

Porter, R. (2000). *Enlightenment: Britain and the Creation of the Modern World*, London: Allen Lane.

Preus, S. (1987). *Explaining Religion: Criticism and Theory from Bodin to Freud*, New Haven & London: Yale University Press.

Priestley, J. H. (1951). 'Schools in the Ryburn Valley', *Journal of the Halifax Antiquarian Society*.

Putnam, R. (2000). *Bowling Alone: The Collapse and Revival of American Community*, New York: Simon & Schuster.

QSR.NUD*IST (1996). *User's Guide*, London: Sage/SCOLARI.

Rankin, M. (2009). *An Introduction to Spiritual and Religious Experience*, London: Continuum.

Rankin, N. (2008). *Churchill's Wizards*, London: Faber & Faber.

Robinson, J. (1963). *Honest to God*, London: SCM Press.

Robinson, E. (1977/1983). *The Original Vision*, New York: Seabury Press.

Rudge, D. W. (2005).'Did Kettlewell commit fraud? Re-examining the evidence', *Public Understanding of Science*, Vol. 14, No. 3: 249–268.

Russell, M. (2003). *Piltdown Man: The Secret Life of Charles Dawson* Stroud: The History Press Ltd.

Sanderson of Oundle (1924). Published by a committee of admirers of Sanderson, London: Chatto & Windus.

Savours, A. (2001). *The Voyages of the Discovery: The illustrated history of Scott's ship*, London: Chatham Publishing.

Scoresby, W. (1820/1969). *An Account of the Arctic Regions with a History and Description of the Northern Whale-Fishery* (2 volumes), Newton Abbott: David & Charles.

Schlich, W. (1891). *Manual of Forestry* (5 volumes), London: Bradbury, Agnew & Co.

Selznick, P. (1992). *The Moral Commonwealth: Social Theory and the Promise of Community*, Berkeley: University of California Press.

Simpson, G. G. (1949). *The Meaning of Evolution*, Newhaven: Yale University Press.

Singer, B. (1957). *Living Silver: An impression of the British fishing industry*, London: Secker & Warburg.

Smith, A. (1999). *The Wealth of Nations* (2 volumes) (introduced by Andrew Skinner), London: Penguin Books.

Smith, A. (1759/2000). *The Theory of Moral Sentiments*, Amherst, New York: Prometheus Books.

Solomon, S. J. (1920). *Strategic Camouflage*, London: John Murray.

Spark, M. (1961/2000). *The Prime of Miss Jean Brodie*, Harmondsworth: Penguin Classics.

Stace, W. T. (1960). *Mysticism and Philosophy*, Philadelphia: J. B. Lippincott.

Starbuck, E. D. (1899). *The Psychology of Religion: An Empirical Study of the Growth of Religious Consciousness* (with an introduction by William James), New York: Walter Scott.

Stirner, M. (1845/1993). *The Ego and His Own* (tr. by Steven Byington; introduced by Sydney Parker), London: Rebel Press.

Stringer, C. B. (1994). 'Evolution of early humans', *The Cambridge Encyclopaedia of Human Evolution* (edited by Steve Jones, Robert Martin and David Pilbeam), Cambridge University Press, 241–251.

Strout, C. (1971). 'The pluralistic identity of William James', *American Quarterly*, 23 (2): 135.

Studdert-Kennedy, G. A. (2006). *The Unutterable Beauty: The Collected Poems of G. A. Studdert-Kennedy*, Liskeard: Diggory Press.

Sunday Graphic (1955). Article on Mrs Margaret Knight, 7 January.

Tacey, D. (2004). *The Spirituality Revolution: The emergence of contemporary spirituality*, Hove and New York: Brunner-Routledge.

Taylor, C. (1989). *Sources of the Self: The Making of the Modern Identity*, Cambridge University Press.

Taylor, C. (2007). *A Secular Age*, Harvard University Press.

Teilhard de Chardin, P. (1960). *The Phenomenon of Man* (with an introduction by Julian Huxley), London: Collins.

Thomson, M. (2006). *Psychological Subjects: Identity, Culture, and Health in Twentieth-Century Britain*, Oxford University Press.

Tressider, R. (1980). *Nottingham Pubs*, Nottingham Civic Society.

Trimble, M. R. (2007). *The Soul in the Brain: The cerebral basis of language, art and belief*, Baltimore: Johns Hopkins University Press.

Van Ness, P. H. (ed.) (1996). *Spirituality and the Secular Quest*, London: SCM Press.

Walters, K. (ed.) (2008). *After War, Is Faith Possible? An Anthology of the Writings of Geoffrey Anketell Studdert-Kennedy ('Woodbine Willie')*, Cambridge: Lutterworth Press.

Walzer, M. (1990). 'The communitarian critique of liberalism', *Political Theory*, 18 (1): 6–2

Weber, M. (1930). *The Protestant Ethic and the Spirit of Capitalism* (tr. Talcott Parsons), London: George Allen & Unwin.

Bruce H. Weber and David J. Depew (eds.) (2003). *Evolution and Learning: the Baldwin Effect Reconsidered*, Cambridge: MIT Press.

Wiener, J. & Stringer, C. (2004). *The Piltdown Forgery*, Oxford University Press.

Wells, H. G. (1927). *The Story of a Great Schoolmaster: Being a plain account of the life and ideals of Sanderson of Oundle*, London: Chatto & Windus.

Wilson, A. N. (1990). *God's Funeral,* London: John Murray.

Wilson, B. (1966). *Religion in Secular Society*, London: C. A. Watts.

Wilson, D. S. (2002). *Darwin's Cathedral: Evolution, Religion and the Nature of Society*, University of Chicago Press.

References

Wordsworth, W. (1994). *Collected Poems*, Ware: Wordsworth Editions Ltd.

Wood Jones, F. (1919). *Man's Place Among the Mammals*, London: Edward Arnold.

Wulff, D. (1997). *Psychology of Religion: Classic and Contemporary* (2nd Edn) New York: Wiley.

Yorkshire Post. Report of Alister Hardy's first ever flight from Bradford to Leeds, Issued in edition of 24 July 1924.

Zinnbauer, B. J., Pargament, K. et al. (1997). 'Religion and Spirituality: Unfuzzying the fuzzy.' *Journal for the Scientific Study of Religion*, 76 (4): 549–564.

Zohar, D. and Marshall, I. (2004). *Spiritual Capital: Wealth We Can Live By*, London: Bloomsbury Publishing.

Notes

Notes to Chapter One

[1] The cottage belonged to Manchester College. Later the unit moved to offices in George Street and then to Westminster College, Oxford. Currently it is based in the University of Wales, Trinity St David at Lampeter. See the Website: www.alisterhardyreligiousexperience.co.uk For a history of the Unit, see John Franklin's *Exploration into the Spirit* published by the Alister Hardy Society at Lampeter in 2006.

[2] For a very full discussion of popular opinion, see Alvar Ellegard's fascinating book *Darwin and the General Reader: The Reception of Darwin's Theory of Evolution in the British Periodical Press, 1859–72* (reprint edition) published by Chicago University Press in 1990.

[3] Published in 1999 in London by John Murray , which incidentally is the same company that published *The Origin of Species* in 1859.

[4] There is a potentially explosive argument waiting to happen. Since the account of Creation in the Qu'ran is the same as in the Old Testament and the Muslim view of the Qur'an is that it is the voice of God, debate about the plausibility of evolution is effectively censored out for most Muslims. This problem is submerged for the time being by the more immediate concern about terrorist violence, but it is one of the fundamental issues underlying the overt conflict.

[5] The name may originate from the title of a book by Tina Beattie, *The New Atheists* published in London by Darton, Longman & Todd, in 2007.

[6] See for example the classic exposition of social construction theory, Peter Berger and Thomas Luckmann's pioneering text book, *The Social Construction of Reality*, published in London by Allen Lane, The Penguin Press in 1967.

[7] There are around 200 households listed under the name Hardy in the Nottingham telephone directory alone, making the identification of family links in the East Midlands a complicated business.

[8] At first glance, visitors to Nottingham castle may not notice that the sandstone cliff on which it stands is made of unusually soft rock which erodes easily, to the extent that in recent years rock falls have threatened to undermine parts of the outer walls of the fortress. Much of the town is built on similarly friable stone and long before the coming of the Normans – and prior to them the Saxons – the ancient Britons called this region *Tigguocabauac,* meaning the place where people live in caves. In the seventeenth century the diarist John Evelyn noted that numbers of people still inhabited the caves, a practice that hung on well into the nineteenth century and partly returned during the Second World War when they were used as air-raid shelters. To this day, beneath its modern surface Nottingham is riddled with hundreds of caverns and tunnels gouged out of the bedrock by hand, many of them in use as storage rooms. Others are tourist attractions, like the former brew house of the castle, in recent centuries turned into the *Trip to Jerusalem*, a cavernous pub in Brewhouse Yard, with a name alluding to the mediaeval Crusades. Alister knew about the caves, for he makes a reference to them in one of his short stories. He can hardly have missed those in the castle rock, and the mystery surrounding them would certainly have stirred his imagination.

[9] The hotel seems to have gone downhill in the latter part of the nineteenth century, judging by newspaper reports at the time. It was finally closed and demolished a few years after the First World War, but the Maypole Yard is still there, forming a large cul-de-sac off Clumber Street, round the corner from Long Row.

[10] This may not have been his exact age, since ages were rounded up to the nearest five in the 1841 census.

[11] Quoted in John Beckett's *The Book of Nottingham*, published in Buckingham by Barracuda Books, 1980, p. 5.

[12] Two of John's sons, Thomas and Henry, had either left home or were absent on the day of the census.

[13] See *A Tour of the Whole Island of Great Britain* (Abridged and Illustrated Edition), edited by P. N. Furbank, W. R. Owens & A. J. Coulson and published by Yale University Press in 1991.

[14] I am grateful to a prominent Nottingham local historian, Ken Brand, for the following remarks referring to the enclosure problem in Nottingham:

From the late eighteenth century mention of enclosure by any Nottingham councillor or candidate was political suicide. After the 1835 Municipal Reform Act there was a more enlightened approach to enclosure, but for several years the so termed 'free-men's rights' and the value of compensation payable were sticking points. In addition Thomas Wakefield (the leading Whig) in particular and some of his cronies were owners of slum properties who would suffer financially should enclosure of the common fields take place, for which action Hawksley was a fervent advocate. In evidence c.1843–4 to the *Royal Commission on the State of Large Towns and Populous Districts,* he said that 'several influential members of the corporation are extensive owners of the small houses inhabited by the working classes in the worst-conditioned districts, and have repeatedly avowed their hostility to the principle of enclosure, under what I believe to be the very erroneous impression that their property would sustain permanent injury by the erection of better, more healthy, and more comfortable dwellings on the enclosed lands.'

It is worth pointing out that Nottingham was in some ways three different towns in the nineteenth century. It remained confined within its historic core up to c.1840, surrounded by its common fields and private estates. It became an enlarged town after the enclosure of its common fields by an Act of 1845. Such was the complexity of the allocation of land experienced by the Enclosure Commissioners that even when they declared the enclosure completed in 1865 another Act of 1867 was needed to finish the uncompleted infrastructure. Then in 1877 a Borough Extension Act of that year brought outlying industrialised parishes within the town. Now of some size, Nottingham was granted city status by Queen Victoria in 1897.

[15] There have been many editions of this work. See for example the Penguin Classics paperback edited by V. G. Kiernan and published as a revised edition in 1987.

[16] From J. R. Martin, 'Report on the Sanitary Condition of Nottingham, Coventry, Leicester, Derby, Norwich, and Portsmouth' *Second Report of the Commissioners for Inquiring into the State of Large Towns and Populous Districts,* Appendix Part II; 1845 (610), XVIII.1, 299.

[17] I am indebted to Ken Brand for this information.

[18] The publication of Adam Smith's masterpiece *The Wealth of Nations* in 1776 strengthened the belief that the stability of the market depends on self-interest, an axiom that continues to dominate economics to this day.

[19] The Duke, who was also absent, was notorious for his hostility to any kind of parliamentary reform. Following the riots his mansion was left derelict for many years until it was renovated to become the municipal museum and art gallery of Nottingham.

[20] 'Chartism is the campaign that came together from 1838 onwards in support of the People's Charter. At a time when the right to vote was severely limited, the Charter demanded the vote for all men (but not women). The Charter was launched by a small radical group called the London Working Men's Association and a handful of parliamentarians, but swiftly gathered support in all parts of Great Britain.' Information taken from www.chartists.net

[21] Information drawn from Richard Tresidder's pamphlet on Nottingham Pubs, published in 1980 by the Nottingham Civic Society.

[22] See Booth's celebrated book on the social and spiritual troubles of the Victorian period, first published in 1890, *In Darkest England and the Way Out*, Liskeard, Cornwall: Diggory Press, 2006.

[23] The Hardys were, on a relatively small scale, businessmen of a type that was characteristic of Nottingham during the industrial revolution. Somewhat later during the nineteenth century Nottingham men with similar entrepreneurial drive founded several of Britain's largest industrial companies. Thus in 1877 Jesse Boot, who was born in the same year as Richard Hardy, began his contribution to the nation's wellbeing by opening the first cash chemist's shop on Goose Gate. Also in 1877 John Player founded his tobacco company with rather more controversial effects on health. Then in 1888 Frank Bowden took over and built up what became the Raleigh Bicycle Company.

[24] Reported in *Kimberley Ale*, George Bruce's history of the Hardy & Hanson Brewery, published in London by Henry Melland Ltd. in 1982. See page 15.

[25] I am grateful for the help of Nicholas Forman Hardy, great-grandson of Thomas Hardy, one of the two founder brothers of Hardy's brewery. Unfortunately neither he nor I have been able to determine the relationship with Alister Hardy's family.

[26] There is an article entitled 'Schools in the Ryburn Valley' published by J. H. Priestley in 1951 in the journal of the Halifax Antiquarian Society. It refers to the innovations created by William Dove when he opened *Making Place College*, as it was called, in 1832. The school had an international reputation and attracted pupils from many other countries. It is a sign of John Hardy's eagerness to take on new ideas that he sent young Richard there. Sadly, when Dove died in October 1865 his successor failed to maintain the methods he had introduced. The school went into decline and eventually in 1880 it was closed.

[27] They were not the first Australian cricketers to play at Trent Bridge, for a team of Australian aborigines had previously toured England in 1868. That precedent led people to the assumption that the group visiting in

1878 were also aboriginals and scurrilous rumours hinted that they were cannibals. As a result a large crowd of curious bystanders gathered at the Midland Station to see their arrival. The *Cricket and Football Times* for May 16 reported that as the train bearing the team steamed into the station, the Australians were greeted by a splendid band playing 'Auld Lang Syne'. They were then welcomed by members of the county cricket club and driven in a coach drawn by four greys to the Maypole Hotel. At that time Richard Hardy's office was on Market Street, just off the Square, so we might imagine him stepping out to join the crowds watching the coach pass by.

[28] From Conan Doyle's poem, 'Bendy's Sermon', first published in *Strand Magazine* for April 1909, pp. 420–4.

[29] Adapted from an article on Bendigo in *Left Lion* an online journal about Nottingham's local culture. See www.leftlion.co.uk/articles.cfm/id/1175

[30] Colwick today is a suburb of Nottingham, alongside a racecourse and a country park. In search of evidence of the original hamlet, I came across an overgrown field oddly isolated in the middle of a housing estate and containing the partly ruined remains of one of the farmhouses, the old Manor Farm. Colwick House itself is gone, replaced by a road of modern dwellings where I had the good fortune to discover John Baggaley who had lived in the old house when he was a child. He was able to point out a large tree, still standing, which had given shade to the main entrance. I am also grateful to him for supplying me with a photograph of the original ivy covered Colwick House taken in 1965.

[31] During a recent visit to Bromley House on Angle Row in Nottingham, which is where Richard Sutton had his offices, I was shown a copy of his brother Henry's collected poems, possibly having been there in Richard Hardy's day.

[32] Now held in the Manuscript Collection in the library of Nottingham University.

[33] By this time they had merged with the Nottinghamshire regiment known as the Sherwood Foresters. The name Robin Hood Rifles survived until very recently as the title of a local cadet unit. I am indebted to Eddie Edwards of the Sherwood Foresters' Museum in Chilwell and Lawrence Barber at the Robin Hood Rifles NCO's club in Nottingham for information about the Robins.

[34] Axwell Hall was built by Sir Thomas Clavering, the seventh baronet. The tenth baronet was the last in the line and died in 1893. Today the Hall is used as an approved school.

[35] Quoted from 'Clydeside Cameos' in *Fairplay*, No. XIII 'Uncle Tom', pp. 101–108. I am grateful to Michael Stewart for providing me with this reference.

[36] This and the following quotations from Trinidad newspapers were researched for me in Port-of-Spain by Radica Mahase, to whom I am most grateful.

[37] I am grateful to Jane Winship, great grand-daughter of Elizabeth for supplying me with this information. The grandson in question was Dick Hardy, Jane's father.

[38] The parish register sheds a small sidelight on social class. There are eight baptisms recorded on page 94 of which the only one officiated at by the vicar is that of Alister Hardy. The other entries are for the children of a postal clerk, fitters, card punchers and the like. Those ceremonies were handled by the curate.

Notes to Chapter Two

[1] The cul-de-sac no longer exists, having been overtaken by extensions to the Boys High School.

[2] The quotation, along with others in this and subsequent chapters, is drawn from the unfinished and unpublished text of an autobiography that Hardy began writing when he was in his late 80s: See Autobiography, p. 4. A copy of the unpublished typescript is held in the archives of the Bodleian Library in Oxford. I am indebted for help and advice in particular to Colin Harris who was in charge of the Modern Manuscripts Room in the Bodleian during most of the period when I was studying Hardy's archive.

[3] Autobiography, pp. 12–13.

[4] The extract is from the opening poem in Robert Louis Stevenson's *A Child's Garden of Verses*, entitled 'To Alison Cunningham from her Boy', and honouring the nanny who was chiefly responsible for Stevenson's upbringing. Available in many editions cf. Everyman's Library, 1992.

[5] *Sketches of British Insects: a handbook for beginners in the study of entomology* by Rev. W. Houghton, MA, FLS, author of 'Country Walks of a Naturalist'; 'Sea-Side Walks of a Naturalist' etc. Illustrated with coloured plates and wood engravings. London: Woodbridge and Sons, 1877.

[6] See the two volumes in The New Naturalist series produced in London by Collins: *The Open Sea: Its Natural History, Part I: The World of Plankton* (published in 1956) and Part II: *Fish and Fisheries* (published in 1959).

[7] Such phenomena appear to exist although very rare, perhaps associated with electrical storms, and are interpreted as manifestations of the supernatural in some cultures, for example, China.

[8] Autobiography, p. 9

[9] My thanks are due to Drs Sandy Pringle and Paul Denny for help with this question.

[10] This is curious and leads to the speculation that Elizabeth, who had been influenced by the strict Calvinism of the Free Presbyterian Church, disapproved of her husband's profession. Perhaps in response

to this, Richard seems to have spent a great deal of time away from home, much of it with his brother officers in the Robin Hoods.

11 What form did his grief take? How did he handle the loss? To whom did he turn for solace? Amateur psychiatrists seeking reductive explanations for Alister's profound religiosity in later life might want to rush in with remarks about the loss of a father at a young age. Taking their cue from Feuerbach or his intellectual descendents Marx and Freud they might assume that following the death there was a subsequent projection of feelings onto an imaginary father figure in the sky, thus generating that notorious opium of the people, the empty solace of religion. I myself do not dismiss certain generalisations about culture, but they can easily sound glib. In addition, the psychologist of religious experience, William James, long ago pointed out that the validity of a phenomenon cannot be determined on the basis of what triggered it off. The reality and validity of religious phenomena, like all other phenomena, must be judged on their own merits, and not on what may be presumed to have originated them. In any case, since we simply do not know the nature of the turmoil in Alister, or indeed if there was any serious disturbance associated with the death of his father, it seems wise to desist from empty speculation.

12 Information kindly provided by Malvern School.

13 Information generously supplied by the librarian of the RIBA in London.

14 And continues to be so. The information about the school is drawn from Pip Land's book *Bramcote School: The First Hundred Years*, published by the Pentland Press Ltd. in 1993. I am grateful to the headmaster, Mr A. G. W. Lewin for his hospitality and for the gift of the book.

15 In the end the bill did not need to be paid. The company was sufficiently impressed by Alister's originality to offer to buy the suit back at cost price.

16 Later the exhibits were shifted to where they still are, in Wollaton Hall, a grand house built in Elizabethan times by Sir Francis Willoughby who was a pioneer of commercial coal mining in the Midlands.

17 He retired in 1911 to enter the House of Commons, where he served as Conservative MP for Holderness and was knighted in 1937.

18 Alister remembered the name of the large public school for girls as Lady Walburga's but on checking up with the archive department in Scarborough Public Library I was informed that there had never been a school of that name in the town. He may have been confusing it with Queen Walburga's School near Harrogate. He was almost certainly thinking of Queen Margaret's which was a Woodward school, founded in Scarborough in 1901 and later moved to Escrick Park south of York.

19 Autobiography, p. 27.

20 *Weekend With Willows*, published by Sutton Publishing in 1986.

21 Wells' short biography is entitled *The Story of a Great Schoolmaster: being a plain account of the life and ideas of Sanderson of Oundle*, published in London in 1927 by Chatto & Windus. Three years previously a committee of admirers of Sanderson edited a more extended account of the organisation of the school under Sanderson, along with a selection of his sermons and scripture lessons. See *Sanderson of Oundle* published in 1924, also by Chatto & Windus. For a forthright and highly readable short article on Sanderson, see Richard Dawkins' piece in the *Guardian* of 6 July 2002, reproduced on the Internet at www.guardian.co.uk/Archive/Article/ 0,4273,4455275,00.html

22 Unpleasant horseplay of this type seems to have been a feature of many English boarding schools at the time. Eventually the tradition was outlawed in Oundle after a boy was severely injured.

23 This was a reissue, in parts, of Kirby's 400+ page book, originally published by Cassell in London in 1903, then revised in 1907.

24 I remember being lectured to about the exemplary teaching methods of Sanderson when I was studying for a Postgraduate Certificate in Education.

25 Autobiography, p. 36. Hardy did have a son, Michael, whom he sent to Marlborough.

26 Autobiography, p. 38.

27 Transcribed from a scripture class by two people labelled X and Y by H. G. Wells (were these perhaps his sons? Alister Hardy thought so; see main text later in this chapter), in *The Story of a Great Schoolmaster*, op. cit. pp. 69–70.

28 Sermon on Faraday, in *Sanderson of Oundle* op. cit. pp. 204–205.

29 Autobiography, p. 41.

30 Referred to by Wordsworth in many of his poems, most famously in his lines written above Tintern Abbey in the Wye valley:

> I have felt
> A presence that disturbs me with the joy
> Of elevated thoughts; a sense sublime
> Of something far more deeply interfused,
> Whose dwelling is the light of setting suns,
> And the round ocean, and the living air,
> And the blue sky, and in the mind of man,
> A motion and a spirit, that impels
> All thinking things, all objects of all thought,
> And rolls through all things.

31 Rebecca was the fieldworker on a programme of research on children's spirituality that I directed at Nottingham University during the 1990s. She came to the notion of a 'personal signature' following a study of the transcripts of research conversations she had with children aged six

and ten in schools in Nottingham and Birmingham. For more on this subject, see the postscript of this book. See also David Hay with Rebecca Nye, *The Spirit of the Child* (revised edition), London: Jessica Kingsley, 2006, pp. 97–98.

[32] 'The concept of synchronicity indicates a meaningful coincidence of two or more events where something other than the probability of chance is involved. Chance is a statistical concept which "explains" deviations within certain patterns of probability. Synchronicity elucidates meaningful arrangements and coincidences which somehow go beyond the calculations of probability.' Taken from publicity material on the back cover of C. G. Jung, *Synchronicity: An Acausal Connecting Principle*, Princeton: Bollingen Paperbacks, 1973.

[33] Autobiography, pp. 41–42.

[34] I remember feeling a similar astonishment and delight when it was demonstrated in the school laboratory that air had weight. Previously, in spite of phenomena such as the wind, or the feeling of the air moving through my breathing apparatus, I had somehow got the notion that it was literally nothing.

[35] Autobiography, note added to p. 42 of main text by Hardy.

[36] Autobiography, p. 42.

[37] There are many editions of this great travel book. See, for example, Wordsworth Editions, 1997.

[38] See for example the edition published by Adamant Media Corporation in 2005.

[39] For example, the edition published by the University of California Press in 1962.

Notes to Chapter Three

[1] Authored by George Bentham and Sir Joseph Hooker, this famous handbook was still in regular use when I was an undergraduate. It took considerable perseverance to master the classification system sufficiently to make it a practical field guide.

[2] Years later, in 1928, Alister was particularly proud to present Professor Ronald Good, head of the newly-founded Botany Department at Hull University, with a set of 230 specimens from his schoolboy collection, where they formed a significant fraction of the herbarium.

[3] Hardy does not identify the house but a search of the Ordnance Survey map suggests one possible candidate, Markenfield Hall, a moated manor house situated on a side road off the A61 between Harrogate and Ripon.

[4] There is a record of Harold Blackburn using the plane very briefly, from 23 to 25 July 1913, to deliver copies of the *Yorkshire Post* newspaper from Leeds to York. It is conceivable that on one or more of those days he landed at Harrogate, giving us an approximate date for one of

Alister's visits to the Stray. Remarkably, the plane still exists. It crashed in Lincolnshire in 1914, but was rediscovered in a farmyard in 1937 and renovated. It is now maintained in working order and occasionally takes to the air, the oldest plane still flying in the UK.

[5] Autobiography, p. 47. Alister was constantly surprised by life and most commonly employed modifications of the word 'Good' to emphasise his astonishment; e.g. 'Good Heavens', 'Good gracious', 'Goodness me', 'My Goodness', etc.

[6] Information taken from Wikipedia: en.wikipedia.org/wiki/Aviation_history

[7] *Yorkshire Post*, 24 July 1914, p. 4. I am grateful to Michele Lefevre, local studies manager for Leeds City Council, for her help in tracking down this news item.

[8] Near Biggleswade in Bedfordshire.

[9] It was not realised at that time that Virginia Creeper damages stone-work. The clean golden sandstone one sees today gives the colleges a very different appearance from that encountered by Alister in 1914.

[10] Probably the most celebrated fraud in biological history. Charles Dawson claimed to have unearthed fossil skull and jaw fragments at Piltdown in East Sussex somewhere between 1908 and 1912, which were thought to be the earliest European human remains until proved a hoax. In fact the jaw was from an orang-utan, whilst the skull bones were human. Various other artefacts found at the site suggested an early Pleistocene date for the fossils, and were supposed to show transitional features between apes and *Homo sapiens*. The fraud was finally uncovered in 1953. See, *Piltdown Man: The Secret Life of Charles Dawson* by Miles Russell, published in 2003 by The History Press Ltd.

[11] See *Schlich's Manual of Forestry* (five volumes), published in 1891 in London by Bradbury, Agnew & Co.

[12] The wood is still used by the university for teaching purposes.

[13] Schlich was ambitious for the subject and argued vigorously for the introduction of a degree course, but the university authorities ruled that forestry was not a sufficiently academic subject to merit a degree, and did not give way until several years later.

[14] The painting is held in the collection of the Tate Gallery in London.

[15] Hardy makes explicit reference to these writers in 'Some memories of Julian Huxley' that he sent to Huxley's widow after his death. Archived correspondence with Juliette Huxley held by the Fondren Library, Rice University, Texas, MS 50 Box 44 f.4.

[16] For a first class overview of the Enlightenment, see Roy Porter, *Enlightenment: Britain and the Creation of the Modern World*, published by Allen Lane in 2000.

[17] For a thoughtful interpretation of the secularism of our time, see Charles Taylor, *A Secular Age,* published by Harvard University Press in 2007.

18 Published in London by John Murray in 1999.

19 *Matthew Arnold: Selected Poems* published by Phoenix in 1998.

20 Autobiography, p. 52.

21 Hardy's first public reference to his Vow was not made until 1984, when he was 88. He mentioned it rather shyly while writing his unfinished and unpublished autobiography.

22 The Museum of Natural History in Oxford was also for many years the home of the Zoology Department, where Hardy was an undergraduate and eventually Professor and Head of the department.

23 The most famous interchange was initiated by Bishop Wilberforce's attempt to lighten the atmosphere by making an ill-conceived joke at Huxley's expense. Turning to Huxley he asked him whether it was on his grandfather's or his grandmother's side that he was descended from an ape. Huxley reported his reply:

> If then, said I, the question is put to me would I rather have a miserable ape for a grandfather or a man highly endowed by nature and possessed of great means and influence and yet who employs these faculties and that influence for the mere purpose of introducing ridicule into a grave scientific discussion I unhesitatingly affirm my preference for the ape.

There are other versions of the occasion which differ radically from Huxley's account. The point at issue was the integrity of a senior bishop in the Established Church, with the plausibility of Darwin's theory temporarily sidelined. The matter is still controversial and is discussed in detail in the two best biographies of Darwin. See Chapter 33 of Adrian Desmond and James Moore's *Darwin* published by Michael Joseph in 1991; also, Janet Browne's *Darwin*, Vol. II, Chapters 3 & 4, published in London by Pimlico Press in 2002.

24 The front page of the *Illustrated Chronicle* for Saturday, 6 March 1915 has three photographs of NCB personnel in training at Bamburgh. One is of a group of 12 officers, including a young looking Lieut. Hardy standing unobtrusively at the back with Col. Garrett in the centre at the front. Alister has drawn a pencil mark pointing himself out, so the cutting was probably sent to a relative or friend. The other two illustrations are of recruits at bayonet drill and watching a demonstration of how to control the bayonet. A later edition of the *Chronicle* dated 28 March has pictures of cycle drill, and shooting practice on the sands at Bamburgh.

25 PBI = Poor bloody infantry

26 *Memoir*, p. 1.

27 Ibid, p. 2. 'It is sweet and right to die for one's country', a line from an ode by the Roman poet Horace quoted by Wilfred Owen in what is probably the best known poem to emerge from the Great War. See *The Poems of Wilfred Owen*, Wordsworth Editions Ltd, 1994.

[28] *Memoir,* p. 5.

[29] Autobiography, p. 59.

[30] More speculatively, one might suppose that if Alister's grandfather Tom Clavering was himself the son of a Durham coal miner, his position in Glasgow society meant that he had every reason to conceal the fact, and remind his children that they belonged to the gentry.

[31] See *Without Parade: The Life and Work of Donald Hankey, A Student in Arms,* published by the Book Guild in Lewes, Sussex in 2003.

[32] See Hankey's essays, *The Beloved Captain; the Honour of the Brigade; an Englishman Prays* (1917), republished in New York by Kessinger Publishing in 2008.

[33] *The Beloved Captain,* op. cit. pp. 1–7.

[34] *After War, is Faith Possible?* is an anthology of the writings of Geoffrey Anketell Studdert-Kennedy ('Woodbine Willie') edited by Kerry Walters and published by the Lutterworth Press in 2008. See also Studdert-Kennedy's collected poems in *The Unutterable Beauty* republished by the Diggory Press in 2006.

[35] Solomon was a Pre-Raphaelite painter best known for very large canvases portraying highly dramatic scenes from the Bible and from classical legend. Paintings by him are held by the Tate Gallery in London and the Walker Gallery in Liverpool.

[36] The Herkomer School in Bushey, not far from London, was an art college founded by a Bavarian, Sir Hubert von Herkomer in 1883 to spread his ideas about the teaching of art from a close inspection of life.

[37] Autobiography, p. 61.

[38] Hardy's opinion of his leader was on the whole rather critical, to the extent that he felt Solomon had been appointed to a post for which he was inadequate, through having the ear of the Prime Minister, Lloyd George. It was true that much could be learned from disciplined study of aerial photographs, as shown by the case of two huge zeppelin sheds in Belgium, not far from Brussels, from which numerous aerial attacks were launched on Britain. The sheds were around seven hundred feet in length and about thirty or forty feet high. They were covered with wire netting on which were laid squares of camouflage looking like vegetable gardens, with artificial cabbages and other plants placed so that they appeared to be continuous with the surrounding allotments. The effect was impressive, but photographs taken on a British reconnaissance flight one morning shortly after sunrise showed odd shadows. Careful examination confirmed the fact that the shadows came from the sheds and subsequent air attacks successfully destroyed them. Solomon went much further. He held obsessively to the belief that photography revealed that much larger tracts of strategically important German landscape (factories, troop movements etc.) were hidden beneath camouflage. Numerous photographs taken on reconnaissance

flights over enemy territory failed to show any convincing evidence in support of Solomon's conjecture. After the war was over, Solomon published a book about his theory, *Strategic Camouflage*, in which he further elaborated his views. But the general consensus was that he was caught into an eccentric obsession. Nevertheless his reputation is partially salvaged in Nick Rankin's book, *Churchill's Wizards* (published in London by Faber & Faber in 2008), in which Rankin makes the case for considering Solomon a major founding father of modern camouflage.

Notes to Chapter Four

[1] The first verse of Hopkins' poem *In Honour of St Alphonsus Rodriguez Laybrother of the Society of Jesus*. See *Gerard Manley Hopkins: a selection of his poems and prose*, by W. H. Gardner, Harmondsworth: Penguin Books, 1953.

[2] See Jack Morrell, *Science at Oxford, 1914–1939: Transforming an Arts University*, published in Oxford by the Clarendon Press in 2007.

[3] Morrell mentions that the zoology department, because it attracted women undergraduates, had a reputation as a marriage bureau. Apart from Alister, V. C. Wynne-Edwards (future Regius Professor of Natural History at Aberdeen University) and Peter Medawar (eventually Professor of Zoology at University College, London and Nobel Prize winner) both met their wives there. See, Morrell, op. cit. p. 268.

[4] Ruskin's enthusiasm even led him to construct a brick pillar inside the building with his own hands, though apparently it was later found to be inadequate and had to be redone by professional builders.

[5] For an entertaining account of the building history see the chapter on Ruskin in Kenneth Clark's *The Gothic Revival*, first published in London by Constable in 1950.

[6] Republished in 1987 as *Textbook of Oarsmanship: A Classic of Rowing Technical Literature*, by Sport Book Publishers, Toronto.

[7] When Ray Lancaster brought him to Oxford and while he was still an undergraduate, he published three academic papers, two of which in Hardy's judgement became classics in their field.

[8] Republished by Dover Publications of New York in two paperback volumes.

[9] Autobiography, p. 76.

[10] Ibid.

[11] The name *Priapulus* is a neologism with the literal meaning of 'small penis', which may be of interest to those who like to indulge in psychoanalytic speculation.

[12] M. Hulot's ungainly style was memorably presented in the films of Jacques Tati. The best known of which is *M. Hulot's Holiday*, first released in 1953.

[13] The Bloomsbury Group was a loose association of intellectuals who met at the homes of Clive and Vanessa Bell and Virginia and Leonard Woolf in the Bloomsbury district of London. They were active in the first half of the twentieth century and included prominently the economist J. M. Keynes, the philosopher Bertrand Russell, the writers E. M. Forster and Lytton Strachey. Ottoline Morrell was also associated with the group and was well known for hosting gatherings at Garsington, where Juliette Huxley encountered them when she was governess to the Morrell children.

[14] *Leaves of the Tulip Tree*, published by Oxford University Press in 1986.

[15] For example:

Isopod Phylogeny

Sing a song of six legs, a new phyletic stage!
Four and twenty Isopods cradled in a cage:
When the cage was opened, out they ran to play,
Wasn't it a jolly thing to have a jolly day!
Mother rocked the cradle between her stegopods:
The youngsters ran about her seven pereiopods;
When they found she'd one pair more than they themselves
They called a hasty conference on oöstegal shelves.
MacBride was in his garden settling pedigrees,
There came a baby Woodlouse and climbed upon his knees
And said, 'Sir, if our six legs have such an ancient air,
Shall we be less ancestral when we've grown our mother's pair?'

The above is taken from *Larval Forms and Other Zoological Verses* by Walter Garstang (with an introduction by Alister C. Hardy), Oxford: Basil Blackwell, 1951. Garstang's verses were often in the form of satirical attacks on Haeckel's theory of recapitulation, the idea that an animal during the course of its development passes through a series of stages that parallel the stages gone through in the long process of evolution of the species. Among the supporters of this view was the Professor MacBride referred to in the third verse of the poem quoted. Garstang argued that the so-called Biogenetic Law, summarised in the phrase 'Ontogeny repeats Phylogeny' was incorrect.

[16] Autobiography, p. 78.

[17] Autobiography, p. 80. See also E. N. Harvey (1925), 'Fluorescence and inhibition of luminescence in Ctenophores by ultra-violet light', J. Gen. Physiol. vol. 7, pp. 331–339.

[18] Autobiography, p. 81.

[19] *An Apparatus for Displaying Historical Charts, etc.* Patent applied for in the United Kingdom and other countries, by A. C. Hardy, Exeter College, Oxford (n.d.).

20 Adapted from a hotel brochure. Parker-Bidder was certainly wealthy, but he was not the drone's club habitué that the story conjures up. He was a competent biologist who lectured in the Cambridge Zoology Department, and since he was Chairman of the Marine Biological Association from 1939 to 1945, Alister had almost certainly met him.

21 Letter dated 27 April 1921, from the Huxley Archive, Rice University, Texas MS 50 Box 6 f.4.

22 Ibid.

23 Ibid.

24 Ibid.

25 Letter dated 12 May 1921, from Huxley Archive, op.cit.

26 Ibid.

27 Letter dated 16 May 1921, from Huxley Archive, op.cit.

28 Ibid.

29 Ibid.

Notes to Chapter Five

1 Alister continued to find the work he had begun in Naples burdensome. In the end he persuaded Professor Goodrich to allow him to curtail the research and return the remaining Welch Scholarship money.

2 See, Cleghorn, J. 1854. On the fluctuations in the herring fisheries. *British Association for the Advancement of Science*, 24, 1854, 124.

3 International Fisheries Exhibition, London 1883, Inaugural Meeting of the Congress, p. 14. Text available online at aleph0.clarku.edu/huxley/SM5/fish.html

4 Ibid.

5 See Garstang's essay, 'The impoverishment of the sea', *Journal of the Marine Biological Association of the United Kingdom*, 6 (1), 1900, 1–69.

6 Autobiography, p. 91.

7 See, A. J. Lee, *The Directorate of Fisheries Research: Its Origins and Development*, published in 1992 by the Ministry of Agriculture, Fisheries and Food, p. 40.

8 Ibid. p. 53.

9 The source of his nickname is obscure. Was he jokingly called Mac by Scottish fishermen visiting Lowestoft because of the contrast between his polite English accent and his Scottish sounding first name?

10 Smith's Knoll is a large sandbank in the North Sea, about thirty miles off the Norfolk Coast. At one time it was an important fishing ground for the herring fleet.

11 Autobiography. p. 92. The cheeky young Flight Lieutenant known to Hardy ended his career in the RAF as Air Commodore Charles Oscar Modin. Whether Alister knew this I have no knowledge.

[12] Claremont pier was constructed in Victorian times and is made of cast iron. It is now in a ruinous condition.

[13] A predecessor of *Bluebirds K3* and *K4* with which Campbell broke the world water speed record on four successive occasions.

[14] The pteropods are small pelagic sea snails that live as part of the plankton for the whole of their life-cycle. The name *Pteropoda* is not much used nowadays. It refers to holoplanktonic molluscs (animals that spend the whole of their life cycle in the plankton) belonging to the orders of *Thecosomata* and *Gymnosomata*. The common feature of the species is that the foot has been adapted into a pair of 'wings' or parapodia that are used for swimming.

[15] See 'Notes on the Atlantic plankton taken off the east coast of England in 1921 and 1922', *Publications de Circonstance, Conseil International pour l'exploration de la mer, Copenhagen,* no. 78.

[16] Autobiography, p. 99.

[17] The quotation is taken from the first volume of Hardy's two volume work, *The Open Sea* entitled *The World of Plankton*, published in the New Naturalist Series by Collins in London in 1956, pp. 75–76.

[18] Ibid, p. 102.

[19] See for example 'A revolutionary development in herring fishing: the plankton recorder in commercial use' written by skipper R. Balls, master of the steam drifter *Violet and Rose*, published in *The Fish Trades Gazette* for 24 February 1934; also 'Science finds the best fishing grounds: no need now to take pot luck by skipper H. K. George of the *Ocean Spray,* in *The Fishing News,* 16 June 1934.

[20] Michael Graham followed Russell as director of the Lowestoft laboratory in 1945 and is a writer who transmits a genuine feel for life aboard the fishing vessels of that time. See his book *The Fish Gate,* first published in London by Faber & Faber in 1943. See also Burns Singer's book *Living Silver: An impression of the British fishing industry,* published by Secker & Warburg in 1957. Singer based his book partly on his experience of meeting a Polish refugee who had been working as deckhand on an Aberdeen trawler, but with the help of members of the Fisheries Laboratory staff, came ashore and got a university degree. Singer himself was based at the lab, in a district of Aberdeen known as Torry.

[21] The herring get caught when they swim into the net, which has a mesh size sufficiently large for the fish to push through it partway, but when they try to release themselves they are unable to because the gill covers act like the barb on a hook, preventing withdrawal.

[22] Named after *HMS Challenger* which made a pioneering investigation of marine biology during a four-year voyage between 1872 and 1876 under the scientific direction of Charles Wyville Thomson, the professor of Natural History at Edinburgh University. Thomson was knighted in 1877.

23 Known since 2002 as the Rationalist Association.

24 The most celebrated argument in favour of dismissing religion as illusion was Freud's *The Future of an Illusion*, first published in English by the Hogarth Press in London in 1928, that is, very shortly after Alister began to reflect on these matters. Freud owes his interpretation of religion to Ludwig Feuerbach, whose hypothesis that religious belief is a projection was debated in the first half of the nineteenth century. However it is unlikely that Alister as a young zoologist was aware of Feuerbach's ideas.

25 See *The Unutterable Beauty: The Collected Poems of G. A. Studdert-Kennedy ('Woodbine Willie'),* republished in 2006 by Diggory Press.

26 These will be discussed in a later chapter.

27 Published for the Rationalist Press Association by A. P. Watts in 1945.

28 See, Pierre Teilhard de Chardin, *The Phenomenon of Man*: With an introduction by Sir Julian Huxley [Translated by Bernard Wall. Rev. ed.], London: Collins, 1960.

29 The atmosphere of this and several other stories is reminiscent of the style of George McDonald's fantasies (*At the Back of the North Wind; Lilith*), making one wonder if Alister read MacDonald when he was a child. Alister's father, Richard, was probably familiar with MacDonald's work, through his relationship with the Nottingham architect, Richard Sutton and hence, MacDonald's friend, Septimus Sutton.

30 In the field of psychotherapy it is commonplace to interpret talk about entering passages, tunnels, mines and caves as symbolic of sexual intercourse, with the passage or tunnel representing the female genitalia. Hardy was almost certainly aware of this Freudian interpretation through his acquaintance with the agenda of the Rationalist Press Association. By the time he was writing his stories, Freud's views had become a matter of popular knowledge (at the same time as being taboo in polite company), via the publication of *The Interpretation of Dreams*, which first appeared in German in 1900, with an English translation in 1913. The example used in that book – in which someone's dream of a 'shaft' is interpreted by Freud as representing the female genitalia – was also used in one of his *Introductory Lectures on Psychoanalysis,* published in 1911. The purpose of this brief excursus is to make it clear that Hardy was aware of psychoanalysis, did not reject Freudian ideas wholesale, but did not think there was only one way of interpreting a symbol. He discusses Freud at some length in Chapter 6 of *The Divine Flame,* which is the second volume of the published version of his Gifford Lectures in Aberdeen University, published in London in 1966. See also Chapter 6 in *The Biology of God*, published by Jonathan Cape in 1975. On the whole, Hardy found Freud a more congenial writer than Jung, who he felt was unnecessarily obscure, though of course the latter was much more positively disposed towards religion.

Notes to Chapter Six

[1] This was the epigraph used by Alister Hardy for his book *Great Waters* published in London by Collins in 1967.

[2] Copy of a letter to an unknown recipient, held in Hardy's Archive in the Bodleian Library, Oxford. From early on, Hardy made a practice of making copies of most of his letters often in longhand (File C1).

[3] From 1901 onwards, the full title was *The Nineteenth Century and After*. The journal ceased publication in 1972.

[4] See, William Scoresby, *An Account of the Arctic Regions with a History and Description of the Northern Whale-Fishery* (2 volumes), 1820, reprinted by David & Charles in Newton Abbott in 1969.

[5] That is to say, whale species that are the 'right' ones to catch because they float on the surface after being killed. In the early days of whaling the hunters were unable to retrieve the bodies of species that sank to the bottom after death.

[6] *Nineteenth Century*, op. cit. p. 720. As an undergraduate in the Natural History Department in Aberdeen University, I remember hearing V. C. Wynne-Edwards illustrating the outcome of uncontrolled exploitation of prey by carnivorous animals, by referring to Peterhead in North-east Scotland. During the nineteenth century it was a major whaling port, but by overfishing its prey it brought the species to the point of extinction, thus ensuring its own 'extinction' as a predator of whales.

[7] Now permanently docked at Discovery Point in Dundee, where it is open to visitors. Alongside the vessel there is an excellent exhibition centre giving an account of the voyages of the *Discovery*. See also Anne Savours' *The Voyages of the Discovery: The illustrated history of Scott's ship*, published in London by Chatham Publishing in 2001, and published and distribute in America by Stackpole Books of Mechanicsburg, Pennsylvania.

[8] For an account of the trip see, for example, *The Silent Landscape: The Scientific Voyage of HMS Challenger* by Richard Corfield, published by the Henry Joseph Press in 2003.

[9] *Nineteenth Century*, op. cit. p. 728.

[10] Dr. J. D. Hooker, friend of Darwin, accompanied James Clark Ross on the voyage of the *Erebus* and *Terror* as surgeon-naturalist (see below).

[11] Admiral Sir James Clark Ross, R. N. (1800–1862) who discovered the North Magnetic Pole in 1831. He made the first extensive series of deep-sea soundings during his voyage to the Southern Seas in 1839–1843 in *HMS Erebus* and *Terror*.

[12] Captain George S. Nares, RN, FRS was in command of *HMS Challenger* during the years 1873–76 when it made its pioneering marine expedition.

13 Sir John Murray (1841–1914), the founder of modern oceanography. John Murray pioneered research on the ocean depths and oceanic sediments and was a leading light in marine biology.

14 William Speirs Bruce was naturalist and surgeon on the Dundee whaling expedition to the Antarctic in 1892 (aboard *Balaena*) and was said to be Scotland's greatest polar explorer.

15 From a photocopy of the original advertisement, filed with *The Nineteenth Century*, Bodleian Library, op. cit. p. 728.

16 Wordie archive, Scottish National Library, Edinburgh. Discovery Committee, letter from H. T. Allen dated 15 October, 1923.

17 Wordie archive op. cit., Discovery Committee, p. 20.

18 Ibid. p. 21.

19 Ibid, Letter dated 24 October 1923.

20 In Ann Savours, *The Voyages of the Discovery*, op. cit. p.110.

21 In *Great Waters*, op. cit. pp. 48–49.

22 For example: Dr N. A. Mackintosh who went on to succeed Stanley Kemp as Director of Research, Dr J. F. G. Wheeler who became Director of Fisheries Research in East Africa and Dr L. Harrison Matthews who eventually became Scientific Director of the Zoological Society of London and a Fellow of the Royal Society. All three joined the shore staff of the Discovery Expedition. Other applicants who were not appointed included N. J. Berrill who became head of the Zoology Department at McGill University in Montreal and C. M. Yonge who was Professor of Natural History at Glasgow University.

23 See Stephen Haddelsey's fascinating book, *Ice Captain: The Life of J. R. Stenhouse* published by the History Press in Stroud in 2008.

24 Savours, p. 110.

25 Wordie archive, Discovery Expedition, letter dated 27 June 1923.

26 During this interim Hardy had the pleasure of returning to an earlier enthusiasm. He chanced to meet the pioneering balloonist Ernest Willows whilst on a visit to the 1924 British Empire Exhibition in Wembley. Their immediate rapport led to Willows taking Hardy along with three friends on a weekend balloon trip from London in the direction of Oxford. Forty years later Alister could still remember every detail of their journey and recorded it in a delightful little book *Weekend with Willows*, published in Gloucester by Alan Sutton in 1986, the year after Hardy died.

27 The shore staff included three zoologists, N. A. Mackintosh, J. F. G. Wheeler and L. Harrison Matthews; see note 22 of this chapter.

28 *Great Waters*, op. cit. p. 51. Specimen jars with hand written labels in Hardy's distinctive script can be seen in the exhibition centre at Discovery Point in Dundee.

29 I am grateful to Professor Phil Rainbow, Keeper of Zoology at the Natural History Museum for pointing out the spot where the trial took place, now built over by the new wing of the museum which contains the excellent Darwin Centre.

[30] *Great Waters*, op. cit. p. 54.

[31] Ibid, p. 58.

[32] Ibid, p. 161.

[33] Ibid, Plate 10, facing p. 160.

[34] Ibid, p.176.

[35] See 'The work of the Royal Research Ship "Discovery" in the dependencies of the Falkland Islands', *The Geographical Journal* LXXII (3), 1928, 209–234.

[36] Quoted by Savours, p. 110.

[37] See 'The *Discovery* Expedition: a new method of plankton research' by A. C. Hardy, in *Nature*, 30 October 1926.

[38] In aiding my understanding of the CPR I am most grateful for the generous assistance given to me by Dr Chris Reid, who was Director of the *Sir Alister Hardy Foundation for Ocean Studies* (SAHFOS) until 2006. The basic principle of the CPR has hardly changed but, after his return from the Antarctic, Hardy redesigned many of the features to produce the form of machine we see today. It is important to note that Alister was not particularly skilled with his hands and the adaptations were often the result of an amalgam of his ideas and the ideas and practical constraints and alterations demanded of him by the engineers who made them a reality. The end point of these Antarctic beginnings has been the spread of the use of the CPR world wide and the establishment in Plymouth of SAHFOS to operate the international Continuous Plankton Recorder Survey.

[39] Gunther's complete journal is held in the archives of the Maritime Museum in Greenwich, where I was able to examine it. I am also most grateful to Gay F. Sturt of the Dragon School, Oxford, for providing me with copies of the extracts from Gunther's journal that appeared in the school magazine, *The Draconian*. See the issues of *The Draconian* for January 1928, pp. 6703–6715; April 1928, pp. 6762–6777; August 1928, pp. 6874–6898.

[40] Maritime Museum, Greenwich. Gunther's journal, p. 52.

[41] Maritime Museum, Greenwich, Gunther archive.

[42] It is, however, jarring to note a number of offensively racist remarks in Gunther's journal, mainly in connection with his observations of different ethnic groups whilst he was ashore in South Africa.

[43] Gunther archive, op. cit.

[44] Hardy archive, Bodleian, file A17: letter to Sylvia Garstang, dated 14 December 1925.

[45] Ibid, p.2.

[46] Ibid. There are many editions of *The Way of All Flesh*, for example in Penguin Classics with an introduction by Richard Hoggart, new impression edition, 2006.

[47] Hardy, letter to Sylvia, pp. 4–5.

48 The statue of St Teresa by Bernini in the church of Santa Maria della Vittoria in Rome had been discussed at length by psychologists of a sceptical frame of mind. The fact that Bernini's portrayal of Teresa in religious ecstasy resembles a person in the ecstasy of sexual orgasm, was sufficient for such critics to dismiss Teresa's experience as nothing but thinly disguised sexuality. It is easier today, in an age less inclined to equate sexuality with impropriety, to say that Teresa's ecstasy was both sexual and religious. And by analogy the ecstasy with which the adolescent Hardy encountered nature in the Northamptonshire countryside could be interpreted as a function of his awakening sexuality and also of his religious or spiritual insight.

49 From, Julian Huxley, *Essays of a Biologist*, Harmondsworth: Penguin Books, 1923, p. 212.

50 Ibid, p. 214.

51 Quoted in letter to Sylvia Garstang op. cit. p. 16.

52 Ibid, p. 24.

53 In Britain during the 1920s the general public were likely to be aware at a popular level of psychoanalysis though often from a critical perspective. However, as an Oxford educated marine biologist, Hardy may have had only the remotest idea of the subject. If so, Huxley's treatment of sublimation would be novel to him, which it appears to be, judging from the way he writes about it. For a review of public knowledge of psychoanalysis in Britain in the 1920s, see Mathew Thomson's *Psychological Subjects: Identity, Culture, and Health in Twentieth-Century Britain*, published by Oxford University Press in 2006.

54 Hardy archive, Bodleian, file A17: letter to Professor Walter Garstang, dated 28 July 1926, p. 1. Garstang's religious opinions are not known for certain, though he seems to have been accepting of the religious intensity of his future son-in-law. He wrote a long poem in 1919 entitled *The Return to Oxford: A Memorial Lay*, which is a commemoration of his colleagues at Oxford who did not return from the war. The following lines imply that he approved of the Christian ethic, contrasting it with:

> ... Berserk dreams
> Of power usurp'd with blood and iron, as though
> Christ had not lived and died and lived again
> In million hearts aspiring to the true
> And just, to bring to earth the peace of God.

55 Contributors include Balfour, Malinowski, Singer, Aliotta, Eddington, Needham, Oman, Brown, Webb and Inge), Sheldon Press, 1925.

56 *Great Waters*, op. cit., p. 290.

57 I am grateful for the advice of Rosalind Marsden, the daughter of Rolfe Gunther, for advice on the personal background to the relationship between her father and Hardy. See also, her very interesting paper,

'The Discovery Committee – Motivation Means and Achievements', *The Scottish Naturalist* 111, 1999, 69–92.

58 Haddelsey, op. cit. p. 169–170.

59 The distance between Kemp and Captain Stenhouse's conception of the work to be done on the expedition came out in the latter's suggestion that 'the surgeon might do duty as the biologist on the scientific staff'. Reported in Rosalind Marsden, 'Expedition to investigation: the work of the Discovery Committee' in *Understanding the Oceans: a Century of Ocean Exploration*, edited by Margaret Deacon, Tony Rice and Colin Summerhayes. Published by UCL Press in London and New York in 2001.

60 *Great Waters*, p. 522.

Notes to Chapter Seven

1 When the First World War broke out Vickers joined up and was commissioned in the 7th battalion of the Nottinghamshire and Derbyshire Regiment (successors of the Robin Hoods beloved by Alister's father Richard). In 1915 he won the Victoria Cross for conspicuous gallantry at the Hohenzollern Redoubt on the Western Front. In his maturity Vickers was to become an outstanding student of organisation theory, and in 1946 he was knighted for his work. He had a humane interest in institutions as totalities, and in this respect his ecological perspective closely paralleled Hardy's emphasis in zoology.

2 One important exception was when Vickers accompanied Hardy on the balloon trip described in *Weekend With Willows*, op cit Chapter 6, note 26.

3 Letter from Geoffrey Vickers, in the Alister Hardy archive, Bodleian Library, Oxford (Box A 18).

4 Hardy Archive, Bodleian Library, File B152.

5 The brother of the novelist Henry James, and first professor of psychology at Harvard University.

6 William James gave the Gifford Lectures in Edinburgh University during the academic sessions of 1901 and 1902. The lectures were published in 1902 with the title *The Varieties of Religious Experience* and are widely recognised as a classic work, arguably the most important of James' publications. His view of religious experience as a natural phenomenon and hence a human universal, led to a shift away from conceiving of such experience as exclusively religious. If we accept James' interpretation, a more appropriate term for this realm would be 'spiritual' within which 'religious experience' becomes a sub-category, though no doubt the largest.

7 Although there is no record of the guest list, a letter dated 14 November 1927 to 'My dear Hardy' from Rolfe Gunther, is preserved in the Bodleian. He wishes Alister and Sylvia well and describes a small gift he

had purchased for them. It was a reproduction of 'the standard bushel measure made in the days of Henry VII. The original, in copper, is in the North Gate at Winchester and it seemed to me that the copy of a bowl I liked was preferable to embarking on a new shape … if you find it unsuitable for any purpose including plankton estimation, Payne & Sons at Oxford [the company is still in existence at 131 High Street] will at any time exchange it for something else'. The gift is perhaps eccentric, but Gunther's friendship with Hardy seems intact at this stage.

8 Much of the material in this section was gleaned from a typescript of Hardy's extensive reminiscences of the early days of the Department of Zoology at the University of Hull. I am indebted to the staff at the Brynmor Jones Library for permitting me to examine this document.

9 The Palmer family, owners of the biscuit company Huntley & Palmers, provided a site for Reading Extension College, which eventually became the University of Reading. Bristol University was established in 1909 on the basis of the pre-existing University College with the aid of a grant from H. O. Wills, the cigarette manufacturer. In 1921 Sir Jesse Boot, the founder of Boots the Chemists, presented a 35-acre site to the city of Nottingham for the provision of a new University College campus.

10 See, T. W. Bamford's *The University of Hull: The First Fifty Years*, published for the University of Hull by Oxford University Press in 1978, p. 48.

11 Ibid, p. 106.

12 Hardy, *Reminiscences*, op. cit. p. 11.

13 Steedman was also intellectually talented and eventually became Professor of Zoology at the University of Bath.

14 Hardy, *Reminiscences*, op. cit. p. 16.

15 Ibid, p. 13.

16 Ibid, pp. 23–24.

17 Ibid, p.31. A very detailed account of the CPR, written by Hardy was published in the first issue of the *Hull Bulletins of Marine Ecology*, in November 1939.

18 Ibid, p. 32.

19 Ibid, p. 33.

20 The German-Anglo Line was a constituent company of the very much larger Hamburg Line.

21 Hardy archive, Bodleian.

22 Gresham was of course not a disinterested party, since the 'oil tax' from which a considerable sum of money was drawn to finance the Discovery Expedition was also an important source of revenue for the Falkland Islands.

23 In 'The Discovery Committee – motivation, means and achievements', op. cit. p. 87.

It seems that after Gunther was removed from his unhappy 'enslavement' there was no attempt to appoint someone else to complete the job. With 25,000 jars of plankton collected during the 1925–27 expedition, the notion of 'completion' is problematic. The *Discovery* spirit collection (meaning the specimens preserved in spirit) was stored in the National Institute of Oceanography in Godalming until the 1990s, when the new Oceanography Centre was opened in Southampton. Unfortunately the storage space in Southampton was limited and the NERC discussed the possibility of getting rid of the collection. Fortunately the new Darwin Centre in the Natural History Museum had the storage space to accommodate the entire specimen collection from the *Discovery* (approximately 65,000 jars). The plankton specimens are likely to be important in relation to the question of global warming, as comparison with current samples will make it possible to monitor the effects of climate change on the Southern Oceans since 1925–27. I am grateful to Professor Phil Rainbow, Dr Martin Angel and Dr Howard Rowe for help in unravelling the fate of the plankton collection.

[24] Hardy stood his ground and discussed this hypothesis at length in the original paper of 1935; see especially pp. 300–322. He also reintroduced the idea in 1967, in Chapter 15 of *Great Waters* op. cit. pp. 350–381.

[25] Reported by Rosalind Marsden in an audio-recorded conversation with the author. Rolfe Gunther was accidentally killed in the most tragic circumstances in 1940. In later years, Hardy was in communication with Gunther's wife Mavis to obtain her approval for the inclusion in his book *Great Waters* of substantial amounts of material from her husband's researches. He also corresponded with Rolfe's brother A. E. Gunther. These actions imply a wish to mend the broken – and by then irreparable – relationship with Gunther.

[26] Hardy reminiscences p. 46. For a detailed account of the research by Hardy and Milne, see their paper, 'Studies in the distribution of insects by aerial currents: experiments in aerial tow-netting from kites', *Journal of Animal Ecology* 7(2), 1938, 199–229.

[27] Personal communication from Jane Winship, Alister Hardy's great-niece.

[28] I am grateful to Hardy's daughter Belinda for passing on this piece of family folklore.

[29] The scope of the work with the CPR continues to increase and in the UK is now the responsibility of SAHFOS – the Sir Alister Hardy Foundation for Ocean Science, based in Plymouth. There are also several sister organisations round the world which use the CPR.

[30] Notes taken at a dinner on 2 May 1930 for A. R. Cleminson, a local industrialist in Hull who also took an interest in the university. Reported in Bamford, op. cit. p.111.

[31] Now known to be Sir John Ellerman, multimillionaire owner of the Ellerman Shipping Company.

32 Kerr had been Regius Professor of Zoology at Glasgow University from
    1902 until 1935. He then turned to politics and was elected MP for the
    Scottish Universities, a position he held until 1950, when the university
    constituencies were abolished. Kerr's professional background meant
    that he was given a hearing when he made the suggestion that a
    committee of engineers and biologists ought to be set up to look into
    the question of using plankton as food.

33 See the article by A. C. Hardy, 'Plankton as a source of food', *Nature*
    147, 695–696 (7 June 1941).

34 Alister himself admitted that there was some degree of neglect of the
    children, which he regretted and commented approvingly on their care
    of their children as superior to his own.

Notes to Chapter Eight

1 Sadly, the financial burden of replacing extremely widespread cracked
   stonework, created by faulty building methods, proved to be far beyond
   what was practical for the university. Therefore much of the building
   has been handed over to Aberdeen City Council, though the Mitchell
   Hall, where graduations take place, has been retained.

2 A colleague of mine remembered being told by his tutor in Aberdeen
   University that 'Your learning is as broad as your accent', which was
   taken as a compliment on both points.

3 Hardy's student Cyril Lucas, who was at the time setting up the
   Oceanography Department in Leith, eventually became the director of
   the Torry lab.

4 Now located a few miles north of Montrose.

5 A reference to Muriel Spark's novel *The Prime of Miss Jean Brodie*,
   available in several editions. See for example the Penguin Classics
   edition published in 2000.

6 Although he is remembered for founding the Natural History Museum
   in Aberdeen, McGillivray was also a forerunner of Hardy in promoting
   field studies. The following note is taken from the website of the Natural
   History Museum in London, www.nhm.ac.uk/nature-online/science-
   of-natural-history/biographies/william-macgillivray/index.html

    He was raised in rural surroundings on the Scottish island of Harris.
    He received a good school education and attended university in
    Aberdeen. From early on, he preferred exploring the outdoors to
    studying inside. He gained expert knowledge of the animals and
    plants of the Scottish Highlands by going on solo field trips, often
    walking hundreds of miles. McGillivray progressed through his
    dedication to his work, gaining experience and honing his skills. In
    1823 he became assistant to the professor of natural history at
    Edinburgh University. Later, the Royal College of Surgeons in

Edinburgh appointed him curator of their museum. In 1841 his talents were recognised when he secured the position of professor of natural history at Marischal College, Aberdeen. Here he transformed the way students were taught by taking them out into the wild and inspiring them with his passion for nature.

7 The museum was open to the public and I visited it many times during my boyhood. My most lasting memory is of gazing in awe at the sheer length of the outline on the ceiling. Alister noticed another small but surprising cultural difference from England when the museum was being redecorated during the Christmas vacation in 1942. When he called in to the department on Christmas Day he was astonished to find the painters at work, for he had not previously encountered the Calvinist habit of ignoring Christmas because of a suspicion of religious festivals as Papist inventions.

8 Still available from the publisher W. W. Norton & Co, New York, 1993.

9 In Hogben's autobiography, *Lancelot Hogben, Scientific Humanism*, published by Merlin Press in Woodbridge, Suffolk in 1998, p. 1.

10 When Hogben decided he disapproved of someone, he tended to become obsessive about it. Thus, he could not resist continuing with his unpleasant character assassination of Carr-Saunders in a footnote:

> It used to puzzle me how anyone so facelessly devoid of charm and with so mediocre intellectual equipment, attained such eminence. It does so no longer. The first rung of the ladder is a place on a minor government committee. If one remains somnolently acquiescent to the pressure group in command, news spreads among civil servants that one is a sound chap due to fill a vacancy on [an] other ministerial committee, somnolently ...

See note 1, Chapter XV in Hogben's unpublished autobiographical notes *Look Back with Laughter,* Birmingham University Archives. A glance at C. P. Blacker's admiring obituary of Carr-Saunders (*Population Studies*, 20 (3), 1967, 365–369) makes one somewhat dubious of Hogben's judgement.

11 Boyd Orr was the founder of the Rowett Institute of Nutrition and Health in Aberdeen University and winner of the Nobel Prize.

12 Bodleian Library, Hardy archive, File A36.

13 Ibid.

14 Ibid. See File A40.

15 Ibid.

16 Ibid.

17 Ibid.

18 Many years after he had returned to his *alma mater* I overheard a colleague refer to him – I think unfairly – as 'the most ruthless gentleman in Oxford'.

19 Private communication.

[20] Bodleian Library, Hardy Archive, File A41.

[21] Ibid, File A44.

[22] Ibid.

[23] Hardy archive, Bodleian, op. cit. File A42.

[24] Hale Carpenter was a lepidopterist who taught and strongly influenced E. B. Ford. It is an interesting side-light on the small world of academia, that Carpenter was the nephew of Estlin Carpenter, at one time Principal of Manchester College, Oxford. Whilst he was a visiting chaplain at Harvard Divinity School, Estlin Carpenter assisted the pioneer in the scientific study of religious experience, Edwin Starbuck, by taking a set of his questionnaires back to Manchester College. The fate of the questionnaires is not known, but conceivably the study of religious experience got off to a small start in Manchester College more than seventy years prior to the arrival of Alister Hardy's research unit in 1969.

[25] Ibid.

[26] Ibid

[27] The name of the school refers to the fact that when it first opened it was housed in Charles Darwin's house in Kent, though whether that influenced the Hardy's choice of school is not known.

[28] From the obituary written in 1995 for the Royal Society by Bryan Clarke, Emeritus Professor of Genetics at Nottingham University.

[29] For a classic study on the function of hierarchies in reducing anxiety, see Isabel Menzies, 'A case study in the functioning of social systems as a defense against anxiety', in Arthur D. Colman and W. Harold Bexton (eds.), *Group Relations Reader*, Sausalito: GREX, 1975.

[30] *Patterns of Behavior: Konrad Lorenz, Niko Tinbergen and the founding of Ethology*, published by the University of Chicago Press in 2005.

[31] Ibid, p. 332.

[32] Later to become Chief Scientific Officer at the Marine Laboratory in Plymouth.

[33] Personal communication.

[34] Fred Holliday told me about another striking example of Hardy's outstanding skill in managing human relations. After the end of the Second World War, the Development Commission set up a number of groups to ensure that there was cooperation between the different laboratories it was funding. One of these was the Herring Group, which was made up by representatives from each of the British fisheries laboratories with a concern for research on the herring. Alister Hardy chaired it for many years. There were wide differences of opinion about the conduct of this research, separating the laboratories, and the group was notorious for the bitterness and anger that erupted during its meetings. Alister's ability to handle these episodes was, in many people's opinion, the only reason that the group did not collapse.

[35] From Desmond Morris' appreciation of Alister in the *Oxford Times*, 31 May 1985.

[36] While he was in Oxford Tinbergen won the Nobel Prize, and the new Zoology Department is called the Tinbergen Building in his honour.

[37] Alister Hardy archive, Bodleian Library, File B134.

[38] The British Library, Cambridge University Library, National Library of Scotland, Library of Trinity College, Dublin and the National Library of Wales.

[39] Many of Taylor's speeches had the quality of sermons. I still remember his address on Graduation Day in the year I completed my degree, in which he 'preached' with great power on the text 'Remember the rock from whence ye were hewn'.

[40] For example Richard Dawkins, who told me that when he was an undergraduate in Hardy's department, he had no idea that he had any interest in religion.

[41] Hardy Archive, Bodleian Library, File B78.

[42] Introduction, pp. xliv–xlviii.

[43] Tinbergen won the Nobel Prize for Physiology or Medicine jointly with Konrad Lorenz and Karl von Frisch in 1973. Though he had an aversion to religion, his relationship with Alister Hardy was very close. See Hans Kruuk's biography, *Niko's Nature: The Life of Niko Tinbergen and his Science of Animal Behaviour*, Oxford University Press, 2003.

[44] In 2002 an American journalist, Judith Hooper, published a popularly written book about Kettlewell's work, *Of Moths and Men: Intrigue, tragedy and the peppered moth* (London: Fourth Estate), which implied, without saying so explicitly, that Kettlewell was a fraud. For a soberly-written contrary view, see David Wÿss Rudge, 'Did Kettlewell commit fraud? Re-examining the evidence', *Public Understanding of Science*, Vol. 14, No. 3, 249–268 (2005); see also, Bryan Clarke (2003). 'Heredity – The art of innuendo', *Heredity* pp. 90, 279–280.

[45] Desmond Morris op.cit.

[46] Confidential communication.

[47] Lucas' memories of Hardy are quoted in N. B. Marshall's obituary, op. cit. p. 257.

[48] Confidential Communication.

[49] On one oft-recounted occasion, fate arranged for Alister to enjoy an undeserved reward. He received an invitation by post to attend a party to celebrate the opening of a new cross-channel ferry service. He presumed the invitation came because he had been using cross-channel ferries for towing CPRs for some time. He caught the train from Victoria Station in London and settled down in the all-expenses-paid First Class section of the train. Some other important looking people who seemed to know each other were sharing the compartment. After a while, when the train was well into the countryside, one of them said:

'Funny that old Hardy isn't here.' Slightly shocked, Alister tumbled to what had happened. The invitation was meant for a marine engineer, also called A. C. Hardy, who had been a consultant for the setting up of the ferry, but had been sent to the wrong address. Having come this far, Alister decided to brazen it out, enjoyed the celebrations which included an excellent dinner, and sent the menu to the other Hardy. Luckily, he had a sense of humour.

50 Published as *The Faith of a Scientist* in *Faith and Freedom* Vol. 2, Part 2, 1949.

51 Published as a pamphlet by the Lindsey Press in 1951.

52 Ibid. p. 19.

53 This will be discussed in the next chapter.

54 Extracted from 'Zoology outside the laboratory' (Presidential address to Section D of the British Association), *Advancement of Science, London:* 6 (23), 1949, 213–223.

55 See, David Hay with Rebecca Nye, *The Spirit of the Child* (revised edition), published by Jessica Kingsley in London in 2006. The authors made a study of the spirituality of primary school children in schools in two large industrial cities in the English Midlands, Birmingham and Nottingham. An analysis of the children's talk on spiritual matters uncovered the fact that the language used was always 'relational' and in contrast to the individualist assumptions of the dominant secular culture.

56 Hardy Archive, Bodleian Library, File A52.

Notes to Chapter Nine

1 Taken from Lord Adam Gifford's Will, reproduced on the Gifford Lectures website www.giffordlectures.org/will.asp

2 Hardy archive, Bodleian Library, File A46.

3 Published in 1919 by Edward Arnold. See also Hardy's articles: 'Was man more aquatic in the past?' *New Scientist*, 7 (1960), 642–45; 'Will man be more aquatic in the future?', *New Scientist*, 7 (1960), 730–33.

4 *New Scientist*, op. cit. pp. 642–643.

5 Published by Souvenir Press in 1972.

6 Ibid, 1982.

7 I am indebted to Elaine Morgan for pointing out this comment by Desmond Morris in, *Animal Days*, London: Jonathan Cape, 1979, p. 100.

8 Hardy archive, Bodleian Library, File C18.

9 Gifford Lectures website, op. cit.

10 Ibid.

11 Hardy archive, op. cit. File C18.

12 Op. cit. Note 9.

13 Alasdair MacIntyre, *Three Rival Versions of Moral Enquiry: Encyclo-paedia, Genealogy, and Tradition*, London: Gerald Duckworth & Co. Ltd, 1990.

14 Published as *The Varieties of Religious Experience: A Study in Human Nature*, London & New York: Longmans, 1902.

15 Sadly Taylor died soon afterwards and missed the lectures he had done so much to promote.

16 Now demolished.

17 Now Emeritus Professor Sir Frederick Holliday.

18 Fred Holliday chaired one of these seminars, as a stand-in for V. C. Wynne-Edwards, who had succeeded Hardy in the Regius Chair of Natural History at Aberdeen. The two men admired each other and in a letter preserved in the Bodleian Library, Hardy expresses the hope that Wynne-Edwards will succeed him in Oxford (Wynne-Edwards did not apply, preferring to remain in Aberdeen). Nevertheless, I know from personal conversation with both Holliday and Wynne-Edwards that the latter disagreed with Hardy's views on religion. Consequently, to avoid unnecessary confrontation, wherever possible he avoided attending the sessions.

19 The novelist George Eliot translated the book into English in the nineteenth century and her version was published in 1957 in New York by Harper Torchbooks, along with an introduction by Karl Barth.

20 Published in 1851 as *Lectures on the Essence of Religion*. An English translation by Ralph Manheim was published in 1967 by Harper & Row in New York and London.

21 *Lectures on the Essence of Religion*, op. cit. pp. 219–221. This of course was a commonplace sceptic's dismissal, taken up by eminent philosophers including Kant, who has a similar discussion in *Religion Within the Limits of Reason Alone*, published in 1793. See the 1960 edition (translated by Theodore M. Greene & Hoyt H. Hudson) published in New York by Harper & Row, p. 163.

22 Published in London by Collins in 1965.

23 This point is argued in two scholarly books by the Jesuit historian Michael Buckley SJ: *At the Origins of Modern Atheism* published in Newhaven by Yale University Press, in 1987, and *Denying and Disclosing God: the Ambiguous Progress of Modern Atheism*, also published by Yale in 2004. Thomas M. Kelly's book *Theology at the Void: the Retrieval of Experience*, Notre Dame University Press, 2002, contains an interesting theological discussion of the same question.

24 Originally published in 1802. Currently available as an Oxford World Classic, edited and with an introduction by Matthew D. Eddy and David Knight. Published by Oxford University Press in 2006.

25 Behind the high table in the dining hall at Christ's College are hung, side by side, portraits of Paley and Darwin. Is it my imagination, or does Paley have a slightly embarrassed look on his face?

26 It is worth adding that whilst Paley is best known for his defence of the argument from design, his own religious faith was based much more on personal experience, hence quite closely linked to the natural theology advocated by Hardy. See, D. L. le Mahieu, *The Mind of William Paley*, University of Nebraska Press, 1976.

27 See *The Blind Watchmaker*, London: Longman Scientific and Technical, 1986.

28 In, *The Meaning of Evolution*, published by Yale University Press in 1949.

29 For a recent example of a piece of research designed to test the traditional hypothesis, see, Elissa Z. Cameron and Johan T. du Toit, 'Winning by a Neck: Tall Giraffes Avoid Competing with Shorter Browsers', *American Naturalist*, 2007, 130–135.

30 *The Living Stream*, op. cit. pp. 144–145.

31 Published in 1991 by Stanford University Press. Durham makes interesting use of Richard Dawkins' concept of the *meme* as the unit of transmission in social evolution, and sets out to show how in certain circumstances it can come into conflict with organic evolution.

32   Lamarck (1744–1829) was to influence Darwin's idea of natural selection because of the problem of blending of parental characteristics. If a beneficial variant of some characteristic were to appear, it would presumably disappear after a few generations as it blended in with the norm. Common sense observation suggested that this did not happen; for example, the Jewish custom of circumcising all male children is several thousand years old, but the practice is still necessary, for as my genetics lecturer said, quoting Hamlet:

> There's a divinity that shapes our ends,
> Rough hew them how we will.

The discovery of particulate inheritance by Gregor Mendel gave an account of the mechanism of natural selection that was unavailable to Darwin and explained the persistence of genetic variations.

33 George Gaylord Simpson was the originator of the term 'Baldwin Effect'. The same idea was put forward at approximately the same time by two other scientists: Conwy Lloyd Morgan and H. F. Osborne. Lloyd Morgan was Professor of Geology and Zoology at University College, Bristol (later to become Bristol University). See his book, *Habit and Instinct*, published by Arnold in 1896. Osborne was an American palaeontologist who published a paper on the same issue in 1896, entitled 'A mode of evolution requiring neither natural selection nor the inheritance of acquired characteristics', in *Transactions of the New York Academy of Science*, 15: 1411–148. For a discussion and evaluation of the Baldwin Effect, see Bruce H. Weber and David J. Depew (eds.), *Evolution and Learning: the Baldwin Effect Reconsidered*, MIT Press, 2003. For a hotly-debated critical discussion of the

complexity and uncertainties in modern evolution theory, see Jerry Fodor & Massimo Piatelli-Palmerini, *What Darwin Got Wrong*, published by Profile Books in 2010.

[34] That is to say, without resorting to Lamarckism.

[35] See, Holden, C. & Mace, R., 'A phylogenetic analysis of the evolution of lactose digestion', *Hum. Biol.* 69, 1997, 605–628.

[36] See *The Levinas Reader* (edited by Sean Hand), Oxford UK & Cambridge USA: Blackwell, 1989.

[37] It also potentially sidesteps the puzzle of accounting for the evolution of altruism. Once an individualistic interpretation of reality becomes accepted as common sense, as is the case in Western European culture, attempts to explain altruism become bogged down in increasingly complex mathematical contortions. Assuming individualism to be axiomatic, in the end such explanations are bound to be trapped into proving that altruism is nothing more than a sophisticated form of selfishness.

[38] For a discussion of social capital see Robert Putnam, *Bowling Alone: The Collapse and Revival of American Community*, New York: Simon & Schuster, 2000; on spiritual capital, see Danah Zohar and Ian Marshall, *Spiritual Capital: Wealth We Can Live By*, London: Bloomsbury Publishing, 2004.

[39] See Alister Hardy, Robert Harvie and Arthur Koestler, *The Challenge of Chance*, published in London by Hutchinson in 1973, p. 13.

[40] Many years later he was to become its President for the four years between 1965 and 1969.

[41] *The Divine Flame*, op. cit. p. 234.

[42] See Persi Diaconis and Frederick Mosteller (1989), 'Methods for Studying Coincidences', *Journal of the American Statistical Association*, Vol. 84, No. 408, 853–861.

[43] Published by Collins in London in 1966.

[44] See Rudolf Otto, *The Idea of the Holy* (translated from the original German by J. W. Harvey), Oxford University Press Paperback, 1958. Appendix IX: A numinous experience of John Ruskin, p. 215.

[45] Reproduced in *The Divine Flame*, op. cit. pp. 116–117.

[46] See Richard Jefferies, *The Story of My Heart* (new edition), London: The Green Press, 2002.

[47] This section has been borrowed from another book of mine, *Something There: The Biology of the Human Spirit*, pp. 29–31. The work of Hardy's Religious Experience Research Unit will be discussed in the next chapter.

[48] Reproduced in J. M. Cohen's introduction to his translation of Pascal's *Pensées*, published in London by Penguin Classics in 1961.

[49] See, J. M. Cohen & J-F. Phipps, *The Common Experience*, London: Rider and Company, 1979, p. 137.

[50] See for example, *Spirituality and the Secular Quest*, edited by Peter H. van Ness, published in London by SCM Press, 1996; also, Benjamin B. Page (ed.), *Marxism and Spirituality: An International Anthology*, Westport, Connecticut: Bergin & Garvey, 1993.

[51] Since that time the debate has become much more complex, especially through the influence of Richard Dawkins in arguing for the gene as the primary replicant or unit of selection (see *The Selfish Gene*, Oxford University Press, 1976). At the other end of the scale, some biologists continue to give credence to the possibility of group selection. The American biologist David Sloan Wilson has put forward an account of the evolution of religion in these terms (see *Darwin's Cathedral: Evolution, Religion and the Nature of Society*, University of Chicago Press, 2002). Somewhat ironically, the originator of the idea of group selection was V. C. Wynne-Edwards, who succeeded to the Regius Chair and was a good friend of Hardy, although not in sympathy with Hardy on religious matters.

[52] Emile Durkheim, *The Elementary Forms of the Religious Life*, tr. J. W. Swain, London: George Allen & Unwin, 1915, p. 416.

[53] Ibid, p. 417.

[54] Durkheim, quoted by Hardy in *The Divine Flame,* p. 69.

[55] Marett, quoted by Hardy in *The Divine Flame,* p. 71.

[56] See Cushing Strout, 'The pluralistic identity of William James', *American Quarterly*, 23 (2), 1971, 135.

[57] The Calvinism that dominated New England stressed the doctrine of predestination, that is, the conclusion that since God has known the fate of every person from time immemorial, there is no way to alter one's destination to heaven as one of the saved, or to hell as one of the damned. For people who believed this doctrine, and many New Englanders did, anxiety to be reassured that one was on the right side of the divide led to the search for signs of salvation. One celebrated hint was the assumption that worldly success was evidence of God's favour and another was the experience of conversion, in which one received an assurance that one was saved from damnation, directly from God. The continuation of the latter conviction lies behind the well known evangelist's question, 'Are you saved?'

[58] In *Unended Quest: An Intellectual Autobiography*, London: Fontana/Collins, 1976, p. 180.

[59] Hardy archive, Bodleian Library, File C25.

[60] *The Sunday Graphic*, 7 January 1955.

[61] Hardy archive, op. cit. File C25.

Notes to Chapter Ten

[1] Unitarian beliefs have a long history within Christianity. The North African Berber priest Arius, who lived in the fourth century AD, taught that Jesus was human but not divine. Arianism was very widespread

during Arius' lifetime and was condemned as heresy at the Council of Nicea in 325.

2 For the history of Harris-Manchester College and an account of the controversy over the move to Oxford, see V. D. Davis' book, *A History of Manchester College from its Foundation in Manchester to its Establishment in Oxford*, published in London by George Allen & Unwin Ltd in 1932. I should add that the current website for Harris-Manchester College makes no mention of Unitarianism. I contacted the Principal, Dr Ralph Waller, and I am grateful to him for the following statement:

> What is really interesting about the College is that it was never Unitarian even though it had a lot of Unitarian influence over the years. It was founded for young men of every denomination and its Governing Body was anybody who subscribed the right amount. In its Foundation documents there is no mention of Unitarianism nor in its Trust Deed of the 1950s. Even though Principals and members of staff and members of the Governing Body were largely Unitarian … We have of course kept a friendly relationship with the General Assembly of Unitarian and Free Christian churches and still train Unitarian and non-subscribing Presbyterian ministers, alongside those of other denominations.

3 *Faith and Freedom*, Summer 1968, p. 110.

4 These issues are investigated in the German philosopher Hans-Gyorg Gadamer's masterpiece, *Wahrheit und Methode,* published in English as *Truth and Method* by Sheed & Ward, in London in 1975.

5 Archives of Harris-Manchester College for 1968.

6 Ibid.

7 See, E. D. Starbuck, *The Psychology of Religion: An Empirical Study of the Growth of Religious Consciousness* (with an introduction by William James), New York: Walter Scott, 1899. Republished in 2009 by General Books LLC.

8 Published by Cresset Press, London in 1961.

9 £1,000,000 in 1961 would be worth approximately £14,000,000 in the year 2000. In other words the sums Hardy was hoping to collect were not negligible.

10 Among these last the name of the Hon. E. R. H. Wills (or 'Bobby' as he preferred to be called) is pre-eminent. Bobby was one of the heirs to the fortune accumulated by the Wills family through the import of tobacco and the manufacture of cigarettes in Bristol. The major charity operated by W. & H. O. Wills is the Dulverton Trust, chaired by Lord Dulverton, but Bobby had a smaller charity of his own, with offices in the Summertown district of Oxford, and called the Farmington Trust after the village in Gloucestershire where he lived. He was to prove a loyal friend to the Unit.

11 Hardy's intention was to turn the stables into a parapsychology laboratory. It never materialised, not least because the person appointed to work in the lab departed after barely a month, having found a better paid job.

12 From Short's Circular dated 26 March 1969, *Archives of Harris-Manchester College.*

13 See Arthur Long's *Unitarian Thought in the Twentieth Century,* Part II, www.unitarianhistory.org.uk/hsthought2.htm

14 Alister had brought together a formidably competent group of consult-ants: Michael Argyle, Psychologist and eventually the Head of the Psychology Department, Fellow of Wolfson College, Oxford; E. E. Evans-Pritchard, FBA, Professor of Social Anthropology and Fellow of All Souls College, Oxford; Reverend Canon David Jenkins, Chaplain and Fellow of the Queen's College, Oxford, later Bishop of Durham; Basil Mitchell, Nolloth Professor of the Philosophy of the Christian Religion, and Fellow of Oriel College, Oxford; Michael Polanyi, FRS, Emeritus Professor of Social Studies, University of Manchester and Gifford Lecturer, University of Aberdeen, 1951–52; H. H. Price, FBA, Honorary Fellow of New College and formerly Wykham Professor of Logic, Oxford; W. H. Thorpe, FRS, Professor of Animal Ethology and Fellow of Jesus College, Cambridge and Gifford Lecturer, University of St Andrews; Dr R. H. Thouless, Emeritus Reader in Psychology and Fellow of Corpus Christi College, Cambridge.

15 It is one of the ironies of the situation that Hardy never came remotely near his objective of accumulating at least £500,000, or managed to link up with the university, whilst the Unit was occupying the cottage on Holywell Street. It was the college authorities themselves who decided to proceed to the merger with the university, taking the name of Harris-Manchester College, and for this purpose required Hardy's Unit to seek another home.

16 In our early research, Ann Morisy and I field-tested Hardy's question by stopping passers-by at random in the city centre of Nottingham and inviting them to respond to it. Quite often people would begin by making a joke of the 'presence or power' that influenced them, for example saying 'Yes, my bank manager', or 'My mother-in-law'. But having made the wisecrack, most people would go on to say: 'I was not being serious; I know what you mean', and go on to describe a moment which clearly fell within the category we had chosen to investigate. See David Hay & Ann Morisy, 'Reports of ecstatic, paranormal or religious experience in Great Britain and the United States: a comparison of trends', *Journal for the Scientific Study of Religion* 17, 1978, 255–268.

17 The following description is borrowed from Wikipedia: The Kinsey Reports are two books on human sexual behavior, *Sexual Behavior in the Human Male* (1948) and *Sexual Behavior in the Human Female*

(1953), by Dr. Alfred Kinsey, Wardell Pomeroy and others. Kinsey was a zoologist at Indiana University and the founder of the Kinsey Institute for Research in Sex, Gender and Reproduction, more widely known as the Kinsey Institute. The research astounded the general public and was immediately controversial and sensational. The findings caused shock and outrage, both because they challenged conventional beliefs about sexuality and because they discussed subjects that had previously been taboo.

[18] Taken from Hardy's account of the first eight years of the work of the Religious Experience Research Unit, in *The Spiritual Nature of Man*, published by the Clarendon Press in Oxford in 1979.

[19] Published by Rand McNally in Chicago in 1965.

[20] Dr Mason of Yarra Theological Seminary kindly let me read the draft of an unpublished paper, entitled 'Toward further research on religious experience'. The ideas in this section are his.

[21] Hardy's colleague, the Professor of Botany in Oxford, C. D. Darlington, took an extreme view of the importance of genetics. See his interesting but much criticised book, *The Evolution of Man and Society*, published by Allan & Unwin in London, 1957.

[22] For an interesting discussion of this well-known divide, see W. T. Stace's *Mysticism and Philosophy*, Philadelphia: J.B. Lippincott, 1960.

[23] I have discussed this problem in detail in 'Asking questions about religious experience', *Religion* 18, 1988, 217–229.

[24] A computer search of scientific publications in this area demonstrates their exponential increase since the turn of the century. Evaluation of this body of evidence is by no means complete, but even now the view that spiritual experience is associated with a distinct pattern of changes in the brain is becoming more and more plausible. Even as the present biography of Hardy went to the publisher, I became aware of Iain McGilchrist's *The Master and His Emissary* (published by Yale University Press in 2009), a dazzling tour of the neurophysiology of the brain and its relationship to the making of western culture. Dr McGilchrist also brought to my attention Michael R. Trimble's book *The Soul in the Brain: The cerebral basis of language, art and belief*, published in Baltimore by Johns Hopkins University Press in 2007.

[25] This is a question that was examined by Mike Jackson, a staff member of the Unit. His findings were published after Hardy died. See Jackson and Fulford's paper, 'Spiritual experience and psychopathology', *Philosophy, Psychiatry & Psychology* 4, 1997, 41–90.

[26] Published by SCM Press in London in 1963.

[27] *Archives of Harris-Manchester College, Oxford.* Letter from Edward Robinson to Sir Alister Hardy, dated 20 December 1969.

[28] At the same time Brian Carter, a graduate in Religious Studies from Lancaster University, joined the Unit, and in 1971 Michael Walker, a zoology graduate from Hardy's own department, also came to spend a

year at the Unit. Tim Beardsworth returned to work on his book, *A Sense of Presence*, which was published by the RERU in 1977. Others who worked at the Unit in the early days included Joan Crewdson, appointed as Hibbert Trust Research Fellow in 1971, Vita Toon, an Oxford theology graduate who was Curator of the Records from 1970 to 1975, and Carolyn Wilde, a philosopher.

29 Published first in Oxford by RERU in 1977. In 1983 The Seabury Press of New York published an American edition, with an introduction by John H. Westerhoff III and a foreword by Alister Hardy.

30 The Swiss psychologist and philosopher Jean Piaget proposed a Stage Theory of the development of children's thinking that dominated educational training programmes during the latter part of the twentieth century.

31 In the UK, Ronald Goldman applied Piaget's Stage Theory to religious education. See Goldman's book *Religious Thinking from Childhood to Adolescence* published in London in 1964. There is a critical discussion of Goldman's views in David Hay with Rebecca Nye, *The Spirit of the Child* (revised edition), London: Jessica Kingsley Publishing, 2006. See especially Chapter 3.

32 From *Edwin Muir: an Autobiography*, London: Hogarth Press, 1954.

33 The quotation from Rilke which Edward chose as his opening epigraph is as follows:

> Be patient towards all that is unsolved in your heart and try to love the questions themselves like locked rooms ... Do not now seek the answers, that cannot be given you because you would not be able to live them. And the point is, to live everything. Live the questions now. Perhaps you will then gradually, without noticing it, live along some distant day into the answer.

34 The complete list of people with whom Edward had research conversations included: Peter Baelz, Carmen Blacker, Christopher Bryant, Monica Furlong, Lev Gillet, Rosalind Heywood, Martin Israel, Raynor Johnson, Kallistos Ware, Michael Whiteman and Freda Wint.

35 The trusts included the Dulverton, Hibbard, Instone Bloomfield, Moorgate, Phyllis and Spalding Trusts. There was a steady flow of income from numerous private individuals, though their generous grants did not halt the erosion of reserves.

36 Personal communication from Quentin Bone.

37 The full list of Alister's choice of records was:

> A memory of early childhood,
> *You Are My Honeysuckle, I Am The Bee*
> And a memory of going to musical comedies with his mother in Harrogate,

Strauss' *The Waltz Dream*
The Tyneside song, in broad Geordie dialect, as a reminder of the Cyclists' Battalion,
The Blaydon Races
Recalling his days at the Stazione Zoologica in Naples,
Santa Lucia
When he was about to depart for the Antarctic aboard the *Discovery,*
The Fairy Song from the opera *The Immortal Hour*
As a memory of the voyage on the *Discovery*, a sea shanty,
What shall we do with the drunken sailor?
A memory of being with his wife, Sylvia; Noel Coward's *Bitter Sweet,*
Whenever spring-time breaks through again, I'll see you again
And finally, part of Grieg's *Peer Gynt* Suite.
His single most important record was *I'll see you again.*

[38] See my research article, 'Religious experience amongst a group of postgraduate students: a qualitative study', *Journal for the Scientific Study of Religion* 18, 1979, 164–182.

[39] The details of the findings are to be found in David Hay & Ann Morisy, 'Reports of ecstatic, paranormal or religious experience in Great Britain and the United States: a comparison of trends', *Journal for the Scientific Study of Religion*, 17 (3), 1978, 255–268.

[40] Reported in Andrew M. Greeley, *The Sociology of the Paranormal: a reconnaissance*, Sage Research Papers in the Social Sciences, 1975.

[41] The full details are available in David Hay & Ann Morisy, 'Secular society/religious meanings: a contemporary paradox', *Review of Religious Research* 26, 1985, 213–227.

[42] Ibid.

[43] See Back and Bourque's paper, 'Can feelings be enumerated?' *Behavioral Science* 15, 1970, 487–496.

[44] Published by Jonathan Cape in London.

[45] The Templeton Prize is awarded annually to a person who, in the opinion of the judges, has contributed most notably to Progress in Religion. The late Sir John Templeton founded the prize with the conscious intention of emulating the Nobel Prize and because he considered religion to be the most important of human activities, he set the amount of the prize so that it is always greater in financial value than the Nobel awards. Among past prize winners are Mother Teresa of Calcutta, Brother Roger of Taize, Sarvepalli Radhakrishnan, formerly President of India, and the novelist Aleksandr Solzhenitsyn.

[46] Other members of the Hardy family, including Alister's son Michael and his wife Anne, were in the front row of seats in the Hall.

[47] From the text of the address Hardy had prepared for the Guildhall ceremony.

[48] Taken from Dawkins' introductory paragraph to an extract from Hardy's *The Open Sea*, in *The Oxford Book of Modern Science Writing* (edited by Richard Dawkins), Oxford University Press, 2008, p. 127.

[49] In addition, had he been aware of it, one might wonder what his feelings would have been, knowing that probably the best known modern critique of religion on Darwinian grounds is by someone who as an undergraduate sat admiringly in his lectures in the Oxford Zoology Department. Knowing Alister, I think he would have been quite thrilled, for Richard Dawkins takes the subject seriously and has returned religion to a prominent place in public debate.

[50] Personal communication from members of Hardy's family.

[51] Published in London by Collins in 1984.

[52] With text from *The Cotswolds* by John Moore, published in London by Collins in 1984.

[53] *Weekend with Willows* was published in the year after Hardy's death by Alan Sutton Publishing in Gloucester.

Notes to the Postscript

[1] Much of this Postscript is an adaptation of Chapter 9 of my book *Something There: The Biology of the Human Spirit*, published in the UK in 2006 by Darton, Longman & Todd, and in the United States by Templeton Press in 2007. The book can be consulted for an extended account of the concept of relational consciousness. I have also borrowed material from the book I wrote with Rebecca Nye, *The Spirit of the Child* (revised edition published by Jessica Kingsley Publishers in 2006). Finally, some of the text is reproduced from my 2007 Alister Hardy Memorial Lecture

[2] See Penguin Classics Edition (edited by Andrew Skinner), p. 119.

[3] Starring Michael Douglas in the role of Gordon Gecko. Directed by Oliver Stone, written by Stanley Weiser and Oliver Stone. First shown in 1987.

[4] *Sources of the Self: The Making of the Modern Identity*, Cambridge University Press, 1992.

[5] See David Hay and Ann Morisy, 'Secular society/religious meanings: a contemporary paradox', *Review of Religious Research* 26 (3), 1985, 213–225.

[6] Because this response was so frequent, we wondered whether the stereotype of people who say they have never had any religious/spiritual experience, would be the reverse, i.e. described as rational and clear-headed. There were some who fitted this expectation, but the descriptive adjectives that were most often given were so negative that we created a list of them:

> [People who say they have never had any religious/spiritual experience were described as:] apathetic, bitter, conformists, cowards,

dull, emotionless, hard, ignorant, insecure, insensitive, know-alls, lacking capacity, liars, materialists, mean, miserable, morally lax, narrow-minded, over-controlled, sceptics, self-centred, sneerers, superficial, too busy, unaware, unimaginative, unintelligent, unpleasant and weak.

Needless to say, we did not find any evidence to confirm these negative stereotypes, but they do suggest the existence of a considerable amount of anger against 'society' for creating a taboo on what people feel is a vitally important aspect of their personal experience.

[7] See Peter Brierley's report, *Religious Trends No. 1: 1999/2000*, London: Christian Research Association, 2000. For an account of the decline of the religious institutions in the UK, consult Steve Bruce's provocatively titled book, *God is Dead*, published by Blackwell in 2002. See also Callum Brown, *The Death of Christian Britain*, published by Routledge in 2000.

[8] See David Hay and Gordon Heald, 'Religion is good for you', *New Society*, 17 April 1987. An example of the struggle against cultural bias was provided by the publication of this article. A major purpose of the text was to point out that religious experience is a perfectly ordinary feature in many, possibly a majority of people's lives. This theme was severely undermined by the picture editor's choice of illustrations (over which we had no control). They featured a number of distinctly odd people and gave the impression that such experience was weird and eccentric. See also, David Hay and Kate Hunt's *The Spirituality of People who Don't Go to Church*, Final Report, Adult Spirituality Project: Nottingham University, 2000.

[9] Brierley, op. cit.

[10] Lambert, Y. (2004), 'A turning point in religious evolution in Europe', *Journal of Contemporary Religion,* 19 (1), 29–45.

[11] See David Tacey, *The Spirituality Revolution: the emergence of contemporary spirituality*, Hove and New York: Brunner-Routledge, 2004.

[12] See Bryan Zinnbauer et al. 'Religion and Spirituality: Unfuzzying the fuzzy', *Journal for the Scientific Study of Religion*, 76 (4), 1997, 549–564. I should add that, at the time Hardy was writing, the distinction between 'religion' and 'spirituality' was not as clear as it is today.

[13] See her book *Human Minds*, published in London by Allen Lane at the Penguin Press in 1992.

[14] In *Self-Abandonment to Divine Providence* (tr. by Algar Thorold), London: Burns & Oates, 1933.

[15] Published by Basil Blackwell as *Being and Time* (tr. John Macquarrie & Edward Robinson), in Oxford in 1962.

16 See the *User's Guide for QSR.NUD*IST*, published by Sage software SCOLARI in 1996.

17 Let me here reemphasize the importance of Iain McGilchrist's scholarly book, *The Master and His Emissary*. The first half of the book is an extremely thorough account of the neurophysiology of the brain as it relates to transcendence. McGilchrist's expert knowledge of neurology makes his writing vital and complementary to the work of Hardy's Unit.

18 See Katherine Kirk et al., 'Self-transcendence as a measure of spirituality in a sample of older Australia twins', *Twin Research* 2 (2), 1999, 81–87.

19 For a review of this measure, see C. R. Cloninger et al., *The Temperament and Character Inventory: A guide to its development and use*, St Louis, Missouri, Washington University Center for Psychology of Personality, 1994. To understand Cloninger's perspective, I have also consulted his book *Feeling Good: The Science of Wellbeing*, published by Oxford University Press in 2004.

20 Consult Juko Ando et al., 'Genetic and Environmental Structure of Cloninger's Temperament and Character Dimensions', *Journal of Personality Disorders*, 18 (4), 2004, 379–393.

21 See Andrew Newberg et al., *'Why God Won't Go Away: Brain Science and the Biology of Belief'*, New York: Ballantine Books, 2001.

22 See Mario Beauregard and Vincent Paquette, 'Neural correlates of a mystical experience in Carmelite nuns', *Neuroscience Letters*, Volume 405, Issue 3, 25 September 2006, Pages 186–190.

23 Newberg himself urges caution in the interpretation of data collected with a SPECT scanner.

24 Figure reproduced from David Hay, 'Altruism and Spirituality as Forms of Relational Consciousness and How Culture inhibits Them', in R. W. Sussman and C. R. Cloninger (eds), *The Origins and Nature of Cooperation and Altruism in Non-Human and Human Primates*, New York: Springer [forthcoming, 2011].

25 See for example, Chapter 5, 'Ethics as first philosophy', in Seán Hand (ed.), *The Levinas Reader*, published by Blackwell in Oxford in 1989.

26 For an exposition on the special case of European atheism, see, Grace Davie's Sarum Theological Lectures, *Europe – The Exceptional Case*, published in 2002 by Darton, Longman & Todd. The atheism of Advaita in India, or in Theravada Buddhism might be cited as evidence to contradict my thesis, but these forms of atheism are in fact intra-religious. They are aspects of a debate about the nature of transcendence and as such are akin to certain mystical movements in Christianity, for example the near monism of someone like the fourteenth-century Dominican mystic, Meister Eckhart.

27 See especially Chapter 7 in W. H. Durham, *CoEvolution: Genes, Culture and Human Diversity*, op. cit. Chapter Nine.

[28] There are many texts on this theme. Possibly the best introduction because he gives a systematic overview of its many dimensions is Stephen Lukes' *Individualism* published in the series Key Concepts in the Social Sciences by Basil Blackwell, in 1973. See also Colin Morris, *The Discovery of the Individual, 1050–1200*, published by SPCK in London in 1972, and Louis Dumont, *Essays on Individualism*, published by Chicago University Press in 1986, also Aaron Gurevich, who disagrees with Morris' claim that individualism appeared in the twelfth century. See his *The Origins of European Individualism*, published by Blackwell in 1995.

[29] For further information on these questions see the articles by Terrence Deacon on 'Biological aspects of language' (pp. 128–133) and C. B. Stringer on 'Evolution of early humans' (pp. 241–251) in *The Cambridge Encyclopaedia of Human Evolution* (edited by Steve Jones, Robert Martin and David Pilbeam), Cambridge University Press, 1994.

[30] The question of the self-awareness of other animals is hotly disputed. It is discussed at length in Marc Bekoff et al. (eds.), *The Cognitive Animal*, Cambridge, MA: The MIT Press, 2002

[31] See for example, Nagy, E. & Molnar, P. (2004), 'Homo imitans or Homo provocans? Human imprinting model of neonatal imitation'. *Infant Behavior and Development*, 27: 54–63.

[32] For a popular discussion of the effect of language on self-awareness, see John McCrone, *The Ape that Spoke: Language and the Evolution of the Human Mind*, London: Picador, 1990.

[33] See Luria's book *Cognitive Development: Its Cultural and Social Foundations* (tr. by Martin Lopez-Morillas and Lynn Solotaroff; edited by Michael Cole), Harvard University Press, 1976. Because of difficulties with Stalinist censorship, these findings were not published in the Soviet Union until the decade of the 1970s.

[34] One only has to think of the way that reading and writing dominate our everyday lives, now added to by the ubiquity of the Internet and the World Wide Web, to begin to see that the mode of action of our consciousness is very different from that of our non-literate forebears. See, for example, John L. Locke's (1998) book, *Why we Don't Talk to Each Other any More: the De-voicing of Society*.

[35] Note for instance the experience of the psychotherapist Eugene Gendlin (1981, 1997), when encountering academically high-flying clients in his Chicago consulting rooms. Gendlin comments on the disconcerting fact that he was unable to help many of them to explore their immediate emotional difficulties because they were isolated from the felt sense of their bodies. Too good a training in academic detachment had crippled them. See also the related arguments from the neurologist Antonio Damasio (1994, 2000) on the importance of the body in relation to emotion and consciousness.

[36] Republished in Penguin Classics in 2004.

37 See *The Protestant Ethic and the Spirit of Capitalism* (tr. by Talcott Parsons), London: George Allen & Unwin, 1930: p. 104. Pastoral need led to the mitigation of the doctrine and it became accepted that one plausible sign of election was material prosperity in this life. Weber's (often-disputed) contention was that this belief encouraged the growth of capitalism in Europe.

38 The teaching of Cornelius Jansen, which split the Roman Catholic Church in France in the mid-seventeenth century. Jansen emphasised the belief that individuals can do nothing to assure their own salvation, all is due to divine grace. Jansenism was centred on the abbey of Port Royal and Pascal was its most prominent lay supporter. The Jansenists were excommunicated in 1719.

39 See *The Self as Agent* (with an introduction by Stanley M. Harrison), London: Faber & Faber, 1995, p. 71.

40 See David Berman's fascinating thesis on hidden atheism in *A History of Atheism in Britain: From Hobbes to Russell*, London & New York: Routledge, 1990.

41 For an overview of scientific approaches to altruism theory, see Lee Alan Dugatkin, *The Altruism Equation: Seven scientists search for the origins of goodness*, Princeton University Press, 2006.

42 See Jean Hampton, *Hobbes and the Social Contract Tradition*, Cambridge University Press, 1988.

43 In *Philosophical Rudiments concerning Government and Society*, Ch. 1, Section 4, 25–26 (quoted in MacPherson 1962: p. 44).

44 *Leviathan* (edited with an introduction by C. B. Macpherson), London: Penguin Classics, 1985.

45 Ibid, p. 228.

46 C. B. Macpherson, *The Political Theory of Possessive Individualism*, Oxford University Press, 1962.

47 *The Passions and the Interests: Political Arguments for Capitalism before its Triumph* was first published by Princeton University Press in 1977, and republished as a Twentieth Anniversary Edition with an foreword by Amartya Sen.

48 Hirschman, op. cit. p. 14.

49 Ibid, p. 40.

50 Ibid. p. 50.

51 Currently available in the two-volume Penguin edition, with an introduction and notes by Andrew Skinner, published in 1999.

52 A distinction must be made between Smith's account of the way things are in capitalist society and his personal view of ethics. Smith's moral philosophy is expounded in *The Theory of Moral Sentiments* (1759), published seventeen years before *The Wealth of Nations*. He has much to say of 'sympathy', which suggests that it is not remote from relational consciousness. The apparent ethical disjunction between the two works has led to much discussion. It must be added that Smith's

rhetoric, particularly in the later chapters of *The Wealth of Nations*, frequently makes clear his distaste for some of the situations he is describing (see Muller, 1993).

53 Pseudonym of Johann Caspar Schmidt.

54 Translated by Steven Byington, with an introduction by Sydney Parker. Published in London by Rebel Press in 1993.

55 Ibid, p. 5.

56 Ibid, pp. 296–7. His lover in Berlin left him in disgust, accusing him appropriately enough of being totally self-centred. She eventually entered religious life and died in 1902 in a convent in London.

57 *The Nihilistic Egoist Max Stirner*, published for the University of Hull by Oxford University Press in 1971.

58 Bruno Bauer, another member of the Young Hegelian group in Berlin and a former theologian.

59 Ibid, p. 31.

60 Ibid, p. 263.

61 Ibid, p. 197.

62 Karl Marx, quoted in Michael Walzer (1990), 'The communitarian critique of liberalism', *Political Theory,* 18 (1), 6–23.

63 Hobbes may have dispensed with religion, but it would be interesting to investigate the theological complexion of his early upbringing. He certainly encountered Calvinist opinions when he was a student at Magdalen Hall in Oxford and this may have encouraged in him a belief in the natural depravity of the species. When he discarded religious belief in his maturity, he would then have been left with depravity, now deprived of saving grace.

64 See *Between Man and Man* (translated by Ronald Gregor Smith), London: Fontana, 1961, p. 64.

65 Ibid, p. 66.

66 Boyer's interesting ideas are a development of his anthropological field work in West Africa. A highly readable account of his views is contained in his book *Religion Explained: The evolutionary origins of religious thought*, published in New York by Basic Books in 2001.

67 See *Bowling Alone: The Collapse and Revival of American Community*, New York: Simon & Schuster, 2000.

Index of Names

Index of Subjects